INTERNET

MARY LOJKINE

LONDON • NEW YORK • SYDNEY • JOHANNESBURG • SINGAPORE • TORONTO • NEW DELHI

In easy steps is an imprint of Computer Step
Southfield Road . Southam
Warwickshire CV47 0FB . England

http://www.ineasysteps.com

Notice of Liability
Every effort has been made to ensure that this book contains accurate and current information. However, Computer Step and the author shall not be liable for any loss or damage suffered by readers as a result of any information contained herein.

Trademarks
All trademarks are acknowledged as belonging to their respective companies.

Printed and bound in the United Kingdom

ISBN 1-84078-214-5

Contents

Questions, questions...

Chapter One

You've heard of the Internet, of course – there can't be many people who haven't. But what is it, exactly? Where did it come from, how does it work and, most importantly, what good is it? This chapter provides the answers.

Covers

Hello...

...and welcome to the Internet. Put your coat over there, grab a drink from the bar and join the party!

To be honest, you're a little late. The invites went out in the mid 1990s, the DJ arrived in 1997 and the Internet has been a big, wild, rock 'n' roll extravaganza ever since. Still, you're here now... and it isn't such a bad time to arrive. The party is settling down and all the guests are getting mellow. The neighbours have been round to complain about the noise and now they're sat over there with a glass of wine, making friends. No more worries on that front. There was an awkward moment when the venture capitalists got upset about the money they'd spilt, but we've mopped everything up and you can hardly see the stain. We've sorted out the problem with the sound system, we've sent someone out for more beer, and the pizzas will be arriving any minute. In short, it's a better party than it was five years ago.

Making the most of the Internet used to require technical know-how, blind faith, a fat wallet and a fair degree of patience. In 2003 you don't need any of those things. It's easy to get connected and it costs very little. The Internet has become more versatile, too. You can access all sorts of information, from today's news to descriptions of the plumbing systems in ancient Egypt, and do all sorts of useful things. You can communicate with your friends, shop for a new home and everything that goes in it, pay your bills, find phone numbers, look up addresses on an interactive map, book your holidays and even file your tax return. The Internet has become an important part of day-to-day life.

This book will drag you on to the Internet, kicking and screaming, and show you all its best features (the kicking and screaming is optional, okay?). You'll learn how to choose a modem, find an Internet service provider, make a connection, browse the Web, dispatch an e-mail, participate in a newsgroup, send an instant message and create a Web page. For starters, though, you might be wondering what the Internet is, where it came from and how it works. This chapter answers all those questions.

Grab a seat, help yourself to pretzels and read on...

What is the Internet?

The Internet is the hottest thing since boy bands, the coolest thing since flares and the best thing since sliced bread. It's in the news, it's on the telly, it has bit parts in your favourite soaps. Your children are using it at school, your workmates swear by it (or at it) and your elderly grandmother keeps asking you how it works. If you haven't heard of the Internet, you must have been living in a cave, on a mountain or in a far-off country, for the last ten years.

But what is it, exactly?

The Internet (or Net) is a computer network that spans the globe. It consists of millions of computers that are physically connected, using wires and cables and satellite connections, so information can pass from one computer to the next.

You might have heard people talking about the 'information superhighway'. In reality, the Internet is more like the entire road network, from the smallest country lane to the largest motorway, along with all the ferries that let you take your car across the sea. Just as the road network lets you drive to any house or building that's actually on a road, the Internet lets you send information to any computer that's connected to the network. Computers that aren't connected are like caves on faraway mountains – the data that's on them, like the people who live in the caves, have no contact with the outside world.

The difference between the Internet and the road network is that information flies from computer to computer at speeds motorists can only dream of. Although it's technically possible to drive from London, England to Sydney, Australia (if you take a couple of ferries), it would take you weeks. On the Internet, data moves so quickly that the distance between computers is irrelevant. It doesn't matter whether the information you need is stored on a computer in your home town, or on a computer on the other side of the world. Either way, it reaches you in seconds.

So that's all there is to it?

Not exactly. Computers and cables are only half the story. To do anything productive with the Internet, you also need software to manage the information and move it about. Otherwise it's just going to sit on a computer, taking up space.

People have all kinds of information they want to share, including facts, figures, stories, pictures, sounds and programs, and all kinds of ways to share it. Some information is private and needs to go to a specific person. Some can be made available to everyone. Some things are only relevant for a short period and must be transmitted quickly. Others may be useful for years to come. If you're inviting a friend to meet you for lunch, you don't want to immortalise your plans in a public forum. The restaurant, on the other hand, might want to advertise its menu to everyone, 24 hours a day.

There are many different ways to send information over the Internet. In general, each method has its own software and procedures. This book deals with four common ways to use the Internet:

- **The World Wide Web (or Web)** consists of millions of magazine-style pages packed with text, pictures, sounds, animations and video clips. They are linked together by electronic cross-references that enable you to jump from page to page. Information on the Web can be accessed by anyone, so it's used for news, reference material, information about products and events, and entertainment. You'll learn more about the Web and the software it requires – a Web browser – in Chapters 3, 4, 5, 6 and 7. Chapter 12 explains how to create your own Web pages.

There's loads of good stuff on the BBC's Web site. Find it at: http://www.bbc.co.uk/

- **Electronic mail (or e-mail)** is the Internet equivalent of letters and faxes. It enables you to send private messages to other Internet users, almost instantaneously. You can also send documents and pictures with your messages. E-mail and e-mail programs are covered in Chapters 8 and 9.

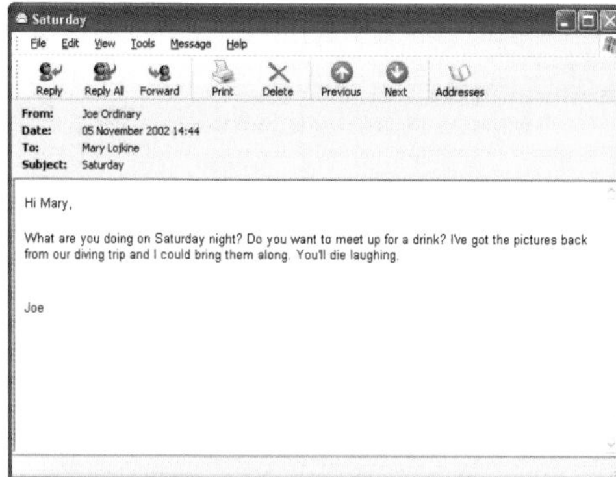

E-mail is ideal for quick notes

- **Usenet newsgroups** are public discussion forums where people exchange gossip, trivia, advice, insults and – very occasionally – news. They're the Internet equivalent of your local pub or social club, although there's no beer (alas). Newsgroups are accessed using a newsreader and are covered in Chapter 10.

- **Instant messaging (or chat)** enables you to conduct live, real-time conversations with other Internet users. You type instead of talking, but otherwise it's like nattering on the phone. Some instant-messaging programs even let you hook up a microphone and speak to people via the Internet. Instant messaging is covered in Chapter 11.

There are other ways to use the Internet and no doubt there'll be many more applications in the future. The important thing to remember is that the Internet provides the infrastructure and the software makes things happen. To return to the road analogy, once the road network reaches your front door, you can take off on a bicycle or a motorbike, or in a car or a bus or a truck, depending on your destination and the amount of gear you need to carry.

Where did it come from?

The Internet turned 30 a few years ago (really, it's that old). Like any 30-something, it has some quirky habits born of its childhood experiences, so it's worth knowing how it evolved.

The Cold War

Back in the days when nuclear holocaust seemed imminent, the US Government decided to connect up some of its computers so scientists and military agencies could communicate more easily. Instead of building a control centre, which an enemy might destroy, the designers created a system where each computer operated independently. Messages travelled by any available route, rather than in fixed patterns. Even if some of the computers were destroyed by a military or terrorist attack, the others could carry on working. The first messages were transmitted in 1969.

The legacy of this period is a robust network that isn't disrupted by computer crashes and power cuts.

The nerd days

In the 1970s several more computer networks were established by military and academic institutions. Eventually they were joined together, creating a network of networks or 'Internetwork'. It was like the building of the Channel Tunnel between the United Kingdom and France: there were arguments about which side of the wires the messages should travel on, but eventually everyone agreed on common standards for transferring information.

This period gave us the term 'Internet'. It was also a time when computers were used primarily by scientists, academics and students (nerds and geeks, basically), so many of the developments were inspired by the desire to discuss *Star Trek* and tell bad jokes.

The age of the Internet

For more about the man who invented the Web, Tim Berners-Lee, visit his Web site at: http://www.w3. org/People/ Berners-Lee/

Everything changed in the 1990s, when the World Wide Web was developed by a British scientist working in Switzerland. Suddenly the Internet was attractive and easy to use, and you didn't need a degree in computer science to see the point. New software was developed by mainstream companies and distributed in cereal boxes (practically). Many more people had access to computers. Millions of them got connected. And people like you started buying books like this.

How does it work?

If you'd like to know more about internal combustion engines and cathode ray tubes, visit the HowStuffWorks Web site at: http://www.howstuffworks.com/

Do you know how the engine in your car works? Or how the cathode ray tube in your television puts a picture on the screen? No? You don't need to know how the Internet works, either, but it's kind of interesting (if you disagree, you can skip this section).

Where's your computer?

Just as your house has a unique postal address, every computer on the Internet has a unique numeric address called an IP number. It consists of four numbers, separated by dots (periods). For example, 212.58.240.32 is the address of the computer that stores the BBC's Web site.

IP is short for Internet Protocol, a set of rules for making up addresses and moving information around the Internet.

I can't remember that!

Numeric addresses are fine for computers, but human beings are better at remembering words. All the important computers on the Internet also have user-friendly names, such as www.bbc.co.uk The Domain Name System (DNS) converts these names into numbers when a computer needs to find something.

Once you've learned how to use a Web browser (Chapter 3), you can test this system. Run your browser and type 212.58.240.32 into the Address bar. You should end up at the BBC's Web site.

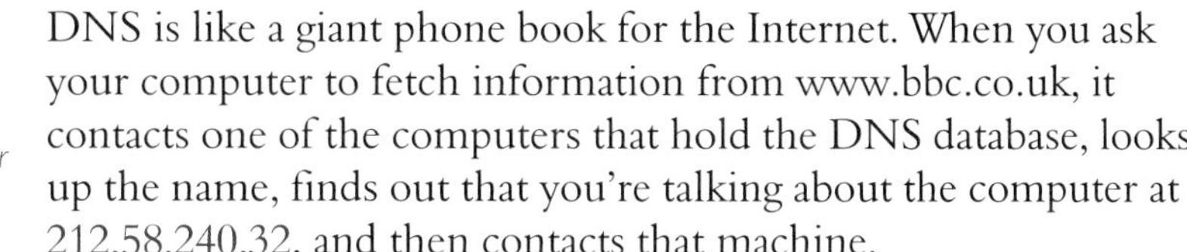

DNS is like a giant phone book for the Internet. When you ask your computer to fetch information from www.bbc.co.uk, it contacts one of the computers that hold the DNS database, looks up the name, finds out that you're talking about the computer at 212.58.240.32, and then contacts that machine.

Let's get moving

You don't want to transmit information in big chunks, because if something goes wrong (such as the military attack the original designers feared), you'll lose everything. It's better to divide the information into small pieces, dispatch the pieces separately, and then reassemble them at the other end.

There's another set of rules for this procedure. Transmission Control Protocol (TCP) explains how to break up a lump of computer data into small 'packets' and add the destination to each one, along with the address of the computer that's sending the data. The packets can then be transferred across the Internet, following the rules laid down by Internet Protocol. When they get to the other end, Transmission Control Protocol takes over again, checks that all the packets are present and reassembles them.

The important thing about this system is that it's very flexible. If there's a problem somewhere along the way, the packets are rerouted to avoid it. They might not all take the same route, and some packets go missing and have to be sent again, but everything gets there in the end. Also, information flows smoothly, because different people's packets can be mixed together. No-one gets to monopolise the wires.

Fun for everyone

The other good thing about this system is that the two important protocols, TCP and IP, can be implemented on almost any computer. Once your computer is physically connected to the Internet (more on that on page 16), you run a small program that creates a TCP/IP interface. This software is usually built in to your operating system (it is part of Windows, for example). It runs automatically when you try to use the Internet.

The TCP/IP software differs from computer to computer, but the rules are the same for everyone. It doesn't matter whether you use a PC or an Apple Macintosh to connect to the Internet, because both computers use the same procedures when they're sending and receiving information. You can think of TCP and IP as a set of road rules that everyone follows, no matter what type of computer they drive. The difference is that on the Internet, people actually follow the rules! If they don't, their data doesn't go anywhere.

The bottom line

You don't need to remember any of this and there certainly won't be a test, but since you've read this far, here's the cheat sheet:

- Each computer on the Internet has a unique address.
- When you transmit data, your computer uses Transmission Control Protocol (TCP) to divide it into small packets.
- Internet Protocol (IP) shifts the packets across the Internet, by any convenient route. TCP reassembles them.
- Any computer that can 'do' TCP/IP can connect to the Net.

Who's in charge?

People used to believe that no-one owned or controlled the Internet. It was the Wild West of computing, a lawless frontier where anyone could set up camp and behave as they pleased. Sadly, the truth isn't quite as exciting.

Mine, mine, all mine

The physical infrastructure of the Internet didn't just spring out of the ground. Every computer, every cable, every wire and every switch belongs to someone. In the early days, most of the hardware was owned by public institutions such as universities. Now much of it is installed and operated on a commercial basis. If a company wants to pull the plug on its computer, it can… but there are so many computers out there that you won't notice the difference. No-one owns enough of the Internet to seize control.

…and you'll do as you're told

All sorts of people have a say in how you use the Internet:

- To get connected, you'll need to sign up with an Internet service provider (see overleaf). You give the company money, it gives you access. As in any other commercial relationship, you're bound by the terms of the contract.
  If you break the rules, you'll be shown the door.
- There are several organisations that set standards and keep everything working. The Internet Society (ISOC) oversees for the development of the Internet. Organisations under its control include the Internet Engineering Task Force (IETF), which deals with technical problems. The Internet Corporation for Assigned Names and Numbers (ICANN) keeps the address book in order and the World Wide Web Consortium (W3C) takes care of the Web.
- Governments are increasingly aware of the Internet. Sometimes they create new laws to deal with it, but often the existing legislation is sufficient. You can't (legally) make threats, libel people, steal copyrighted material or view hard-core pornography on the Internet, any more than you can in real life.

Of course, if you have a complaint about the Internet, no-one is going to admit to being responsible for even the smallest part of it!

How do I join?

You'll find out how to connect to the Internet in Chapter 2. For now, here's a quick overview.

You need four things to join the Internet:

- **A computer.** The simplest option is to use a PC running Windows. You can also use an Apple Macintosh or, if you're looking for a challenge, almost any computer ever invented.
- **A physical connection** between your computer and the Internet. In a perfect world, there'd be Internet cables running down your street, alongside the power lines and phone cables and water pipes. Unfortunately there aren't many towns with hot and cold running Internet, so you'll probably make a temporary connection using a modem – a device that enables computers to communicate with each other via a telephone line. Information travels from your computer to the modem, which sends it down the phone line to another modem, which is attached to another computer, which belongs to…
- **An Internet service provider (ISP).** Internet service providers make it possible for ordinary people to access the Internet from their back bedrooms. They have computers that are permanently wired up to the Internet, and also to banks of modems. Once you've opened an account, you use your modem to make a connection to one of your ISP's modems, and thence to the Internet. Service providers also take care of housekeeping tasks such as storing and forwarding your electronic mail.
- **Internet software.** As you learned earlier, a physical connection is only half the story. To do anything useful, you'll need computer programs that enable you to send and receive information. Most new computers come with everything you'll need. If you have an older model, you can get software from your service provider, from the CDs attached to computer magazines, or from computer shops.

That's all there is to it: computer, modem, ISP, software… Internet.

Why should I bother?

There are many, many reasons why you should drop everything (except this book) and get connected to the Internet:

- **To stay in touch.** It isn't the multimedia glory of the Web that attracts most people, but the practicality of electronic mail. Whether you're communicating with colleagues in the next office or friends on the other side of the world, e-mail is quick, cheap and convenient. Whereas a letter might take a few days to arrive, an e-mail message takes a few seconds – and it costs less to send. And unlike a phone call, it'll never disrupt an important meeting or wake someone up.

- **To meet people.** With over 500 million people using the Net, there are bound to be a few who share your interests. You can find people who want to chat about anything from ancient Greek to football – be it English football, American football, Aussie Rules or soccer – to your favourite television show. Is he cheating on her? Will she keep the baby? There are people who care.

- **It's useful.** Want to know whether it's going to rain? Look out the window. Want to know whether it's going to rain in Spain, next week, when you're there on holiday? Find a forecast on the Internet. You can look up phone numbers, find a map of your neighbourhood, check your bank balance, pay your bills, order flowers for your mother's birthday, see what's on at the cinema and find out which bus to catch.

Get worldwide forecasts from the BBC Weather Centre at: http://www.bbc.co.uk/weather/ or bank with HSBC at: http://www.hsbc.co.uk/

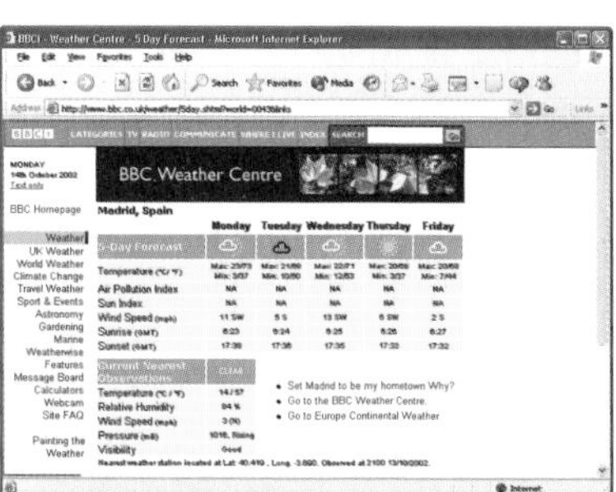

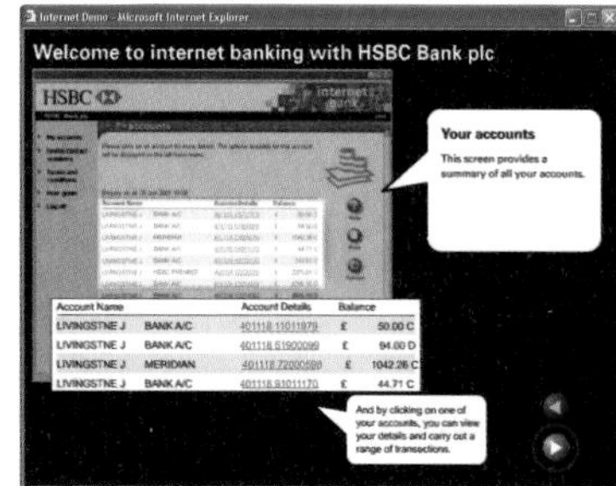

- **It's fun.** The Web isn't just the world's largest magazine, it's also an enormous electronic toy box. There are stories to read, pictures to view, movie trailers to watch, sports highlights to relive and games to play. And every joke ever told is out there somewhere, waiting to be told again.

Watch cartoons and play games at: http://www.shockwave.com/ or enjoy the strangeness of Monty Python at: http://www.pythonline.com/

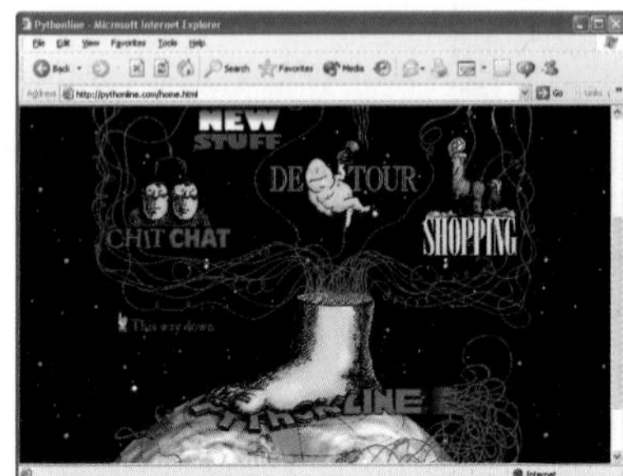

- **It's convenient.** Unlike a public library, the Internet is open 24 hours a day, seven days a week, throughout the year. You don't have to waste time travelling or finding a car park, and when you come across some useful information, you don't have to queue for the photocopier – you just print it out.

- **It's up to date.** Libraries only have the facts that have been around long enough to make it into books. The Internet has the very latest information, including news too new for this morning's paper. And thanks to the power of electronic indexing, it's easy to find the stories you want to read, no matter when they were published. You can flip back to older bulletins and follow a story from its roots.

- **It does the maths.** There are currency convertors that not only give you the exchange rate, but also work out how many Guatemalan Quetzels you'll get for your 23 Honduran Lempira. In the UK, you can even fill in your tax return on the Internet and have your tax calculated automatically.

- **It resolves arguments.** Can't remember who said golf was "a good walk spoiled"? Ask the Internet! What's the shortest English word that contains all five vowels, in order? Ask the Internet! All those snippets of information that have slipped down behind the cushions in your brain are waiting to be rediscovered, whenever you get the urge.

- **To promote your business.** The more people rely on the Internet for information, the more important it is to create a Web site for your business. Without a virtual shop-front in the Internet mall, you're invisible to millions of customers.

Find out more about the 'in easy steps' range from the Computer Step Web site at: http://www.ineasysteps.com/ or go scuba diving with Singapore-based Marsden Bros at: http://www.marsbros.com/

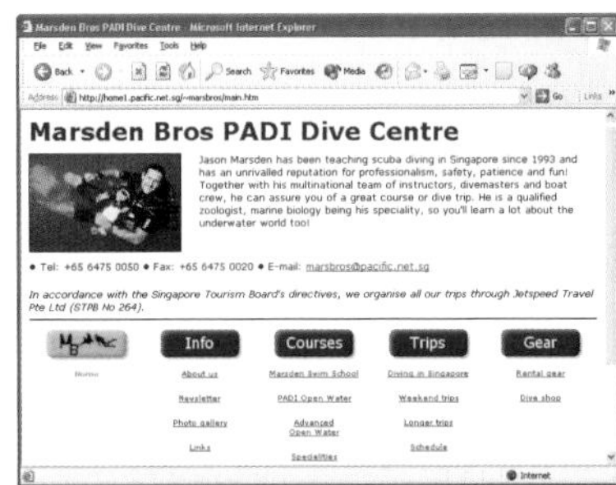

- **To save money.** It costs almost nothing to send an e-mail. You can stop buying newspapers and magazines. Internet shops offer better prices than real-world stores, because their costs are lower. You can download free or cheap software instead of paying for almost-empty shrink-wrapped boxes.

- **To make the most of your computer.** You probably spent a large sum of money on that large lump of beige plastic. It isn't exactly decorative, so you might as well make it useful.

- **It's the future.** When Gutenberg invented the printing press, people probably told him reading was for monks with bad haircuts. In today's world of newspapers, novels, textbooks, bus timetables and warning signs telling you to 'mind the gap', not being able to read is an enormous handicap. In the not-too-distant future, it'll be the same with the Net. Enormous amounts of information are being moved on to the Web and hundreds of services are being computerised. You're going to need to know your mouse from your menu.

But what about...

...the things that go bump in the night? What about the porn merchants peddling dirty pictures, the nasty viruses, the men pretending to be women, the thieves stealing credit-card numbers, the paedophiles preying on small children and the hackers trying to bring down the whole system? What if it all goes horribly wrong?

Truthfully, the Internet does have some dark, nasty corners, just as many towns have dodgy streets that are best avoided in the early hours of the morning. However, if you educate yourself about the problems, a night out on the Net won't leave you with a headache.

If you have children, you're probably concerned about them encountering adult material – or the wrong kind of adult. The best solution is to make Web browsing a family affair. Keep the computer in the living room so you can see what's on the screen.

Teach your children not to give out personal details, such as their full name or your address and phone number, and make sure they understand that people aren't always who they seem to be. If your children are too young to be wary of strangers, they're too young to use the Internet unsupervised.

To avoid computer viruses, start by learning how to recognise a potential threat (try turning to pages 113 and 136). Install antivirus software and update it regularly. To be completely safe, make back-up copies of files that contain important information or would be difficult to replace.

On-line shopping is safer than you think, for two reasons. First, credit card fraud is more of a problem for retailers than it is for consumers, because the retailers usually foot the bill (check your terms and conditions, though). Second, there are many ways of stealing credit card numbers that require much less skill than intercepting Internet transactions. Chapter 6 explains the things to watch out for when you buy things over the Internet.

Hackers go after the rich and famous, which – no offence intended – probably doesn't mean you. If your computer contains valuable or confidential information, such as medical records or military schematics, you should take extra precautions when you connect it to the Internet (and don't leave it in a taxi, either). If you're Joe Ordinary, your documents aren't of interest to anyone else.

Get connected

Chapter Two

This chapter explains how to connect your computer to the Internet. You don't have a computer? Never mind, you'll find out how to choose one. You'll also learn how to choose a modem and an Internet service provider. Throw in a little software and you're on your way.

Covers

Three simple steps

Now you know what the Internet is and where it came from, you're ready to get connected. It's time to make the giant leap from isolated individualism to interconnected bliss.

As with most giant leaps, connecting to the Internet is actually very easy. You don't have to throw yourself into the technological abyss, clutching this book to your chest. You just have to complete three simple steps and presto, you've joined the party:

1. **Sort out your computer.** If you don't have a computer, you'll need to get one. Sorry, there's no way around it. If you've just bought a computer, it probably came with everything you need to connect it to the Internet. You can skip ahead to Step 2. If you've owned your computer for a couple of years, or you've inherited one from another member of your family, you'll have to give it a once-over to see whether it's fit for the job. You may also need to install a modem. Read pages 23–24 to find out more.

2. **Choose an Internet service provider (ISP).** Your service provider acts as a go-between, bridging the gap between your computer and the millions of others that are permanently connected together, forming the Internet. There are lots of ISPs, offering various levels of service, so you'll need to consider all the options and find a company that can make you happy. Pages 26–29 explain what to look for when you're choosing an ISP.

3. **Set up your software.** In most cases, setting up your software is as simple as inserting a CD from your service provider and clicking a couple of buttons. Sometimes you have to do a little more work. If you don't get a CD, or you want to transfer your Internet account to another computer, you may need to set up the software yourself. Follow the step-by-step guide on pages 34-36.

Choose a computer

You can connect to the Internet with almost any type of computer, but if you want an easy life, choose a Windows PC or an Apple Macintosh (Mac). You won't find much else in the shops, anyway.

Boring beige PC or trendy iMac?

If you're trying to decide between a PC and a Mac, consider the following. Everyone hates PCs. Some people like Macs. Despite what the Mac people will tell you, Macs are no easier to use than PCs – but the new iMacs come in nicer colours. Nevertheless, PCs dominate the personal-computer market. If you have a problem, it's easy to find another PC user who can help. When you want to purchase software or hardware, you have many more choices.

The Internet looks much the same from either type of computer.

Use a Windows PC or an Apple Mac to access the National Geographic Web site at: http://www.nationalgeographic.com/

The Web from a Windows PC

The Web from a Mac

Through the square window

If terms such as 'processor' and 'hard disk' mean nothing to you, look out for 'PCs in easy steps', another book in this series. You might also want a copy of 'Windows XP in easy steps – in full colour'.

The book concentrates on accessing the Internet from a Windows PC, because that's what most people have. If you've just bought your PC, it'll have the latest version of the Windows operating system, Windows XP. If you have an older computer running an older version of Windows, such as Windows Me or Windows 98, think about upgrading. Windows XP includes new software that makes it easier to get connected.

If you're buying a new computer, get one with a fast processor, plenty of memory (RAM), a large hard disk and a display that gives you 16.7 million colours at a resolution of 1,024x768 pixels.

Choose a modem

A modem is a box of electronics that converts computer data into audio signals that can be transmitted over a telephone line.

Once you've learned how to connect to the Internet, you can eavesdrop on your modem. Get connected, then pick up the handset of any telephone attached to the same line. You'll hear a hissing noise – that's your modem. Hang up before it gets upset and breaks the connection.

You can think of your modem as a very small office that houses a very small person who reads out the information from your computer. At the other end of the line, another very small person in another modem listens to the incoming data and keys it into the other computer. Occasionally the two people chat backwards and forwards to make sure everything is getting through. From a technological point of view, it's a strange way to communicate (see page 30 for more advanced solutions), but it's cheap and it works.

In, out, shake it all about

Most new computers have an internal modem tucked away inside the system box (sometimes the modem is optional, so check before you buy). You also get a phone cable so you can physically connect the modem to a convenient telephone point. If the nearest point is already occupied, go down to the local electronics store and get a line splitter – an adaptor that lets you plug two telephone cables into the same socket.

For more information about the USRobotics V.92 Faxmodem USB (pictured), visit the company's Web site at: http://www.usr.com/

If you need to buy a modem, get an external model that sits on your desk. It'll be easier to install than an internal one (you don't need a screwdriver, for starters) and you can move it from one computer to another. Pick one that connects to a USB port and you'll only need two cables – one to connect the computer to the modem and another to connect the modem to the phone point.

'Download' means to copy information from the Internet to your computer. When you send information the other way, you 'upload' it.

Make sure your new modem supports V.92, the latest standard for modem communications. A V.92 modem can download data at up to 56kbps (see opposite) and upload it at up to 48kbps. An older modem that uses the V.90 standard will also be okay, if that's what you have. A V.90 modem downloads at up to 56kbps and uploads at up to 31.2kbps.

Those mysterious numbers

Hard-disk manufacturers aren't good at maths and often define a gigabyte as one billion bytes, even though the proper answer is 1,073,741,824 bytes. They believe (rightly) that you won't notice that you only have room for 19.1Gb of data on your 20Gb hard disk.

This page will make your head hurt. It's only in the book because some people like to know exactly how fast their connection is. If you're happy with relative terms like 'slow', 'not so slow' and 'really quite fast', you can skip ahead.

- The smallest unit of data is a bit. If you put eight bits together, you get the next unit, a byte. From there, data is accumulated into bigger, more familiar units. There are 1,024 bytes in a kilobyte (K or Kb), 1,024 kilobytes in a megabyte (Mb) and 1,024 megabytes in a gigabyte (Gb).
- File sizes are measured in kilobytes, or megabytes when you're dealing with large files such as video clips.
- Data-transfer speeds are measured in bits per second (bps). When you get up to 1,000bps, you have a transfer rate of one kilobit per second (kbps). When you reach 1,000kbps, you're transferring data at one megabit per second (Mbps). A rate of 1Mbps counts as 'really quite fast', at least in 2003.
- Now things get tricky. A kilobyte is 1,024 bytes or 8,192 bits. A kilobit is only 1,000 bits. If your connection is running at 1kbps, it takes just over eight seconds to transfer 1K of data. In other words, a small 'k' is different from a big 'K'.
- As a rough guide, you can work out how long it will take to transfer a file by dividing the connection speed by ten. A 56kbps connection can transfer 5–6K of data per second, so a 100K file takes about 20 seconds to download. Even less accurately, it takes about four minutes to download 1Mb of data. In practical terms, 1Mb equates to thousands of words, or a handful of digital photographs, or a minute of CD-quality music, or 10-20 seconds of video.
- To make things worse, people sometimes abbreviate 'kbps' to 'K'. A 56K connection is really a 56kbps connection.
- There are reasons why file sizes and data-transfer speeds are measured differently, but they're complicated to explain. Try to keep your 'K's and 'k's in order... and remember that your files will get there eventually, even if you don't.

Choose a service provider

Your Internet service provider is your new best friend, at least when it comes to the Internet. It reaches out a hand, enabling you to seize hold and become part of a giant chain of people (and computers) stretching all around the globe.

At your service

Internet service providers vary greatly. Some provide a bare-bones service aimed at expert users looking for a low-cost option. Others offer more support for beginners, or extra features for business people, or games servers for people who want to run around and shoot things. In general, though, an ISP does five things:

- **It provides connectivity.** The main role of an ISP is to help people access the Internet. It has a powerful computer that is permanently connected to the Internet, and also to a bank of modems. You connect your computer to the ISP's computer, via the telephone system. Information passes from your computer to your modem, which sends it down the phone line to the ISP's modem, which passes it on to the ISP's computer, which sends it on to other computers – and vice versa. Your computer is (temporarily) part of the Internet.
- **It provides software and technical support.** If you have a relatively new computer, you'll have all the software you need, but setting it up can be complicated. Some service providers give you a setup CD that configures your computer automatically. Others help you out over the telephone or have Web sites that answer your questions.
- **It takes care of your mail.** You can only receive electronic mail while your computer is connected to the Internet. When it is off-line, your ISP stores your messages in an electronic mail box on its computer. It also helps you dispatch your outgoing messages.
- **It provides a home for your Web pages.** If you want to create your own Web pages and share them with other people, you'll need to store them on a computer that's permanently connected to the Internet. And who do you trust with a computer like that? Many ISPs give you a few megabytes of space that you can use for your Web site.

When your computer is connected to the Internet, it is 'on-line'. When it is not connected, it is 'off-line'. Information can also be 'on-line' (available on the Internet) or 'off-line' (not available).

- **It provides additional services.** Most ISPs give you access to Usenet newsgroups (see Chapter 10). Some enhance their service with extras such as game servers for multiplayer gaming, global roaming so you can access the Internet when you're overseas, and reception or forwarding of faxes. A few – notably AOL and CompuServe – have private discussion forums and extra content that's only available to members.

Everyone has their price

One of the more difficult things about connecting to the Internet is working out how much it's going to cost. In most countries there are lots of ISPs, big and small, all competing furiously for the small amount of money you're prepared to part with. You'll have to sift through all the deals to find one that suits.

There are two things you might have to pay for: the phone calls you make to connect to the Internet and the services provided by your ISP. In some countries local calls are free, so you only have to worry about the ISP charges (don't get smug, they'll be higher). In other places your calls can be the most significant expense.

There are four basic charging schemes:

- **Pay as you go.** In the UK, there are many ISPs that offer a 'free' service. It costs nothing to open an account and there are no monthly charges. The ISP funds its services by taking a percentage of your call charges. You don't pay any extra for the calls, your phone company just makes a bit less, because it shares the profits with the ISP. However, if you need help and have to call the technical-support line, you're charged a premium rate to cover the cost of staffing the help desk.

- **Unmetered access.** With an unmetered deal, you pay a flat monthly fee that covers your phone charges *and* the services from your ISP. This arrangement is available in countries where ISPs can get together with phone companies to offer a joint package. You may also be able to sign up for a cheaper deal that only gives you access during off-peak hours.

- **Flat-rate subscriptions with calls on the side.** In the UK, subscription-based services used to be the norm. You paid a flat monthly fee to your ISP and settled your phone bill

Watch out for deals that seem too good to be true. An ISP that isn't making any money won't be able to invest in new equipment, won't offer a reliable service and may not be in business for long.

separately. The monthly fee got you unlimited access to the full range of services, including technical support, and kept the ISP on a firm financial footing. There are still ISPs that operate on this basis, in the UK and elsewhere.

- **Metered subscriptions.** In countries where there's no charge for local calls, people spend more time on the Internet and ISPs have to ration their resources. Some offer subscriptions that entitle you to use the Internet for a set number of hours each month, or to transfer a fixed amount of data. If you go over your allotment, you pay an extra charge. These deals can be good value if you don't use the Internet very much.

You'll also come across more complicated offers that combine Internet access with other benefits, such as reduced rates for long-distance calls. *Always read the fine print very carefully.* Be wary of deals that require you to make a long-term commitment. You might not find the Internet useful (unlikely), or you might use it more than you expect, or market conditions might change, making other packages more attractive.

The secret's in the sauce

To find out what's available in your area, flick through a couple of Internet magazines. You'll probably find a directory listing all the local ISPs. If you don't, look at the ads.

There are lots of things to consider when you're comparing ISPs:

- **Price.** Try to work out how much you'll spend each month, including the cost of your phone calls. As a rough guide, even a light user will spend 5–10 hours on-line. If you have school-age children or run a business from home, you might clock up 25–50 hours. In the worst-case scenario, there are 744 hours in a 31-day month...

- **Service.** How many e-mail addresses do you get? It's nice to have a separate address for each member of the family. How big is your mail box? You don't want it to overflow if you go away for a few days. Also, can you access your messages via the Web (see Chapter 9)? How much space do you get for your Web site? More is always better. What extra features does the ISP offer, and do they sound at all useful?

- **Access numbers.** Make sure you can reach your ISP with a local phone call. In the UK, most ISPs use special phone numbers that are charged at the same rate as a local call, no matter where you are. In other countries, you may need to find an ISP that has an access number or 'point of presence' (PoP) in your local call area.
- **Modem support.** Check that your ISP supports the latest modem standard (V.92 at the time of writing). Also, make sure it has plenty of modems so there's always one to connect to. A subscriber-to-modem ratio of 15:1 is okay.
- **Technical support.** If you have computer-savvy friends who are willing to help you out, you may not need technical support. If you're the chief boffin and everyone is counting on you to solve all the problems, find out how much you'll pay for calls to the helpline. Check the hours – a helpline that's open during working hours isn't much use if you plan to use the Internet in the evening and at weekends.
- **Options for the future.** For now, you'll probably be content with connecting via a modem, but in time you might want something faster. Find out whether it'll be possible to upgrade to a broadband connection (see overleaf) if your Internet use increases.
- **Terms and conditions.** All good ISPs have a set of terms and conditions, sometimes referred to as an 'acceptable use policy'. Make sure you can abide by the rules.
- **Reputation.** Any fool can set up an ISP. The difficult thing is providing a reliable, profitable service that makes everyone happy, not just on the day they sign up but in the long term. Choose an ISP that has been around for a while and has a well-established infrastructure and a good reputation. If possible, get a recommendation from a friend.

Changing ISPs is a nuisance – you lose your e-mail address, for example. At the same time, you aren't marrying the company, so don't spend too long fretting over all the options. Pick an ISP and get on with it! If things don't work out, you can try again. It's easier to make the right choice with some experience behind you.

The need for speed

Until now, this chapter has assumed you're going to use a modem and phone line to connect to the Internet. It's the best (cheapest, easiest, most versatile) option for a beginner. However, there are alternatives, so let's take a quick diversion and check them out.

The problem with modems is that they're slow. Computer data is converted into an analogue signal, which creeps down the line and then has to be converted back into its original, digital form. What you really want is a high-speed, digital connection.

Not fast enough: ISDN

Integrated Services Digital Network is a system for transmitting digital information over an ordinary telephone line. You use an ISDN adaptor instead of a modem and you can transfer data at up to 128kbps. That's only two to three times as fast as a modem connection, so ISDN isn't terribly exciting. Don't bother.

Super zippy: ADSL

Asymmetric Digital Subscriber Line is a new technology. Like ISDN, it enables you to transmit digital data over your phone line, but the speeds are much greater. Most services offer download speeds of 512kbps, making ADSL around ten times faster than a modem connection. The upload speed is 256kbps, so you receive data faster than you can send it (in other words, the connection is asymmetric). Most people download a lot more information than they upload, so that isn't normally a problem.

HOT TIP

Both ADSL and cable are technically capable of much greater download speeds than we're seeing today. You can expect even zippier connections in the future.

Beyond the speed, ADSL has two advantages: the connection is 'always on', so your computer connects to the Internet whenever you power it up, and you can still use your phone line for voice calls – the data signal doesn't interfere with your conversations. You need an ADSL modem, microfilters for all your telephone sockets and an ISP that supports ADSL. Normally you pay a flat monthly fee, although some ISPs offer metered subscriptions that allow you to transfer a fixed amount of data.

Also super zippy: Cable

If you live in an area with cable TV, you have a nice fat fibre-optic cable running past your front door. Hook up a cable modem and you can connect to an Internet channel that transmits data instead of long-forgotten soaps and strange sporting events.

Most cable services offer download speeds of 512kbps or 1Mbps (upload speeds are slower). As with ADSL, the connection is 'always on' and doesn't interfere with your television and/or telephone services.

Broadband for everyone?

ADSL and cable are called 'broadband' services because they give you a lot of 'bandwidth' or data-carrying capacity. If accessing the Internet with a modem is like filling a swimming pool with a garden hose, using broadband is like pumping water through one of the big, fat hoses that fire fighters use. Instead of tidying your desk while you wait for Web pages to arrive, you can view them immediately. Multimedia files such as sounds and videos download in seconds instead of minutes, or minutes instead of hours.

A broadband connection enables you to enjoy the movie trailers on Apple's Web site. Find them at: http://www.apple.com/trailers/

With broadband, the Internet is always available, so you don't have to make a special effort to check your e-mail, look at a weather forecast or track down a fact. Broadband is fabulous, and once you've experienced it, you'll never go back to a modem connection.

Nevertheless, broadband isn't always the best option for beginners. It might not be available in your area – you have to be close to a telephone exchange or have cable in your street. Both ADSL and cable services are relatively new and you may encounter technical hiccups, particularly on installation. Broadband is also expensive – you have to use the Internet a lot to get good value from it.

In the future, everyone will have some type of high-speed connection. For now, you have to look at the services available in your area and decide whether they're worth your attention.

Snip the wires

If your job keeps you dashing hither and thither, collecting frequent-flyer miles and drinking bad coffee in roadside cafés, the issue isn't the speed of your connection, but its portability. You need Internet-to-go, in the form of a wireless connection.

Is that a phone in your pocket?

You can connect to the Internet using that top fashion accessory of the 1990s, a mobile phone. You need a special modem, either built in to the phone or installed in your laptop computer; a means of connecting your phone to the laptop; and a lot of patience. This type of connection is very, very slow. It's okay for collecting e-mail messages, but you'll only want to use the Web in emergencies – when your client needs a report yesterday, or when you have a lot of money riding on the cricket score.

It's the World Wide Web... except it isn't

To compensate for the slowness of wireless connections, some clever person invented Wireless Access Protocol (WAP), a system for accessing cutdown Web sites from a mobile phone. It isn't really the Web, because you can only access sites that have been designed for this purpose, and it isn't much good, because phones have tiny screens and can't display enough information. Ignore it.

Things can only get better

Coming soon to a mobile-phone network near you: a system called General Packet Radio Service (GPRS), closely followed by third-generation services (3G). These natty acronyms conceal new network technologies that will facilitate much faster data transmissions. You'll be able to lie on the beach with your laptop, browsing the Web as you brown your buttocks. Hardware companies are also developing pocket-sized devices that will combine colour screens, cameras and Internet access with standard mobile-phone features such as annoying ring tones. You'll only need one device to stay in touch by voice, fax, e-mail and video.

GPRS services are already available in some countries – contact your local mobile phone networks for details.

Set up your software

If you opt for ADSL, cable or a wireless connection, your ISP should help you install the hardware and set up your connection. You can skip ahead to Chapter 3.

Assuming you haven't been lured away by the high speed of broadband or the high technology of wireless connections, it's time for the final phase of the Internet three-step: setting up the software. This is easier than it might sound.

In most cases you get a CD from your service provider. Simply insert it into your PC and follow the on-screen instructions. The software on the disc configures your computer, telling it the phone number to dial and any special settings to use.

Find out more about UK ISPs Virgin.net and Freeserve from their Web sites at: http://www.virgin.net/ and http://www.freeserve.net/ respectively.

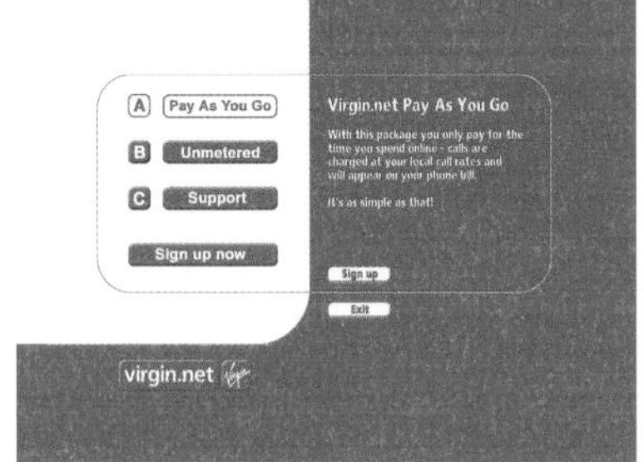

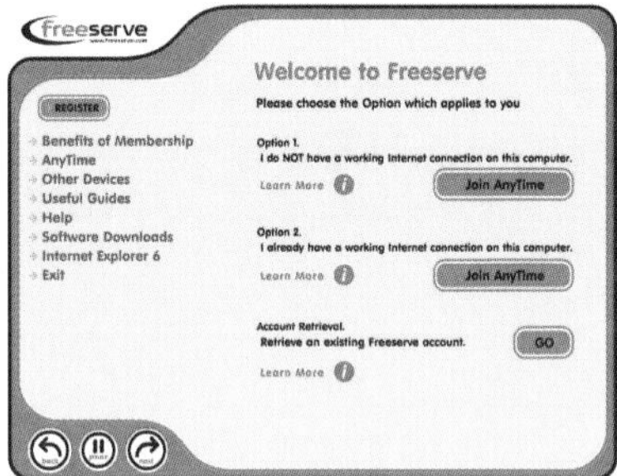

You'll probably be asked to choose a user name and password. The user name forms part of your e-mail address (see page 119), so choose it carefully. A user name that has your friends in stitches may not seem as amusing when you're applying for a job. Your password should be easy to remember, but difficult for other people to guess (see page 100). Some service providers assign passwords automatically to prevent people from choosing very obvious ones, such as names or birth dates.

Do it yourself

Sometimes you'll need to set up your software by hand. Your service provider may not give you a CD or you may want more control over the setup process. If you need to reinstall Windows, writing down and re-entering your details takes less time than hunting out a CD you haven't used for months.

To connect to the Internet, Windows needs to know how to reach your service provider. Your modem needs to be installed correctly (follow the manufacturer's instructions) and you need to enter your service provider's phone number. Windows also needs your user name and password so it can identify you when it connects. If your ID isn't acceptable, you won't get through the door.

Windows XP has a New Connection Wizard that helps you enter all this information. You'll need the following details:

- Your service provider's phone number (the modem number, not the number you call to speak to someone).
- Your user name and password.

Later on, you'll also need:

Turn to page 121 to find out how to set up Outlook Express so you can send and receive e-mail. Page 155 explains how to access newsgroups.

- Your e-mail address.
- The addresses of your service provider's mail servers (normally there are two, one for sending mail and another for receiving it).
- The address of your service provider's news server.

It's a good idea to record this information and keep it somewhere convenient – but not anywhere too obvious, because you should keep your password secret. If there's anything you don't know, call your service provider.

1. Click the Start button and select All Programs> Accessories> Communications> New Connection Wizard

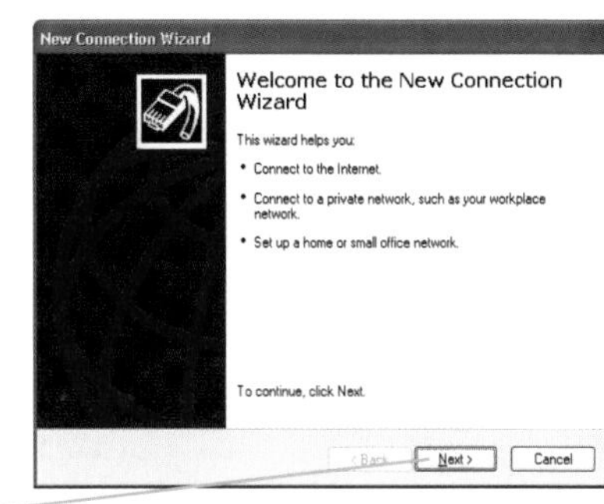

2. Click Next to continue (and at the end of step)

If you're setting up an office computer and will be dialling out through a switchboard, fill in the 'If you dial a number to access an outside line...' section of the Location dialogue box.

3. The Location Information dialogue box may pop up and ask you where you are. Select your country and enter your area code, if applicable. Click OK to continue

4. When you get back to the New Connection Wizard, select 'Connect to the Internet'

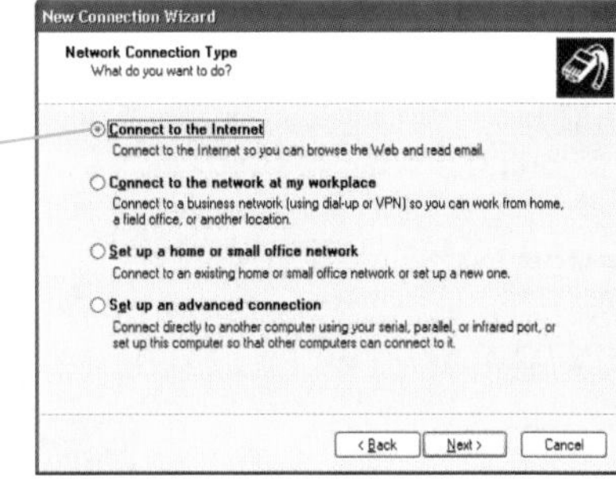

5. Select 'Set up my connection manually'

6. Select 'Connect using a dial-up modem'

7. Fill in the name of your Internet service provider

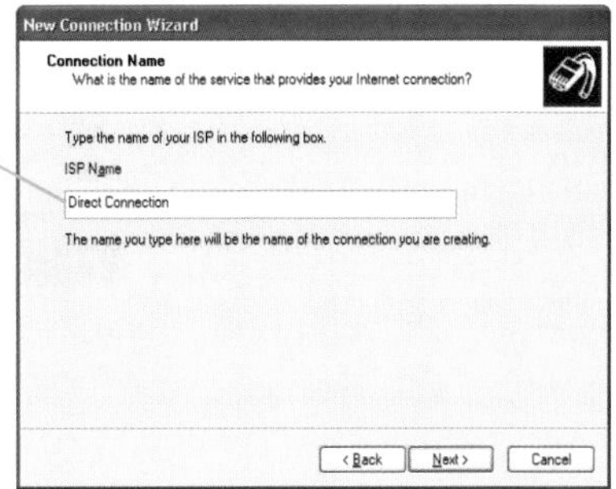

8. Enter your service provider's access number. Including the dialling code if it is different from your own dialling code

9 Enter your user name and password. The password characters are hidden, so you have to enter it twice. Leave the bottom three options selected if everyone in the family is sharing your account. If other people will use their own accounts *from this computer*, deselect the first option

If you decide to have a shortcut icon on your desktop, you'll be able to connect to the Internet by double-clicking it. However, you won't normally need to do that, because Windows will prompt you to connect when you run an Internet program – see overleaf.

10 If you want a shortcut icon on your desktop, select that option

11 Click Finish to create the connection and close the wizard

You can use the Connect To menu option to connect to the Internet – just select your service provider. However, you won't normally need to do that – see above and overleaf.

12 Click the Start button. You should have a Connect To option on the right-hand side of the Start menu

Make connections

If you are running old or badly designed software that doesn't prompt Windows to connect to the Internet, you may need to open the connection yourself – see the HOT TIPs on the previous page.

When you run an Internet program, Windows checks whether you are connected to the Internet. If you aren't, it prompts you to dial your service provider.

1 To run Internet Explorer, the Web browser built in to Windows XP, click the Start button and select Internet from the left-hand side of the Start menu

If you select the 'Connect automatically' checkbox, Windows will make connections without waiting for you to click the Connect button. Generally that's a bad idea, because you can run up big bills by connecting accidentally.

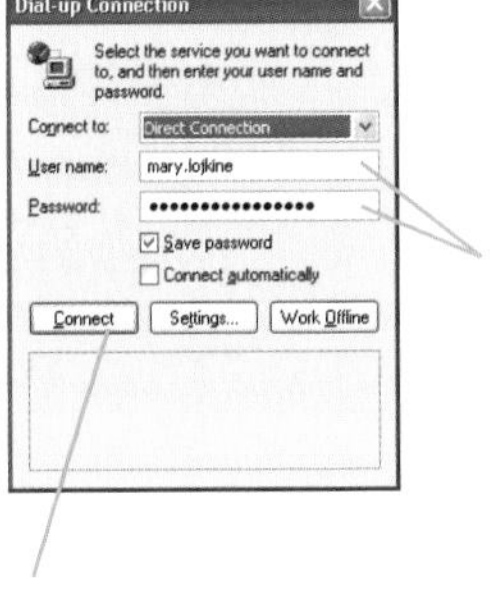

2 The Dial-up Connection dialogue box appears. Your user name and password should be filled in – if they aren't, enter them

3 Click the Connect button. You should hear your modem dial and then connect. Status messages appear at the bottom of the box

Opening a connection to the Internet is often referred to as 'logging on'. Likewise, 'logging off' means closing the connection.

4 A yellow speech bubble lets you know that the connection has been established

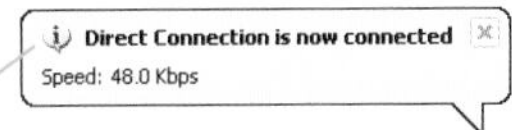

5 Internet Explorer displays a Web page like this, or a page from your service provider's Web site

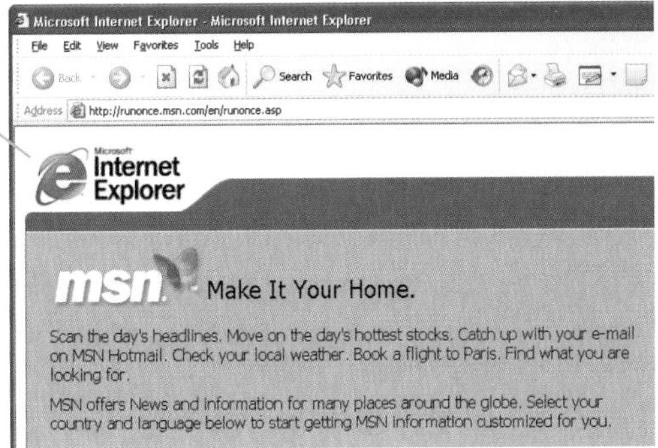

6 You're ready to learn how to browse the Web (see Chapter 3)

7 When you have finished using the Internet, you need to disconnect. Go to the notification area at the right-hand end of the Windows taskbar. Look for an icon that shows two computers joined together

Don't get the Disconnect and Close buttons confused. When you click the Disconnect button, you end your Internet session. When you click Close, you simply close the dialogue box, without disconnecting your computer from the Internet. To check that you've disconnected correctly, pick up your telephone receiver. You should hear a normal dial tone. If you hear a roaring, hissing noise, you're still connected.

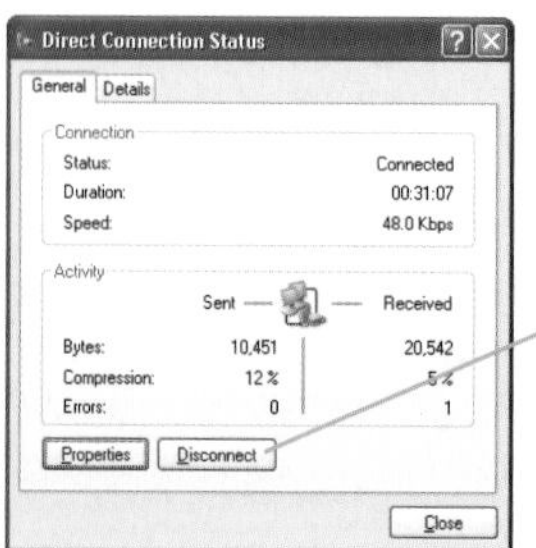

8 Double-click the icon to bring up the Status dialogue box. Click the Disconnect button to close the connection

Ready, change settings, go

Some of the connection settings are specific to Internet Explorer, but most of them apply to most Internet programs. If you use a program that requires you to open the connection yourself, you may have to disconnect manually as well.

Your connection settings determine how and when your computer connects to the Internet. You can alter them so it only connects when you want it to and disconnects automatically when the connection is idle. That way you don't need to worry about running up a huge phone bill or missing important calls because you've accidentally left the computer connected.

1 Click the Start button and select Control Panel from the right-hand side. Select 'Network and Internet Connections', then 'Set up or change your Internet connection'. The Internet Properties dialogue box appears, with the Connections section at the front

2 If you have accounts with several service providers, all the possible connections are listed. Select the one you use most frequently and click Set Default

3 Select 'Never dial...' to make connections manually using a shortcut icon or the Connect To section of the Start menu (see page 36). The 'Always dial...' option enables your computer to make connections as required and is the best choice

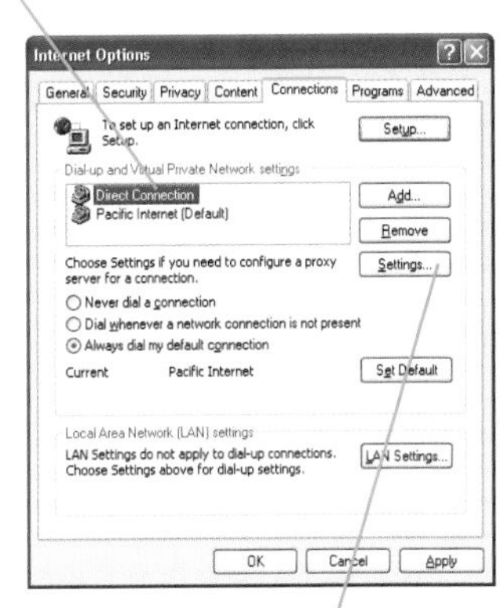

4 To fine-tune the options for a particular ISP, select it and click Settings. This opens the dialogue box shown overleaf

A proxy server stores copies of all the Web pages that have been viewed by people who use your service provider. If there's a copy of the page you want to see, your Web browser can download it from the proxy server more quickly than it could fetch it from the original Web site. In some countries proxy servers are also used to prevent people from accessing undesirable material.

5 If your service provider has a proxy server, select this checkbox and enter the address

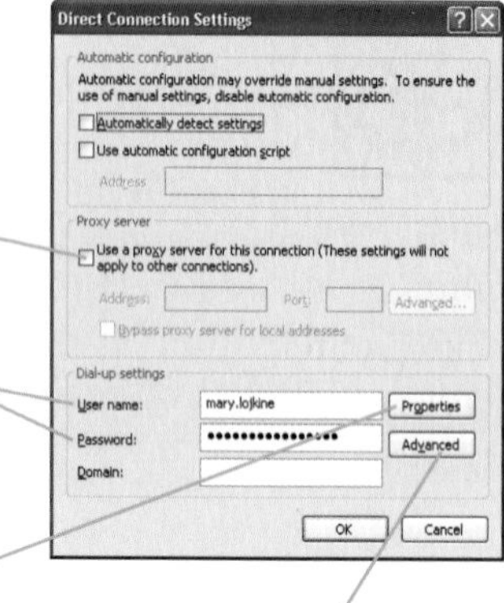

6 If your user name or password changes, update your details here

7 If your service provider's phone number changes, click Properties and enter the new one

8 Click Advanced for further options

9 If all your service provider's modems are busy, your computer waits for a few seconds and then tries again. Tell it how many times to redial and how long to wait between attempts

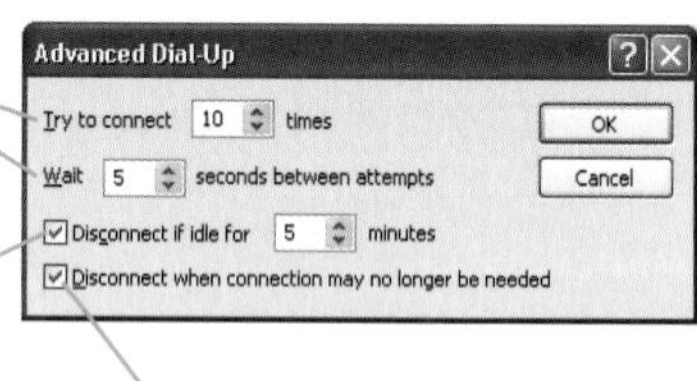

10 Select 'Disconnect if idle' to close the connection if you don't seem to be doing anything. You may want to reduce the idle time

11 Select 'Disconnect when connection may no longer be needed' to end your session if you've closed all your Internet programs

12 Click OK three times to close all the dialogue boxes

Click around the Web

The World Wide Web is the Internet's friendly face. It's colourful and attractive and provides straightforward, easy-clicking entertainment. This chapter covers the concept, the software and the address system, then sends you off to browse.

Covers

Chapter Three

What is the Web?

The World Wide Web has been such a success that many people think it *is* the Internet. In reality, it's just one aspect of it – the prettiest and most popular one. Everyone likes the Web because it's attractive to look at, easy to use and packed with information.

But what is it, exactly?

The Web consists of over a billion pages of text and graphics. Since they are designed to be viewed on a computer screen, they can also contain multimedia elements such as animations, sound files and video clips. It's like a gigantic, full-colour magazine, with built-in speakers and a television screen in the centre.

Web pages are held together by a system of electronic cross-references called hyperlinks. Instead of physically turning the pages, you use your mouse to click on a piece of text – or a graphic – that is electronically connected to another page. The beauty of this system is that it doesn't matter where the other page is located. It might be stored on the same computer as the first one, or on another computer on the other side of the globe. Also, one Web page can be linked to many others. The whole thing is held together by a tangled web of electronic connections that stretches all around the world – hence 'World Wide Web'.

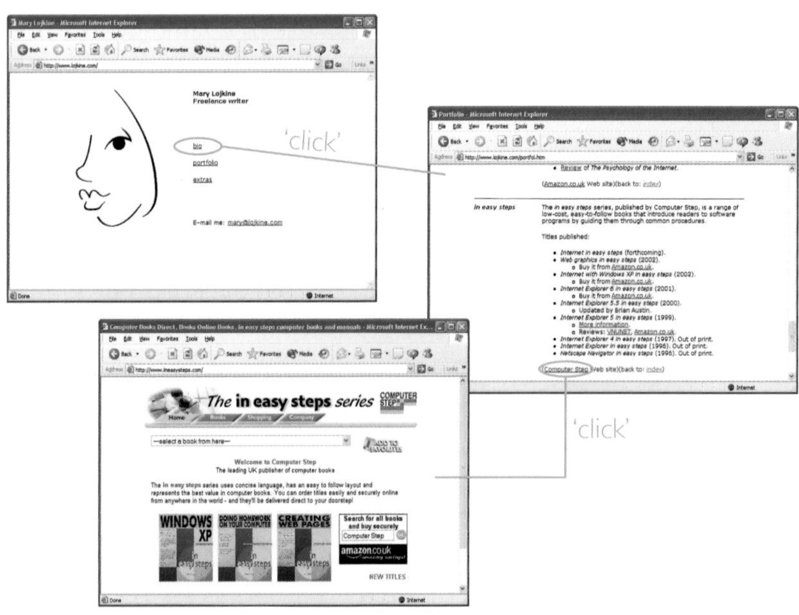

If you know exactly where a Web page is stored, you can tell your computer the address and go straight to it. If you don't know the address, there are various ways to find it (you'll learn more about searching for information in Chapter 4). However, one of the great things about the Web is that you can find things you didn't know you were looking for, simply by following the hyperlinks. For example, you might start on a Web page about penguins, which points you towards an artist who makes paper penguins, who recommends the electronic incarnation of Bristol Zoo, which diverts you to the Bristol section of the BBC's Web site, and before you know it you're reading about a new battery that makes electricity from leftover food.

A Web site is a collection of related Web pages. They all belong to the same person, group or company and they're all on the same topic.

Anyone can create a Web site, so there's a huge range of material to explore. Many newspapers publish an on-line edition. You can read the latest stories or click back in time to find out how a situation developed. Universities and museums use the Web to share information about their research and educate Joe Public. Government bodies have sites that keep you informed about everything from political developments to parking charges and companies provide screeds of information about their products. You can check all the techy details before you hand over your cash.

Catch the news on the CNN Web site at: http://www.cnn.com/ or visit Ancient Afghanistan at the British Museum at: http://www.thebritishmuseum.ac.uk/

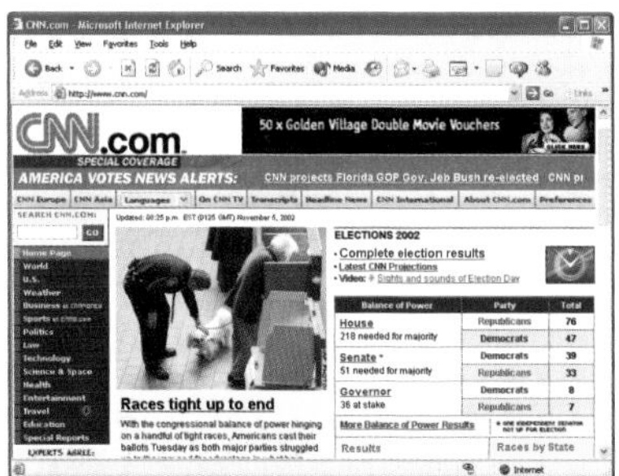

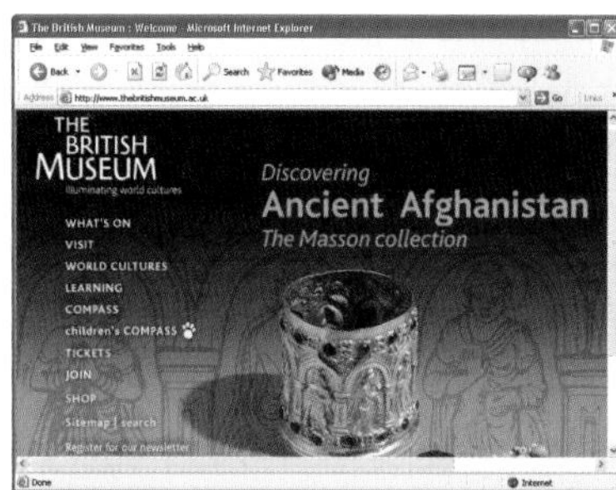

There are also millions of Web pages created by private individuals who simply have a passion for their subject, be it penguins, pop stars or their personal, day-to-day life. Sometimes the Web feels like a giant scrapbook, packed with pictures and comments from anyone and everyone, be they famous or unknown, expert or amateur, completely ordinary or deeply strange. That's another great thing about it: you get a complete cross-section of views.

Choose a Web browser

You need a Web browser to view or 'browse' the Web. It's a specialised piece of software designed to display Web pages and follow the links between them. Browsers also store the addresses of your favourite pages so you can find them again (see page 66).

Netscape's browser has had several names. In the beginning, it was Navigator. Then it was combined with a couple of other Internet programs to create a do-it-all package called Communicator. Now this package is also known as Netscape – so in theory it's Netscape's Netscape. In practice, people use whichever name they remember first: Navigator, Communicator or Netscape.

There are two Web browsers in common use: Microsoft's Internet Explorer and Netscape's Navigator. Navigator was the first really successful Web browser, but aggressive marketing by Microsoft has pushed Internet Explorer to the fore. By the end of 2002 it was estimated that around 95 per cent of Internet users were running Internet Explorer, leaving fewer than five per cent using Navigator. A small number of people use other browsers, notably Opera.

The two main browsers are more similar than different and have many features in common. Web pages don't always look exactly the same in both browsers, because some sites are designed to take advantage of special features of one or other program. However, it's unusual to see significant differences.

For science aplenty, visit the Web site of New Scientist magazine at http://www.newscientist.com/

Internet Explorer

Navigator

This book concentrates on Internet Explorer, partly because of its overwhelming popularity and partly because it's included with Windows, so most people have a copy. To learn more about the alternatives, visit the following Web sites:

Netscape Communications at: http://www.netscape.com/
Opera Software at: http://www.opera.com/

Internet Explorer at your service

Internet Explorer is also known as 'IE', 'MSIE' or 'Explorer'.

To run Internet Explorer, click the Start button and select it from the left-hand side of the Start menu.

Like most Windows programs, it has a title bar, menu bar and toolbars across the top of the window and a status bar at the bottom. The most important areas of the screen are:

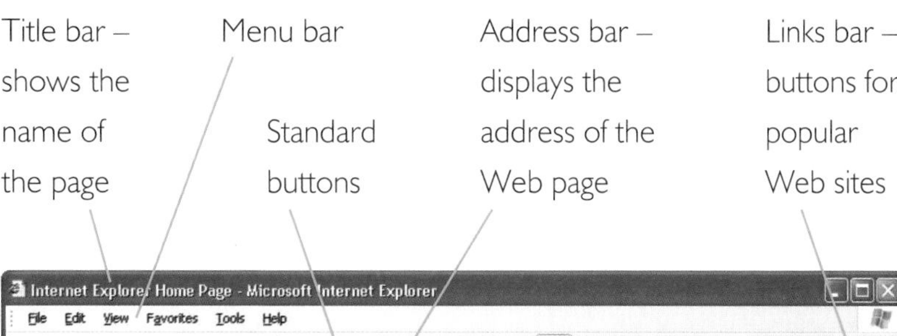

If you use a CD from your service provider to set up your Internet connection (see page 33), it may customise Internet Explorer. Don't be alarmed if your version looks slightly different.

For news about Internet Explorer, plus how-to articles and advice, visit Microsoft's Web site at: http://www.microsoft.com/windows/ie/

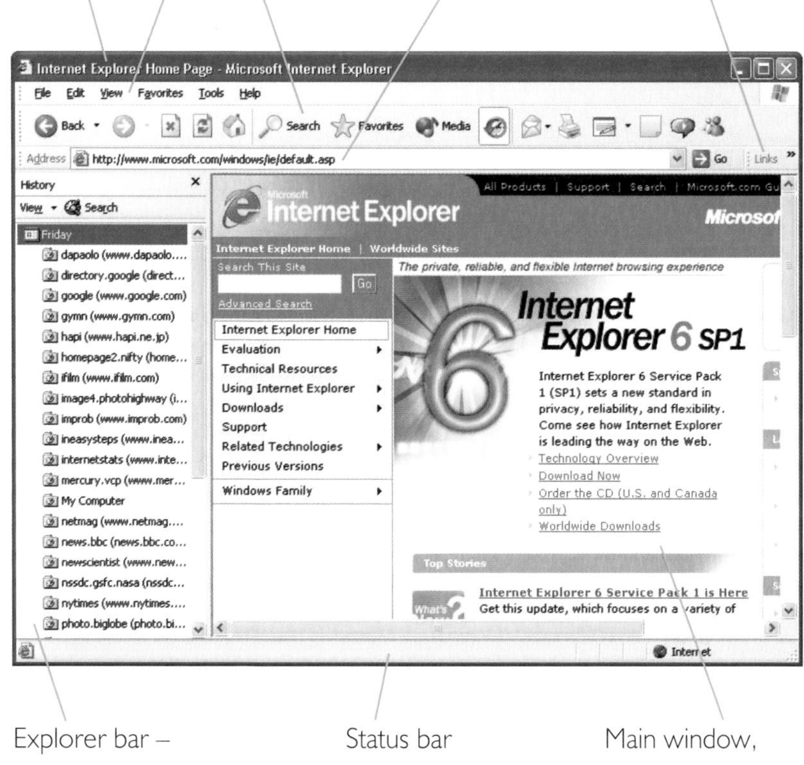

You can customise Internet Explorer by rearranging the toolbars or turning off some of them – see page 57.

Crack the address code

The Worldwide Web Guide at the back of this book contains lots of addresses for you to try.

Once you're comfortable with Internet Explorer's interface, you're ready to go somewhere. Every Web page has a unique address, sometimes known as a Uniform Resource Locator (URL). You've probably seen Web addresses in newspapers and on television.

The address for Microsoft's Internet Explorer Web page is:

Address http://www.microsoft.com/windows/ie/default.asp

The http: indicates that you're dealing with a Web page

This is the name of the Web server – the computer where the page is stored

This section tells your browser which folder the page is stored in

This is the name of the document that describes the page

HTTP is short for HyperText Transfer Protocol, a set of rules for transferring Web pages. If you see an address beginning with https, you're looking at a secure Web page – see page 98.

Internet Explorer assumes you are looking for a Web page, so you don't have to type the http:// at the beginning. If you're looking for the main page of a company's site, you can also leave out everything after the first single slash. To find the main page of Microsoft's Web site, you would enter: www.microsoft.com

Understanding Web addresses

You don't have to understand how Web addresses are constructed, you just have to type them correctly. However, they can provide clues about where a page is located and who it belongs to.

Web addresses never contain spaces, but they can include hyphens and some other punctuation. Sometimes they are case sensitive, so if you see a capital 'T' in an address, don't type a lower-case 't'.

The name of the Web server usually has three or four sections:

www.microsoft.com
www.bbc.co.uk

The first section (www) is used to distinguish between different computers belonging to the same organisation. It's known as a host name. The middle section (microsoft or bbc) is usually the owner's name. The last section (.com) or last two sections (.co.uk) tell you what type of organisation owns the address, and sometimes where it is located. Collectively, the last two or three sections (microsoft.com or bbc.co.uk) are known as a domain name.

The rules for domain names reflect the haphazard evolution of the Internet. The most common single-section endings are:

.com	commercial entity (but also used by individuals)
.org	organisation (usually non-profit)
.net	Internet-related business (such as an ISP)
.int	international body (such as the United Nations)

There are three 'global' top-level domains that are reserved for US organisations. They are .edu (education), .gov (government) and .mil (military).

These endings are known as global top-level domains, because the owner can be based anywhere in the world. Seven new ones have recently been added: .aero (air transport), .biz (businesses), .coop (co-operatives), .info (information), .museum (museums), .name (individuals) and .pro (professionals).

For a complete list of country codes, visit the Web site of the Internet Assigned Numbers Authority (IANA), at: http://www.iana.org/cctld/cctld.htm

Two-section endings consist of an organisation code and a country code: .uk (United Kingdom), .fr (France), .de (Germany), .za (South Africa), .au (Australia), .nz (New Zealand), .sg (Singapore) and so on. The organisation codes differ from country to country. In the UK, the most common endings are:

.co.uk	equivalent to .com
.org.uk	equivalent to .org
.net.uk	equivalent to .net
.ac.uk	academic institution (but not a school, which would have a .sch.uk address)
.gov.uk	government

Other countries have similar organisation codes, although it's quite common to use .com instead of .co and .edu in place of .ac.

If you don't know an organisation's Web address, you can quite often guess it, simply by following the rules. For example, suppose you're looking for the Singapore Web site of electronics giant Sony. Two possibilities spring to mind:

http://www.sony.co.sg/
http://www.sony.com.sg/

If you try them both, you'll find the second address is correct.

Enter an address

If you know the address of the Web page you wish to visit, enter it into Internet Explorer. There are three ways to do this:

If you type ineasysteps and press Ctrl+Enter, www. and .com are added for you.

1 Type the address into the Address bar, then click the Go button or press the Enter key. Internet Explorer finds and displays the page

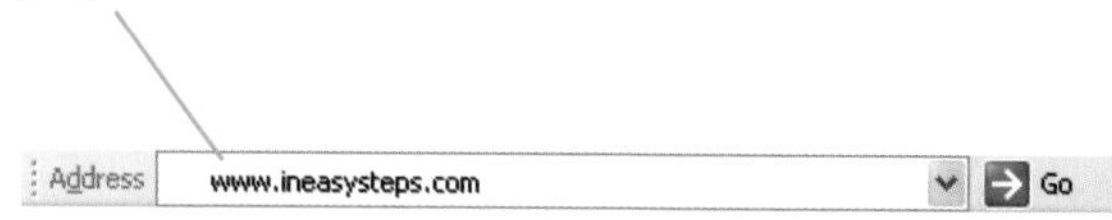

You can also click the arrow at the right-hand end of the Address bar for a list of addresses you've entered recently. This list only shows addresses you've typed yourself.

2 Once you've visited a few sites, Internet Explorer tries to anticipate your typing. If you see the right address in the drop-down list, click on it. You don't have to press Enter

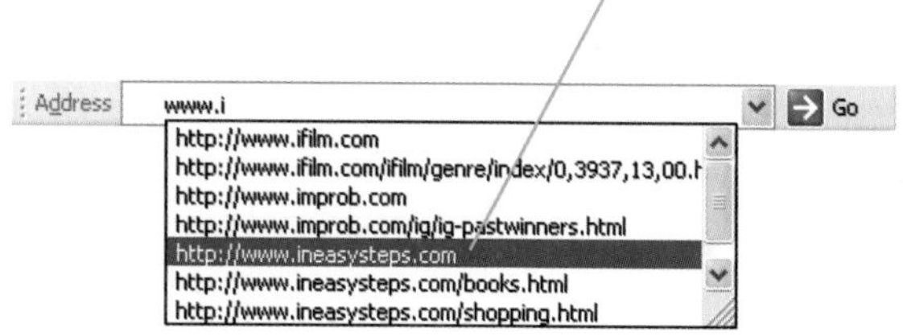

If you don't want Internet Explorer to complete your addresses, turn off this feature under Tools>Internet Options>Content>AutoComplete. To clear the list of addresses, go to Tools>Internet Options>General and click Clear History.

3 The third option is to select Open from the File menu or press Ctrl+O. Both actions bring up the Open dialogue box. Type an address or select one from the list. Click OK

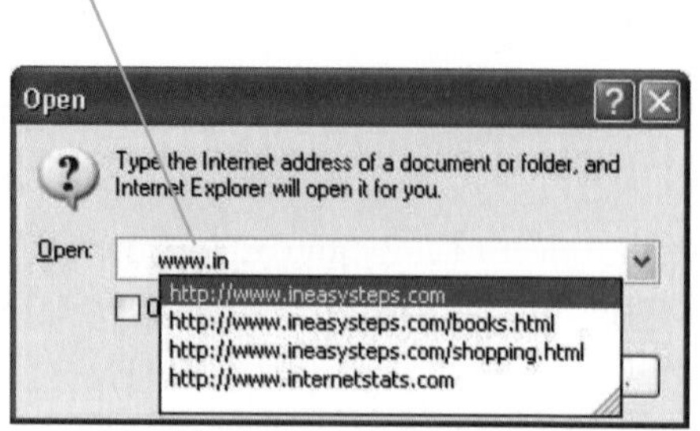

Oh no, it didn't work!

The Internet is constantly evolving: Web sites come and go and computers are moved or upgraded. It's also subject to bugs and bad connections, so sometimes Internet Explorer gives you an error message instead of displaying the page you want to see.

Don't be surprised if you see something quite different. Some Web sites have their own error messages with more specific information.

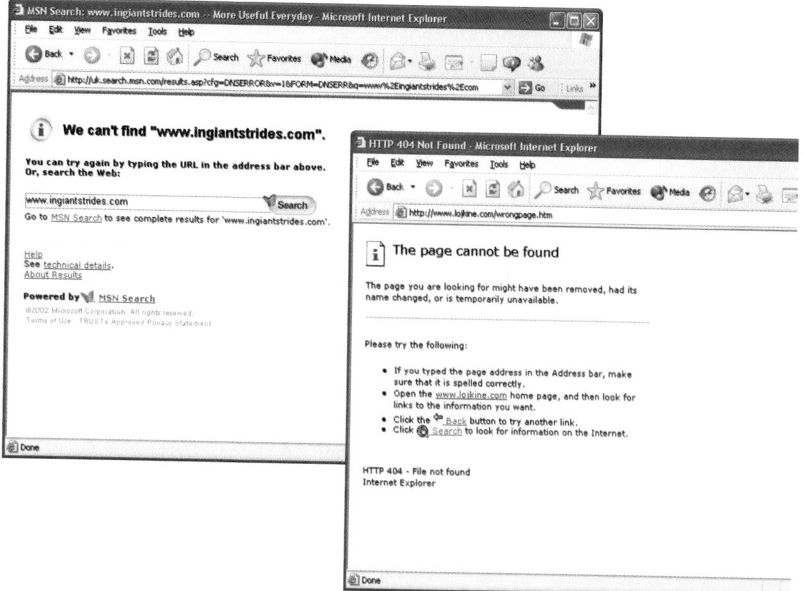

The vast majority of errors arise because:

- You've typed the address incorrectly. Try again, checking the characters carefully before you click Go or press Enter.
- The computer where the page is stored is temporarily out of action. Try again in a few hours.
- The page you want has moved. If this is the case, Internet Explorer displays the address of the main page of the Web site. Click it and try to find the page from there.

Click the links

If you could only get to Web pages by typing in addresses, browsing the Web would be time-consuming and tedious. Fortunately you can use hyperlinks to get about more quickly.

Almost every Web page is linked to anything from one to a hundred or more other pages. Links are usually indicated by coloured, underlined text, and you move to the linked page by clicking this text. For example:

Links can also take you to another section of the same page. For example, long Web pages sometimes have a list of the major subheadings at the top. Clicking on a heading takes you to the relevant subsection.

1 Here's a page from Google's Web directory. If you click the blue, underlined text that says 'Computers'...

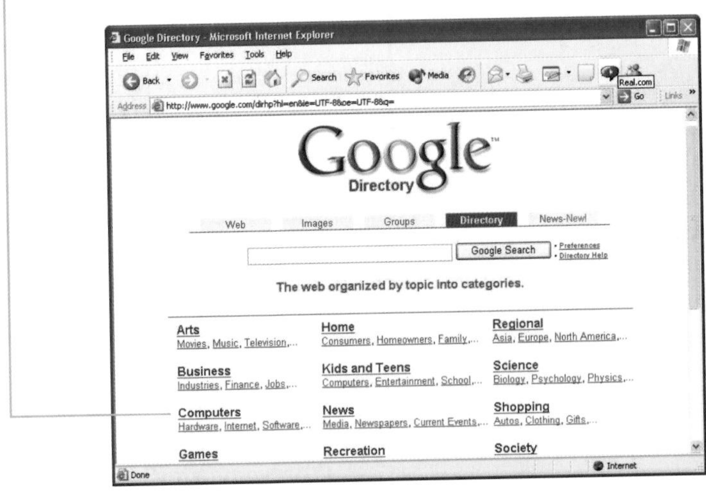

To find out more about Google, turn to page 63 or visit its Web site at: http://www.google.com/

2 ...you are taken to this page, which lists the Computers subcategories. Choose a topic and click again to go to another page

Linked text isn't always blue or underlined. However, you can tell when the mouse pointer is over a link, because it changes into a pointing hand. While you're pointing, check the Status bar. You should see the name of the file or site at the other end of the link. The linked text changes colour after you've clicked it so you can see where you've been.

Graphics can also be used as links – see page 77.

Taking the scenic route

When you click on a link, the new page normally replaces the original one. If you want to display both pages at once, you can load the second one into a new window. This trick is useful when you want to make a detour or compare two Web pages.

Sometimes clicking on a link opens a new window automatically. Web designers can decide how each link should work.

1 Suppose you've found an interesting site in Google's listings. You want to visit it, but you also want to keep the directory on your screen. Hold down Shift when you click the link, or right-click the link and select Open in New Window from the pop-up menu

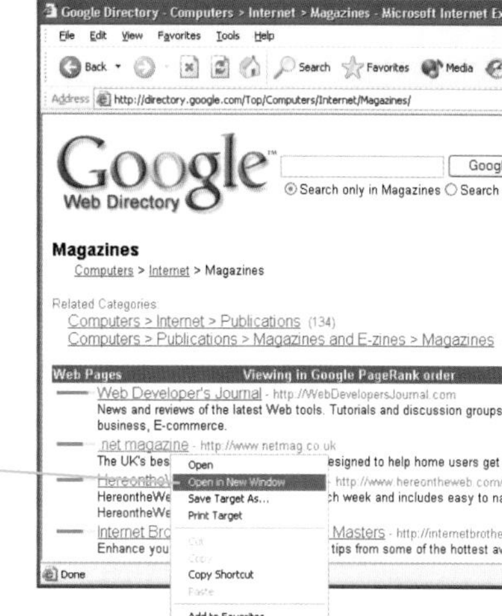

UK Internet magazine .net has an on-line home at: http://www.netmag.co.uk/

2 The linked site gets its own window

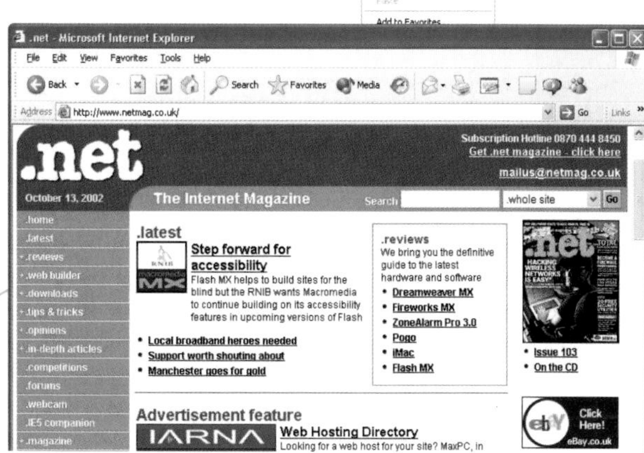

Quick ways to get about

It's easy to get disorientated when you're browsing the Web. There are lots of directions to head in and it's hard to remember where you've been. Internet Explorer helps you retrace your steps.

1 To return to the page you just left, click the Back button or press Alt+Left Arrow

You can use the History bar to return to any page you've visited in the last two or three weeks – see page 69.

2 To go back several pages, click the arrow to the right of the Back button. Select the page you want to revisit from the drop-down list

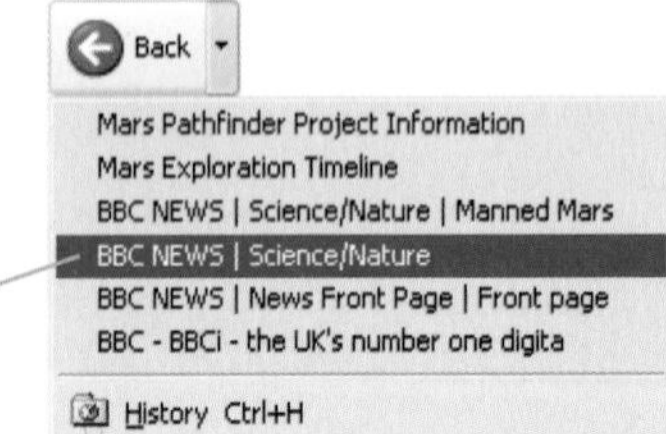

3 Once you've gone back a few pages, you may want to go forward again. Click the Forward button or press Alt+Right Arrow. To go forward several pages, click the arrow to the right of the Forward button

4 If you get lost, you can start again by clicking the Home button or pressing Alt+Home. This takes you to your home page – the page Internet Explorer looks for each time you run it (see page 72)

The logo in the top right corner is animated when a page is downloading and becomes static when the transfer is complete. You can click on links as soon as you see the text – you don't have to wait for the rest of the page to arrive.

5 If a Web page is taking too long to appear, click the Stop button, select View>Stop or press Esc to abort the download

6 If you change your mind and want to see the rest of a half-downloaded page, click the Refresh button, select View>Refresh or press F5 to reload the page. You should also click Refresh if you think Internet Explorer isn't displaying a page correctly

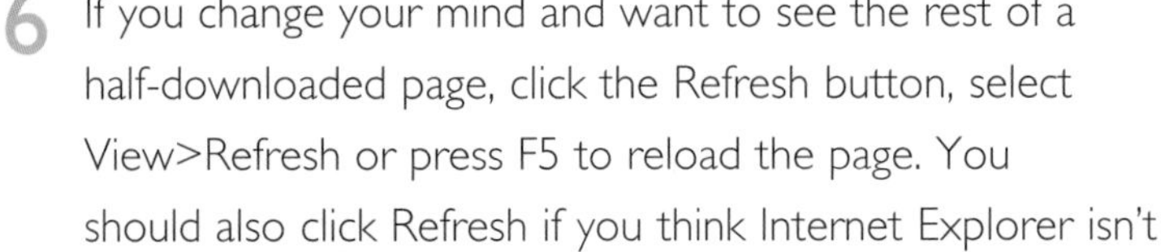

Print a Web page

If you're gathering information for a report or project, you might want to print out relevant Web pages.

You can also click the Print button on the toolbar, but you'll bypass the Print dialogue box.

If you're only interested in a couple of paragraphs of text, highlight them with the mouse before you go to File>Print. In Step 2, choose 'Selection'.

1 To print the current page, pull down the File menu and select Print. Alternatively, press Ctrl+P

2 Decide whether to print the whole document or specified pages (see overleaf)

3 If the page has frames (see page 93), click the Options tab

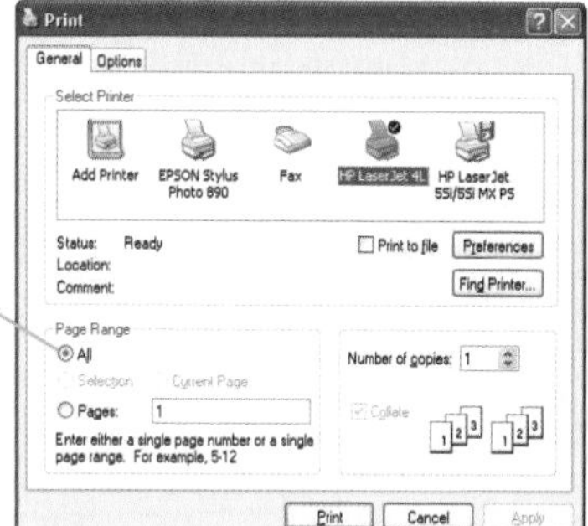

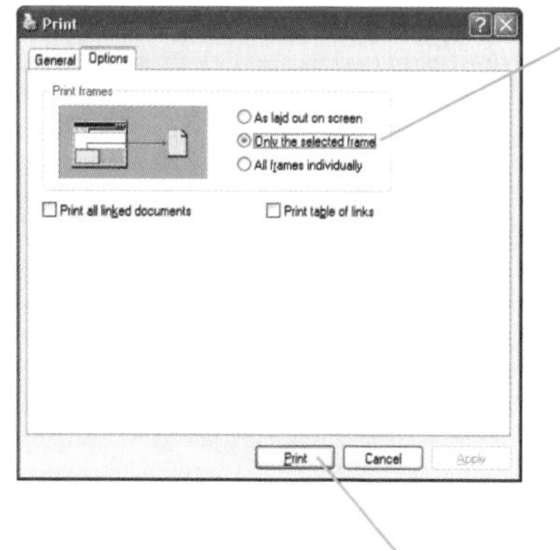

4 Decide whether to print all the frames, or just the selected one (the one you clicked in most recently)

5 Click the Print button to print the page

Print Preview

Because Web pages are designed to be viewed on a monitor, they don't always print the way you expect them to. If you use Internet Explorer's Print Preview function, you get more control over the output. Sometimes it's enough to make the difference between wasting paper and producing a useful printout.

1. To preview your printout, select File>Print Preview

To decode the header and footer codes in the Setup box, click the Help button ? in the top right corner, then click on the 'Header' or 'Footer' settings.

2. To change the margins, header, footer and/or page orientation, click the Setup button

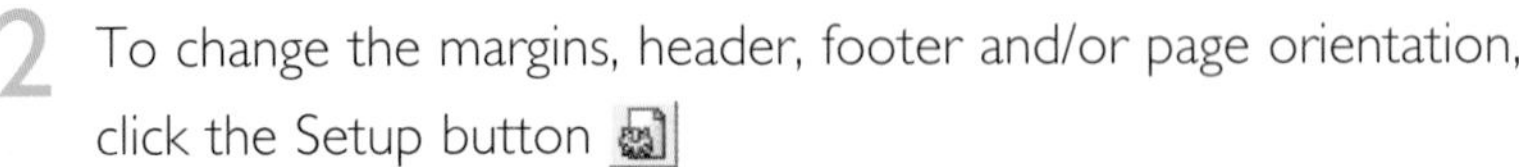

3. Use this set of controls to move from page to page

4. Use this set of controls to zoom in or out

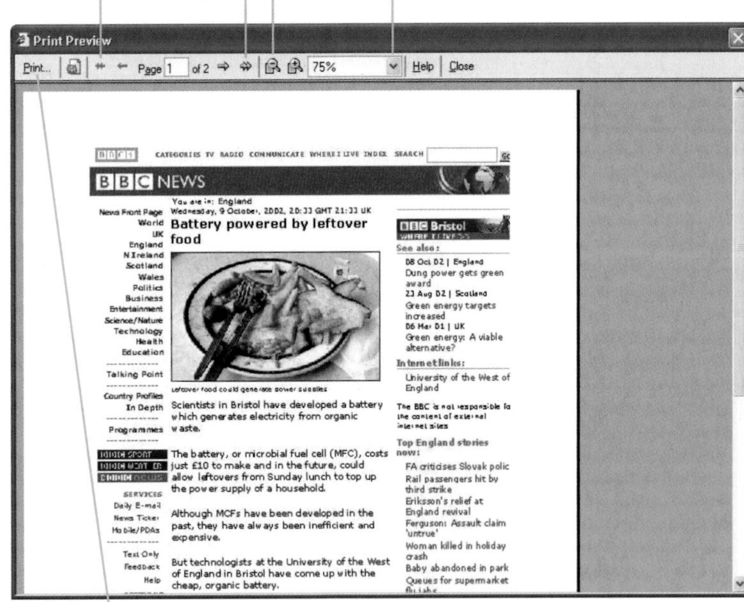

Get the latest news from the BBC News Web site at: http://news.bbc.co.uk/

5. Once you're happy, click the Print button

6. Use the 'Print range' option (Step 2, previous page) to print specific pages

Save a Web page

You can also make a reference copy of a Web page by saving it on to your hard disk. That way you can reload it whenever you want, without the expense of logging on and downloading it again.

Don't forget that material on the Web is protected by copyright. Keeping copies for personal reference is unlikely to get you into trouble, but you mustn't reuse or redistribute text, images, sounds or videos without permission.

1 To save a Web page, select File> Save As. This brings up the Save As dialogue box

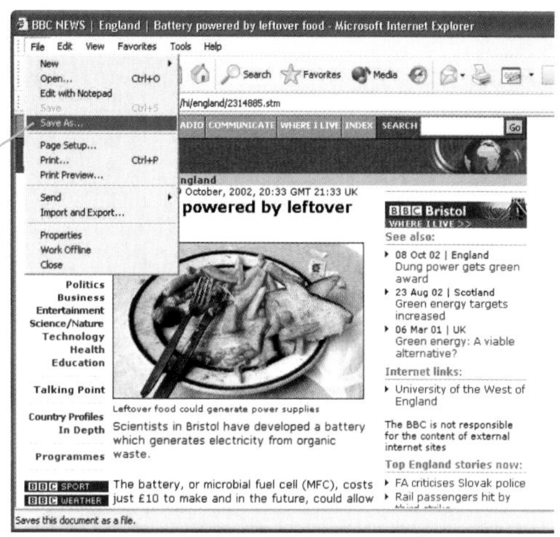

Pictures aren't included in the document that described a Web page. They are stored and downloaded separately, then dropped into place – see page 74.

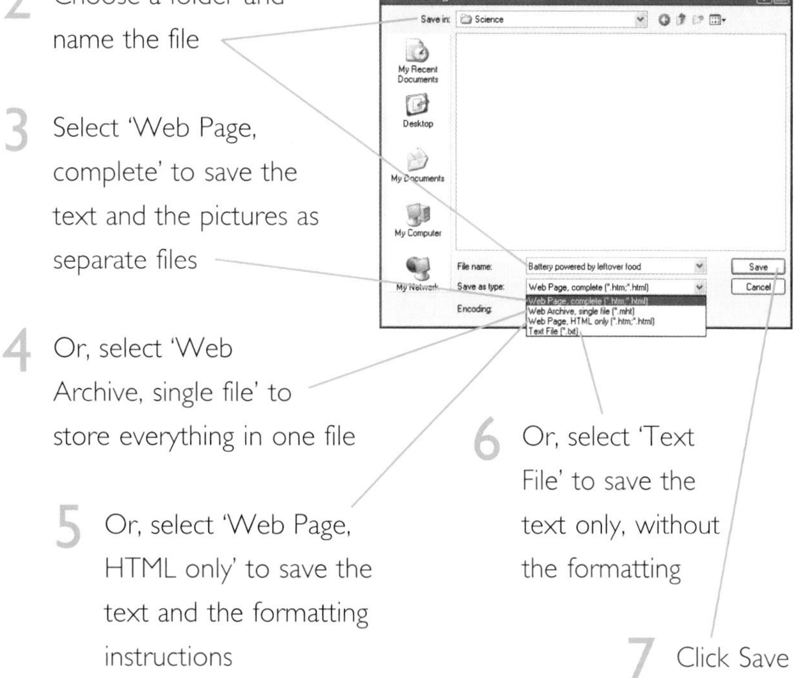

2 Choose a folder and name the file

3 Select 'Web Page, complete' to save the text and the pictures as separate files

4 Or, select 'Web Archive, single file' to store everything in one file

5 Or, select 'Web Page, HTML only' to save the text and the formatting instructions

6 Or, select 'Text File' to save the text only, without the formatting

7 Click Save

See page 76 for more about file extensions.

8 'Web Page, complete' produces a `.htm` file for the page and a folder full of picture files

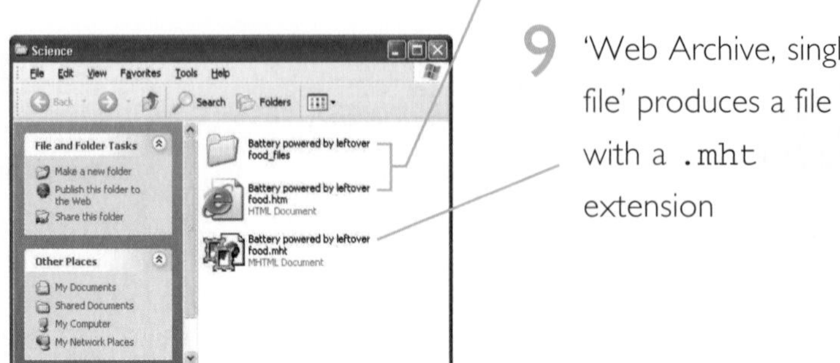

9 'Web Archive, single file' produces a file with a `.mht` extension

10 Either way, you can load the page back into Internet Explorer by double-clicking on the file. Alternatively, select Open from Internet Explorer's File menu. Click the Browse button to find the file

Make yourself at home

Internet Explorer's toolbars are very flexible. You can arrange the Menu bar, Standard buttons, Address bar and Links bar to suit yourself, or turn off some of these toolbars to create more space.

You can also turn toolbars on or off from View>Toolbars.

1 To turn off a toolbar, right-click on an empty section of the Standard buttons. A pop-up menu appears. Deselect the toolbar you no longer want to display

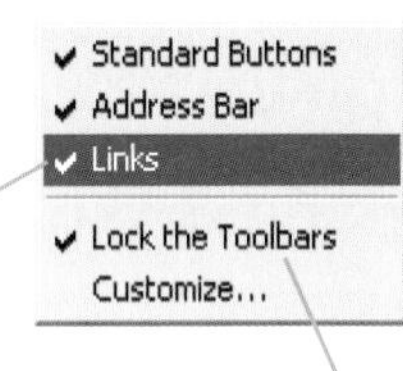

2 If there is a checkmark beside Lock the Toolbars, the toolbars are locked. Deselect this option to unlock them

The toolbars have to be at the top of the window. You can't move them to the side or the bottom or turn them into floating tool palettes.

3 To move a toolbar, use your mouse to grab the grey handle at the left-hand end. Drag it up, down or across

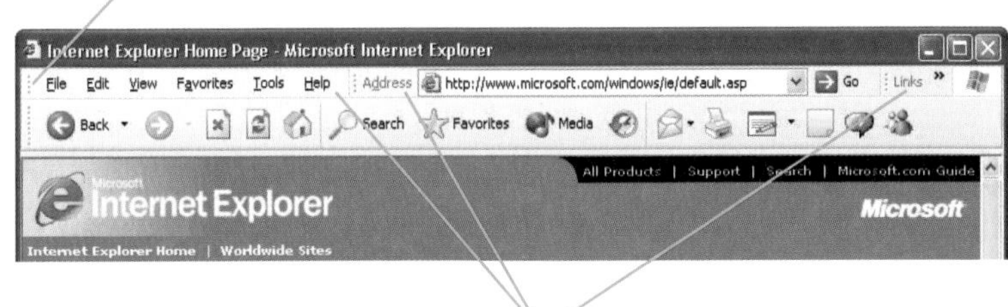

4 You can have several toolbars on the same line

Turn to page 71 to find out more about the Links bar.

5 To expand a toolbar so it occupies the full width of the window, double-click on its handle. Double-click again to put it away

6 If you find you're moving the toolbars by accident, right-click on an empty section and reselect Lock the Toolbars

Customising the Standard buttons

Once you've got used to Internet Explorer, you can make your mark on the Standard buttons. You might want to add buttons for more advanced features or remove buttons for tools you don't use. You can also turn off the text labels and reduce the size of the buttons to create a more compact toolbar.

1 To customise the Standard buttons, right-click on an empty section of the toolbar. Select Customize from the pop-up menu

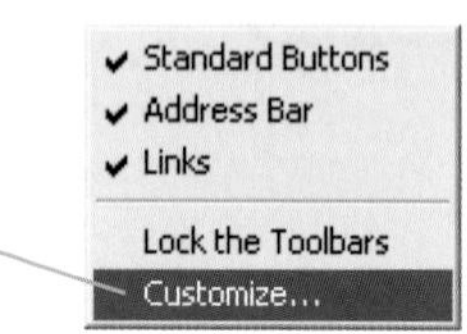

Separators are grey lines that can be used to divide the toolbar into sections. Add as many as you need to keep your toolbar tidy.

2 To add a button, select it from this list and click Add

3 To remove a button, select it from this list and click Remove

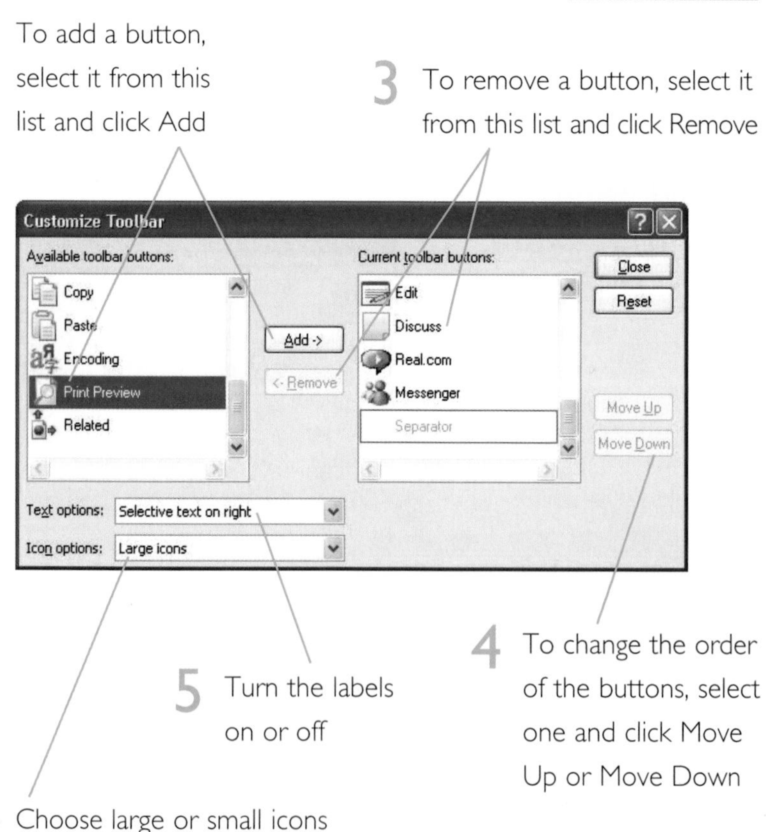

4 To change the order of the buttons, select one and click Move Up or Move Down

5 Turn the labels on or off

6 Choose large or small icons

7 Click Close to finish or Reset to undo all your changes

Lost and found

You've been browsing the Web for hours and you still haven't found what you were looking for. Time for another chapter, then. This one shows you how to avoid the dead-ends and diversions and go straight to a relevant Web site. It also explains how to record the locations of useful sites so you can find them again quickly.

Covers

Chapter Four

Finding information

Imagine visiting an enormous bookshop, with shelving spread out over ten floors and millions of books on every conceivable subject, all at bargain prices. Sounds fabulous... except the books are arranged in no particular order. The novels are mixed up with the non-fiction and the books aren't sorted by author or subject. How frustrated are you? Very!

Sometimes the World Wide Web feels like that. You know the information you need is out there somewhere, but finding it involves sifting through a few billion Web pages spread out over millions of computers. Clearly you can't just follow the links from page to page – your children's children might be growing old by the time you reached your destination. You need a way to find information more quickly.

See the Worldwide Web Guide at the back of this book for the addresses of several popular Web directories and search engines.

The Web has produced two answers: directories and search engines. Directories are like Yellow Pages for the Internet (or like the Worldwide Web Guide at the back of this book). They list Web sites by topic and subtopic, enabling you to focus in on the area of interest. For example, if you're looking for an explanation of Albert Einstein's Theory of Relativity, you select Science, and then Physics, Relativity and so on. Web directories work well when you're researching a broad area.

Search engines are more efficient when you're looking for specific information. They enable you to search through a vast database that indexes all the text on every Web page. You type in a few words – 'Albert', 'Einstein' and 'relativity', perhaps – and the site returns a list of all the Web pages where they appear. In most cases you get a brief extract that helps you work out which pages are relevant. If you choose your words with care, you can jump straight to a Web site that answers your question.

Big Web sites often have mini search engines that only index their own pages. You'll also come across specialised search engines that accept queries in plain English or look for specific types of material, such as news stories, pictures or music files.

Web directories

Web directories are intuitive and easy to use. You select the category that best describes the information you're looking for, then select the most relevant subcategory, and so on.

The Yahoo! Web directory started out as a list of useful Web sites put together by David Filo and Jerry Yang, students at Stanford University. Their personal 'sort out the Internet' project has evolved into a behemoth that's one of the best-known and most-visited sites on the Web. These days it's far more than a directory and you'll have to push your way past numerous other services to find the lists of Web sites. Nevertheless, it's a good place to start if you want to browse the Web by category.

Yahoo! also has local directories for many regions and countries. Try some of these:

- *Yahoo! UK & Ireland http://uk.yahoo.com/*
- *Yahoo! Australia & NZ http://au.yahoo.com/*
- *Yahoo! Singapore http://sg.yahoo.com/*

1 Browse to Yahoo!'s main site at: http://www.yahoo.com/ Scroll down until you find the Web directory section

2 Suppose you want to find an on-line phone directory for the UK. Click the 'Reference' link

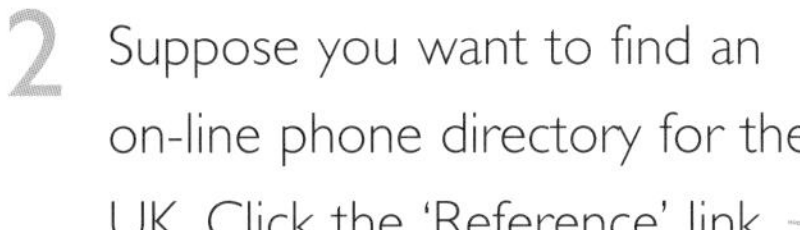

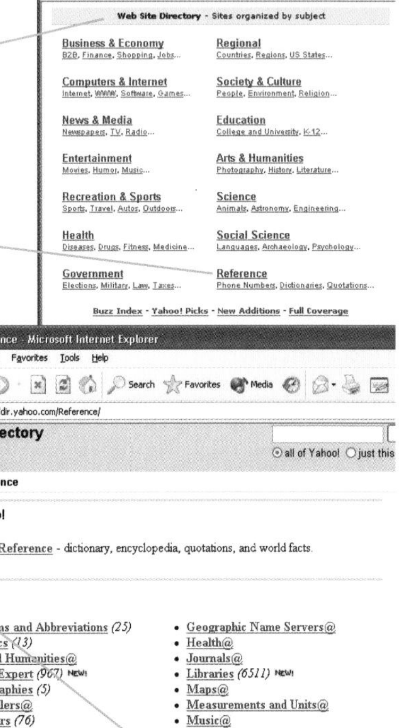

3 You get a new set of categories. Select 'Phone Numbers and Addresses'

4 No sign of a UK phone directory, so try 'Web directories'

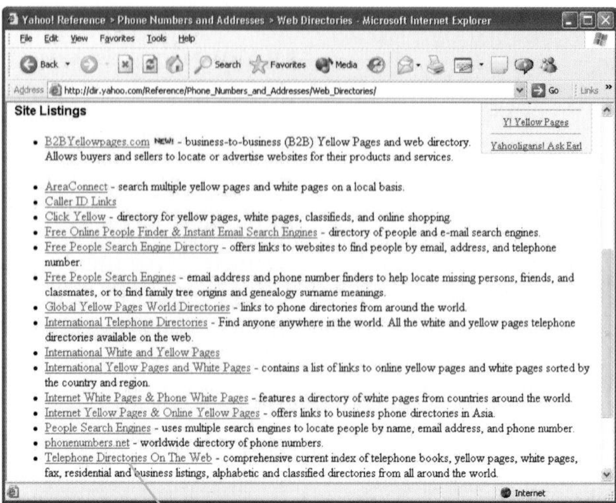

5 Now you get a list of Web sites. Still no UK directory, but there's a site called Telephone Directories On The Web. Follow the link

The useful Telephone Directories On The Web site lives at: http://www.teldir.com/

6 Click the 'United Kingdom' link on the main page of the Telephone Directories site

7 Success! You get a whole list of on-line phone directories

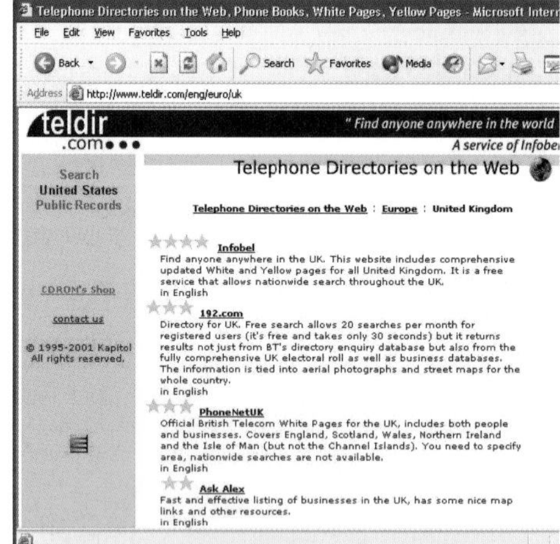

That was a fairly typical Web-directory experience. Sometimes you find exactly what you want, very quickly, but often a little lateral thinking is required. In this case you found a site that lead you, in clickity-click Web fashion, to the information you needed.

Search engines

Search engines are more efficient but not as intuitive. You spend less time clicking and more time thinking, a trade-off that might not seem appealing on a lazy Sunday afternoon. However, once you've mastered a search engine, you can get results very quickly.

The name Google is a play on googol, the mathematical name for an exceedingly large number consisting of a one followed by 100 zeros.

Google was also born at Stanford (clearly a university that attracts neat geeks and encourages them to tidy up the Internet). Founders Larry Page and Sergey Brin set out to create a system for retrieving the best and most relevant Web pages on any given topic.

Like most search engines, Google aims to index every word on every Web page. Uniquely, it also ranks Web pages according to the number of links that point to them – so if a lot of people like a Web page and link to it, the page gets a good ranking. It's very efficient and has a simple, uncluttered design.

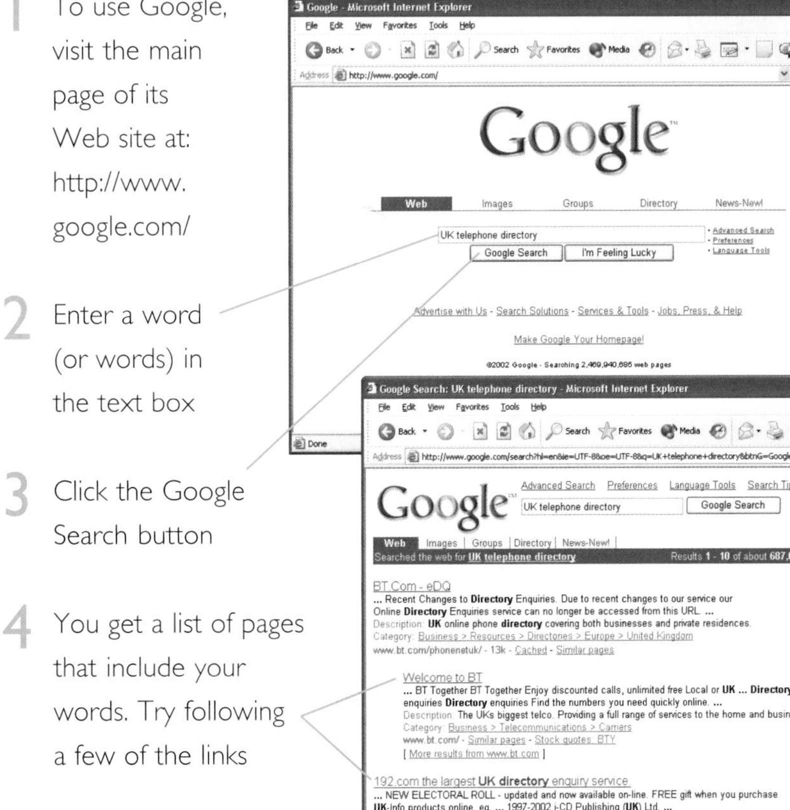

1. To use Google, visit the main page of its Web site at: http://www.google.com/

2. Enter a word (or words) in the text box

3. Click the Google Search button

4. You get a list of pages that include your words. Try following a few of the links

The words you enter are known as keywords or search terms. Internet Explorer remembers the words you have entered previously – see the HOT TIP on page 93.

If you're a gambler, click the I'm Feeling Lucky button instead of Google Search. You'll bypass the list and go straight to the top-ranked Web page.

5 You get ten results on each page. Use the links at the bottom (or click the yellow 'o's) to move through the pages

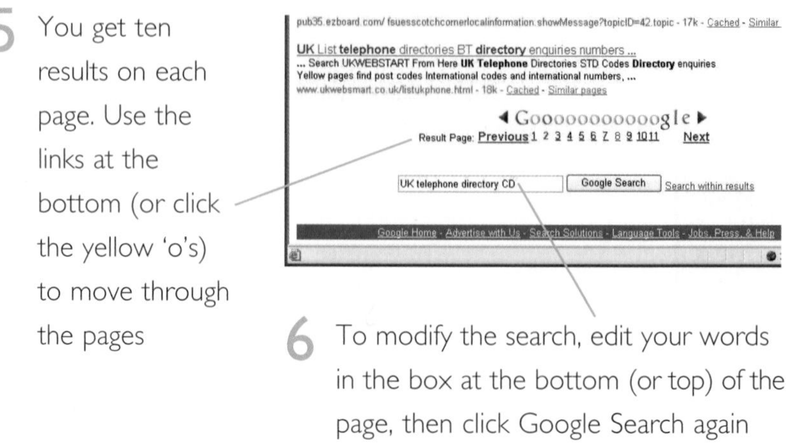

6 To modify the search, edit your words in the box at the bottom (or top) of the page, then click Google Search again

Always add the quotes when you're looking for a specific sequence of common words.

7 To search for a phrase, enclose it in double quotes ("")

8 Google only lists pages that contain your words in that exact sequence

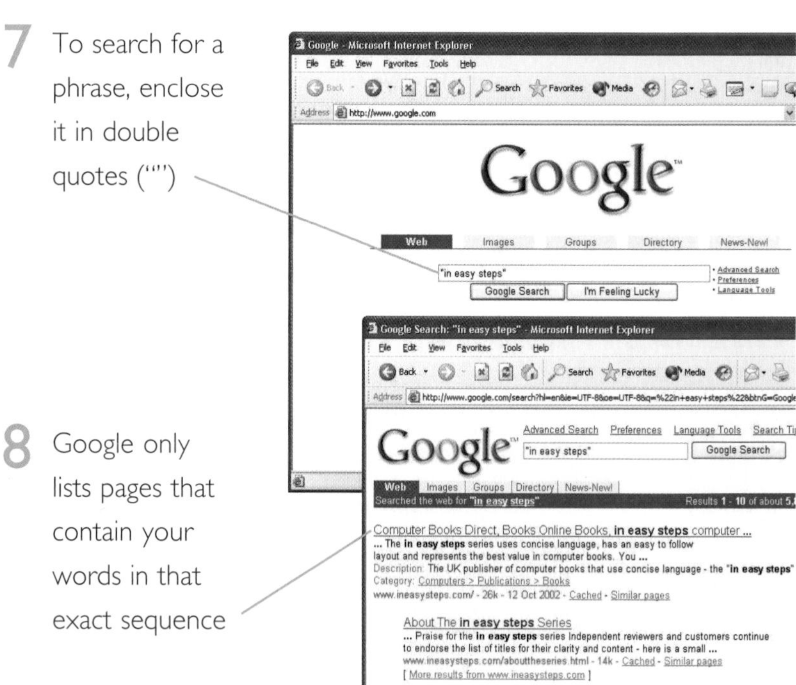

Searching the Internet involves getting into the mindset of a computer. You have to learn how to ask questions that can be answered by a moron with silicon for brains. Remember that the search engine knows nothing about your subject and you'll find it easier to get results.

Successful searching

Searching the Internet can be frustrating, but with practice you'll be able to locate information quickly and efficiently.

Bear the following in mind:

Internet Explorer has a built-in search feature – click the Search button to activate it. It's easy to use but not as efficient as Google.

- Decide whether you're searching or browsing. If you're looking for general information about a broad topic, such as relativity, use a directory to find sites that concentrate on that subject. If you're looking for a specific person or event, use a search engine.
- Read the instructions! Most search engines have special features that help you refine your search. However, they're all different and what works with one won't necessarily work with another. Once you've found a search engine you like, stick with it – the others may find a slightly different selection of sites, but you won't miss much.
- Think words, not concepts. Search engines look for Web pages that contain your keywords, so don't try to describe the concept. You'll get better results by thinking of terms that are likely to appear in the text of a relevant page.
- Refine your search with phrases and extra terms. Most engines allow you to specify that two or more words should appear together, or that the Web pages must contain some words and not others.
- Be specific. If you cast your net too widely, you'll pull in lots of rubbish.
- Use alternatives. Try 'movie' as well as 'film', and don't forget that 'football' is 'soccer' in many parts of the world.
- Check your spelling, especially when you're entering names. Some search engines are case sensitive and will distinguish between 'Reed' and 'reed'. If you're uncertain (why haven't you read the instructions?), stick with lower case.
- Use specialised services, if appropriate. For example, Google has options that enable you to search for images, news stories or messages posted in Usenet newsgroups (see Chapter 10).

Favourite places

Once you've gone to all the trouble of finding a useful Web site, you'll want to remember where it is. Rather than writing down the address, add the site to Internet Explorer's Favorites menu.

Find out all you ever wanted to know about movies from the Internet Movie Database at: http://www.imdb.com/

1. To create a Favorite for the current page, select Add to Favorites from the Favorites menu

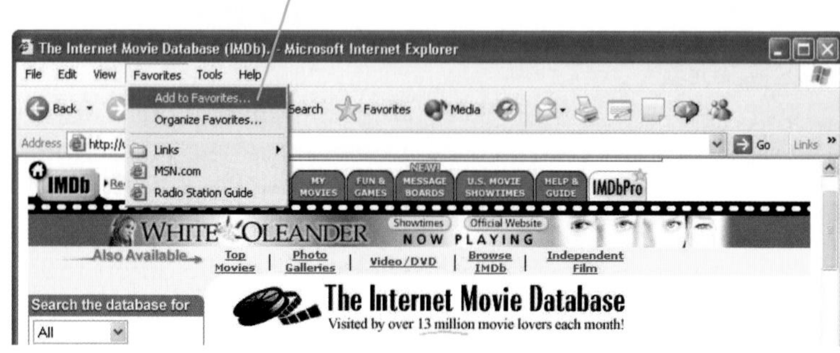

You can also right-click on the page and select Add to Favorites from the pop-up menu. Right-click on a link to create a Favorite for the Web page at the other end.

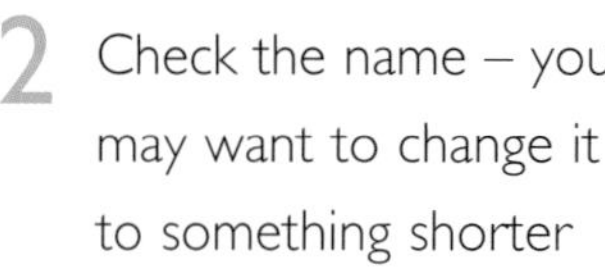

2. Check the name – you may want to change it to something shorter

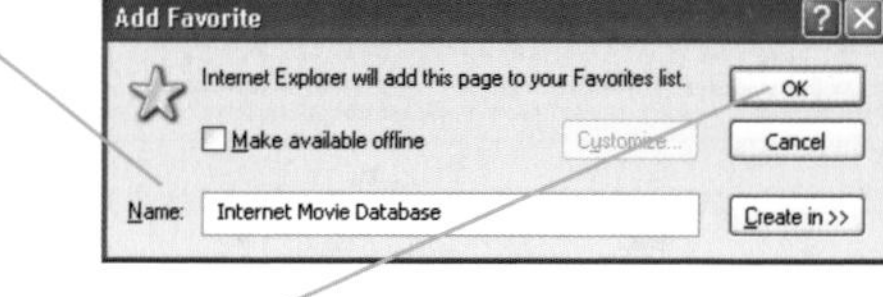

3. Click OK to create the Favorite

4. You can return to this page whenever you want, simply by selecting it from the Favorites menu

Keep things tidy

Before long your Favorites menu will be as much of a mess as the Internet. To tidy it up, organise the entries into folders. This creates submenus and makes it easier to find the site you want.

You'll already have a Links folder – see page 71.

1 Go to Favorites> Organize Favorites

2 Click the Create Folder button

3 Type in a name and press Enter

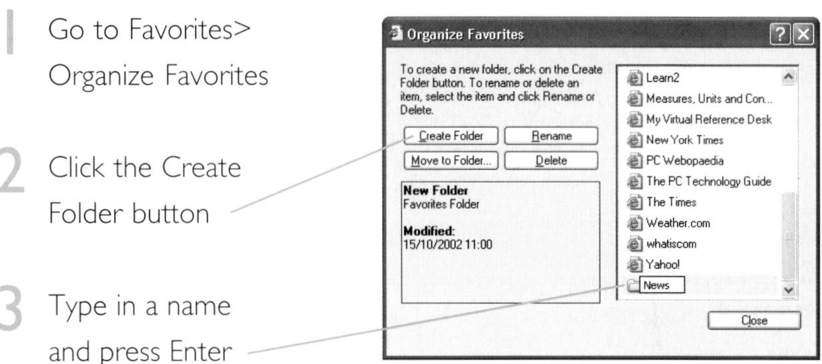

You can also drag Favorites to the correct folders.

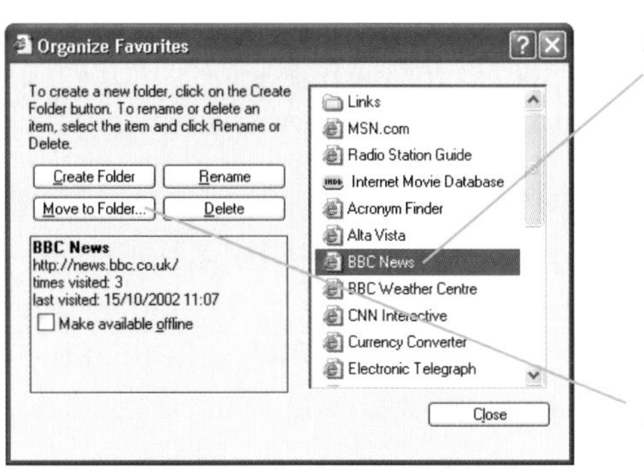

4 Select a Favorite that needs to be moved into the new folder. Internet Explorer displays its details on the left

5 Click Move to Folder

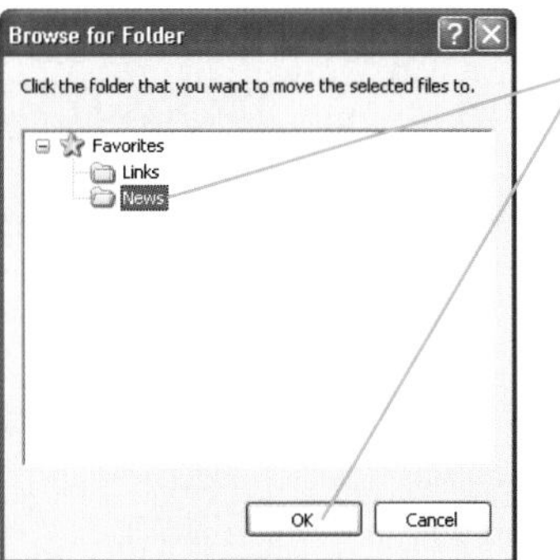

6 Select the folder. Click OK to go back to the Organize Favorites dialogue box

7 Click Close to finish organising your Favorites

To save a new Favorite straight into a folder, click the Create in>> button (see Step 2 on page 66). Select the folder, then click OK.

8 Your Favorites menu now has submenus. To access a folder, hold the mouse pointer over its menu entry until the submenu appears

You can also reorganise your Favorites by dragging them around with the mouse. Open the menu and point to an entry with the mouse. Press and hold the left mouse button, pause for a second or two, and then drag the Favorite or folder to a new location. You can move it to a specific position by looking out for the black divider that appears when the mouse pointer is between two items.

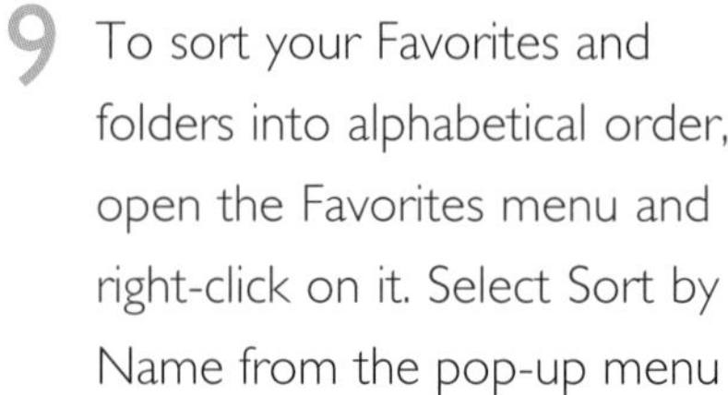

9 To sort your Favorites and folders into alphabetical order, open the Favorites menu and right-click on it. Select Sort by Name from the pop-up menu

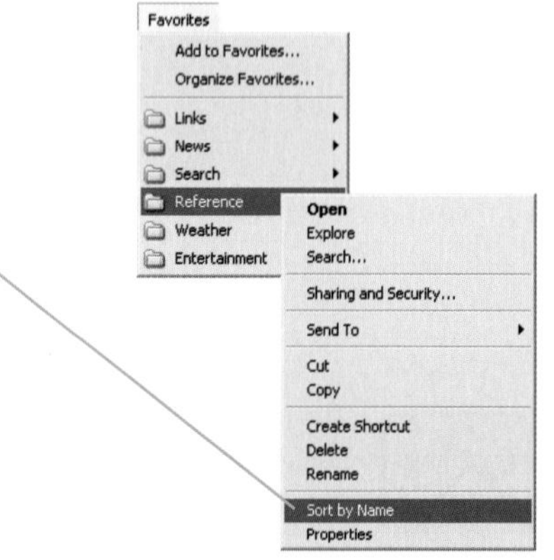

10 Repeat for each of your submenus

All your Web sites in a bar

The Favorites bar gives you another way to view and organise your Favorites. It's more convenient than the menu, but it intrudes on the main window.

1 Click the Favorites button to open the Favorites bar

Click the Organize button to bring up the dialogue box shown in Step 1 on the previous page. You can also drag your Favorites around the bar to reorganise them.

2 Click a folder to see a list of Favorites

3 Click a Favorite to open a Web page in the main window

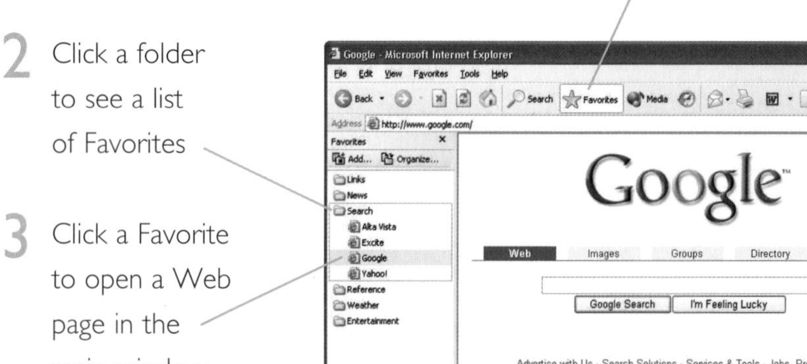

Ancient history

If there's any chance you might want to return to a page, it's a good idea to make a Favorite for it. However, all isn't lost if you forget. You can use the History bar to return to pages you've visited in the last couple of weeks.

To tell Internet Explorer how long to keep the records for, go to Tools>Internet Options and click the General tab. In the 'History' section, specify the number of days.

1 Click the History button to open the History bar

2 Click the correct day, then click the site where the page resides

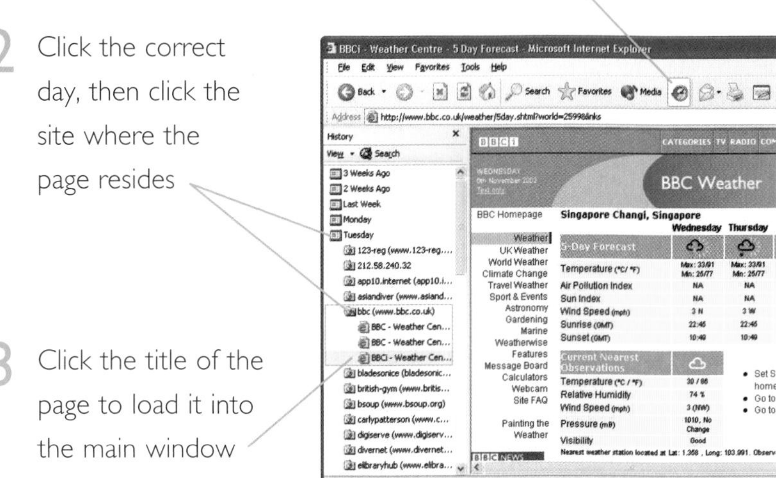

3 Click the title of the page to load it into the main window

4 If you can't find the page you want to see, click the View button to sort the History bar another way

5 Select By Site if you know where a page was, but can't remember when you last visited it

6 Or, use By Most Visited to bring your favourite sites to the top

7 Or, use By Order Visited Today to review today's browsing

8 Still no luck? Click the Search button instead. Enter a keyword and click Search Now to hunt through your history

Internet Shortcuts

An Internet Shortcut is a Favorite that lives on your Windows desktop, rather than in the Favorites menu. Double-click on it to run Internet Explorer, connect your computer to the Internet and go to the specified page.

Internet Shortcuts are useful for sites you go to frequently. For example, you could use a Shortcut to the BBC's News site to start Internet Explorer first thing in the morning. Later in the day you might want to use a search engine or visit an entertainment site.

If you can see your desktop alongside Internet Explorer's window, you can make Shortcuts using the 'page' icon at the left-hand end of the Address bar. Drag it on to the desktop to make a Shortcut for the page. This trick is handy when you want to make a temporary note of the address of a Web page.

1 To create an Internet Shortcut, right-click on the background of the Web page and select Create Shortcut from the pop-up menu. Alternatively, go to File>Send>Shortcut To Desktop

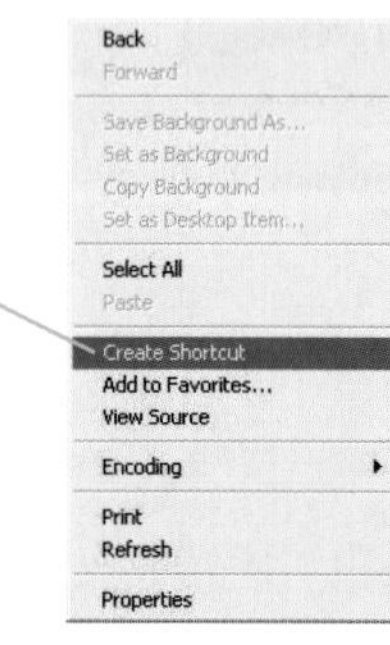

2 A dialogue box appears. Click OK to create the Shortcut

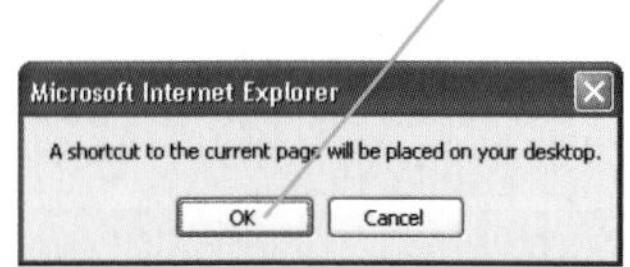

3 The Shortcut is placed on your desktop. To give it a better name, click on it once, wait a couple of seconds and then click again. Type in a short, descriptive name

4 Double-click the Shortcut to start Internet Explorer and load the specified page (if Internet Explorer is already running, double-clicking just takes you to the page)

Links bar

The Links bar provides another way to access your favourite sites. Initially it contains buttons for sites selected by Microsoft or your service provider. You can replace these with your own top choices.

1 To display the Links bar, double-click on its handle (see page 57)

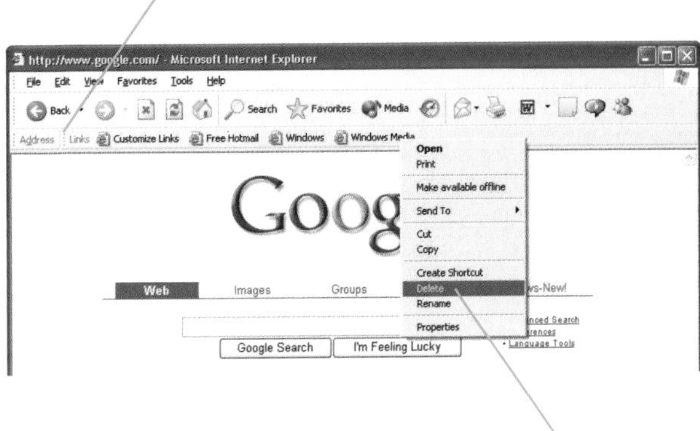

2 If you don't find the default links useful, right-click on them and select Delete from the pop-up menu

You can also use your mouse to drag the page icon from the Address bar to the Links bar.

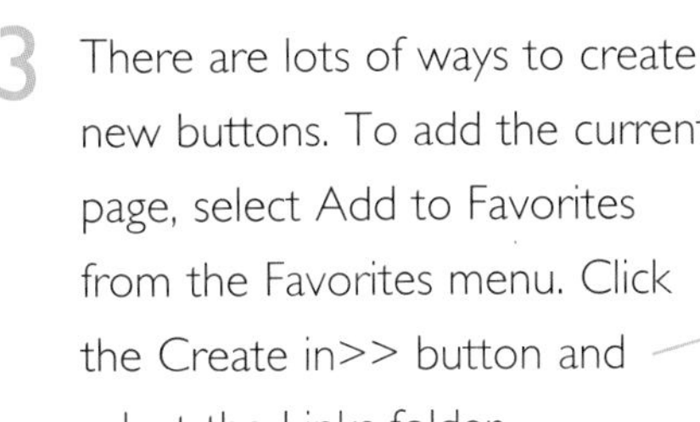

3 There are lots of ways to create new buttons. To add the current page, select Add to Favorites from the Favorites menu. Click the Create in>> button and select the Links folder

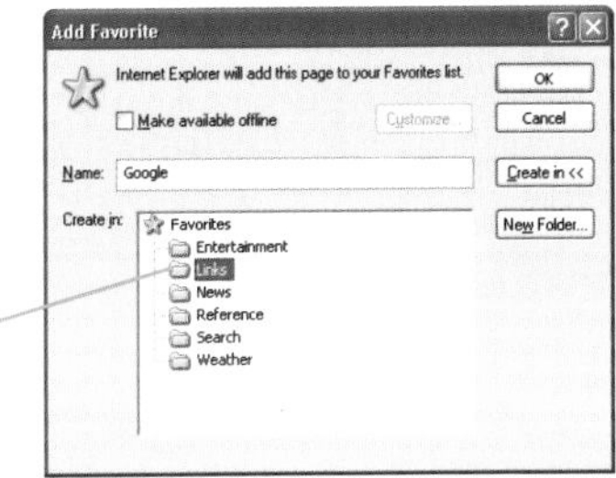

Why do some sites have fancy icons? This is up to the Web designer – if they create a special icon, Internet Explorer uses it. To change an icon, right-click on it and select Properties. Click the Change Icon button and choose another design.

4 Alternatively, open the Favorites bar and drag a Favorite on to the Links bar. Place it between the existing buttons – a black divider appears when the mouse is in the right place

Home page

The term 'home page' has several meanings. It can also refer to a personal Web page or the main page of a Web site.

Internet Explorer looks for the home page each time you run it. You're also taken to this page when you click the Home button or press Alt+Home.

The default home page is usually one of your Internet service provider's Web pages, although you may be taken to one of Microsoft's Web pages instead. You don't have to stick with the default setting – you can change the home page to any page you visit often or find useful, such as a news site or search engine.

1. To change the home page, browse to the site you'd like to use. Select Tools>Internet Options and click the General tab

If you know the address, you don't have to browse to the page. Just open the Internet Options dialogue box and type it in.

2. Click Use Current to change your home page

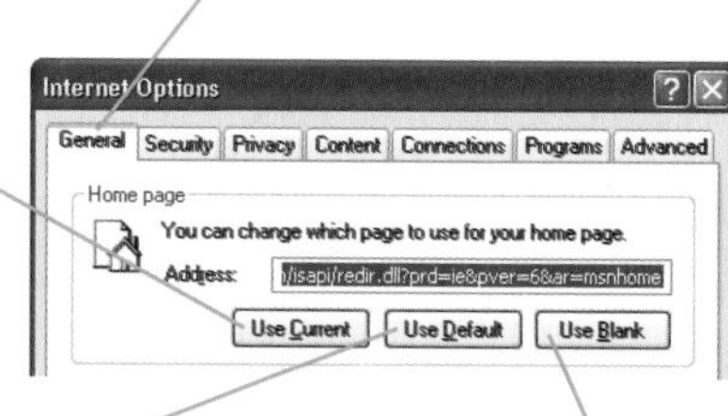

3. Or, click Use Default to revert to the home page that was specified when you installed Internet Explorer

4. Or, click Use Blank if you often want to run Internet Explorer without connecting to the Internet. It will load a blank page from your hard disk instead of running the connection software

Lights, camera, cue music, action

Chapter Five

Like the pages in a book or magazine, Web pages can include pictures – no surprises there. Unlike printed pages, however, they can also include sounds, music, animations, videos and other interactive goodies. This chapter explains how to enjoy the fun stuff that brings the Web to life.

Covers

Multimedia mayhem

Before the Web, the Internet consisted almost entirely of words and numbers. If you wanted anything as exotic as an image or a sound bite, you had to know how to find it and what to do with it once you'd copied it on to your hard disk. Multimedia wasn't even a word, let alone something any ordinary person could enjoy.

The illustrated history

The first Web browsers couldn't display pictures. Then along came a Web browser called Mosaic. It was able to combine text and images, enabling people to create (moderately) attractive Web pages. Mosaic gave birth to Netscape Navigator, which prompted Microsoft to create Internet Explorer, and the rest is history.

Images might not sound like a big deal, but they changed the face of the Web. They made it colourful and interesting, gave it personality and boosted its appeal. When the Internet was a big heap of words, no-one wanted to cover it in newspapers or magazines, let alone on television. Now it pops up everywhere.

For space-related material, including still images, sounds and videos, visit NASA's Spaceflight Web site at: http://spaceflight.nasa.gov/

The Web five years ago...

...and in its current glory

Sum of its parts

A Web page looks like a single document, but it's really a patchwork of different files. When you enter a Web address, your browser downloads a document that contains the text, plus instructions for displaying the page. The instructions are written in HyperText Mark-up Language (HTML), a special language used to format text and add hyperlinks. They also include details of any images that need to be inserted. Once your browser has read the instructions, it downloads the images and assembles the page.

Each image is stored in a separate file, so a Web page with three pictures is put together from four files: one that contains the text, plus three more for the images. This 'sum of the parts' approach explains why the text usually appears first. Until it reads the instructions, your browser doesn't know anything about pictures.

The full monty

Once there were pictures, people started to think it would be cool if you could attach sound samples to Web pages. Why settle for a picture of Charlie Chaplin when you could be listening to him say... no, maybe that isn't the best example. But how about a video clip from one of his movies? That would be better than a still.

Today's Web browsers don't just display static pages. They can also handle sounds, music, videos and animations. You can watch highlights from a big sporting event, look at stills of the decisive moment, listen to an interview with a key player and read the opinions of expert commentators. It's better than being there.

Newer, better, faster, more

As with images, each sound bite or video clip is stored in a separate file. The problem is that people keep inventing new ways to store this type of material. There are dozens of different formats for sounds and videos, and the list just keeps growing (see overleaf). A Web browser can't be expected to recognise all the different types of multimedia file, let alone know how to handle them.

A helper application displays extra material in its own window. Plug-ins and ActiveX controls are more tightly integrated with the browser and the multimedia file is blended into the Web page.

Programmers have developed a nifty way to sidestep this problem. When a browser encounters a file it doesn't understand, it hands it off to another program. These extra programs are known as helper applications, plug-ins or ActiveX controls.

You can think of the extra programs as the electronic equivalent of extra blades for your food processor. Each time you want to do something new, you install a small program that enables Internet Explorer to slice, dice, shred and otherwise process the data. Most of the add-on programs are free and straightforward to install.

File formats

Programs that can create files generally save them in their own, native format. For example, Microsoft Word saves documents in the .doc format. However, most programs can understand a number of standard file formats. They may also be able to open files from rival programs.

The .htm and .html file extensions indicate that the document was created using HyperText Mark-up Language (HTML).

This is another technical diversion that you can skip if you aren't in the mood. However, it's easier to make sense of multimedia if you know a little bit about file formats.

A file format is a set of rules for storing a particular type of information. There are different formats for text documents, numerical data, pictures, sounds, video clips and so on. What's more, there are lots of different formats for each type of data.

On a PC, the format of a file is indicated by a three-letter extension at the end of the filename. For example, story.txt is a basic text file, whereas This is my life.doc is a Microsoft Word document. The extension is separated from the main section of the filename by a dot. Other types of computer have different rules, so you may encounter longer file extensions on the Internet. On a PC, the proper extension for a Web-page document is .htm, but on some other systems it is .html

Windows has an annoying habit of hiding these extensions, but you can take control and force it to display them.

1. Click the Start button and select My Computer from the menu

2. Go to the Tools menu and select Folder Options. Click the View tab

3. Scroll down the Advanced Options list until you find 'Hide extensions for known file types'. Click this option to deselect it

4. Now you can see what you're dealing with!

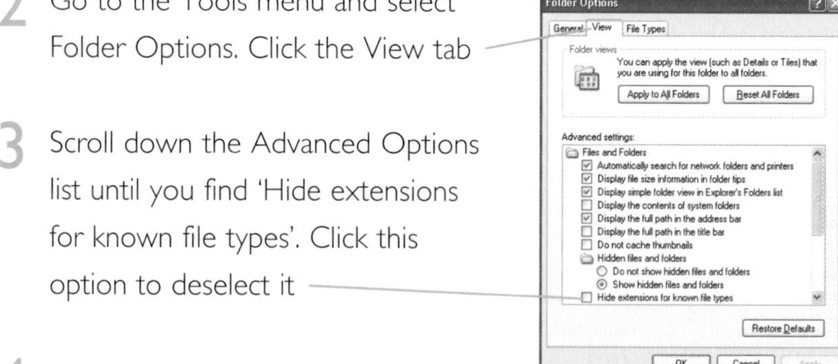

File extensions are often used to describe files. For example, a friend might offer to e-mail you a .jpg of their kids. What they're really offering you is an image file in the JPEG format.

The right image

There are three standard file formats for images on the Web: .gif, .jpg (.jpeg on systems that have longer extensions) and .png.

You might think there isn't much to viewing images. You open a Web page, you look at the pictures, end of story. To be honest, that's all you *need* to do… but there are a few extra tricks that are worth knowing.

Click the pictures

Images aren't just used to make Web pages pretty, they can also help you get from one place to the next. Web designers can turn images into links so a click takes you to another Web page, or sometimes to another image.

There are three common types of linked images:

Many Web sites have their logo at the top of each page. Clicking the logo usually takes you back to the main page.

- **Buttons.** Many Web sites use icons and toolbars to help you navigate. For example, the Yahoo! Web directory (see page 61) has buttons that take you to special sections of the site.

- **Image maps.** Some images contain more than one link. For example, the Disney Web site opens with this theme park graphic. Clicking on the various areas takes you to different sections of the Web site. Photographs can also be turned into image maps. You might come across group photographs where you can click on each person to go to their Web page.

Experience the Magic Kingdom without leaving home at the Disney Web site at: http://www.disney.com/

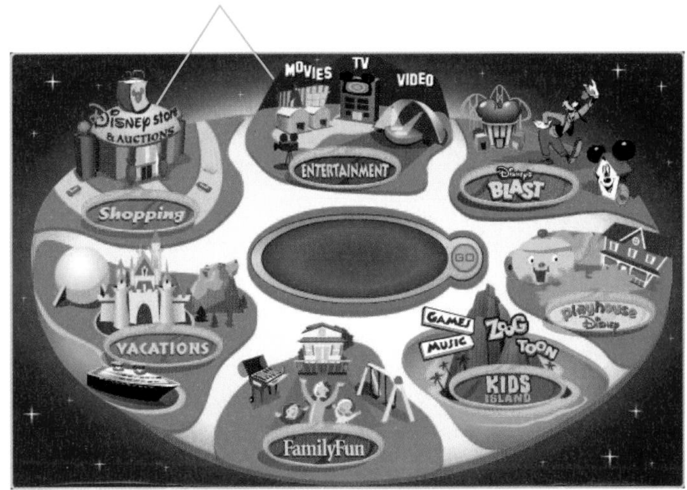

- **Thumbnails.** Large images take a long time to download, so Web designers often show you small preview versions first. For example, Aardman's Wallace and Gromit Web site has galleries with stills from all their movies. Click the small images to see larger versions in a separate window.

Wallace and Gromit have a cracking good Web site at: http://www.aardman.com/wallaceandgromit/

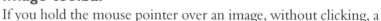

Not sure whether an image is linked to anything? Move the mouse pointer over it. It turns into a hand if the image is clickable.

Image toolbar

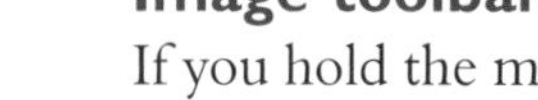

If you hold the mouse pointer over an image, without clicking, a toolbar may appear. It makes it easy to do things with the image.

Holding the mouse pointer over something, without clicking, is known as 'hovering' or 'pointing'.

1. Save the image
2. Print the image
3. Attach the image to an e-mail message so you can send it to a friend (see Chapter 8)
4. Open the My Pictures folder

The Image toolbar doesn't appear when you hover the mouse pointer over very small images.

Sometimes another button may appear in the bottom right hand corner of the image. It only shows up when you're viewing an image on its own, rather than as part of a Web page. It appears because Internet Explorer has resized the image to fit it into the window.

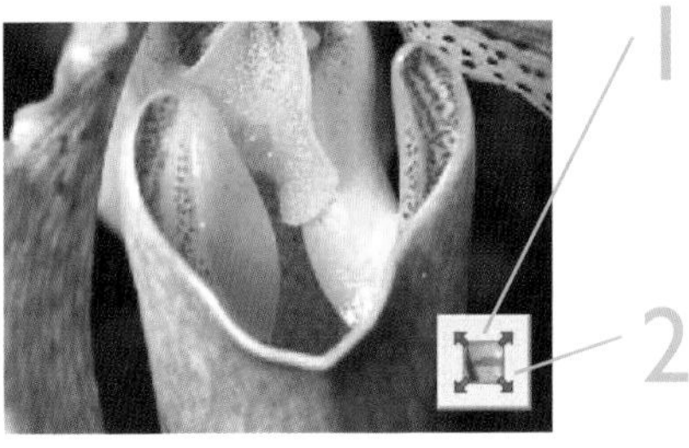

1 Click the button to expand the image to its normal size. Use the scroll bars to move around

2 Click again to make the image fit into the window

Other tricks with pictures

If you see an icon with a red cross ☒ where an image should be, Internet Explorer either can't find or can't display the image file.

Right-clicking on an image produces a pop-up menu with several useful options.

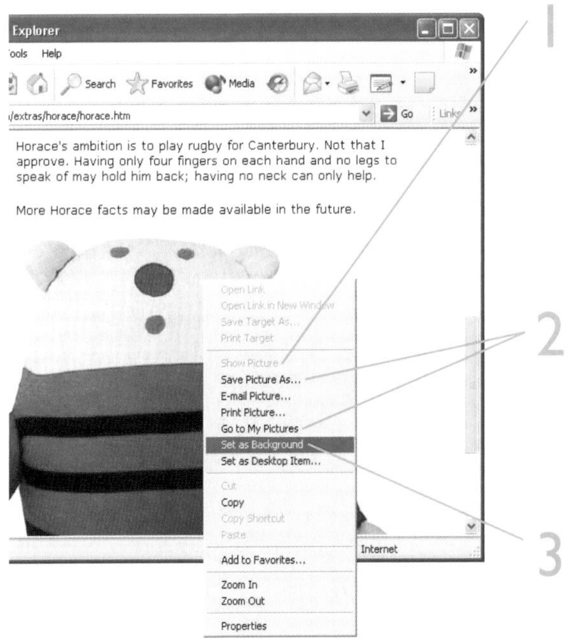

1 Select Show Picture if an image isn't being displayed. It won't always help, but try it anyway

2 The next four options duplicate the buttons on the Image toolbar

3 Select Set as Background to use the image as wallpaper on your computer desktop

Animated antics

Some animations are very similar to image files and Internet Explorer simply inserts them into the page. Others are saved in a specialised animation format and require add-on software.

Very flash

The Flash format is used for intro screens, animated menus and special effects. The software for creating the animations comes from Macromedia and has become very popular because the files are small and download quickly.

You'll need to install Flash Player to view Flash animations. The simplest option is to get it from Macromedia's Web site.

1. Visit Macromedia's Web site at: http://www.macromedia.com/downloads/ Find a link for Flash Player and click on it

2. Click the Install Now button to download and install the player

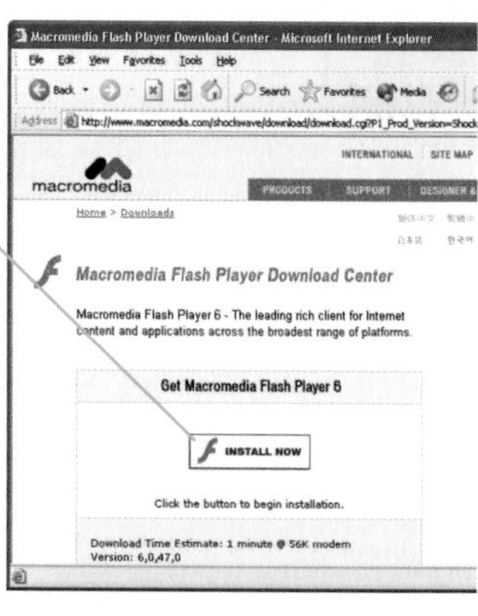

3. A security warning appears. Read it, then click Yes to continue

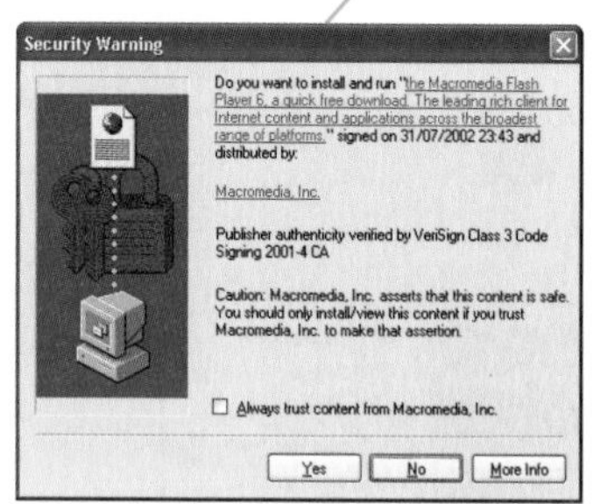

Whenever you see a warning message like the one in Step 3, check the name of the program (at the top) and the name of the company that produced it (in the centre). If you aren't sure what the program does or you don't recognise the company, click the No button to abort the installation.

4. Once the player is installed, a brief animation is displayed

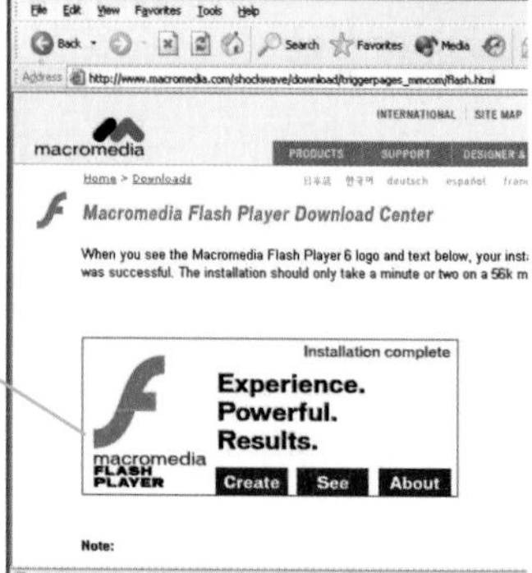

5. That's it!

If you visit a Web site with Flash animations before you install the player, Internet Explorer may display a message prompting you to install it. Simply follow the on-screen instructions. Alternatively, the Web site may have a button or link you can click to start the installation procedure. Either way, you should still see the warning message (Step 3, previous page) asking whether you want to install the player. Check that everything is in order before you proceed.

You can view animations as soon as the installation is complete. You don't have to restart your computer or close Internet Explorer. The Flash Player just does its stuff, automatically, whenever it is required. You don't see it working, you only see the results.

To see Flash in action, try visiting movie Web sites. The stylish Men in Black site is at: http://www.meninblack.com/

Flash is used for high-tech sites with novel interfaces

Shockingly good

People often confuse Flash and Shockwave. They both come from Macromedia and they do similar things. However, the players aren't interchange-able – you need both of them to enjoy all the multimedia on the Web.

Flash has a big brother called Shockwave. Like big brothers the world over, it's a tad more sophisticated than its sibling and can be used to combine text, graphics, animation, digital video and sound into games, interactive movies and multimedia documentaries.

You need the Shockwave Player to view Shockwave files. You install it in exactly the same way as the Flash Player. The download just takes a few minutes longer because it's a bigger program.

Once you've installed the player, try the Shockwave games on Shockwave.com at: http://www.shockwave.com/

Make some noise

The Internet is alive with the sound of music... and people talking, birds singing, swords clanging on armour and anything else you might want to listen to (plus a few things you'd rather avoid, such as the squalling of a hungry baby). Sounds are used to inform and educate, to entertain and to provide atmosphere.

There are many different file formats used for sounds, but they can be divided into two basic groups:

- **High-quality sound formats** such as .wav (Windows audio), .mp3, .mid (or .midi), .aif (or .aiff), .au and .snd. These formats are used for short sound bites, synthesized music and CD-quality recordings. You have to download the file before you can play the sound.
- **Streaming sound formats** such as .ra and .ram (from RealNetworks) and .wma (used by Windows Media Player). These formats are designed to deliver audio in real time. The data is compressed so one minute of sound takes one minute to download. The audio 'stream' is played as it arrives and there's no waiting around. Streaming formats are used for recorded sound, live broadcasts and Internet radio.

Playing sound clips

Some Web sites have background tunes that play automatically. If the music annoys you, try clicking the Stop button.

With a little help from Windows Media Player, Internet Explorer can play sound clips in the high-quality, non-streaming formats.

1. To play a sound clip, click the link that leads to it
2. You can play the clip in Internet Explorer, or in its own window. Click Yes to play it in Internet Explorer

HOT TIP

Deselect the 'Remember my preference' checkbox before you click Yes. You want to keep your options open at this stage.

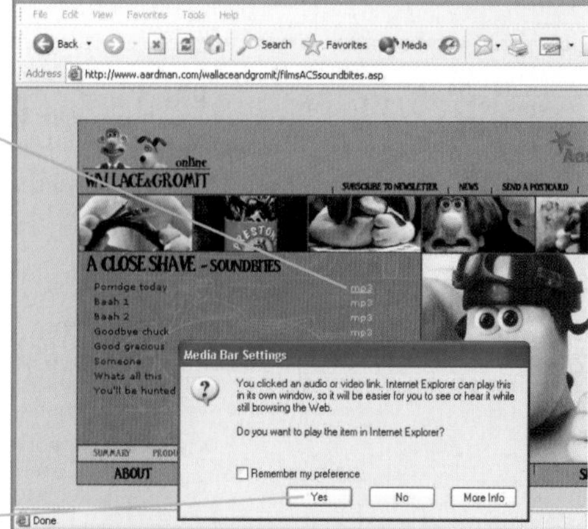

3 The Media bar appears on the left-hand side of the main window. The sound clip is downloaded and played

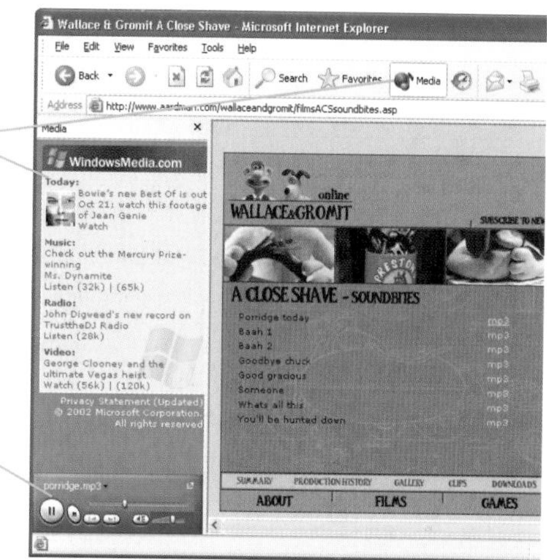

4 Use the tape-deck style controls to adjust the volume or replay the clip

5 Try another clip. This time, click No when you're asked if you want to play the clip in Internet Explorer

To change the style of the Windows Media Player window, click Skin Chooser and pick a design.

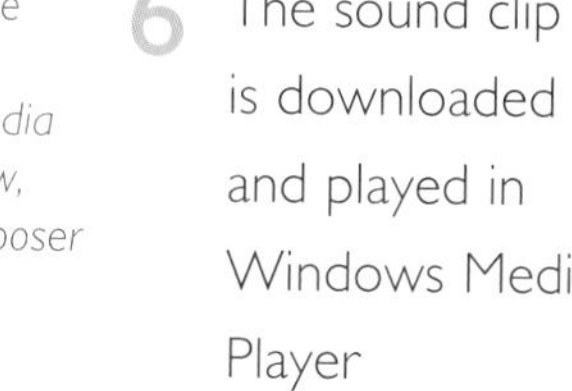

6 The sound clip is downloaded and played in Windows Media Player

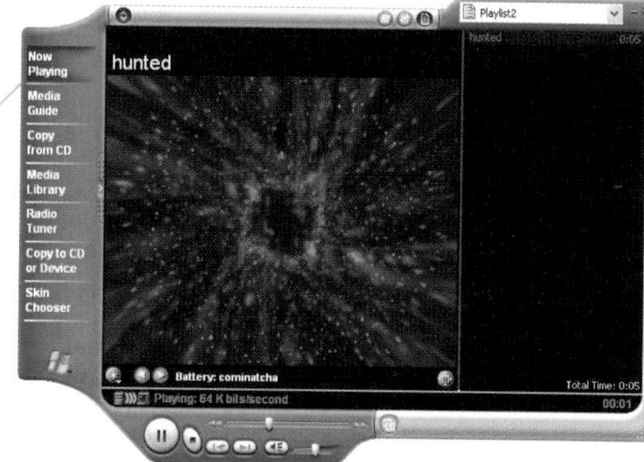

To reset your preferences, click the Media button to display the Media bar. Click Media Options (near the bottom of the bar), then select Settings>Reset Preferred Types. Click Yes to confirm.

7 Once you've decided which method you prefer, you can leave the 'Remember my preference' checkbox selected

Internet Explorer remembers separate preferences for each type of sound file. You can opt to play .wav files in the Media bar and .mp3 files in Windows Media Player, for example.

Saving sound clips

System sounds include the fanfare that plays when you turn on your computer and the beep that announces that you've done something wrong. To change these sounds, open Control Panel and select 'Sounds, Speech and Audio Devices'. On the next page, select 'Change the sound scheme'.

Sometimes you'll want to save a sound clip to your hard disk. You might want to keep a copy so you can play it again in the future or use it to replace one of your system sounds.

1 To save a sound clip, right-click on the link that leads to it. Select Save Target As from the pop-up menu

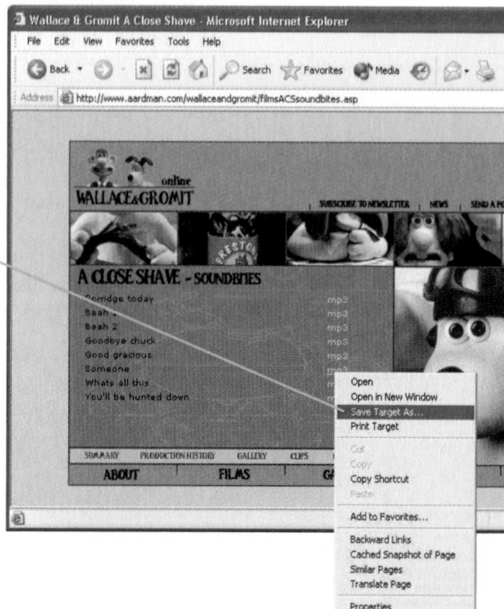

2 Choose a folder for the file and make sure it has a sensible name – one you'll recognise later on

3 Click Save

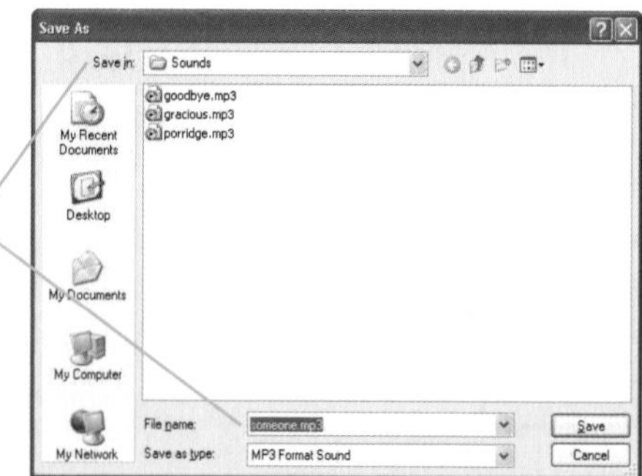

4 Once the download is complete, click the Open button to play the file

5 Or, click Open Folder to open the folder, or Close to go on saving files

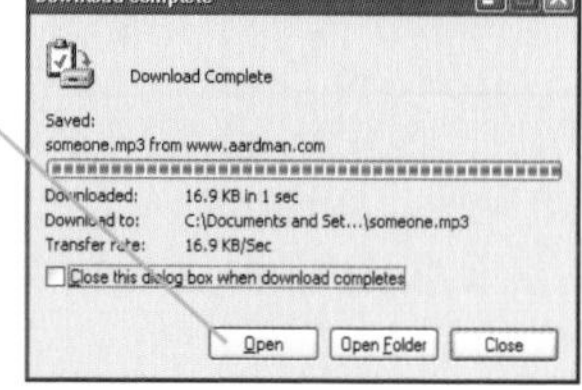

What's so special about MP3?

There is nothing inherently evil about the MP3 format. It's only controversial because it has been used to distribute pirated music.

You might have noticed a big fuss about the MP3 format over the last couple of years. The music business has been waving its arms in the air and wailing, mostly because of the copyright issues.

When music is saved in the MP3 format, all the sounds you don't actually hear are removed. If a loud note and a soft note are played at the same time, and the pitch is similar, the loud note masks the soft one, so there's no need to record both sounds. Eliminating the redundant sounds reduces the size of the file by a factor of around 12. This means that a four-minute song can be squeezed into a 4Mb .mp3 file, without sacrificing the sound quality. Purists with expensive hi-fis can tell the difference, but the music is good enough to play around the house or in your car.

If you have a 56kbps modem, a 4Mb file takes 12–15 minutes to download. That might sound like a while, but it's endurable if you want the song. On a high-speed broadband connection, the download takes about a minute.

To learn more about MP3 and download free music that has been made available without violating anyone's copyright, visit MP3.com at: http://www.mp3. com/

MP3 is great if you want to record a song and put it on your Web site for everyone to enjoy. It doesn't have quite the same appeal for record companies. It's very easy (but illegal) to convert music from a CD into a collection of .mp3 files and share them with other Internet users, saving them the bother and expense of purchasing their own discs. However, it's hard for musicians to earn a living if everyone is getting music for nothing – hence the controversy.

You can play .mp3 files with Windows Media Player. It's best to save large files to your hard disk, then play them (see opposite). Some people prefer to use a specialist MP3 program such as Winamp (from Nullsoft at http://www.nullsoft.com/).

If you want music wherever you go, numerous companies manufacture portable MP3 players. They are similar to personal stereos, but use memory instead of tapes, CDs or Mini Discs. You download music from the Internet (or create .mp3 files from the CDs you own) and transfer it from your computer to the player.

Streaming sound

Playing streaming sound is similar to playing clips (see page 82). There are three main differences:

- You don't have to wait for the sound file to download.
- Depending on the format, you may need extra software.
- You can't normally save streaming sound.

Some Web sites transmit streaming sound in Windows Media format. You can play the stream using Windows Media Player. Others use the RealOne format, which requires the RealOne Player (formerly known as RealPlayer). Download it from the RealNetworks Web site at: http://www.real.com/

There are two versions of the RealOne Player: a basic version, which is free, and a 'Plus' version, which you have to pay for. You may have to look carefully to find the link for the free version.

1. Visit the RealNetworks Web site and follow the links for the free version of the player
2. Follow the on-screen instructions to download the installation program and save it on to your hard disk (see page 110 for more on downloading program files) 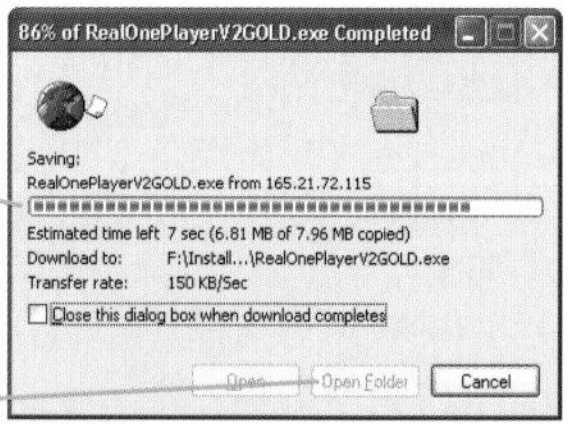
3. Once the download is complete, click the Open Folder button
4. Double-click the file to start the setup routine

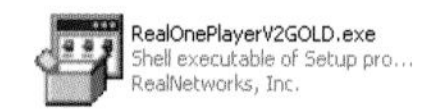

5. Follow the on-screen instructions to install the player. Older versions of the software are removed automatically

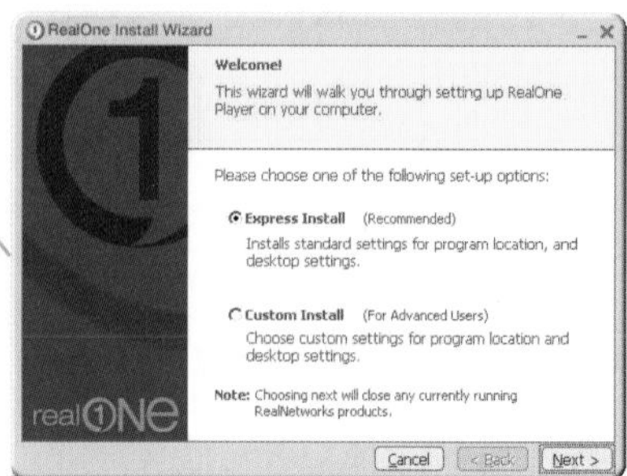

Tuning in to Internet broadcasts

Streaming sound can be used for prerecorded material, such as interviews, or for live broadcasts. For example, many radio stations stream their broadcasts to listeners all over the world.

To listen to Virgin Radio over the Internet, visit its Web site at: http://www.virginradio.co.uk/

1 To play prerecorded material or tune in to a live broadcast, click the button or link that leads to it

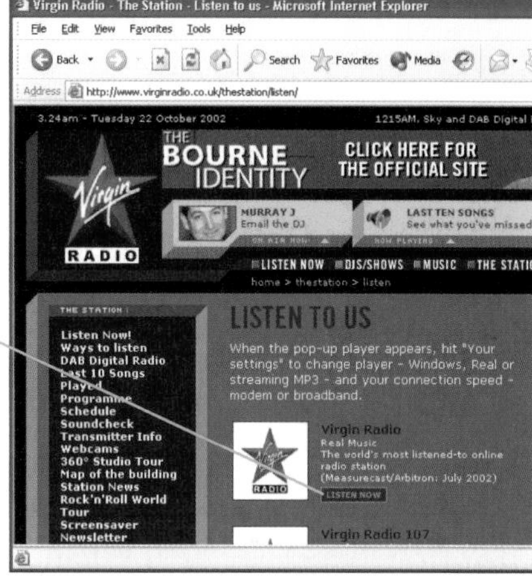

2 You may be offered a choice of formats. Select your player and connection speed

To find a broadcast, run Windows Media Player and click the Radio Tuner button, or run RealOne Player and click the Radio button. You can run both players from the Programs section of the Start menu.

3 There is a short pause while your computer locates the stream and then the music begins to play. Use the controls to adjust the volume

There are lots of different ways to present streaming sound. Some sites have simple links that activate Windows Media Player or RealOne Player; others have customised player windows like the Virgin Radio console shown above. When in doubt, click the link and see what happens!

Watch a video

Playing videos is very similar to playing sounds:

- You click a link to download the video and activate a player.
- There are many formats for video files. Some have to be downloaded before you play them; others can be streamed.
- You need more than one player to view everything.

The main difference is that video files are larger than audio files and take longer to download.

Some video files can be played in Windows Media Player, some require RealOne Player and others need a player you've yet to encounter: the QuickTime Player.

File format	Best player
.asf, .wmv (Windows Media)	Windows Media Player
.rm, .ram (RealMedia)	RealOne Player
.mov, .qt (QuickTime movies)	QuickTime Player
.avi, .mpg (or .mpeg)	Any of the three players

If you install all three players, the right one will be activated when you click a link that leads to a video file.

Installing QuickTime Player

You can download the QuickTime Player from Apple's Web site at: http://www.apple.com/quicktime/

Like the RealOne Player (see page 86), the QuickTime Player comes in two flavours. There's a basic, free version and a 'Pro' version that you have to pay for.

1 Visit Apple's Web site and follow the links for the free version of the QuickTime Player

2 Select the correct version and enter your details

3 Click Download QuickTime

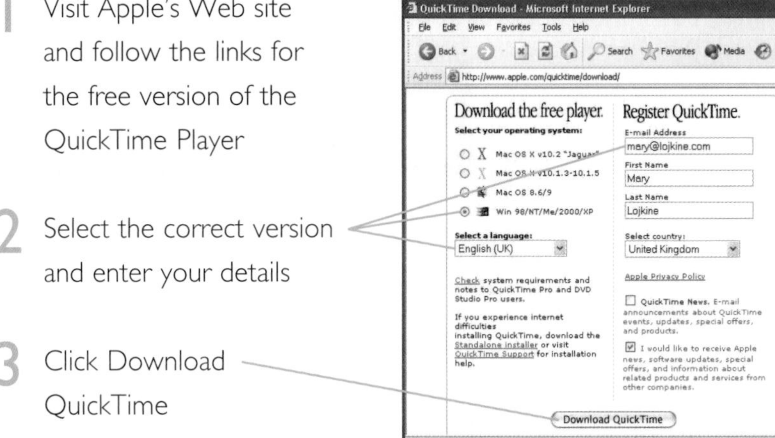

4. When the security warning appears, check the details. If everything looks okay, click Yes to proceed

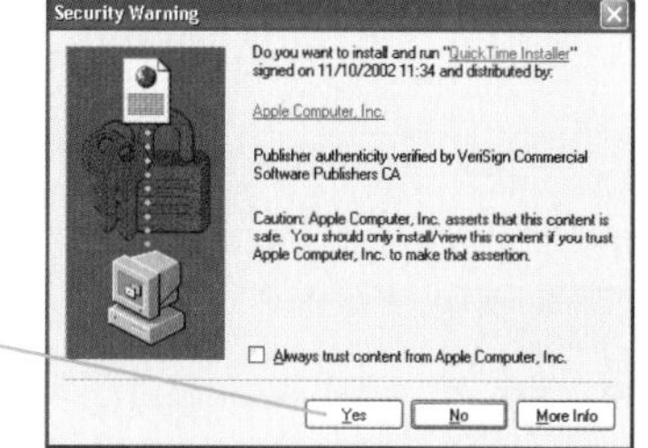

5. The setup routine runs automatically. Follow the on-screen instructions

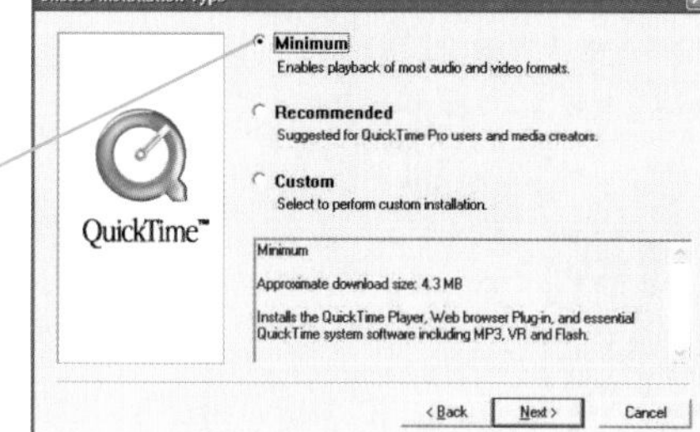

There are lots of optional extras for the QuickTime Player. You can add them later on – the player will let you know when they are required.

6. Choose the Minimum installation – it has enough bits and pieces to get you started

7. The installer downloads all the components and installs them

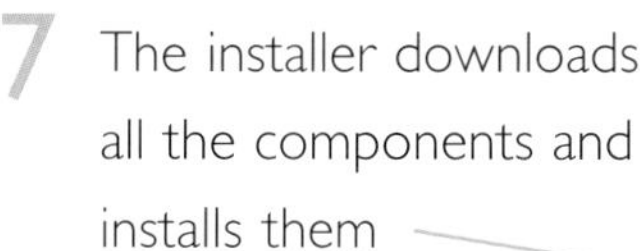

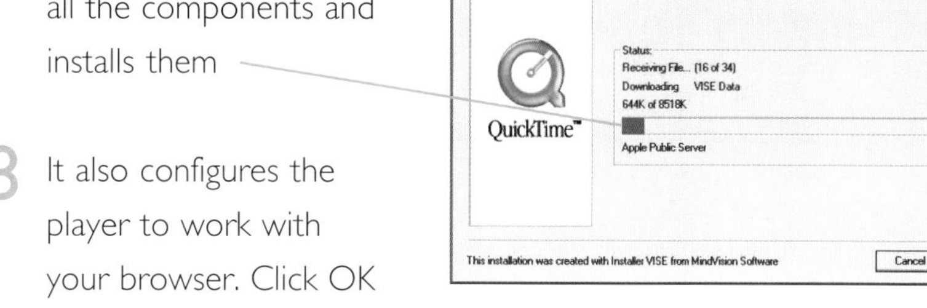

To change your QuickTime settings, open Control Panel. Select 'Other Control Panel Options' from the left-hand side, then select QuickTime.

8. It also configures the player to work with your browser. Click OK to accept the default settings – you can change them later if you encounter problems

You've now installed three different add-ons in three different ways. Flash Player was downloaded and installed automatically (see page 80). RealOne Player had to be downloaded and installed by hand (see page 86). QuickTime Player was downloaded automatically, but you had to install it yourself.

Most add-ons are installed using the Flash Player method, where everything just happens. You won't normally have to install them by hand – although it isn't difficult, as you've seen.

Playing video clips

The exact procedure for playing a video clip depends on the format, but clicking the link that leads to it is always a good start.

The NASA site is unusual. Most Web sites only provide videos in one or two formats.

1. NASA's Spaceflight Web site offers some movies in all three formats

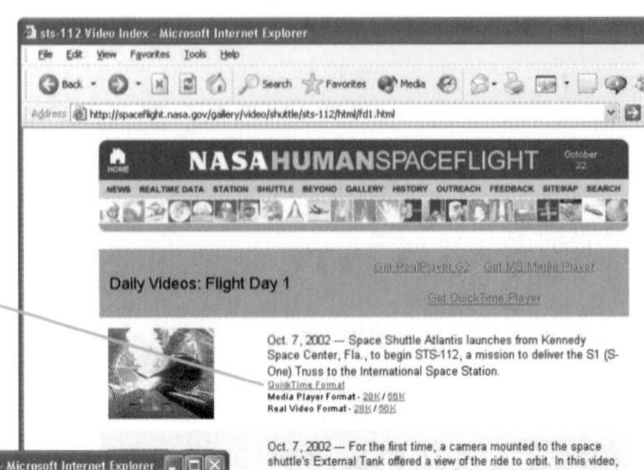

QuickTime videos can also be integrated into Web pages that include text, images and so on.

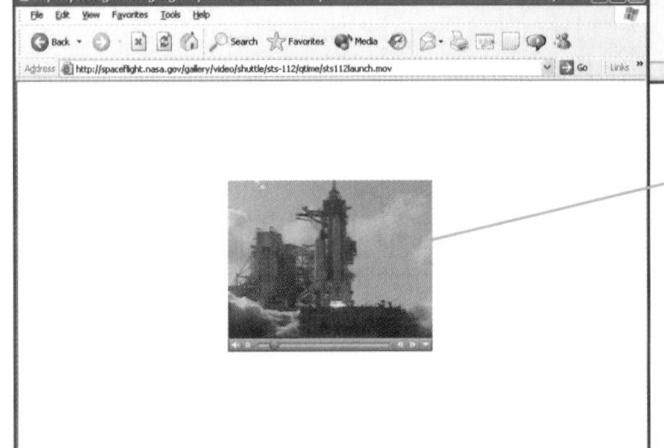

2. If you click the QuickTime link, the video clip is played in the centre of the browser window

To save a video clip, follow the instructions for saving sound clips on page 84. Saving video files to your hard disk before you play them often gives better results than playing them directly off the Web. As with sounds, some types of video file can't be saved.

3. If you click the Windows Media link, you can play the video clip in Internet Explorer's Media bar or in Windows Media Player

4. If you click the Real Video link, the clip is played in RealOne Player

Streaming video

Since streaming sound is used for Internet radio, you might expect streaming video to be used for Internet television – and you'd be right. The catch is that video involves a lot more data than sound, so it's much harder to crush the files to the point where one minute of video takes one minute to download with a 56kbps modem. It's really only feasible when there isn't much happening in the video – for example, when it consists of someone reading the news. More dynamic broadcasts have to be compressed to the point where all you get is a sequence of disjointed frames.

BBC News broadcasts brief bulletins from its Web site at: http://news.bbc.co.uk/

A high-speed broadband connection can carry at least ten times as much data as a modem connection. Broadcasts designed for this type of connection don't have to be compressed as much and they're a lot more fun.

Playing streaming video is just like playing streaming sound. Follow the instructions on page 87, or just click the link that leads to the broadcast and see what happens. If you can't find anything to watch, try the following sites:

Real.com Guide at: http://realguide.real.com/
WindowsMedia.com at: http://www.windowsmedia.com/

A panoramic view

A panoramic image provides a 360-degree view of a scene or location. When you view the image, you feel as if you're standing next to the photographer. You can spin round and look in any direction, or zoom in or out, and sometimes there are clickable 'hotspots' that take you on to other images. Panoramas are used to show you the interiors of houses, hotels and museums; to put you into areas of outstanding natural beauty; and to take you to places you're unlikely to visit personally, such as the surface of Mars.

Panoramic images are created by taking a series of overlapping photographs, then stitching them together into cylinder or sphere. Since the final image isn't flat, you need special software to view it.

There are two common formats for panoramic images:

- **QuickTime Virtual Reality** (QuickTime VR or QTVR). The files have a .mov extension and are viewed with QuickTime Player – see page 88.
- **iPIX**. Files have a .ipx extension and are viewed with the iPIX plug-in, which is available from the iPIX Web site at: http://www.ipix.com/ The plug-in installs itself, just like Flash Player – follow the instructions on page 80.

Once you've installed the viewers, panoramas are downloaded and displayed automatically.

Take a virtual tour of the Louvre on the museum's Web site at: http://www.louvre.fr/louvrea.htm/ This site uses the QTVR format.

1. To explore the image, hold down the mouse button and pan left, right, up or down

2. To zoom in or out, press Shift or Ctrl (QTVR) or use the plus (+) or minus (–) keys (iPIX)

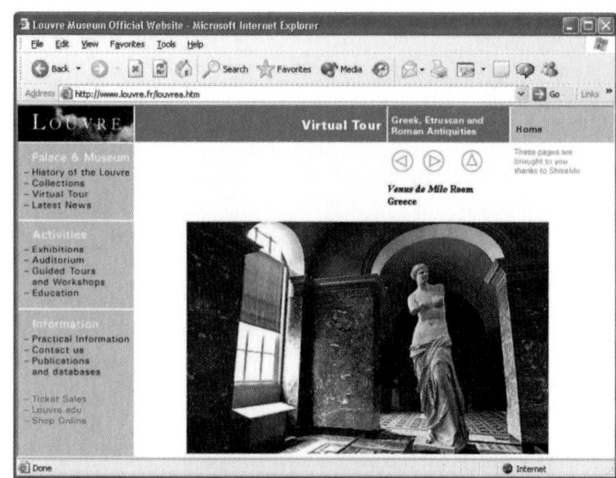

Interactive Web pages

Web designers can also spice up their pages by adding interactive elements such as pop-up menus, forms, calculators and simple games. Some of these items are built in to the document that describes the page; others are downloaded separately and dropped into place by your Web browser.

Fill in the form

Internet Explorer can remember all the things you've typed into forms. When you start typing a keyword into a search engine, for example, it may display a list of similar words you've typed before. If one of the entries on the list is correct, click it. To turn this feature on or off, or clear the list of entries, go to Tools>Internet Options. Click the Content tab, then click the AutoComplete button.

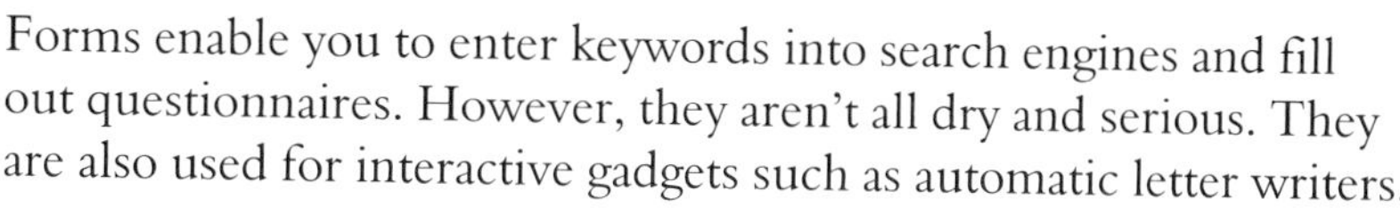

Forms enable you to enter keywords into search engines and fill out questionnaires. However, they aren't all dry and serious. They are also used for interactive gadgets such as automatic letter writers.

Forms are just like dialogue boxes, except the text boxes, drop-down lists, radio buttons and checkboxes are part of the Web page. Once you have filled in the blanks, you click a button to send the data back to the computer that hosts the Web site. You'll get a response – another Web page – a few seconds later.

Here's a form from Railtrack's Web site:

UK travellers can check train times on-line using Railtrack's Web site at: http://www.railtrack.co.uk/

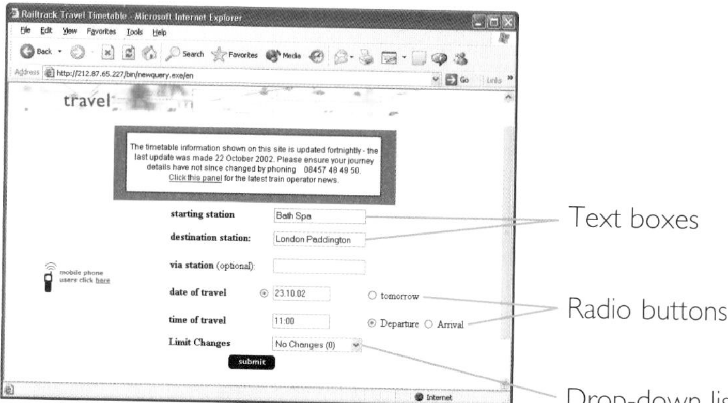

When you fill in your requirements and click the Submit button, you're given a list of suitable trains.

You've been framed

Frames divide the main window into two or more 'panes' that can be scrolled or updated separately. They enable Web designers to display several documents at once. Clicking a link in one of the frames can change its contents, or change the contents of the other frames, or take you to an entirely different Web page.

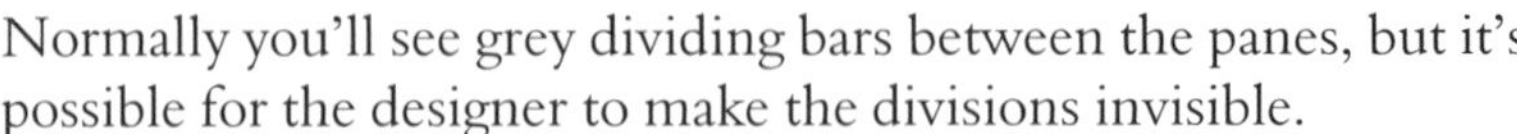

Normally you'll see grey dividing bars between the panes, but it's possible for the designer to make the divisions invisible.

Many people find frames annoying, because they are disorientating and make it difficult to print Web pages. They aren't as popular as they used to be and you won't come across them very often.

Follow the script

It's possible for a malicious programmer to use scripts to access private information or cause problems on your computer – see page 115 for more on this and similar hazards.

A script is a set of instructions that is included in a Web page. You don't see the script on the screen, but it tells Internet Explorer what to do when you click a button or enter some text. Scripts are used to display dialogue boxes, carry out simple calculations and add special effects such as scrolling messages. They can also change the formatting of a Web page at a specified time, or in response to your mouse movements, mouse clicks and keystrokes. Items can appear or disappear, move around, change colour and so on.

You're most likely to notice scripts when something goes wrong. If Internet Explorer comes across instructions it doesn't understand, it displays an error symbol at the left-hand end of the Status bar. Sometimes you can ignore the problem – you may still be able to get the information you need, even though the page isn't being displayed properly. If you can't, all you can do is e-mail the site's designer with details of the error.

Enjoy a cup of Java

Java was developed by Sun Microsystems. To find out more or see some applets in action, visit the company's Web site at: http://java.sun.com/

Java is a programming language that enables Web designers to create small programs or 'applets' that can be added to Web pages. Like image files, applets are stored separately from the main Web-page document and slotted into place by your browser.

The thing that makes Java special – and the reason there's been some hype about it – is that a single Java program can run on many different types of computer. It's a two-part system: as well as the applets, you have the Java Virtual Machine, which is built in to your browser. It acts as an interpreter, converting the standard code into something your computer understands.

Java hasn't been as successful as people expected, so it's possible to use the Web for months without encountering an applet. If you do come across one, it'll run automatically.

It's a rich man's world

Chapter Six

People used to think the Internet was all about sex… but they were wrong, it's all about shopping. You can buy everything from books, CDs, videos and popcorn to bookshelves, hi-fis, video recorders and microwave ovens… and then apply for a credit card, overdraft or mortgage. Chapter 6 shows you how to empty your wallet without losing your shirt.

Covers

Spend and save

In real life, spending and saving go on opposite sides of your personal profit-and-loss statement. Money you spend is money you don't save, and vice versa.

On the Internet, shopping and banking have a lot in common. In both cases, you protect your assets by keeping your personal details private. No matter how generous you are, there are some things you don't want to share – and your credit card and bank account numbers are high on the list. Whether you're spending money in on-line stores or moving it from one account to another, Web browsers encrypt your instructions so they pass across the Internet safely, away from prying eyes.

Shop until you drop

On-line shopping has a lot to offer, both for shopaholics and for people who have to be dragged into town on a leash:

- **It's convenient.** You can order almost anything, at any time of the day, and have it delivered to your door.
- **It's efficient.** Rival stores are only a mouse-click apart. And once you're inside, you don't have to traipse about, trying to work out whether the socks are near the shoes (which would be logical) or in some separate universe (which seems more likely). If you can't find them, you click the Search button.

Marks & Spencer sells socks over the Internet at: http://www.marksandspencer.com/ Amazon sells books about socks (and many other things) at: http://www.amazon.com/

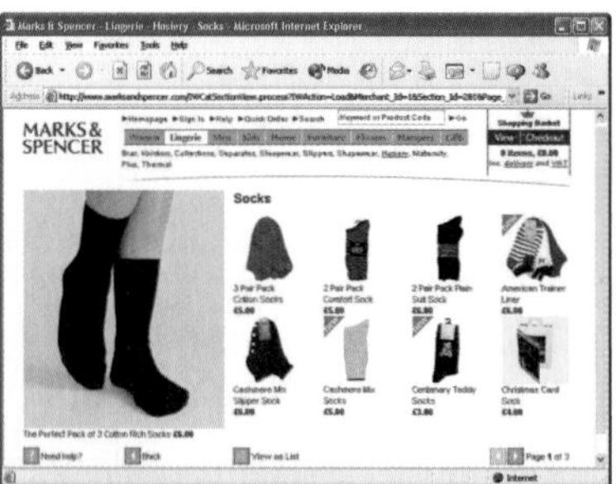

- **You can browse in peace.** Even when an on-line store is busy, you feel as if you're the only customer. You don't have to push through the crowds and shop assistants don't pop out from behind the racks to ask if they can 'help' you.

- **There's lots of information.** Some stores don't just tell you about their products, they also allow other customers to record their opinions. And if you want a detailed technical specification, you can click across to the manufacturer's site.
- **The range is amazing.** The Internet has everything from big-name department stores to specialist dealers selling items that are far too obscure for the high street.
- **It's global.** You can buy all sorts of things from all sorts of countries. And when your friends move to New Zealand and have a baby, you can order a cuddly toy from a store in their part of the world.
- **You'll save money.** On-line stores don't have the overheads of their high-street rivals, so they can offer better deals.

The only drawback is that you can't handle the merchandise. It's difficult to tell whether your bum will look big in a dress you've ordered on-line, although most stores offer exchanges or refunds.

A bank on your desk

If you have any money left after your on-line spree, Internet banking is the answer. You can check your balance, transfer money between accounts and pay most of your bills. It's much more efficient than writing cheques and putting them in the post. You can see exactly what's happening in your accounts, even at two in the morning, and it's easy to stay on top of things.

Pay your bills with NatWest's on-line banking service at: http://www.natwest.com/

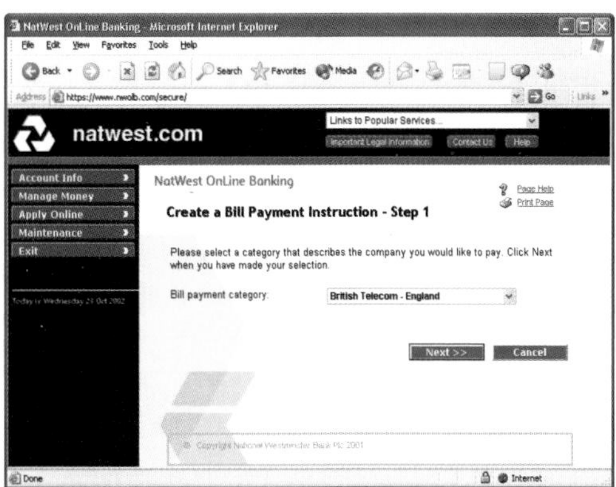

Safe and secure

Shopping and banking inevitably involve transmitting your credit card number and bank account details over the Internet. Before you do that, though, you need to make sure they won't go astray.

Do not enter your credit card number into insecure forms or include it in e-mail messages. The same rules apply to any other confidential information.

Shops and banks that do business on-line use secure servers to collect sensitive information. When you're accessing a Web page on a secure server, all the data you send is encrypted to protect it from eavesdroppers. Sophisticated mathematical procedures turn confidential information into gibberish and then unravel it again at the other end. Anyone who tries to intercept the transmission ends up none the wiser.

Secure connections are slower than regular ones, so shops normally use an ordinary server for their product pages, then switch you over to a secure one when you're ready to make a purchase – usually as you approach the check-out. Banks use secure connections for anything that is specific to your account, including balance checks, transfers and bill payments. Product brochures and marketing fluff live on an ordinary server.

There are several ways to identify a secure server:

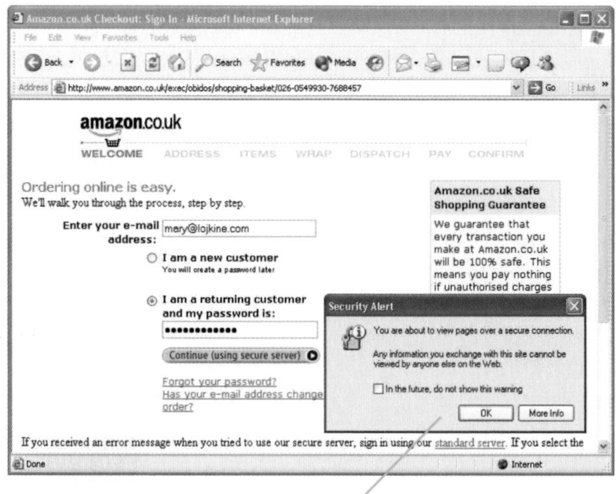

Internet Explorer informs you that you're opening a secure connection. The warning message should appear before you are asked for your credit card number

2 Check the Address bar. Secure Web addresses begin with https:// rather than the usual http://

If a Web site uses frames (see page 93), it's hard to tell whether it is secure. Right-click within the frame that holds the order form and select Properties to check the status of the connection.

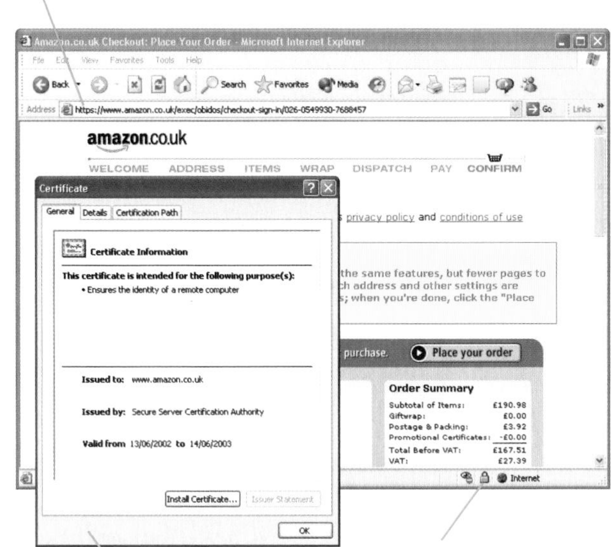

3 A padlock icon appears at the right-hand end of the Status bar

4 Double-click the padlock to see the site's security certificate. Check the address – it should match the site you're viewing

5 Internet Explorer displays another warning when you leave the secure server

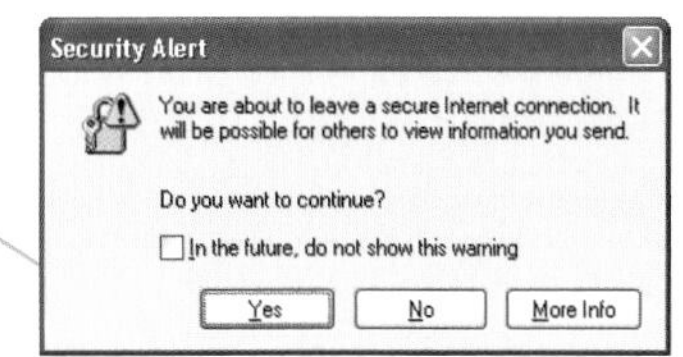

Get into the habit of checking for the warning messages and padlock before you make a transaction. Some people turn off the warnings (by selecting the 'In the future, do not show this warning' checkboxes), but it's better to leave them on. On-line shopping and banking warrant both a belt (the warning messages) and braces (the padlock icon).

Passwords

Passwords are the bane of Internet users' lives. If you aren't thinking up a password for a site you've just discovered, you're trying to recall the one you chose last week.

Many on-line shops keep a record of your payment and shipping details so you don't have to re-enter them every time you buy something. When you're ready to make a purchase, you enter your user name and password and the site 'remembers' who you are and where you live. Banks also use password systems to confirm your identity. They tend to be stricter about the form of your password, but the principle is the same.

If you start using message boards (see Chapter 10), you'll need a user name and password for each one. Some regular Web sites also require you to log on, so they can keep track of your visits. Before you know it, you've got dozens of passwords to remember.

Choosing passwords

Never reveal the password that you use to connect to the Net to anyone you meet on-line, even if they claim that they work for your service provider and need your details to prevent a problem with your account. Anyone who asks for this information is up to no good.

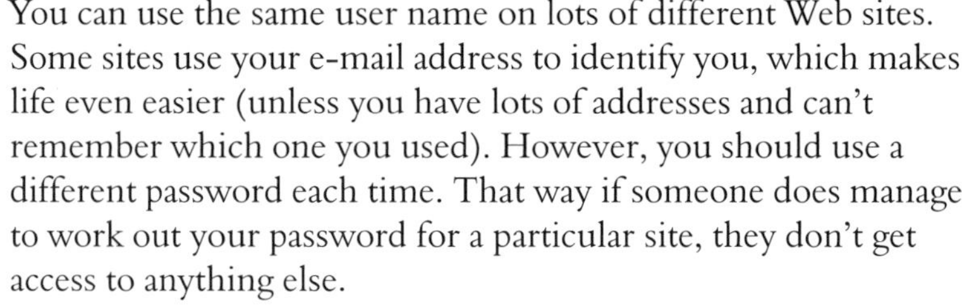

You can use the same user name on lots of different Web sites. Some sites use your e-mail address to identify you, which makes life even easier (unless you have lots of addresses and can't remember which one you used). However, you should use a different password each time. That way if someone does manage to work out your password for a particular site, they don't get access to anything else.

There are two common ways for someone to break your password: they can guess it, or they can use a program that works through a dictionary, trying every word. Try to choose passwords that are immune to both types of attack.

- Don't use your name or user name, or the names or nicknames of your partner, children or pets.
- Don't use your date of birth, ID number, telephone number, licence plate or any other easily obtainable information.
- Don't use place names or any word found in a dictionary.
- Use a mixture of letters, numbers and punctuation (if permitted). Use both upper-case and lower-case letters and make each password at least six characters long.

- One good option is to choose a consonant, then add one or two vowels, then choose another consonant, and so on until you have a nonsense word that's meaningless but pronounceable (which makes it easier to remember). For example, you might use 'zigoonad' or 'rumiatop'.
- Another trick is to think of two short words, then separate them with a number or punctuation character, producing passwords such as 'cat8cups' or 'run$free'.

Remembering passwords

You may find you have to write down some of your passwords. Keep the list somewhere safe (and not too obvious). Don't write down the passwords you use for on-line banking – make a special effort to remember them. You have too much to lose if someone gets access to your bank accounts!

If you log on to the Internet from home and lead a blameless life, choosing good passwords is less important than finding some way to remember the ones you've already picked.

Internet Explorer can remember many passwords for you. It doesn't do this by default; instead, it asks if you want this feature turned on the first time you type a password into a Web site. If you click Yes, it offers to remember each password you enter.

You may want to use this feature for sites where your password simply gives you access. It's less of a good thing on shopping sites, because it may enable family members to access your account and make purchases with your credit card.

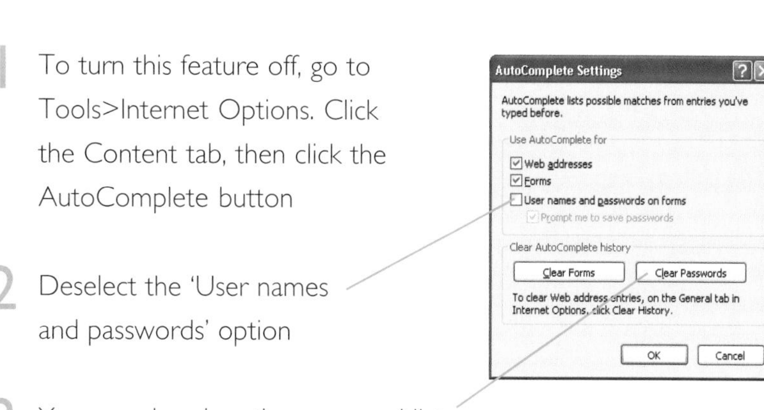

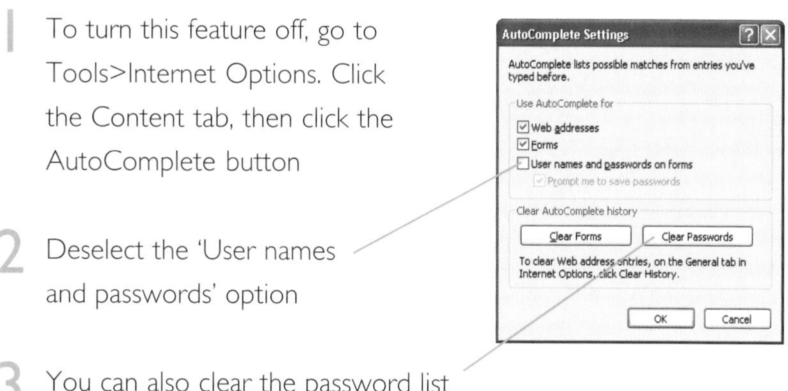

1. To turn this feature off, go to Tools>Internet Options. Click the Content tab, then click the AutoComplete button
2. Deselect the 'User names and passwords' option
3. You can also clear the password list

Sensible shopping

On-line shopping is convenient, easy and fun… but it isn't quite like going to a real-world shopping mall. There are different things to watch out for and the whole process may seem strange at first. To make sure your on-line shopping expeditions are safe and successful, stick to a few simple rules:

- **Start somewhere familiar.** For your first few purchases, stick to companies you know or sites recommended by people you trust. Once you've learnt how to recognise a reputable shop, you can be more adventurous.
- **Look around the Web site before you buy.** Can you find the company's street address and phone number? How much will delivery cost? What happens if your items aren't in stock? Will the company take the goods back if there's a problem? Good shopping sites provide plenty of details about their services. Look for a Customer Service, Help or FAQ (Frequently Asked Questions) section and read through it carefully.

BlackStar sells videos and DVDs from its site at: http://www.blackstar.co.uk/

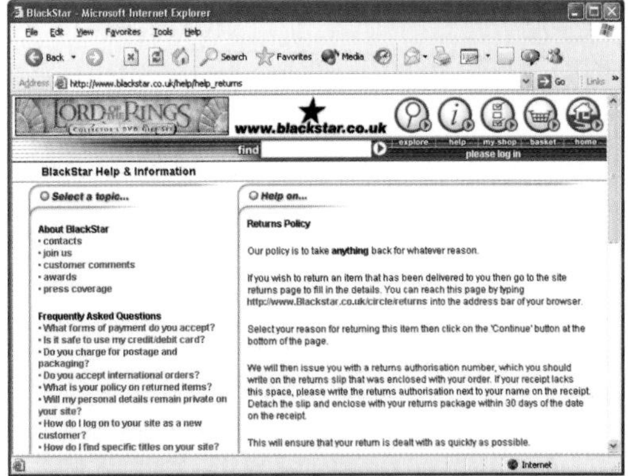

Read the small print before you make a purchase

- **Make contact.** If you aren't sure about a company, ask for a catalogue or call up with a question. See how the company treats a potential customer: do you get a quick and helpful response or an unwelcoming silence?
- **Use your credit card.** If you live in the UK, always pay with a credit card – you have more protection when you do.

In other countries, check with the issuer of your credit card to find out what your rights and responsibilities are.

- **Double-check your order before you submit it.** Have you selected the right size, the right colour and/or the right number of items? For that matter, have you selected the right items? It's easier to make mistakes when you don't have the goods in your hands.

Fat Face sells casual clothes for men and women at: http://www.fatface.co.uk/

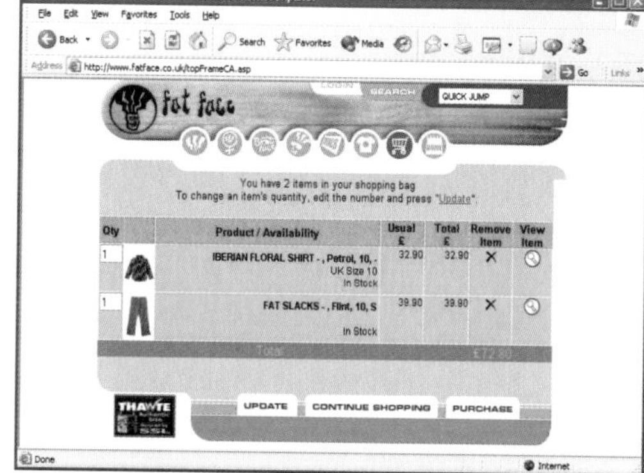

Check all the details of your order carefully

- **Keep a record of your transactions.** Print out details of your order (see page 53) and file any confirmation e-mails you receive. Usually there'll be an order number that you can quote if you have any queries.
- **Check your credit card statements.** Go through your bill each month and make sure you can account for all the purchases. If you see a retailer or amount that you don't recognise, call your credit card company. Be doubly vigilant if you pay your bills automatically with a direct transfer from your bank account. It's easier for a rogue purchase to slip past if you aren't writing a cheque each month.

Internet shopping can save you time and money and enable you to buy things you wouldn't normally get in the shops. Don't be put off by all these warnings – if you shop sensibly, it can be safer than walking down the street with a bulging wallet in your back pocket.

Buying from overseas

The ease with which you can make purchases from overseas is one of the special joys of Internet shopping. You can buy specialist items that aren't available locally; take advantage of lower prices in other countries; or order presents for friends and relations who live elsewhere. However, there are some special considerations when you shop overseas:

- **Will they deliver, and how much will it cost?** Before you get all excited about tracking down the final item for your priceless collection of whatever, find out whether the store delivers to your country. If it does, check the cost – you may need to ask for a quote. Shipping costs can be surprisingly reasonable or staggeringly exorbitant, depending on the delivery method, and it pays to shop around.
- **Will it work?** Be particularly careful when purchasing electrical equipment, telephone equipment, anything involving radio signals (including radio-controlled toys), videos and DVDs. Standards for these items vary from country to country.
- **Is it guaranteed?** What happens if something goes wrong? Do you have to ship the item(s) back to the country of origin? Dealing with overseas merchants is almost always more hassle than dealing with local companies and the costs can mount up. Avoid buying items that are likely to break down. It's better to purchase them locally, even if you have to pay a little extra.
- **Will you have to pay duty and/or tax?** Your fabulous bargain may not seem as attractive when it's accompanied by a big bill from your local tax and customs people. On the other hand, you may be able to avoid sales tax in the country of origin. Do the sums before you submit your order.

UK shoppers can find out about their liability for tax and duty from the Customs and Excise Web site at: http://www.hmce.gov.uk/

Brochures and forms

As well as being a great place to shop, the Internet comes in handy when you need to research your purchases.

Most big companies have Web sites, and if they manufacture products or provide services, you can be pretty sure they'll be promoting them on-line. Many companies provide everything from detailed technical specifications to lists of the available colours – far more information than you'd get from most shop assistants. There's a better chance of it being right, too.

PDF is short for Portable Document Format. It was designed to enable people to share documents even if they were using different software on different types of computer. Unlike Web pages, which are designed to be viewed on the screen, PDF files are optimised for printing. The designer has more control over the layout, so they can make the pages look nice or cram in lots of details.

Companies that have printed brochures sometimes provide on-line versions in PDF format. A .pdf file is an electronic facsimile of a paper document. You can view it, using a program called Acrobat Reader, and you can print it, but you can't edit it.

You can get Acrobat Reader from Adobe's Web site at: http://www.adobe.com/

1 Follow the links to the download page and select the correct version of Acrobat. Download it on to your hard disk (see Chapter 7)

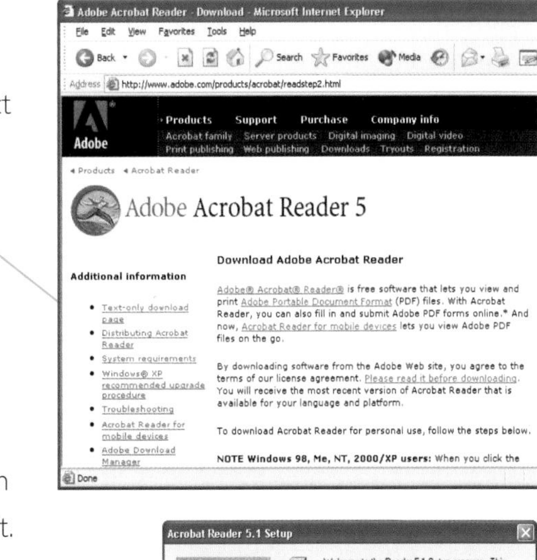

2 Open the folder containing the downloaded program and double-click on it. You may have to wait while extra files are downloaded

3 Follow the on-screen instructions to install Acrobat Reader

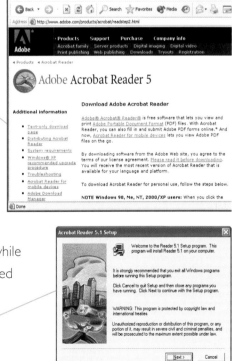

The PDF format is also used for application forms. If you want to open a new bank account, for example, you may be able to download the application form from the bank's Web site, print it out, fill it in and send it off. In the UK you can even download tax return forms from the Inland Revenue Web site at: http://www.inlandrevenue.gov.uk/

You can run Acrobat Reader as a stand-alone program or use it from inside Internet Explorer.

Suppose you want to look at one of the product brochures on Adobe's Web site.

1. Click the link that leads to the .pdf file to open it in Internet Explorer

2. Acrobat Reader's toolbars appear inside Internet Explorer's main window. Use the tools to view, save and/or print the document

3. When you're finished, use Internet Explorer's tools to navigate back to the original Web page or on to somewhere else

4. Alternatively, right-click on the link to the .pdf file and select Save Target As to save it on to your hard disk

5. Open the folder that contains the .pdf file and double-click it

6. The file is opened in a standalone Acrobat Reader window

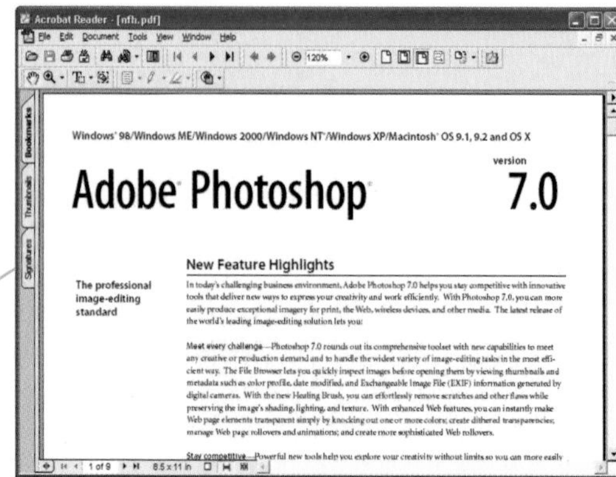

Fancy filework

The Net is awash with free software, try-before-you-buy-ware and add-ons and upgrades for commercial programs. This chapter explains how to grab all the files you want without downloading the things you certainly don't want: viruses, Trojan horses and worms.

Covers

Chapter Seven

Get your free software here!

If there's one thing Internet users have in common, it's computers. Like it or loathe it, almost everyone who uses the Net is beholden to a computer of some sort. And if there's one thing computer users have in common, it's their rapacious appetite for software. Seems as if you're always short of a program to do this or a utility to do that. Unsurprisingly, the Internet has evolved into a giant buffet that enables you to pile your plate with new software.

You'll find six different types of software on the Internet:

- **Commercial programs.** Instead of buying shrink-wrapped boxes from a computer store, you can purchase software on-line. You pay with your credit card (see Chapter 6), then download the program(s) on to your hard disk.
- **Demos and trial versions.** Many software companies appreciate that using a program tells you a lot more than reading about it. Rather than trying to describe their whizzy new application, they let you download a trial version. Most demos lack one or two key features – for example, you may not be able to save or print your documents.
- **Add-ons and upgrades.** Software companies also use the Internet to distribute freebies such as small utilities, document templates and 'patches' that fix minor problems.
- **Drivers.** A driver is a small program that enables your computer to communicate with an add-on device such as a printer or a camera. Drivers get updated regularly.
- **Shareware.** Shareware programs are distributed on a 'try-before-you-buy' basis. You're allowed to use a shareware program for a while to find out whether you like it (unlike a trial version, it should give you access to all the important features). If you find it useful, you pay a registration fee. You'll usually get an enhanced version with extra features as a reward for your support.
- **Freeware.** The Internet is full of small programs you can simply download and use, free of charge. Some are too small to be worth marketing commercially. Others are produced by hobby programmers who enjoy sharing their creations.

The shareware system relies on people paying for the programs they find useful. The registration fees help pay for further development, leading to new versions with extra features. If you use a shareware program regularly, do the decent thing and send the programmers some money.

Find your programs

Downloading programs is easy (see overleaf). Finding software to download can be a little more challenging, especially if you have a particular task in mind, rather than a specific program.

If you're looking for commercial programs, demos, add-ons and upgrades or driver software, start by visiting the software or hardware company's Web site. Usually you can guess the address. For example:

Adobe is at: http://www.adobe.com/
Epson is at: http://www.epson.com/
Symantec is at: http://www.symantec.com/

Spot the pattern? If guessing doesn't work, use a search engine (see page 63). Once you've found the site, look for a Products, Support or Download section.

Sometimes you need a program to do a particular job. For example, you might be looking for an icon editor. Start by visiting one of the sites that catalogue downloadable software. Two of the best are:

Download.com at: http://download.com.com/
Tucows at: http://www.tucows.com/

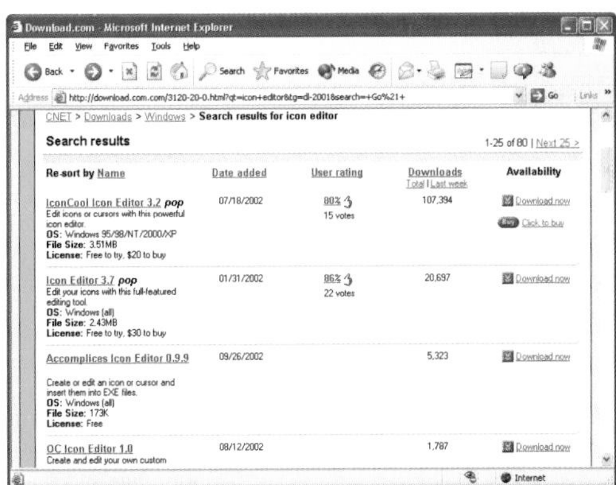

Download.com has details of thousands of programs

These sites let you search by program name or keyword. You can find all the icon editors, then use the descriptions, reviews and user ratings to make a decision. Either download the program directly or click through to the developer's Web site for more details.

Haul down the files

Internet Explorer enables you to fetch and run a program in a single operation, but you'll almost always want to save it on to your hard disk instead. You can experiment with your new software once you've disconnected from the Internet.

Find Herman Compute's Icon Editor program at: http://www.hermancompute.com/

1 To download a program file, click the link that leads to it

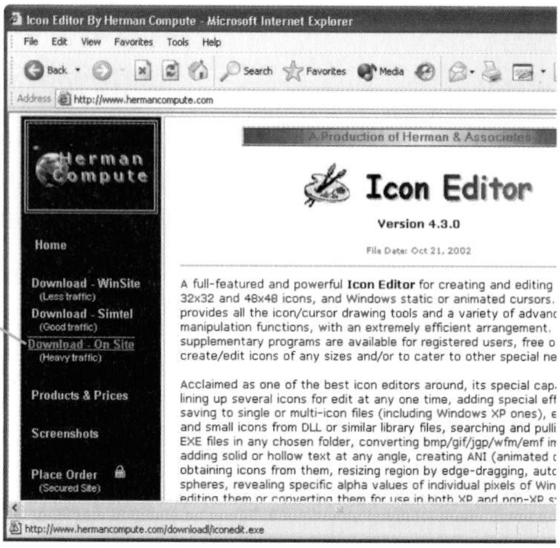

There's always a chance that a downloaded program might contain a virus. Don't click the Open button unless you are absolutely, positively, utterly sure the program doesn't contain anything nasty. See page 113 for more antivirus advice.

2 Internet Explorer asks whether you want to open (run) the file or save it on to your hard disk. Click Save

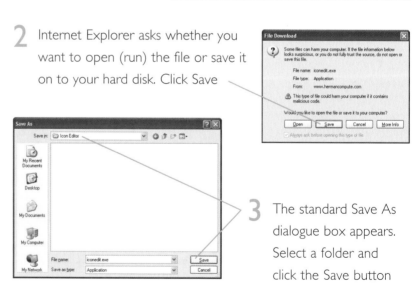

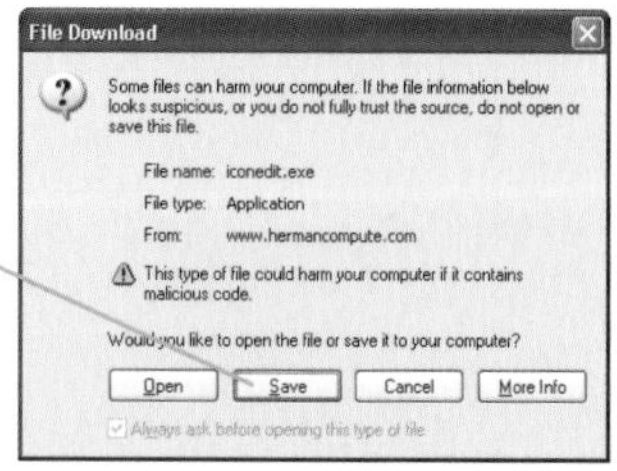

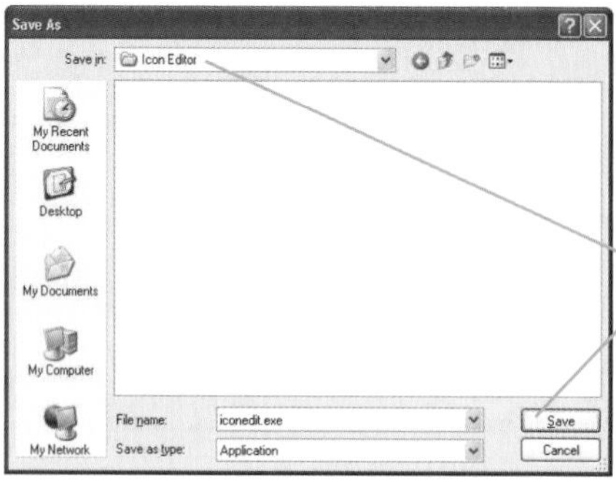

3 The standard Save As dialogue box appears. Select a folder and click the Save button

4 The file is downloaded on to your hard disk – this often takes several minutes. You can continue browsing or switch to another program and carry on working

5 Once the download is complete, you have three options. Click Open to run the program straight away

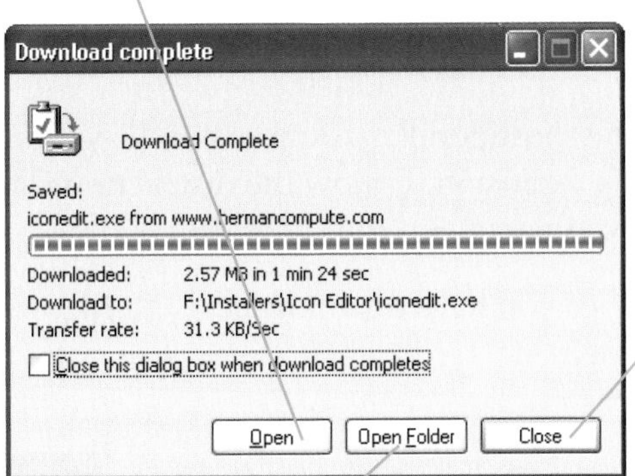

7 Or, click Close to close the dialogue box and go on with something else. Don't forget to go back and deal with your new program later on!

6 Or, click Open Folder to find the downloaded file on your hard disk. Double-click on the program's icon to run it

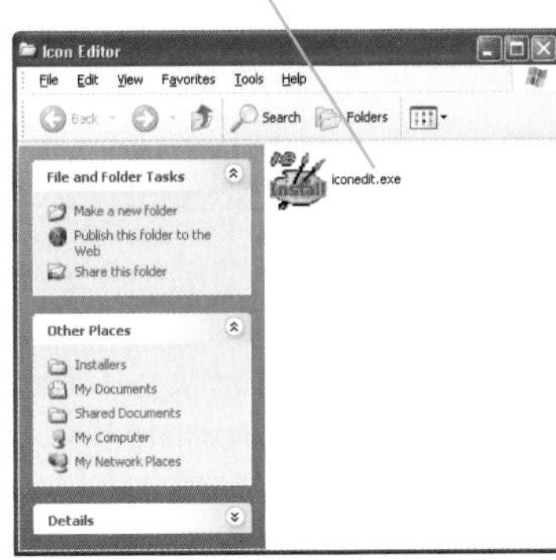

Compressed files

Software companies often use compression programs to 'archive' the program files linked to their pages. Creating an archive packs everything – setup utility, documentation, help files and the program itself – into a single, neat package. The archive is smaller than the original group of files, so it downloads more quickly.

See page 76 for more about file extensions.

The most popular compression programs produce archives with a .zip extension. Follow the instructions on the previous two pages to save them on to your hard disk.

Once you have downloaded a .zip file, you'll need to decompress or 'unzip' it.

You may also come across other types of archive. Self-extracting archives have an .exe extension and unzip themselves automatically when you double-click the original file. Archives with names ending in .hqx, .sit, .sea, .gz, .Z, .tar or .gtar contain Apple Macintosh or Unix files. It's unlikely you'll be able to use the files in these archives, so it's best to avoid them.

1. Open the folder containing the file. Double-click it
2. Windows displays the contents of the .zip file. To unzip it, click 'Extract all files'

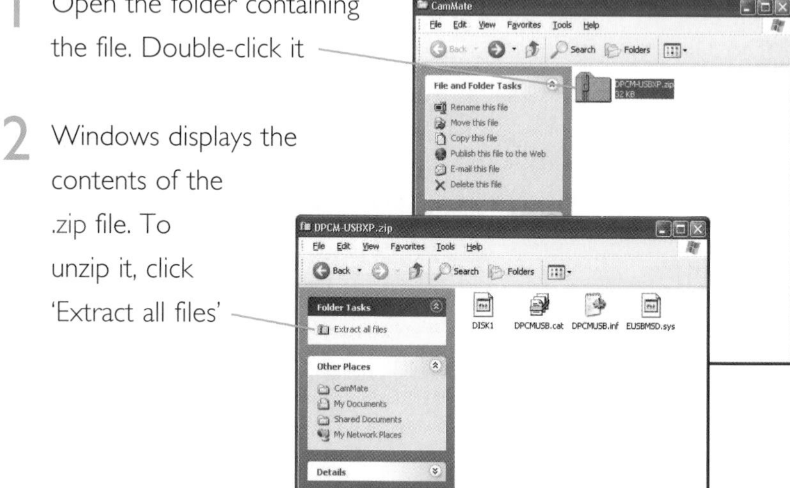

3. The Extraction Wizard helps you unpack the files into a new folder

Keep your computer healthy

There are several types of malicious programs, including viruses, worms and Trojan horses. A virus attaches itself to other programs. A worm can replicate independently and doesn't need to attach itself to a program. Trojans don't replicate – they just cause damage if you make the mistake of running them.

A computer virus is a small piece of program code that attaches itself to other programs. When you run the infected program, the virus copies itself to another program or causes your computer to do something untoward. Some are just irritating, but others may damage or destroy your files.

Programs versus data

A program file contains instructions for your computer. When you run the program file, for example by double-clicking it, your computer follows the instructions.

A data file simply contains information. Many data files are associated with particular programs. For example, Windows normally associates .htm (Web page) files with Internet Explorer. When you double-click a data file, Windows runs the associated program and displays the data.

Viruses attach themselves to program files. When your computer runs the program file, it carries out all the normal instructions, plus some extra ones added by the virus. This is how viruses make copies of themselves or cause strange things to happen – they weave their instructions into other programs.

How do you tell the difference between a program file and a data file? It isn't always easy. Try looking at the file extension. If the filename ends with .exe, .bat, .com, .shs, .vbs or .scr, you're definitely looking at a program. If it ends with something else, it might be a program file. In other words, sometimes you can be sure you're dealing with a program, but you can never be sure you aren't – so treat everything with caution!

Most viruses are spread by e-mail (see page 136).

Macro viruses

Some data files can contain macros – small fragments of program code that are used to automate common procedures. For example, an Excel worksheet might include a macro that displays a dialogue box when someone tries to enter data. Rather than keying numbers directly into the worksheet, they type them into the dialogue box, which provides hints and tips to help them get everything in the right place.

Since macros are basically small programs, they can contain viruses. Macro viruses are a particularly sneaky development, because the files they infect don't look like programs – they look like normal word-processor or spreadsheet data files. Macro viruses are most commonly found in Microsoft Word or Excel documents, although they can infect files from other programs. They've become very common in recent years and even documents from reputable sources may be infected.

Inoculate your computer

Antivirus programs check all the files you download, looking for known viruses and warning you about them. They also make periodic sweeps of your hard disk.

Virus checkers work well as long as you remember three things:

- The virus checker has to be running to detect a virus. Most programs run automatically each time you turn on your computer, then lurk in the background, checking every file that you save, copy or download.

You'll probably have to pay an annual fee to get new versions of the database for your antivirus program.

- Virus checkers rely on a database that contains details of all the known viruses. If your database is out of date, you may 'catch' a new virus that the program doesn't recognise. Companies that produce antivirus software usually let you download the latest version of the database from their Web site. Some programs do this automatically; others require you to get the update yourself. Whatever the procedure, make sure your database is up to date.

Be choosy about the sites you download from. Stick to large, well-managed file libraries or get software directly from the company that created it. It's also a good idea to make regular back-ups of files that contain important data.

- To give your virus checker the best possible chance of detecting a virus, always save suspect files on to your hard disk. Never open program files, Word or Excel documents from within Internet Explorer or Outlook Express.

Virus checkers detect macro viruses as well as the regular sort. Recent versions of Word and Excel can also protect you against these pests. Consult the Help file to find out how to use this feature. If you're using a very old version that doesn't have macro virus protection, use a virus checker on any Word or Excel files before you open them.

Other security problems

Back in Chapter 5 you installed several add-on programs so you could enjoy multimedia files such as sounds and videos. You also learnt that Web pages can contain scripts – fragments of program code that add interactive elements. Both these technologies could potentially be abused to cause problems for your computer. On the other hand, they help make Web sites dynamic and interesting.

The security settings complement the activities of your virus checker. They can help you avoid problems a virus checker might miss, but they don't protect you from viruses.

Internet Explorer provides four security settings – High, Medium, Medium-Low and Low – that enable you to trade off excitement against security when you're browsing the Web. The settings cover all kinds of interactive content, file downloads and communication with insecure sites (see page 98).

- **High** prevents you from downloading anything that could cause problems, keeping you safe but cutting you off from some of the more exciting aspects of the Web.
- **Medium** is less severe: it bans some unsafe content and warns you about the rest.
- **Medium-Low** is the same, but without the warnings.
- The **Low** setting provides hardly any protection.

1 Go to Tools>Internet Options, then click the Security tab

The Local Intranet zone contains the computers on a local computer network, such as a company's internal network. The Trusted Sites and Restricted Sites zones can be customised to include sites you feel good or bad about. You can use a different setting for each zone, if you're so inclined. However, the Internet zone is the important one.

2 Choose the Internet zone

3 Move the slider to High (at the top) to eliminate potential hazards

4 Medium security exposes you to some risks, but enables you to enjoy interactive Web content. You are warned about potential hazards

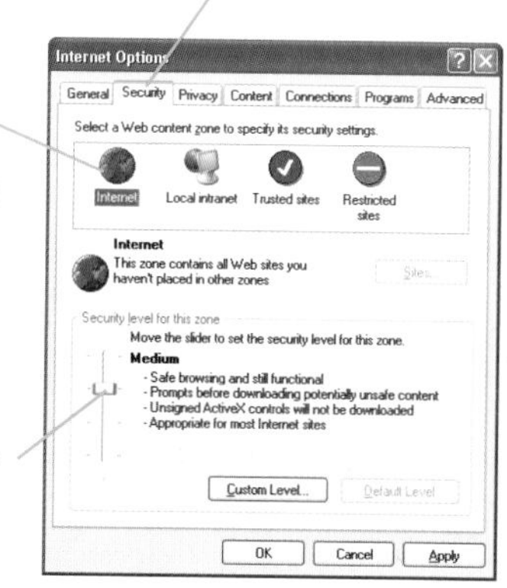

5 Don't use the Medium-Low or Low settings for general browsing

File transfer protocol

This chapter has focused on downloading program files with a Web browser, because that's what most people do. It isn't the most efficient approach, but it's easy and convenient, and perfectly adequate if you don't download files very often.

In the days before Web browsers, people used a different system known as File Transfer Protocol (FTP). As you might expect from the name, it was entirely about transferring files and no use for anything else.

You can still use File Transfer Protocol today. All you need is an FTP program, such as GlobalSCAPE's CuteFTP or Ipswitch's WS_FTP. Find out more and/or obtain copies of these programs from the following Web sites:

GlobalSCAPE at: http://www.cuteftp.com/
Ipswitch Software at: http://www.ipswitch.com/

FTP programs show the files on your computer on one side of the screen and the files from a computer on the Internet on the other side. To move a file from one computer to the other, you simply select it and click a button or drag it across with the mouse.

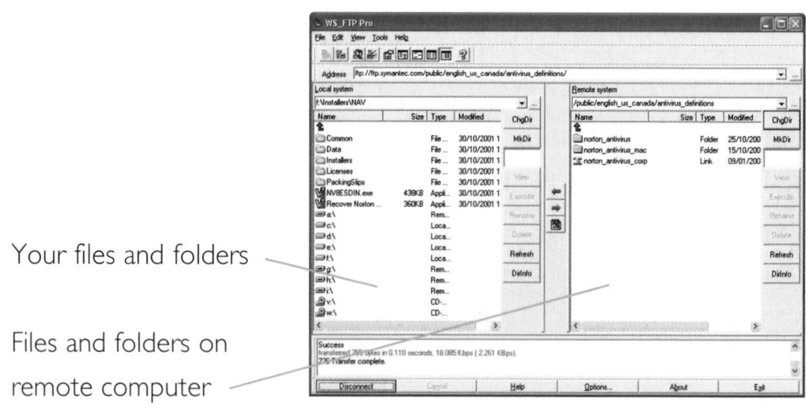

You may want to learn more about FTP if you decide to create your own Web site (see Chapter 12), because it makes it easy to upload your pages.

Send me an e-mail

Chapter Eight

Electronic mail is quick, quiet, cheap, convenient, courteous… and easy to send and receive. What more could you want? Find out how it works, how to keep your addresses and messages in order, and how to sidestep viruses and junk mail.

Covers

E is for e-mail

E-mail is short for electronic mail, the Internet equivalent of letters and faxes. However, it's better than both of those:

- **E-mail is quick.** It only takes a couple of minutes to send a message to someone, no matter where in the world they are. A letter might take days or even weeks.
- **E-mail is cheap.** Even if you pay for your connection by the minute, you won't run up a significant bill sending e-mails, because all the time-consuming activities take place off-line. You only have to be connected to the Internet when you're sending or receiving messages. You can read your mail and write replies after you have disconnected.
- **E-mail is convenient.** You don't need to find an envelope, buy a stamp or look for a mail box. You can do everything from home, at any hour of the day.

E-mail is great for queries with straightforward answers. If you need to discuss something, it's better to use the telephone. Don't try to carry out complex negotiations by e-mail.

- **It helps you stay in touch.** E-mail is great for contacting people who are perpetually on the phone or out of the office. Instead of spending half the day playing telephone tag, you can e-mail your queries and comments and let them respond when they can. It also makes it easier to deal with people in different time zones. Sending an e-mail is more considerate than calling at an awkward hour.
- **You can send people files.** You can attach text documents, pictures, sound clips and program files to your messages. If you're collaborating on a project, you can send people editable documents instead of expecting them to re-enter information from a letter or fax. It's also a great way to share holiday snaps and family photographs.
- **You can do mass mailouts.** Printing newsletters and mailing them out to customers or club members can be expensive and time consuming. With e-mail, you simply compose a message and send it to everyone on your mailing list. It's a great way to inform people about special offers and upcoming events.

To send an e-mail to someone, you just need to know their address, which will look something like:

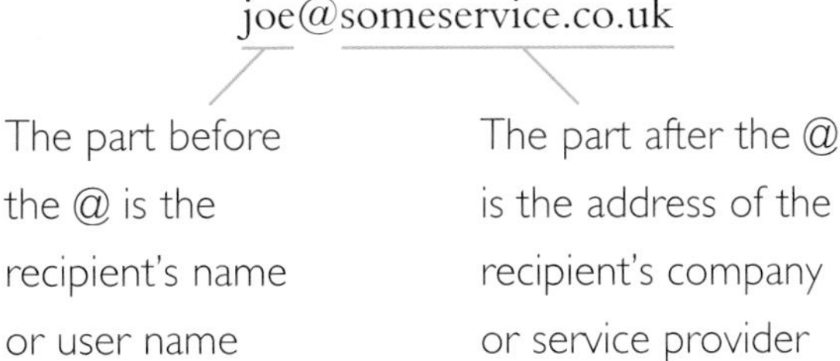
joe@someservice.co.uk
The part before the @ is the recipient's name or user name
The part after the @ is the address of the recipient's company or service provider

When you send an e-mail message, it crosses the Internet very quickly. If the recipient's computer is permanently connected to the Internet, for example via a company network, it reaches them in a couple of minutes.

If the recipient uses a modem to connect to the Internet, your message is delivered to their service provider. It is deposited in their mail box and waits there until they log on and check for new e-mail. It's like sending a letter to someone with a post-office box: they don't know your message is there until they go to the post office and open their mail box. Most people check their mail at least once a day, but some people only log on occasionally – in which case it may be a while before you get a reply.

Choose a mail program

You can also sign up for a Web-based mail service and send and receive mail using your browser – see Chapter 9.

You need an e-mail program to send and receive e-mail messages. Most programs have four basic functions:

- They let you compose messages in a word processor-style window. Usually you can add formatting and insert pictures.
- They dispatch your messages and check your mail box for incoming mail.
- They enable you to read and file the messages you receive.
- They store the addresses of the people you correspond with.

Popular e-mail programs include Microsoft's Outlook Express (included in Windows) and its big brother Outlook (supplied with Microsoft Office), Netscape's Mail and Qualcomm's Eudora. All these programs enable you to send messages to any Internet user, including people with other e-mail programs. You only need to have the same e-mail program as your friends if you want to send messages with very complicated formatting.

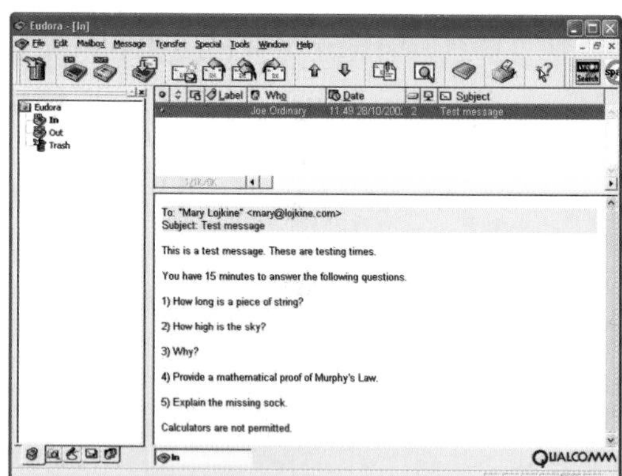

Eudora can display messages created with Outlook Express, and vice versa

This book concentrates on Outlook Express. It was designed as a companion program for Internet Explorer and is included with Windows, so it's a good choice for beginners. For information about the alternatives, visit their Web sites:

Netscape Communications: http://www.netscape.com/
Qualcomm: http://www.eudora.com/

Introducing Outlook Express

Outlook Express isn't just an e-mail program; you can also use it to access Usenet newsgroups (see Chapter 10). It has quite a lot in common with Outlook, the mail program supplied with Microsoft Office, but it's more specialised. Outlook Express is optimised for sending mail over the Internet, whereas Outlook also has features for communicating with colleagues over a company network.

If you used a CD from your service provider to configure your Internet connection (see page 33), you've probably set up your account already.

1. To run Outlook Express, click the Start button and select it from the left-hand side of the Start menu
2. The first time you do this, you may be prompted to fill in the details of your e-mail account. You'll need to know your e-mail address and the addresses of your service provider's mail servers (if you don't have this information, call your service provider)
3. Enter your name
4. Click Next to continue (and again after each step)
5. Enter your e-mail address
6. Enter the addresses of your service provider's mail servers

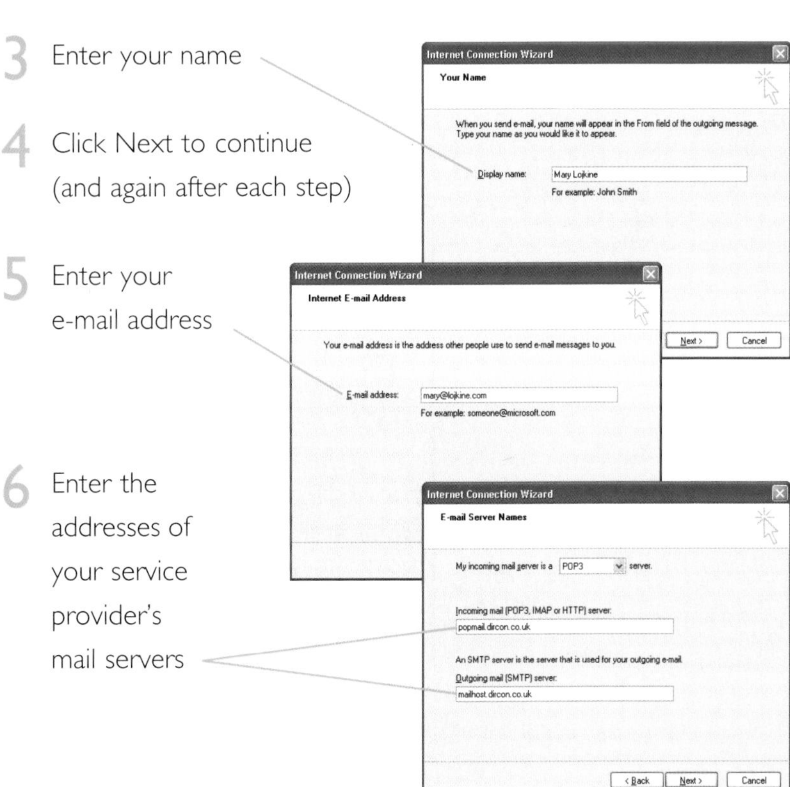

When you collect e-mail, you have to send your user name and password twice: once to connect to your service provider and again to access your mail box. Windows XP can automate both log-ins.

7 Fill in your user name and password. Usually these are the same as the ones you use to connect to the Internet (see page 33), but some service providers give you a separate user name and/or password for e-mail

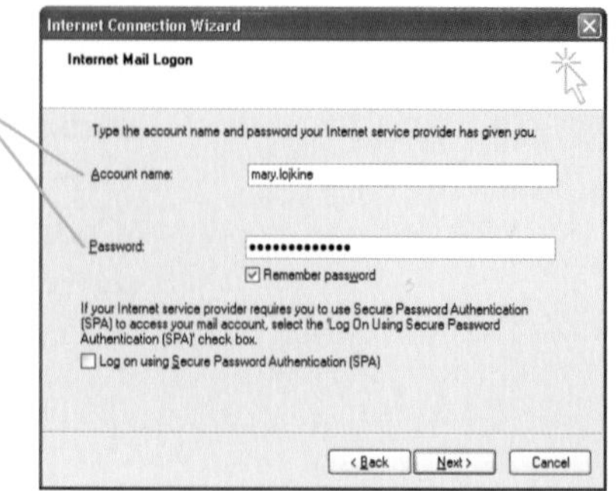

8 Click Finish. Outlook Express prompts you to connect, then checks for new mail. When it has finished, disconnect (see page 38)

Make yourself at home

The Outlook Express window is divided into several panes:

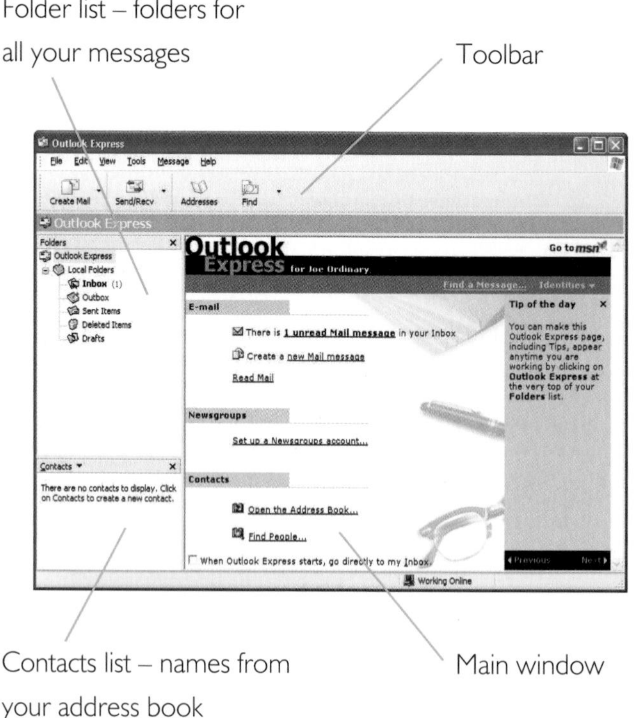

1. Select Inbox from the folder list to open your Inbox. The main window is divided in two:

Message list – lists all the messages in this folder

Preview pane – displays the selected message

2. Drag the grey dividing bars to adjust the relative sizes of the panes

3. To make further changes, go to View>Layout

4. Select the items you want to display

5. Click Customize Toolbar to add or remove toolbar buttons, change the button size or hide the text labels

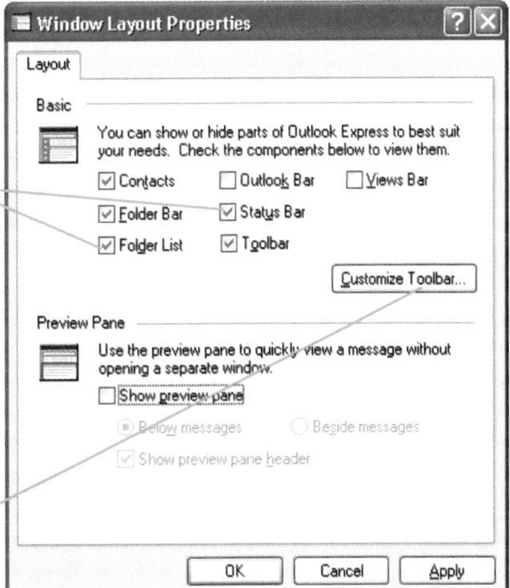

It's a good idea to turn off the preview pane. If you leave it on, Outlook Express automatically displays the latest message each time you download your mail. Some viruses can be caught by previewing a message – see page 136.

Send an e-mail

You have to be connected to the Internet to send a message, but you don't have to be on-line while you compose it. It's best to write your messages before you log on, then send them all in a batch. You can collect any new messages at the same time (see opposite).

1 To write a message, click the Create Mail button, select File>New>Mail Message or press Ctrl+N

If you have one of the Microsoft Office applications, you can spell-check your message. Click the Spelling button, select Tools>Spelling or press F7.

2 A New Message window appears

3 Enter the e-mail address of the recipient

4 Fill in the Subject: line

5 Compose your message

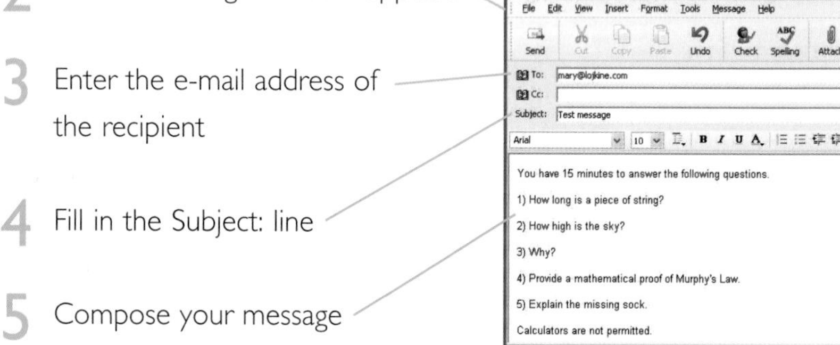

To determine whether Outlook Express sends messages immediately, go to Tools>Options and click the Send tab. If 'Send messages immediately' is selected, it will send each message as soon as you click the Send button. If you use a modem to connect to the Internet, deselect that option. You can then collect messages in your Outbox and send them in batches.

6 Click the Send button or press Alt+S. If Outlook Express is set up to send messages immediately, it dispatches the message

7 If Outlook Express is not set up to send messages immediately, it transfers the message to the Outbox

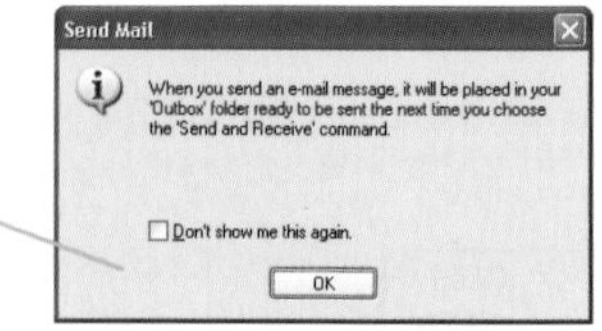

8 When you're ready to send the messages in your Outbox, click the Send/Recv button or press Ctrl+M.
Outlook Express connects to the Internet and dispatches them

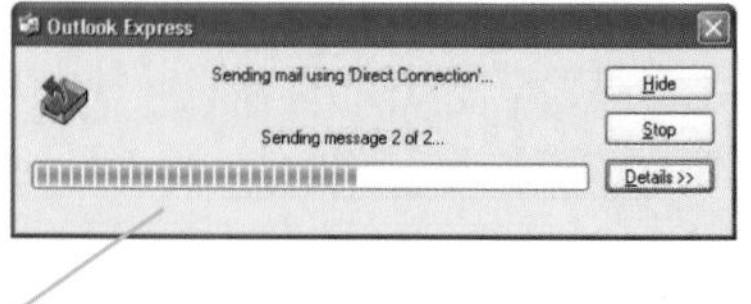

Receive messages

To make Outlook Express check for new messages automatically, go to Tools>Options. Click the General tab and select the 'Check for new messages every xx minutes' checkbox.

Unlike 'real' mail, e-mail messages aren't delivered to your door – or in this case, computer. When someone sends you an e-mail, it's delivered to your service provider's mail server, which puts it into your personal mail box. You must then log on and collect it.

1 To check your mail box, click Send/Recv. Outlook Express connects to the Internet (if necessary), sends any messages waiting in your Outbox and fetches any new mail. The new messages are placed in your Inbox. You can log off and read them in your own time

2 Select the Inbox folder to see the messages you have received

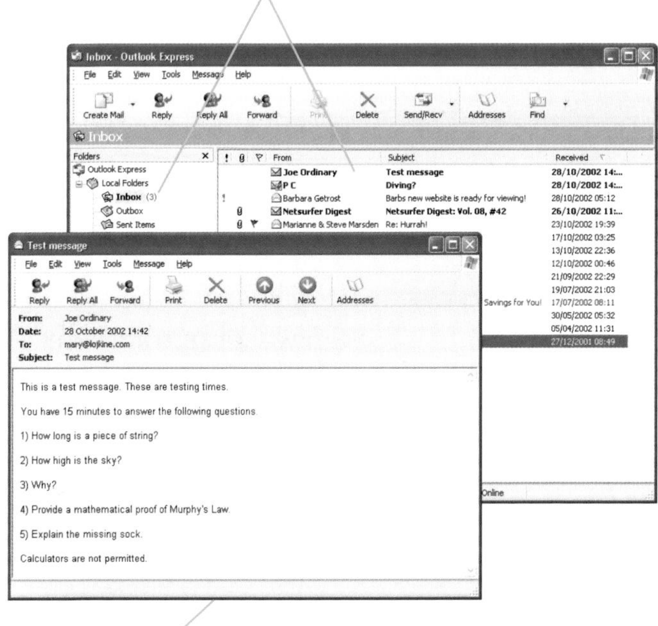

3 Double-click on a message to display it in a separate window

To print a message, open it, then click Print. You can also select File>Print or press Ctrl+P.

Reply and forward

It's easy to reply to an e-mail message, because Outlook Express automatically adds the correct address.

You don't have to open a message to reply to it – simply selecting it in the message list will do.

1 To reply to a message, click on its entry in the message list to select it. Click the Reply button, select Message>Reply to Sender or press Ctrl+R. Outlook Express opens a New Message window

2 The To: and Subject: lines are already filled in

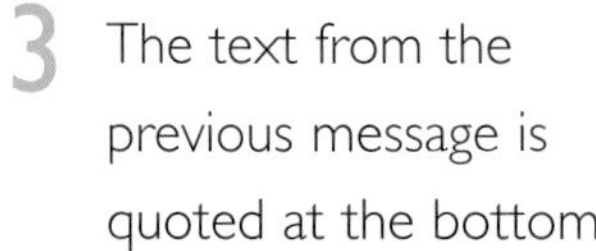

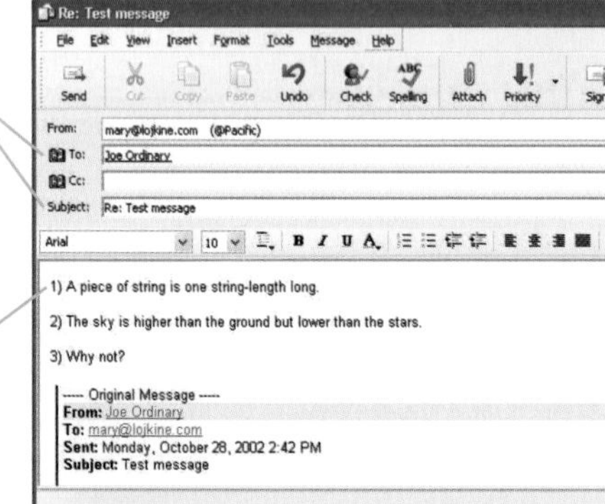

3 The text from the previous message is quoted at the bottom

4 Type your reply

5 Delete any superfluous material from the bottom section, then send the message as usual

Quoting is useful when you're dealing with people who receive a lot of mail. If you delete everything except the part of the message to which you're responding, it's easy for them to see what you're on about. However, you can turn this feature off if you find it a nuisance. Go to Tools>Options and click the Send tab. Deselect 'Include message in reply.'

Forwarding messages

You can also divert an e-mail message to a friend or to someone who is better able to respond to the sender.

1 To forward a message, select it and click the Forward button. Alternatively, select Message> Forward or press Ctrl+F. Enter the new address in the To: line

2 Add any comments you wish to make above the quoted text, then send the message

Address book

The Address Book enables you to store all the e-mail addresses you use regularly. You can then add them to messages more easily.

1 To open the Address Book, click the Addresses button, select Tools>Address Book or press Ctrl+Shift+B

It's even easier to add the address of someone who has sent you an e-mail message. Select the message, then go to Tools>Add Sender to Address Book.

Outlook Express may automatically add people you reply to. To turn this option on or off, go to Tools>Options and click the Send tab.

2 To add an address, click the New button and select New Contact. You can also select File>New Contact or press Ctrl+N

3 Fill in the person's name and (optionally) nickname

4 Enter their e-mail address and click Add. Repeat if they have several

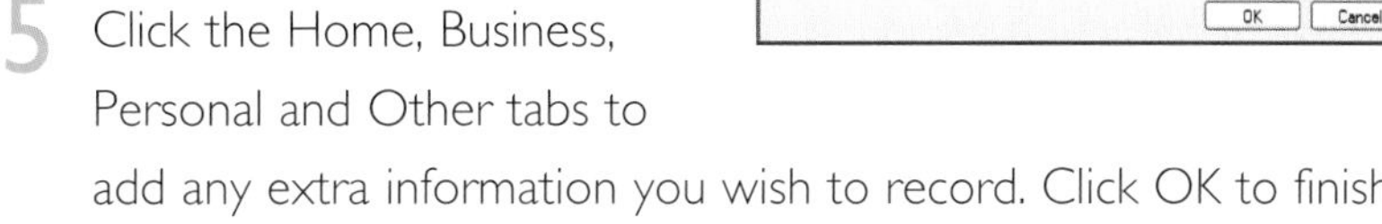

5 Click the Home, Business, Personal and Other tabs to add any extra information you wish to record. Click OK to finish

To access the Address Book from the New Message window, click the address book icon at the left of the To: line.

6 You can now enter the person's name or nickname in the To: line of your messages. Outlook Express will look up the address when you send the message. Alternatively, double-click the person's entry in the Contacts list to create a pre-addressed message form

Organise your messages

Initially you have five e-mail folders: Inbox, Outbox, Sent Items, Deleted Items and Drafts.

- New e-mail is deposited in the Inbox (see page 125).
- Outgoing e-mail waits in the Outbox (see page 124).
- Once a message has been dispatched, it is moved to the Sent Items folder so you have a copy.
- If you select a message and click Delete, select Edit> Delete, press Delete or press Ctrl+D, it ends up in the Deleted Items folder. You can rescue it if necessary.
- If you close a message without sending it, Outlook Express asks if you want to save the changes. Click Yes to move the message to the Drafts folder so you can finish it later on.

DON'T FORGET

The Deleted Items folder is like the Windows Recycle Bin – it stores items you think you won't need again until you're ready to get rid of them for good. To empty the folder, select Edit>Empty 'Deleted Items' Folder.

Sort your e-mail

As well as placing your e-mail in these folders, Outlook Express enables you to sort the messages in each one.

HOT TIP

To change the column headings, right-click on one of the tabs and select Columns...

To sort your messages, click one of the grey tabs at the top of the list. Click again to reverse the sort

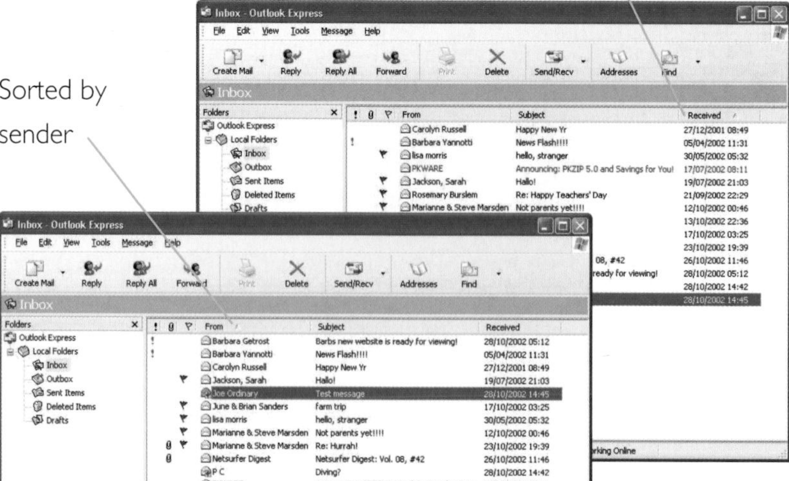

A small grey arrow within the tab tells you which column is being used to sort the messages. It points upwards for a regular sort and downwards for a reverse sort.

Create your own folders

Some messages can be deleted as soon as you've read them, but there'll be others you want to keep. Create some extra e-mail folders and file them away tidily.

1 To create a new e-mail folder, go to File>Folder>New

2 Enter a name

3 To create a new top-level folder, select Local Folders. To add a subfolder, select one of your existing folders

If the folder ends up in the wrong place, use the mouse to drag it around the Folder list.

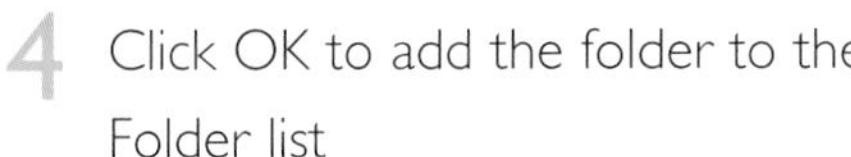

4 Click OK to add the folder to the Folder list

5 Use the mouse to drag messages into the new folder. You can also select them (hold down Shift or Ctrl to select several at once), then go to Edit> Move to Folder. Select the folder and click OK

If you can't remember where you filed an important message, click the Find button, go to Edit> Find>Message or press Ctrl+ Shift+F. You can search by subject or sender, or look for messages that contain a word or phrase.

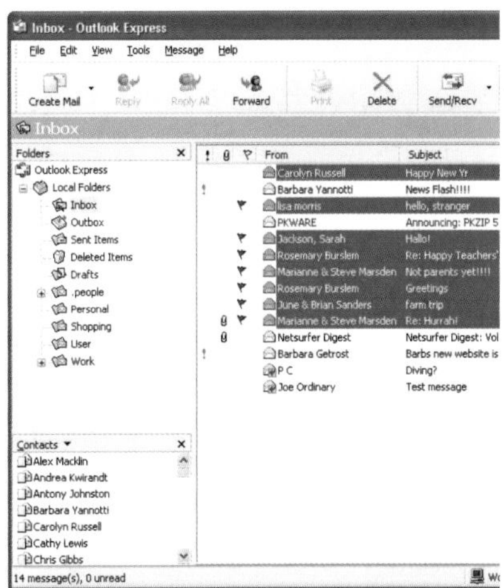

Formatted e-mail

Outlook Express enables you to format your e-mail messages so they are as attractive as Web pages (the formatting is added using HTML, the language used to create Web pages).

Formatted mail is fun and can be useful when you're trying to catch someone's eye. However, it's only a good idea if you're sure the other person uses a program that can handle HTML mail. Formatted messages look awful in older e-mail programs and some people find them irritating. If in doubt, stick to plain text.

1 Use the New Message window's Format menu to switch between Rich Text (HTML) and Plain Text. A formatting bar appears when Rich Text is selected

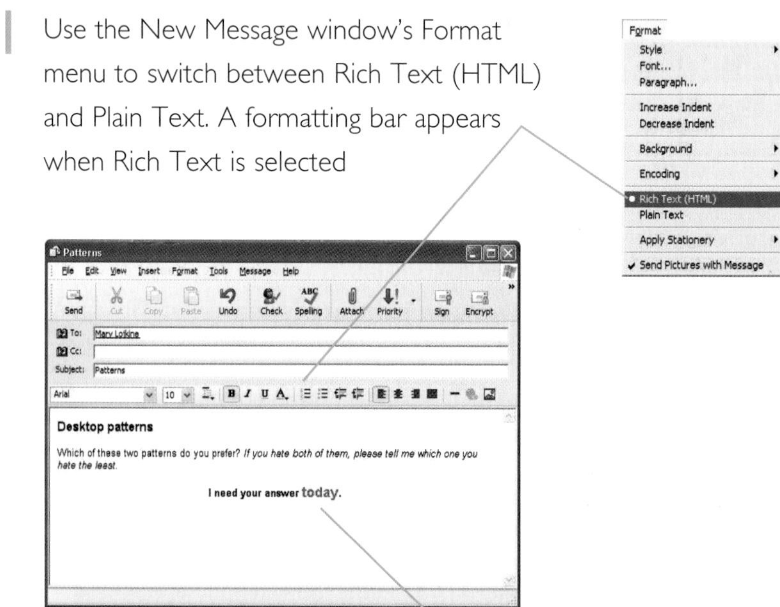

Stick to fonts that the other person is likely to have: Arial, Comic Sans, Georgia, Impact, Times New Roman, Trebuchet and Verdana.

2 Use the drop-down lists and buttons to format your text

The picture must be saved in the .gif or .jpg format.

3 To add a picture, click Insert Picture or select Insert>Picture. Click Browse and locate the picture file. Click OK

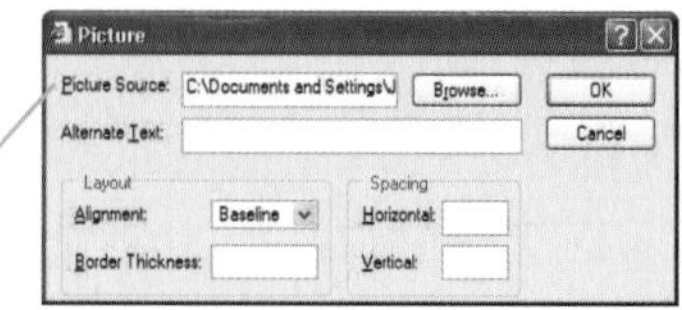

4 To add a horizontal line, click Insert Horizontal Line or select Insert>Horizontal Line

5 To create a fancy backdrop for your text, go to Format>Background. Select Color to choose a solid colour, or Picture to insert an image

6 If you're inserting an image, click Browse to locate the file, then click OK

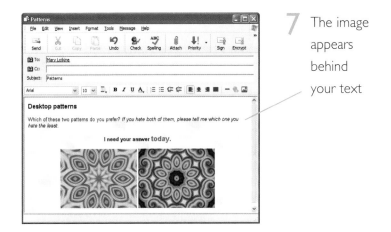

7 The image appears behind your text

Plain or fancy?

You don't have to format your messages. Experienced Internet users regard e-mail as a fast and easy way to communicate. They will be happy to receive quick notes in Plain Text format and may not be impressed by multicoloured messages.

You can tell Outlook Express to use Plain Text by default.

1 Go to Tools>Options and click the Send tab. Under 'Mail Sending Format', select 'Plain Text'

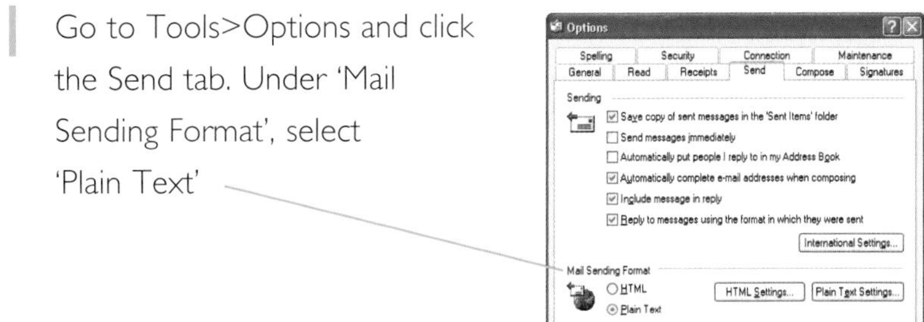

Stationery

Outlook Express comes with predesigned Stationery that can add a touch of class to your correspondence or help you celebrate special occasions. However, Stationery is formatted mail (the fact that it was formatted by someone else makes no difference), so it's only a good idea if you're sure the recipient can display it.

To specify a default Stationery design, go to Tools>Options. Click the Compose tab, select 'Mail:' and pick a design.

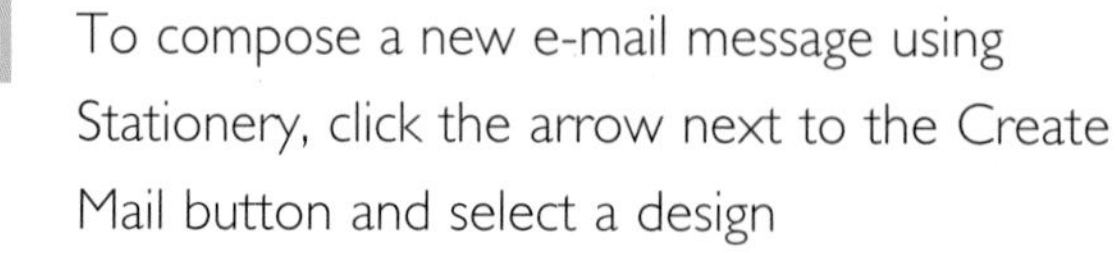

1. To compose a new e-mail message using Stationery, click the arrow next to the Create Mail button and select a design

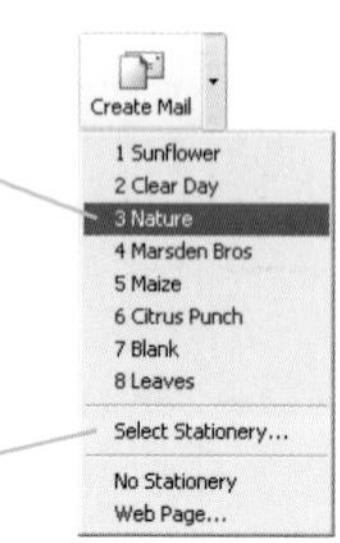

2. The menu only lists a few of the designs. Click Select Stationery for more choices

To design your own Stationery, go to Tools> Options and click the Compose tab. Click the Create New button to run the Stationery Wizard.

There's also a Download More button that takes you to Microsoft's Web site, where you'll find lots of extra designs.

3. Complete and send your message as usual. You can add additional formatting if you wish

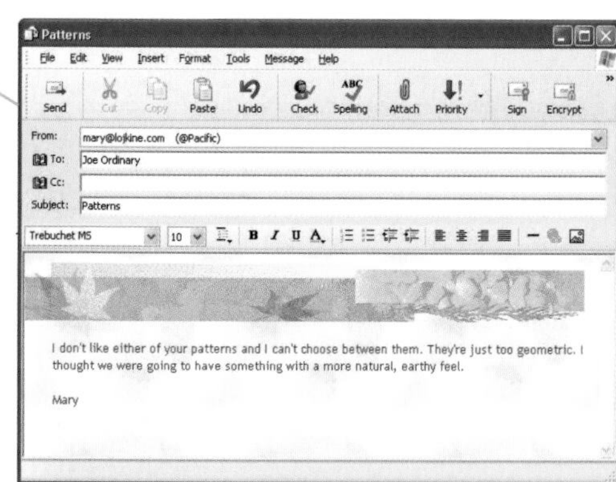

4. You can also add stationery to a message that you're halfway through composing. Make sure Rich Text format is selected (see page 130), then go to Format> Apply Stationery

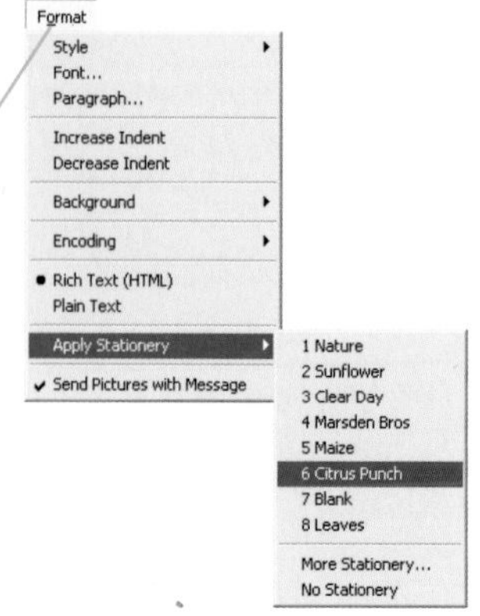

Signatures

A signature is a short piece of text that is appended to the end of every message you send. If you're sending messages from work, it could include your contact details. For personal messages, you might use a catch phrase or favourite quote. Keep it short, though – long signatures soon become tiresome.

You can create several signatures. You might use different ones for business and personal messages. However, you'll have to sign your messages manually – see below.

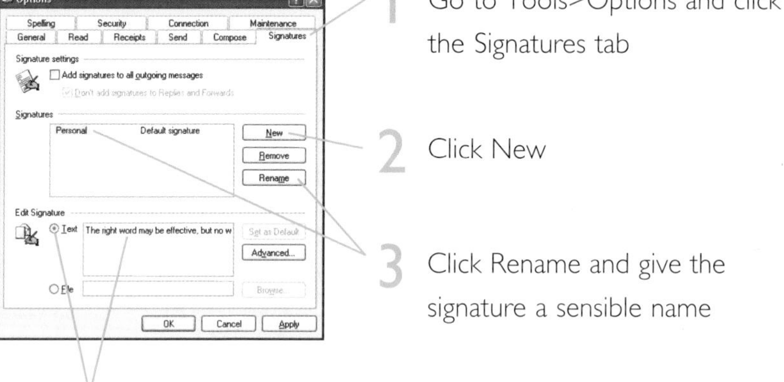

1 Go to Tools>Options and click the Signatures tab

2 Click New

3 Click Rename and give the signature a sensible name

4 Select 'Text' and enter the text you want to add to your messages

If you only want to sign some of your messages, don't select 'Add…'. Instead, use the Insert>Signature menu option to add your signature manually before you send your messages.

5 If you want to sign all your messages, select the 'Add signatures to all outgoing messages' option at the top of the dialogue box

6 Click OK

7 The signature text is added to the end of every message you create

Attachments

You can e-mail pictures, document files and programs to friends and family. If you have a digital camera or microphone, you can bring your messages to life with snapshots or recordings. More prosaically, being able to exchange files by e-mail is handy when you're working from home.

1. Compose your message (see page 124) and click the Attach button. Alternatively, select File Attachment from the New Message window's Insert menu

You can attach any kind of file, but don't send your friends large files without warning them first. Make sure they have the right software for viewing your files.

2. Find the file(s) you want to send – you can select several files at once by holding down Shift or Ctrl

3. Click Attach

If you change your mind about one of the files, right-click on its entry in the Attach: line, then select Remove from the pop-up menu.

4. The files are added to the message

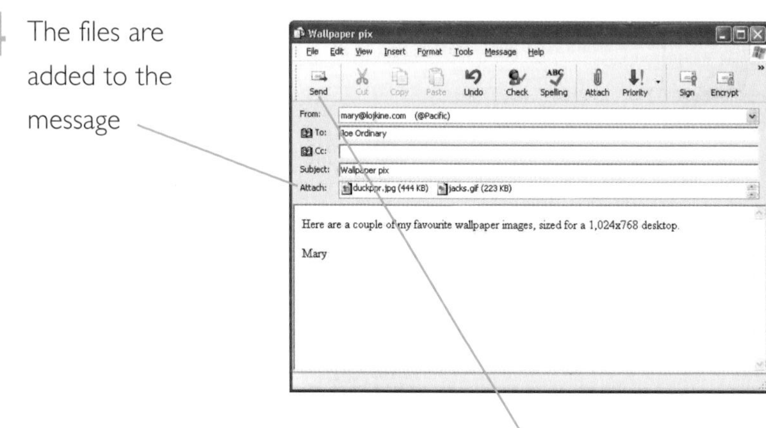

5. Send the message in the usual way

Receiving attachments

When you receive a message with attached files, you have two main choices: open the files or save them on to your hard disk. It is usually better to save them.

If you receive a file from someone you don't know, don't open it. The safest option is to delete the entire message. Alternatively, save the file on to your hard disk and check for viruses before you open it. This also applies to Word and Excel documents, which can carry macro viruses (see page 113).

1 If you see a paperclip icon in the message list, the associated message has one or more files attached

2 When you open the message, the attached files are listed at the top. In some cases – for example, when a .gif or .jpg image has been attached – the file is displayed at the end of the text

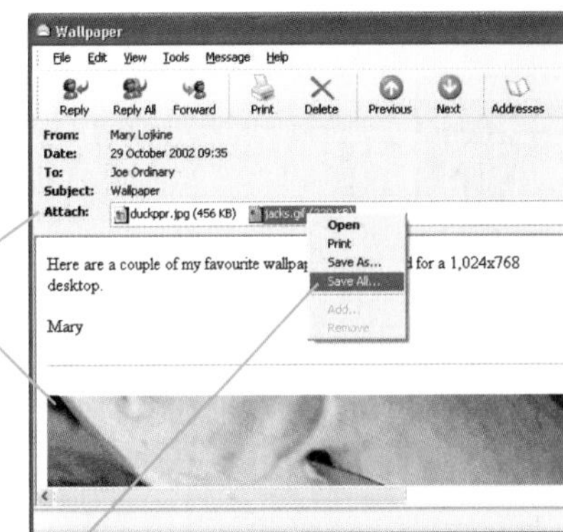

3 Right-click on a file to open it or save it. You can also save all the files at once

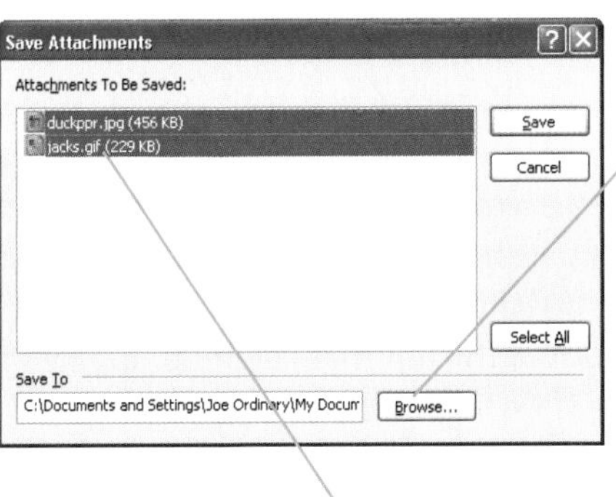

4 Click Browse and choose a folder

5 Select the files you want to save and click Save

Viruses by e-mail

Viruses are designed to spread themselves as widely as possible. The malicious programmers who produce viruses want to get their creations on to as many computers as possible, as quickly as possible. Over the last few years they've figured out how to harness the power of e-mail to distribute viruses. You are almost certain to receive an infected e-mail at some point, so it's worth learning how to recognise a problem and protect your computer.

There are several things you should know about viruses that are transmitted by e-mail:

People used to tell beginners that they couldn't catch a virus simply by opening an e-mail message. With the advent of formatted mail, that's no longer true.

- Most viruses travel as attachments. However, there are some that hide themselves in the body of a formatted message. You can catch this type of virus simply by previewing or opening the infected message.
- If a friend or colleague picks up a virus, they may pass it on unwittingly. The virus may secretly attach itself to every message they send, or go through their address book and send fake messages to everyone they know. Each message carries a copy of the virus.
- Some viruses can fake (or 'spoof') the From: address in the e-mails they send out. Suppose you have two friends, Joe and Tina, and Joe catches the Klez virus. It goes through his computer, looking for e-mail addresses, and finds Tina's address. It then creates a fake message that appears to be from Tina and sends it to you. You are running a virus checker (of course) and it sounds the alarm. Since the message came from Tina, you tell her to check her computer, but she says she doesn't have the virus. She is right – it is Joe's computer that is sending out the messages. You can even receive an infected message that appears to have come from your own computer.
- Some viruses can also attach random files from your computer to the messages they send out. This can be embarrassing if they choose confidential documents.

Keep your computer healthy

Avoiding viruses is mostly a matter of common sense:

- Run a virus checker and keep its database up to date (see page 114). Make sure it is set up to check e-mail messages as well as files that you download or copy on to your hard disk.
- Turn off Outlook Express' Preview pane (see page 123).
- Tell Outlook Express to use a high level of security when opening messages. To do this, run Internet Explorer and go to Tools>Internet Options. Click the Security tab, then select the Restricted Sites zone. Make sure its security level is set to High (see page 115). Switch to Outlook Express and select Tools>Options. Click the Security tab. Under 'Virus Protection', set 'Select the Internet Explorer security zone to use' to 'Restricted sites zone (More secure)'.

This trick is useful when you get a message that sounds legitimate. For example, if you've sent a query to an on-line shop, you may not recognise the name of the person who replies. By checking the Properties box, you can at least find out whether they work for the company you've been communicating with.

- Don't open e-mail messages from strangers – delete them. If you aren't sure whether a message is legitimate, right-click on its entry in the message list and select Properties. You can then see the sender's e-mail address, which may include the name of their company.
- Be suspicious if a friend sends you a message with an unusual or unlikely subject, especially if it has attached files. Give them a ring and see if they actually sent the message.
- Set up your computer to display file extensions (see page 76) and learn to recognise the dangerous ones (see page 113). Watch out for filenames with double extensions, such as picture.gif.exe. It's the letters at the end (in this case, .exe) that count.
- Always save attached files on to your hard disk before you open them. Saving the files gives your virus checker a second chance to inspect them.
- Don't yell at your friends when they send you viruses. They may have done so unwittingly, or the virus may have come from somewhere else. Concentrate on finding the source and stamping out the infection.

Virus hoaxes

There are a number of virus hoaxes that do the rounds by e-mail. The best-known example is a message that tells you not to open messages with 'Good Times' in the subject line. Doing so will delete your files and destroy your processor – or so the story goes.

The warning is a hoax and the virus it describes does not exist. However, the Good Times e-mail is almost as troublesome as a real virus, because people waste a lot of time forwarding the message to their friends, calling their systems manager and so on.

If you receive a warning that you think might be a hoax, don't pass it on 'just in case'. You'll get your less knowledgeable friends worried over nothing, and those with more experience will sigh deeply as they delete your message.

How can you tell whether a virus warning is a hoax? Be suspicious of any warning message that:

- Contains lots of exclamation marks!!!!!
- Tells you something dreadful will happen if you open an e-mail message with a particular title.
- Promises total destruction of your hard disk, your processor, your entire computer, your home…
- References a technical-sounding organisation you've never heard of and can't find on the Web.
- Encourages you to pass it on to all your friends.

You can find out whether your message is a well-known hoax by looking it up on one of the following Web sites:

CIAC Internet Hoaxes, at:
http://hoaxbusters.ciac.org/

Symantec's Anti-virus Resource Center, at:
http://www.symantec.com/avcenter/

Junk mail

The ease with which you can send e-mail or create Web pages encourages some people to abuse these services. You shouldn't believe everything you read on the Web and you shouldn't take every e-mail message seriously.

Platefuls of spam

Unsolicited commercial e-mail is known as 'spam' (after a Monty Python sketch set in café where every dish contains spam). You can expect to receive messages offering you miracle cures, better credit ratings, all manner of improvements to your sex life, x-rated pictures, vinyl siding for your house (?!) and so on.

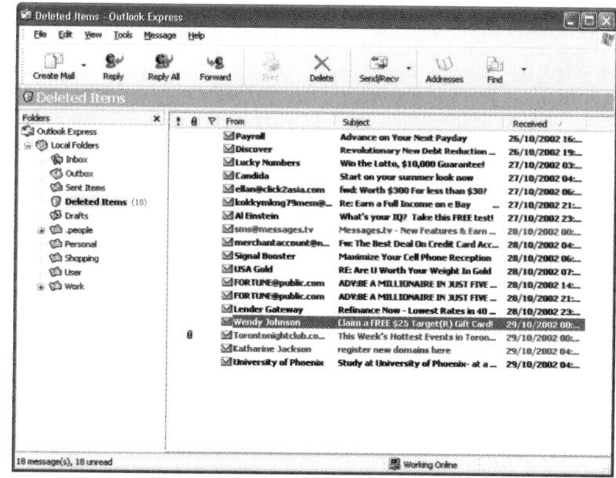

Spam is annoying but unavoidable – it's a fact of Internet life

If you notice that you are getting a lot of messages from a particular address, select the next one, then go to Tools>Block Sender. Future messages from that person will be consigned to the bin.

There's very little you can do about junk mail. The best option is to delete it, unopened. Some messages claim that if you reply to a particular address, or reply with 'remove' in the Subject: line, your name will be removed from the mailing. Don't bother doing this. Often the company just wants to confirm that their messages are getting through. You may receive even more spam if you send any kind of reply.

Chain letters

There are two sorts of chain letters. One type has a list of names and promises you enormous wealth if you send a small sum of money to the person at the top. You're then supposed to add your name and redistribute the message. It's mathematically impossible for most of these schemes to pay off, and they're probably illegal.

Many service providers will close your account if they catch you forwarding this kind of junk.

The other type promises you good luck if you forward it to all your friends and bad luck if you don't. Some of these messages are very unpleasant and you should delete them. You aren't doing your friends any favours by sending them messages that threaten all sorts of dire consequences if they 'break the chain'.

The Craig Shergold story is an urban legend – a tale that keeps being told, regardless of its veracity. You can find many more in The AFU & Urban Legends Archive, at: http://www.urbanlegends.com/

There are also some well-meaning chain letters that ask you to send cards to a sick child – usually Craig Shergold, a boy with cancer – who is trying to get into *The Guinness Book of Records*. There's actually some truth to this story, which dates back to the late 1980s. However, Shergold got his record, had an operation and got on with his life, so there's no need to send a card.

Scams and frauds

There are numerous scams circulating the Internet, some of which are quite convincing. Be suspicious of anything that sounds too good to be true and learn to recognise the most common tricks.

One of the most serious scams is the Nigerian Advance Fee scam (also known as the 419 fraud). Victims receive a message purportedly from someone in Nigeria (or a similar country). The sender claims they have access to a large sum of money and need help to get it out of Nigeria. If the victim helps the writer, they'll receive a share of the profits.

Once a victim is hooked, the writer starts to request money – for example, to bribe government officials. Victims are also encouraged to travel to Nigeria or a neutral country to complete the deal. They may then be threatened with violence, held hostage or murdered.

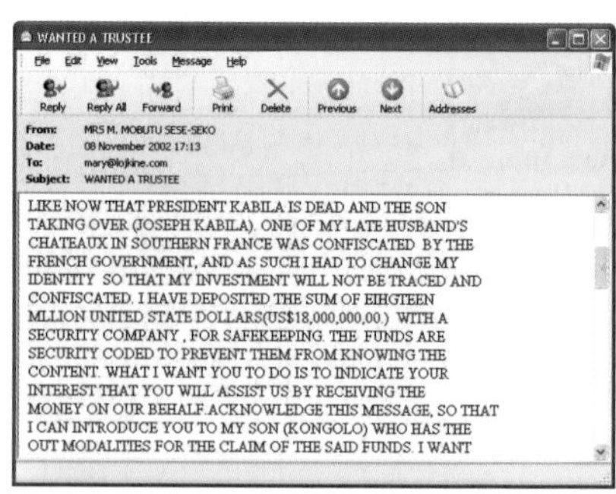

From: MRS M. MOBUTU SESE-SEKO
Date: 08 November 2002 17:13
To: mary@lojkine.com
Subject: WANTED A TRUSTEE

LIKE NOW THAT PRESIDENT KABILA IS DEAD AND THE SON TAKING OVER (JOSEPH KABILA). ONE OF MY LATE HUSBAND'S CHATEAUX IN SOUTHERN FRANCE WAS CONFISCATED BY THE FRENCH GOVERNMENT, AND AS SUCH I HAD TO CHANGE MY IDENTITY SO THAT MY INVESTMENT WILL NOT BE TRACED AND CONFISCATED. I HAVE DEPOSITED THE SUM OF EIHGTEEN MLLION UNITED STATE DOLLARS(US$18,000,000,00.) WITH A SECURITY COMPANY , FOR SAFEKEEPING. THE FUNDS ARE SECURITY CODED TO PREVENT THEM FROM KNOWING THE CONTENT. WHAT I WANT YOU TO DO IS TO INDICATE YOUR INTEREST THAT YOU WILL ASSIST US BY RECEIVING THE MONEY ON OUR BEHALF.ACKNOWLEDGE THIS MESSAGE, SO THAT I CAN INTRODUCE YOU TO MY SON (KONGOLO) WHO HAS THE OUT MODALITIES FOR THE CLAIM OF THE SAID FUNDS. I WANT

For more information about this scam and many others, visit Internet ScamBusters at: http://www.scambusters.org/

Mail on the move

Off to see the world… or making a trip to Little Tiddlytown on the Marsh, home of your company's head office? Either way, Web-based mail services enable you to collect your messages from any computer with an Internet connection.

Covers

Chapter Nine

Web-based mail

A cybercafé is the Internet equivalent of a public telephone. It has computers that are connected to the Internet and you pay a half-hourly or hourly fee to make use of them. Cybercafés are common in cities that attract a lot of travellers.

Web-based mail systems enable you to send and receive messages from any computer that's connected to the Internet, using a Web browser. You can check your mail using a computer at work, at a friend's place or in a cybercafé, without having to set up an e-mail program or enter lots of personal details.

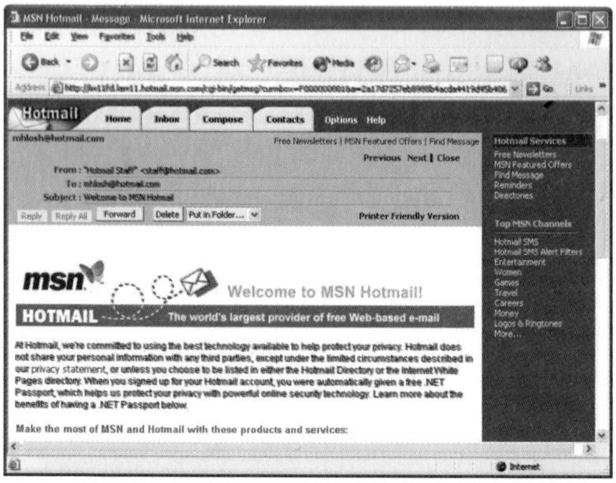

You can access a Hotmail account from anywhere

Web-based mail is great when you're travelling. Instead of lugging around a laptop or making expensive phone calls, you can stay in touch by popping into cybercafés or using computers in public places such as libraries and airports. Your friends and relatives can always contact you, without needing to know where you are, and you can send them a day-by-day account of your adventures.

Some service providers offer Web-based access to your regular e-mail account. That way you get the best of both worlds: you can use Outlook Express to send and receive mail when you're sat at your primary computer, and check your messages from a Web browser when you're away from your desk.

Web-based mail is also useful when you want to send personal messages from a company computer. Some organisations frown on people using company facilities for personal correspondence. They may not want people to mistake you for a company spokesperson. Also, you may want to keep some of your correspondence private. Your systems administrator can intercept any messages you send through your company's mail server, which can be embarrassing when you're applying for another job or flirting with a co-worker.

The downside of Web-based mail systems is that you have to be connected to the Internet to read or write messages. If you're only going to be sending e-mail from home, it's better to use a regular mail service. You'll spend less time on-line and you'll be able to take advantage of the extra features of a dedicated e-mail program such as Outlook Express.

Choose a mail service

There are thousands of Web-based mail services and most of them offer free accounts. Popular services include:

Fastmail at: http://www.fastmail.fm/
Hotmail at: http://www.hotmail.com/
Mail.com at: http://www.mail.com/
Yahoo! Mail at: http://mail.yahoo.com/

To track down the address of your dreams, visit the Internet Email List site at: http://www.internetemaillist.com/ It catalogues Web-based mail services by company name and domain names (addresses) offered.

There are also many smaller services that offer amusing addresses such as joe@madmanmail.com or tina@tough.com

When you're choosing a Web-based mail service, keep the following points in mind:

- **Will it still be operating a year from now?** Internet businesses come and go at an alarming rate. Choosing a service that's supported by a large company increases your chances of an enduring relationship.
- **If the service is free, how is it funded?** Many services add a tag-line to every message you send, promoting themselves to all your contacts. You might not find that acceptable for business mail. Most services display adverts on their Web pages and some sell your details to marketing companies.

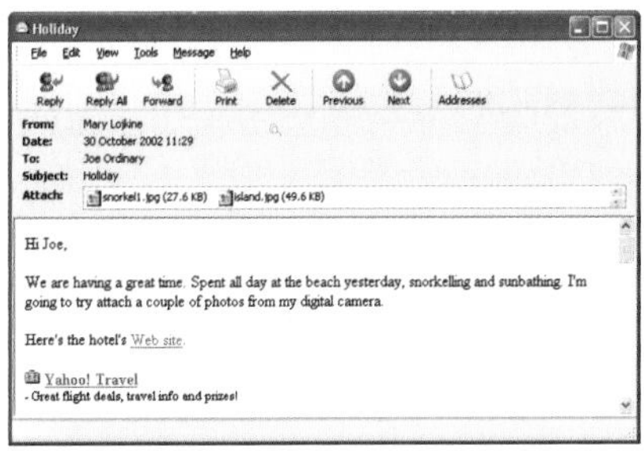

- **What addresses are available?** Can you have something simple, or will you be joe567542@someplace.com?
- **What do you get?** How much space will you have for storing messages? Can you set up an address book? Can you attach files to your messages? Is there a spell-checker?
- **What options are available?** Some companies offer a fairly basic free service, then give you the option to pay for extras such as removal of the adverts, more storage space or access to your messages from a regular e-mail program.

Regular e-mail services are often described as 'POP3' mail services. The acronym is short for Post Office Protocol 3, the normal method for receiving messages via a mail box (see page 125).

Open an account

Once you've chosen a Web-based mail service, opening an account is straightforward. Choose a user name and password, enter some personal details and you're in business.

Suppose you've decided to open a Yahoo! Mail account:

Other Web-based mail services have different procedures for opening an account, sending messages and so on. However, the basic principle doesn't change – you do everything from your Web browser.

1. Visit the Yahoo! Mail Web site at: http://mail.yahoo.com/ and follow the links to sign up for a new account. You can open a free account or pay for extra features

Note that Yahoo! Mail may change your address to reflect your location, making you joe@yahoo.co.uk or tina@yahoo.com.sg

2. Choose an ID (you can only use letters, numbers and underlines) and password. Answer the security question and fill in your personal details

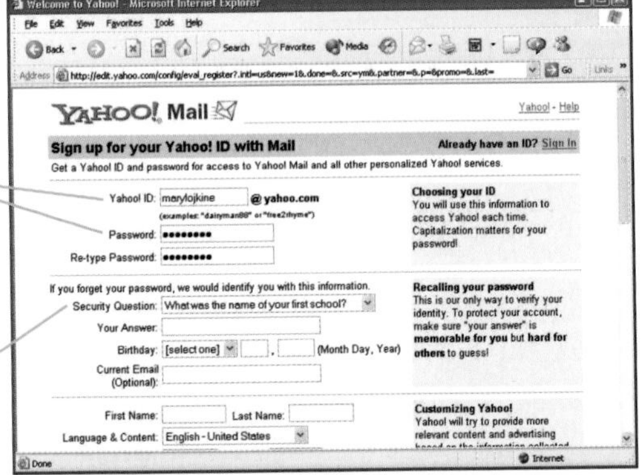

Always read the Terms of Service carefully. They tell you what to expect from the service.

3. Read the Terms of Service and confirm your acceptance of the rules

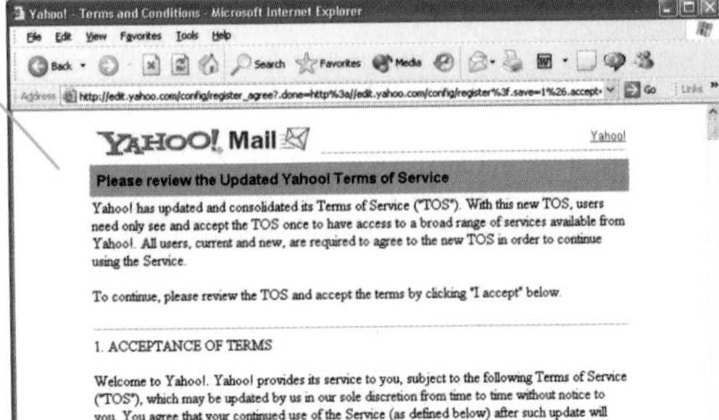

4 You'll then be taken to your on-line mail box

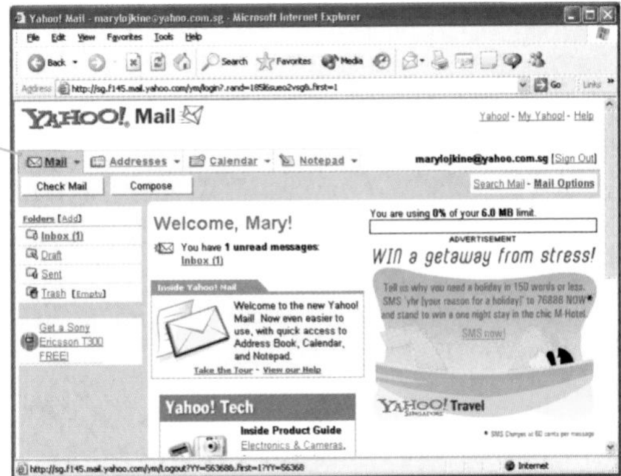

5 When you return to the Yahoo! Mail site from your own computer, it remembers your user name – you just have to enter your password. If you access the site from another computer, you have to enter both your user name and your password

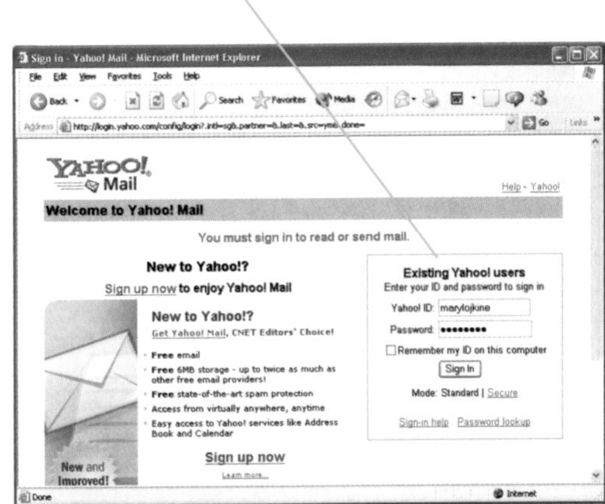

Read your mail

You can read your mail from any computer with a Web browser and an Internet connection.

1 Go to the Yahoo! Mail site and log in to your account

2 Select the Inbox to view your messages

3 Click one of the messages

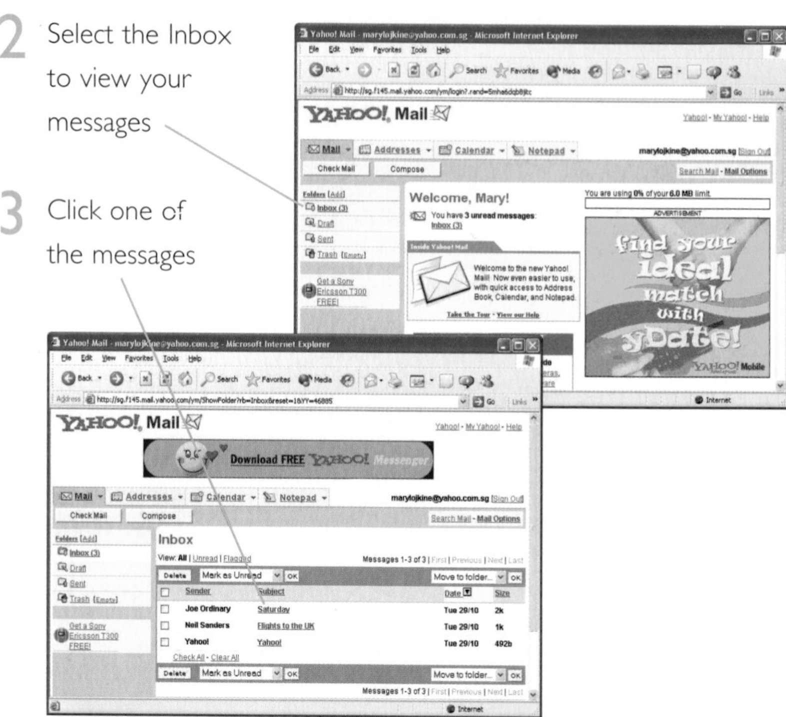

4 The message is displayed

Send a message

Sending messages is equally straightforward. Yahoo! Mail lets you format your messages, add clickable Web links and attach files from your hard disk.

1 Log on to Yahoo! Mail. To create a new message, click Compose. To reply to an existing one, open it and click Reply

2 Enter the address and subject

3 Compose your message

4 To send files with your message, click Attach Files

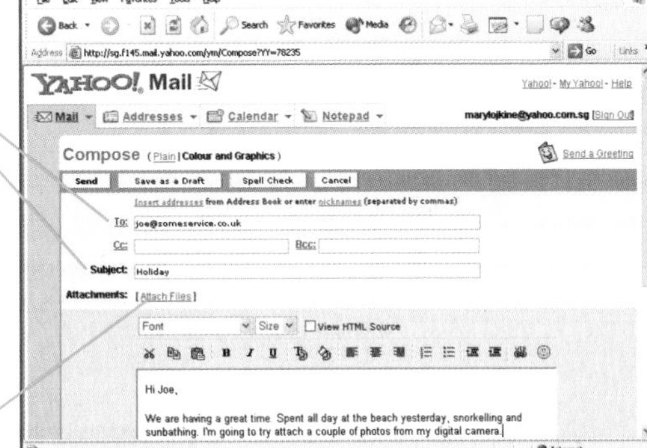

HOT TIP

To add a clickable link, select the text you want to link from, then click the Create Hyperlink button. Fill in the address of the page you want to link to.

5 Click the Browse button(s) and find the file(s) you want to include. Click Attach Files

6 The files are added to the message

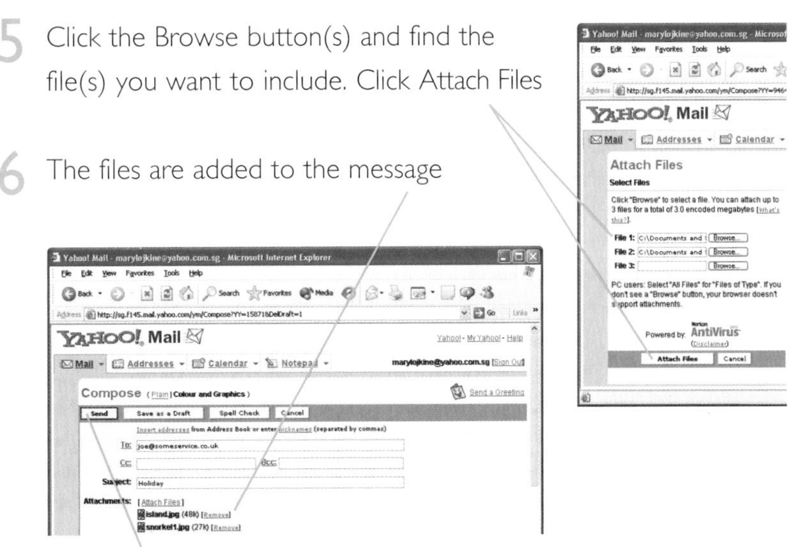

7 Click the Send button to dispatch your message

Use the Address Book

The Address Book stores the addresses of people you write to regularly, so you don't have to type them in each time.

You can also open a message and click the 'Add to Address Book' link.

1 To add someone to your Address Book, click Addresses. Select the 'Add a New Contact' option or click Add Contact

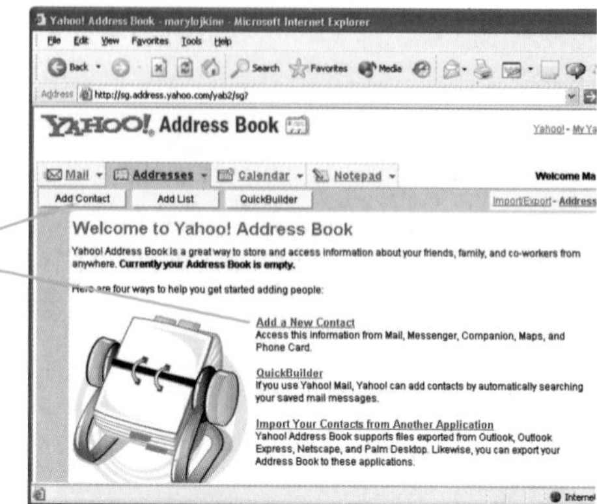

2 Fill in their details and click Save Contact

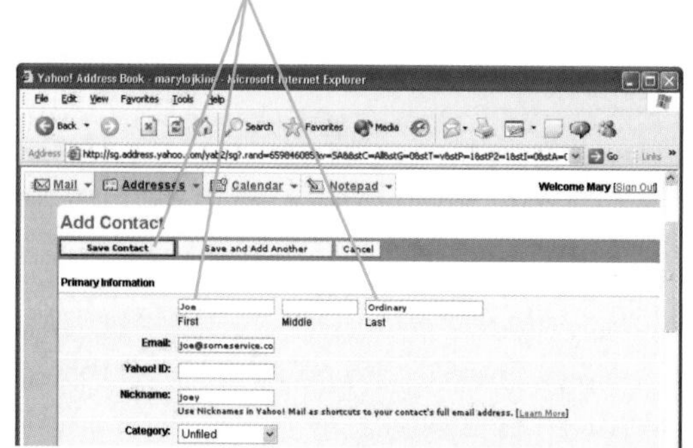

3 Next time you want to send a message to this person, click the 'Insert addresses' link or enter their nickname

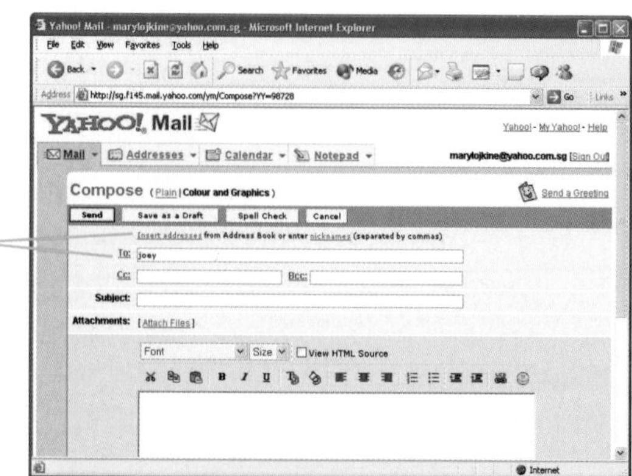

Make friends on-line

Even with millions of people on-line, the Internet can be a lonely place. This chapter explains how to use message boards and newsgroups to meet people who share your interests. Fire out a few opinions and you'll soon be making friends.

Covers

Chapter Ten

Where are all the people?

At any time of the day, there are millions of people using the Internet, but it hardly ever feels crowded. You never get elbowed by a passing stranger or pushed out of the way, and you never have to queue. Sometimes it feels as if you have the whole World Wide Web to yourself, which is great… but also kind of lonely.

If you want to meet Internet users who share your interests, stop browsing and start interacting. Get involved in message boards and newsgroups, where you can share your thoughts and opinions. You'll soon come across people who agree (or disagree) with your point of view, and before long you'll be having free and frank exchanges on all sorts of subjects. It's a great way to make friends.

Leave a message

Message boards are also known as forums.

Message boards enable you to express your opinions via the Web.

Some message boards function like the letters pages of a newspaper. The Webmaster asks a question or proposes a topic and visitors can add their remarks. For example, the BBC News Web site has 'Talking Point' areas where you can comment on the issues of the day.

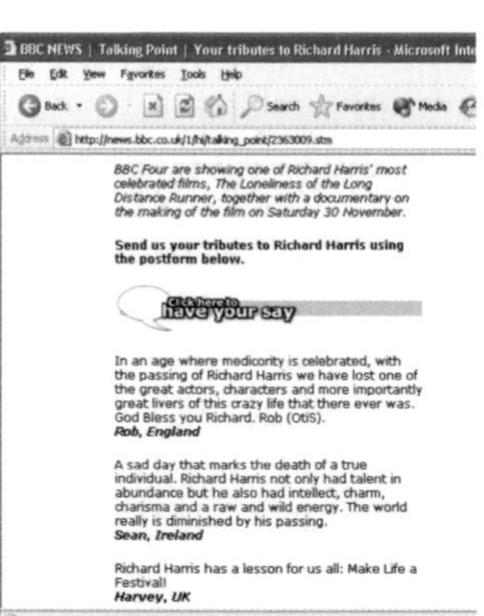

Other message boards are more conversational. Someone makes a comment, someone else replies, a third person adds something, and the original person responds to the points raised by the others. Most boards confine themselves to a single topic. For example, there are message boards dedicated to scuba diving, photography, physics, movies and, of course, computers.

Did you hear the news?

Usenet newsgroups are completely separate from the Web. They were created to enable Internet users to exchange gossip, trivia, advice, insults and – very occasionally – news.

You can think of a newsgroup as a public mail box for messages on a particular topic. Anyone can post a comment, and anyone else can read it and upload a reply.

The name Usenet is derived from 'User Network.' Usenet is a network of computers (news servers) that store news messages.

Unlike Web pages, newsgroups aren't stored in a specific place. All the messages are copied from one news server to the next, so you don't have to connect to lots of different sites. You just download the latest messages from your service provider's news server.

alt.who.what.where?

There are over 50,000 newsgroups, although some service providers only carry the more popular ones. Each group is dedicated to a different topic and its name tells you what to expect. For example, there's a newsgroup called:

rec.arts.movies.reviews

Each section of the name reduces the scope. In this case rec stands for recreation, arts and movies are self-evident and the group only carries reviews. There are a dozen other movies groups, 100 other arts groups, and over 600 rec groups in total.

There are also newsgroup hierarchies for different countries. There are lots of uk groups, for example. You'll also come across groups for people from Australia (aus), New Zealand (nz), South Africa (za), Singapore (sg) and many other places.

rec is only one of dozens of top-level categories. Other important categories include:

- **Alternative** (alt). The alt hierarchy is one of the liveliest sections of Usenet. Some of the groups are pretty wild, but most are just odd. It's also a nursery for new newsgroups.
- **Computing** (comp), for everything from hardware and software to artificial intelligence and home automation.
- **Miscellaneous** (misc). Things that don't fit anywhere else.
- **Usenet** (news), for discussion about Usenet. The news.announce.newusers group has advice for beginners.
- **Recreation** (rec), for hobbies, sports, arts and music. The rec groups are friendlier than the alt groups and it's easy to find your way around, so rec is a good place to start.
- **Science** (sci), for mathematics, physics, engineering, chemistry, biological science, medicine, psychology and philosophy – everything except computing.
- **Social** (soc), for social issues such as culture, religion, politics, history and mental health.

Use a message board

Web-based message boards are easy to use. If you've used Web-based mail (see Chapter 9), you'll find the procedures familiar. The main difference is that your message isn't sent to a specific person. Instead, it is displayed publicly for everyone to read.

If you're interested in scuba diving, Scuba Board is a good place to start. Find it at: http://www.scubaboard.com/

1 Like most message boards, it is divided into forums for different subjects. Select a forum to see the topics under discussion

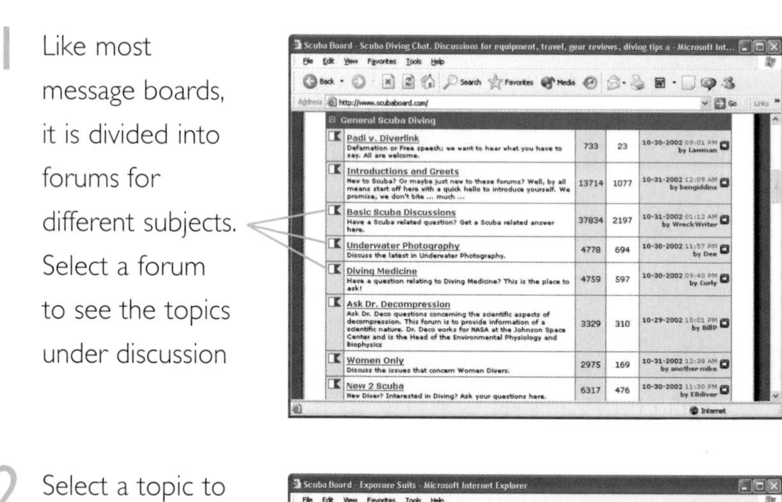

2 Select a topic to see what people have to say

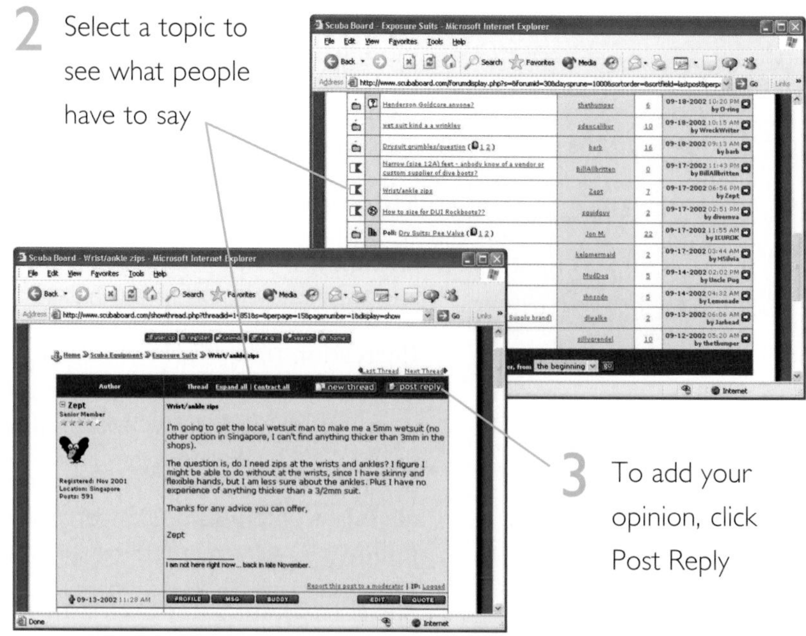

3 To add your opinion, click Post Reply

Most message boards allow anyone to read messages. If you want to post replies, you'll probably have to register. You'll acquire yet another user name and password and you'll have to agree to another set of terms and conditions.

4 You may have to register before you have your say

5 Give your response a title

6 Enter your comments

7 Scroll down and click Submit Reply

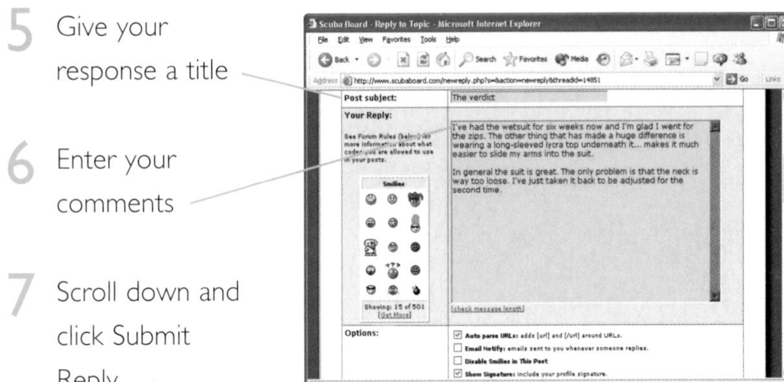

8 Your message is added at the bottom of the page

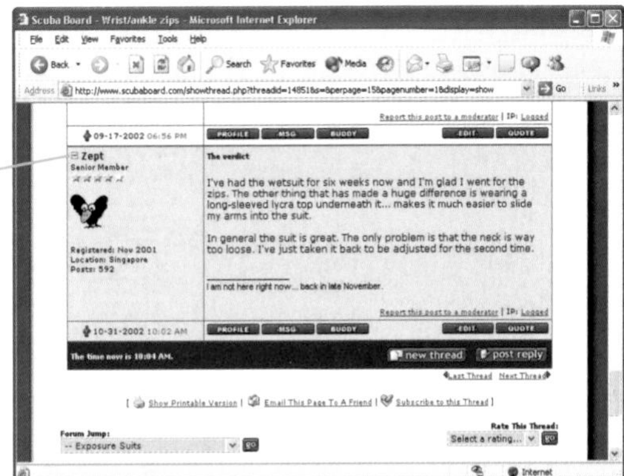

There are lots of other message boards that use similar procedures (often because they use the same software to run the board). To find a message board on a particular subject, use a search engine such as Google (see page 63).

Most message boards are friendly and welcome newcomers. However, it's a good idea to familiarise yourself with the general rules for polite behaviour before you start posting messages. See page 161 for information about 'Netiquette'.

Choose a newsreader

Whereas message boards are part of the Web, newsgroups are completely separate. You'll need a specialised program called a newsgroup reader or newsreader to access them.

Reading and posting newsgroup messages is similar to reading and sending e-mail, so some mail programs – including Outlook Express – can double as newsreaders. This is a good option for beginners because you already have the software and know how to use the basic features.

If you find yourself spending a lot of time reading newsgroups, you might want to get a dedicated newsreader such as Forté's Agent or Microplanet's Gravity. These programs have extra tools that help you filter out the rubbish and concentrate on the conversations you find interesting.

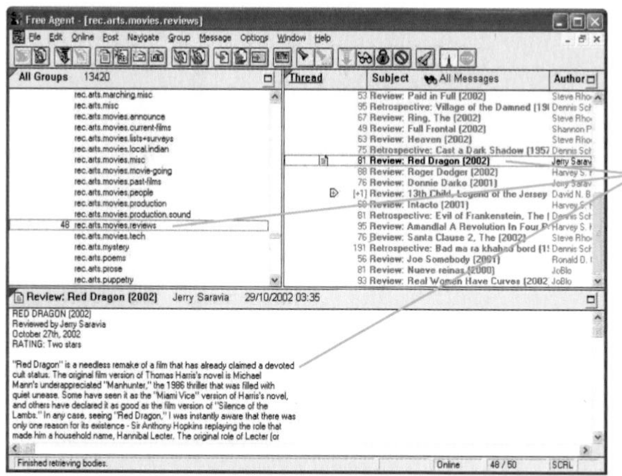

Agent lists newsgroup names on the left and message titles on the right. Message text appears at the bottom

Find out more about Agent and Gravity from the following sites:

Forté at: http://www.forteinc.com/
Microplanet at: http://www.microplanet.com/

Find some newsgroups

The rest of this chapter explains how to use Outlook Express to access newsgroups. The first thing you need to do is find out the address of your service provider's news server and set up Outlook Express to connect to it.

1. Run Outlook Express and select Tools>Accounts. Click Add and select News

2. Enter your name and e-mail address, clicking Next after each step

3. Fill in the address of your service provider's news server. You don't normally have to log on

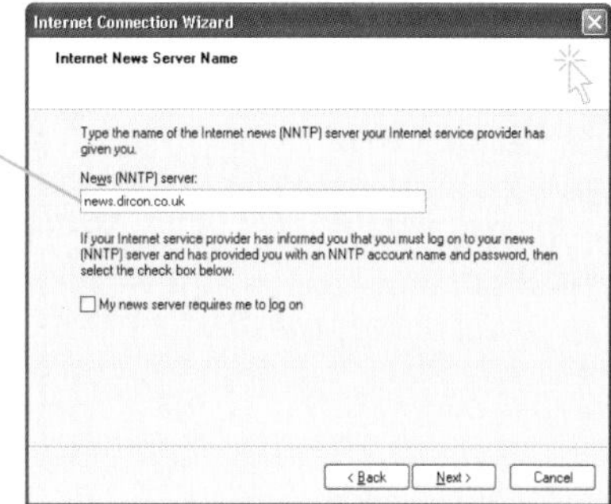

4. When you get back to the Internet Accounts dialogue box, click the News tab. You should see an entry for your news server. Select it and click the Properties button to give it a sensible name

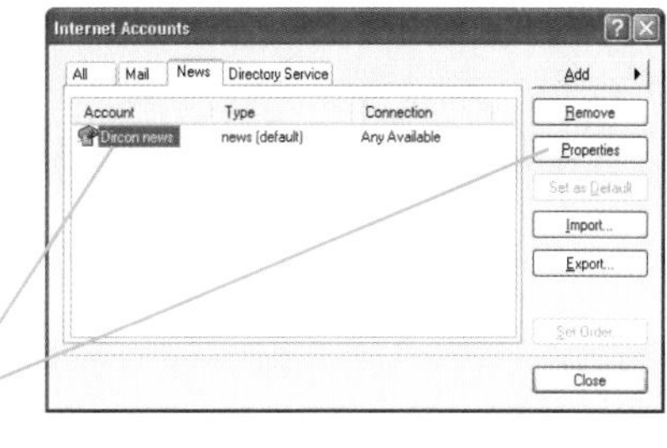

5. When you click Close, Outlook Express asks if you want to download newsgroups. Click Yes

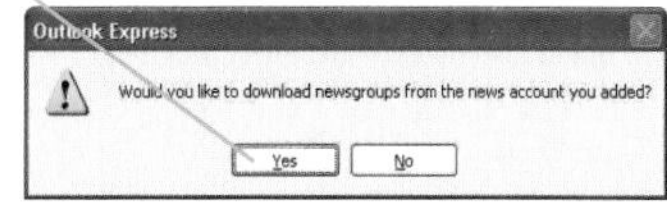

6 Outlook Express downloads the names of the newsgroups carried by your service provider. This process takes a few minutes, but you only have to do it once

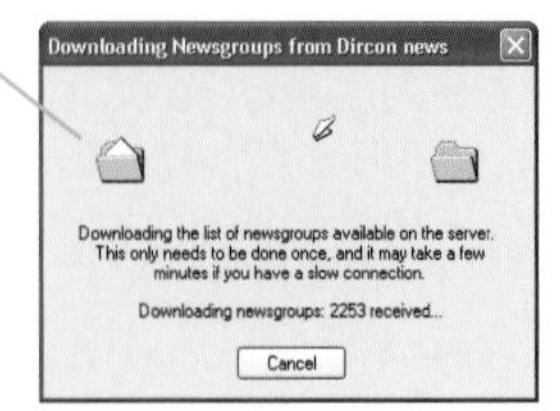

Subscribing to a newsgroup isn't like subscribing to a magazine or joining a club. You don't have to pay and you won't be added to a membership list. Subscribing just tells Outlook Express you're interested in a newsgroup – it's like making a Favorite for a Web site.

7 The newsgroup list appears. You need to select some newsgroups and 'subscribe' to them

8 Scroll down the list until you find a group that looks interesting, then select it and click the Subscribe button

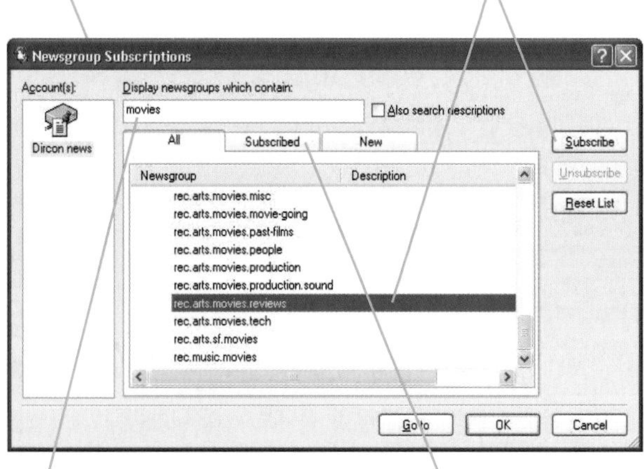

9 To find groups covering a particular subject, type a word that might appear in the name into the 'Display...' box

10 Click the Subscribed tab to see a list of the groups you have selected

11 If you want to add more groups later on, select your news server from the Folders list. Click the Newsgroups button or select Tools>Newsgroups. You won't have to download the list again

Read the news

Reading newsgroup messages is slightly different from reading e-mail. Instead of downloading all the messages, which might take some time, Outlook Express only fetches the headers (the parts that contain the subject lines, senders's names and so on). You then download the ones that sound interesting.

1 Select your news server from the Folder list to display your subscribed newsgroups

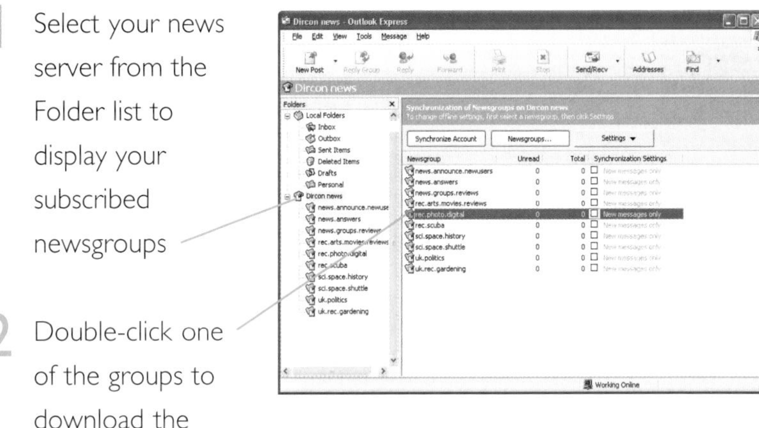

2 Double-click one of the groups to download the message headers

Some groups are very busy and receive hundreds of new messages each day. To tell Outlook Express how many headers to fetch, select Tools> Options and click the Read tab. Enter a number in the 'Get xx headers...' box.

3 Click a title to download and display the body of the message

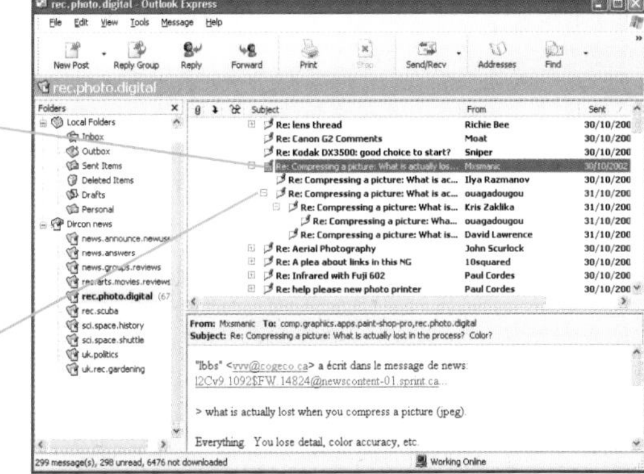

4 Outlook Express displays on-going conversations as 'threads', with the responses immediately below the original message. Click the plus ⊞ and minus ⊟ icons to expand and contract the threads

Work off-line

To reduce the amount of time you spend on-line, mark the messages you want to read and download them all at once. You can then disconnect and read the messages off-line.

1. Select your news server from the Folder list

News messages don't stay on the server forever; your service provider keeps clearing them out to make way for new ones. If a group is very busy, they may only be accessible for a day or two, so check popular groups regularly. You can search for old messages using Google's Group search at: http://groups.google.com/

2. Select all your newsgroups, then click the Settings button and select Headers Only

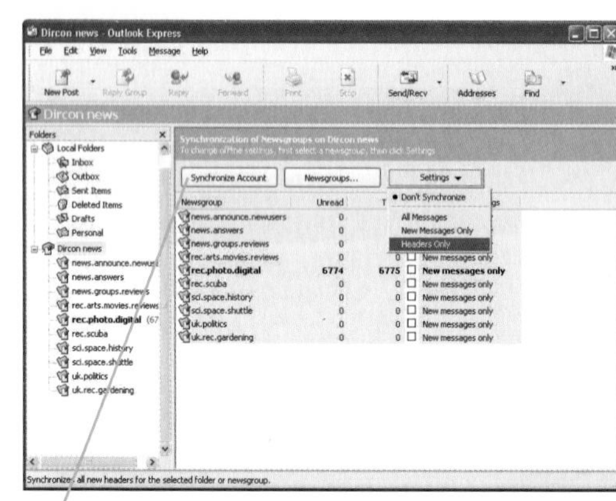

3. Deselect the checkboxes of any groups you don't want to bother with today

4. Click Synchronize Account. Outlook Express connects to the Internet and downloads the headers of any new messages sent to any of the selected groups

5. Log off and select File>Work Offline

6. Double-click on one of your newsgroups. Scroll down the list of messages and select one that sounds interesting

If you read more than half the messages posted to a group, you're better off selecting New Messages Only (rather than Headers) in Step 2 and fetching everything. Use the Headers option at least once before you do this, though, to establish a starting point.

7 Mark the message for downloading. To do this, go to Tools>Mark for Offline>Download Message Later. You can also mark an entire conversation (thread), or all the messages in the group

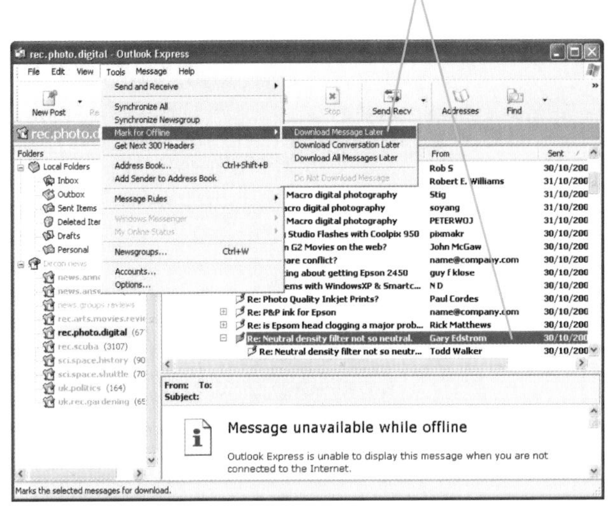

You can mark messages more quickly by clicking in the column where the arrows appear.

8 Mark all the other interesting messages, then repeat for the other newsgroups. Marked messages have blue arrows

9 When you've finished, select Tools>Synchronize All or go back to the list of groups and click the Synchronize Account button again

10 Outlook Express downloads the marked messages

11 Log off and select Work Offline again. Select a newsgroup, then select one of the messages you marked (its icon will now be a complete page, rather than a torn one). You'll be able to display the message in the Preview Pane

Have your say

Read the opposite page before you start posting messages – lots of things are considered rude on Usenet.

Posting messages is similar to sending e-mail (see page 124), but you address the message to the newsgroup.

1 To create a new message, first check that you're viewing the right newsgroup. Click New Post, select Message>New Message or press Ctrl+N

You can also respond to a poster privately, using e-mail. Click Reply to Author, select Message>Reply to Sender or press Ctrl+R to create a pre-addressed form.

2 To respond to a message, select it. Click Reply to Group, select Message>Reply to Group or press Ctrl+G

3 Either way, Outlook Express launches a pre-addressed New Message window (if you're responding to an existing message, the original text is quoted – see page 126)

4 Fill in the Subject line and compose your message

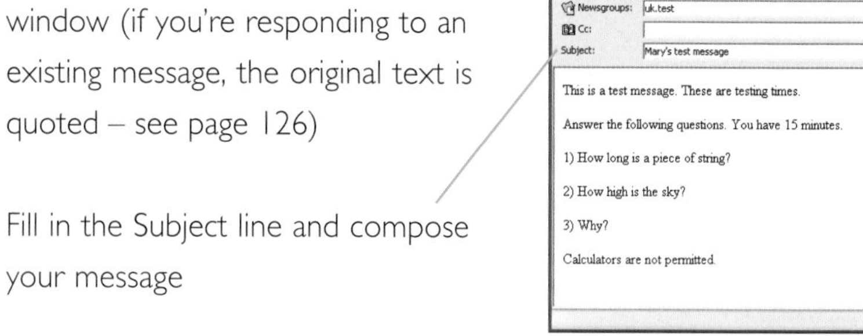

5 Click Send, select File>Send Later or press Alt+S to transfer the message to your Outbox

Want to practise? Post a message to the alt.test or uk.test newsgroups. These groups were created for people who want to experiment with their software.

6 Click Send/Recv or Synchronize Account to upload the message. You'll see it in the newsgroup next time you check for new messages

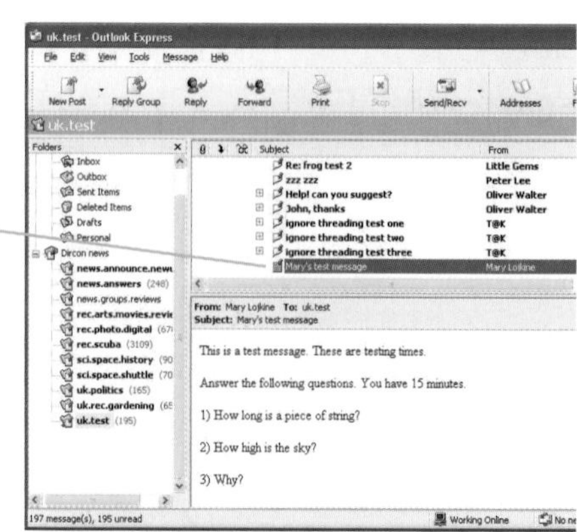

Netiquette

Usenet has a reputation for being hostile to beginners or 'newbies'. While it's true that some groups are hard to break into, most welcome anyone who displays a little common sense and courtesy. In particular, try to adhere to the following guidelines, known collectively as Netiquette.

Most FAQs are posted in the relevant newsgroup(s) at regular intervals. You can also find FAQs for many newsgroups in the Internet FAQ Archives at: http:/www.faqs.org/faqs/

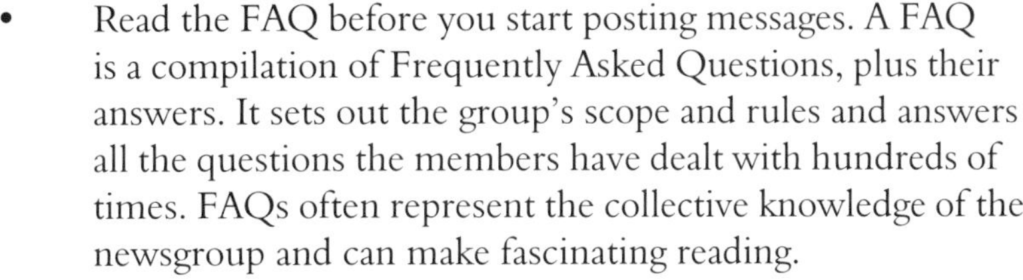

- Read the FAQ before you start posting messages. A FAQ is a compilation of Frequently Asked Questions, plus their answers. It sets out the group's scope and rules and answers all the questions the members have dealt with hundreds of times. FAQs often represent the collective knowledge of the newsgroup and can make fascinating reading.
- Avoid posting the same message to several groups at once. This is known as cross posting and it irritates the people who end up downloading your message several times.

Usenet is packed with jargon. Other terms you're likely to encounter include 'flame', which refers to an abusive message. Some groups tolerate and even encourage flaming; others expect members to be civil.

A 'troll' is a message designed to provoke angry responses and start a 'flame war'. If you aren't sure what you're getting yourself into, 'lurk' for a while. Lurkers read the messages but don't contribute anything. It's a good way to find out what's acceptable in a newsgroup.

- Don't ever post the same message to lots and lots of newsgroups. This is known as spamming and it irritates everyone. Sadly, you'll encounter lots of spam on Usenet, especially in the alt groups.
- Don't format your messages (see page 130). Many newsreaders can't display Rich Text messages, so stick to Plain Text format.
- If you're replying to a message, don't quote more of the original than is necessary – most people won't want to read it all again. It's helpful to quote the sentence or two you're actually responding to, though.
- Avoid posting messages that just say, 'Me too,' or, 'I agree.' Wait until you have something interesting to contribute.
- Don't type your message in upper case. This is known as SHOUTING, AND IT MAKES YOUR MESSAGE DIFFICULT TO READ.
- If you use a signature (see page 133), keep it short. Four lines is considered the maximum acceptable length.

Sorry, what?

Most people can't type well, so they use smileys and acronyms to speed things up. They can also clarify people's comments.

Smileys

Smileys are also known as emoticons. Don't use too many – some people think they're silly.

It's difficult to communicate your emotions in a brief text message to a stranger. This can lead to arguments, especially if you're prone to bluntness or sarcasm. Many people get round this problem by using 'smileys' – little faces made out of keyboard characters – to convey their state of mind.

There are dozens of different smileys. The three you're most likely to encounter are:

:-)	happy
;-)	winking or 'only joking'
:-(	sad or disappointed

(Turn the book 90 degrees to the right to see the faces.)

Acronyms

Found an acronym you can't decipher? Try the Acronym Finder, at: http://www.acronymfinder.com/

Common phrases are often abbreviated to their initials, producing TLAs (Three-Letter Acronyms) and ETLAs (Extended TLAs). You'll also see phonetic abbreviations.

Common acronyms and abbreviations include:

AFAIK	As far as I know
B4	Before
BTW	By the way
F2F	Face to face
FYI	For your information
<g>	Grin
IMO	In my opinion
IMHO	In my humble opinion
IMNSHO	In my not so humble opinion
ISTM	It seems to me
ISTR	I seem to recall
IRL	In real life (meaning, off the Internet)
L8R	Later
ROFL	Rolling on floor laughing
RSN	Real soon now
RTFM	Read the 'flipping' manual

Chat with your mates

Instant messaging enables you to hold conversations over the Internet by typing messages back and forth. It's spontaneous, convenient and absurdly popular. This chapter explains how it works and gets you clacking on your keyboard.

Covers

Chapter Eleven

Instant messaging

When you communicate by e-mail, message boards or newsgroups, the conversations can be frustratingly laconic. Messages sometimes go unanswered for hours or even days. If you find that annoying, you'll probably prefer instant messaging.

When you send an instant message, it pops up on the other person's screen immediately – assuming they are on-line and have activated their messaging program. It's the Internet equivalent of using your mobile phone to send a text (SMS) message.

The big difference between instant messaging and the other services is that messaging enables people *who are on-line* to communicate with other people *who are on-line.* It's a real-time, interactive activity that needs a live connection.

The no-fuss, no-muss service

When you run an instant-messaging program, it notifies a central server that you're connected to the Internet and ready to receive messages. The server acts as a giant, global 'in/out' board and keeps track of everyone's status.

You don't have to hunt through millions of names to find out whether your friends are on-line. Your messaging program automatically checks the status of your 'contacts' or 'buddies' and displays a list of people you can send messages to. This system makes instant messaging one of the simplest and friendliest Internet applications. The software tells you who is available and you double-click a person's name to send them a message. There are no addresses to remember (or forget).

Choose a messenger

When you're browsing the Web or sending e-mail, it doesn't matter if you use a different program from your friends. There are rules governing the format of Web pages and e-mail messages, so everyone can muddle along together.

Instant messaging isn't quite as organised. The software companies are all fighting for a share of the market and don't seem to be able to agree on anything. In general, if you have program A from company A is for Annoying, you can only communicate with other users of program A. You won't be able to send messages to people who use program B from company B is for Botheration. This is a very frustrating state of affairs, but there isn't much sign of a solution. All you can do is ask your friends which program they use and go with the majority decision.

Choices, choices

Windows Messenger has been updated since Windows XP was released. Get the latest version from Windows Update or the .NET Messenger Service Web site.

If you have Windows XP, you already have an instant-messaging program called Windows Messenger. Friends who use older versions of Windows can install a similar program called MSN Messenger. It doesn't have Windows Messenger's more advanced features, but people with MSN Messenger can exchange messages with people with Windows Messenger, and vice versa.

You can download the latest versions of Windows Messenger and MSN Messenger from the .NET Messenger Service Web site, at: http://messenger.microsoft.com/

Other popular messaging programs include AOL Instant Messenger (AIM), Mirabilis' ICQ ('I seek you') and Yahoo! Messenger. You can get more information about them from the following Web sites:

AOL at: http://www.aol.com/
Mirabilis at: http://www.icq.com/
Yahoo! at http://www.yahoo.com/

The rest of this chapter concentrates on Windows Messenger, since you probably have it already.

Get a .NET Passport

To find out more, visit the .NET Passport Web site, at: http://www.passport.com/

You'll need to sign up for a .NET Passport before you can use Windows Messenger.

.NET Passport is a centralised password service run by Microsoft. Once you have a Passport, you can use your e-mail address and Passport password to log in to any Web site that uses this technology. The advantage of this system is that you only have one password to remember. However, if someone else discovers your password, they can pretend to be you on a number of sites.

You'll be prompted to create a Passport when you install Windows XP or try to access Microsoft services such as Hotmail (see page 143) and Windows Messenger. Alternatively, you can sign up from the User Accounts section of Control Panel.

1. Click the Start button and select Control Panel, then click User Accounts. If several accounts are listed, select your own. Click 'Set up my account to use a .NET password' to activate the .NET Passport Wizard

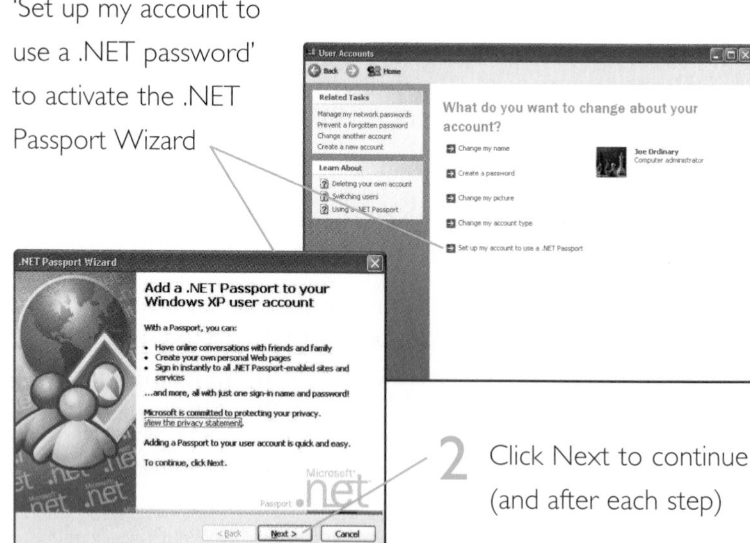

2. Click Next to continue (and after each step)

If you have an e-mail account with Hotmail or MSN.com, you already have a Passport. Enter the address and corresponding password to add the Passport to your Windows XP user account.

3. When you're asked if you have an e-mail address, click Yes

4. Enter your e-mail address

5 Think up a password and enter it twice

6 Choose one of the questions and enter the answer

7 Fill in your country. You may be asked for your region and postcode

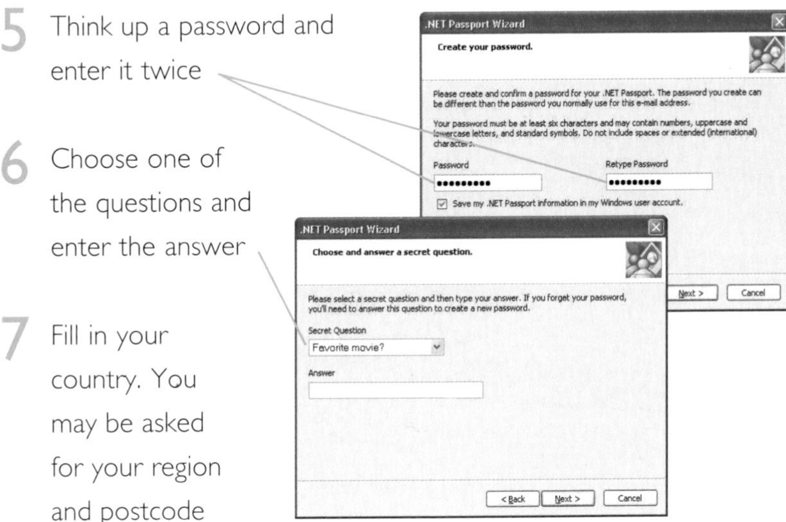

8 Read the Terms of Use and select 'I accept the agreement' if you're happy with them

9 Decide which details you want to share with sites that you log on to using Passport

10 You're done. Click Finish to close the wizard

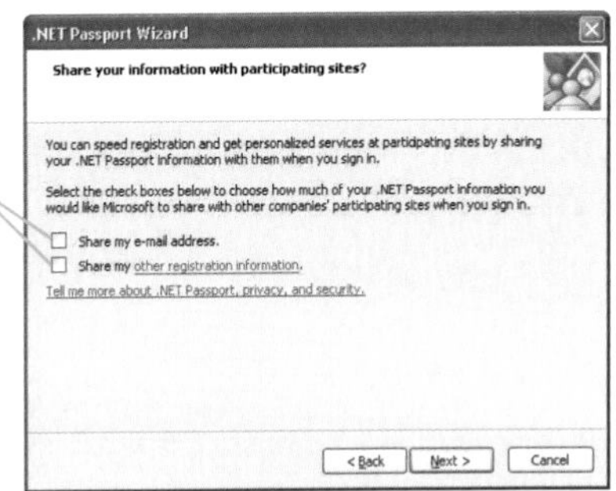

11 You'll be sent an e-mail requesting that you verify your address. Click the enclosed link

12 The link takes you to the Passport Web site. Follow the on-screen instructions to sign in and confirm your identity

Ready for a chat?

Windows Messenger may run automatically when you power up your computer. If it doesn't, you'll need to start it yourself.

1. Look for an icon showing a green, stylised person in the notification area at the right-hand end of the Windows taskbar. Double-click it to open the program window

2. If you can't find the icon, click the Start button and select All Programs, then Windows Messenger

If you select the 'Sign me in automatically' option, you won't have to enter your details next time.

3. Either way, Windows Messenger may prompt you to sign in. Click the link to get started

4. Enter your e-mail address and password and click OK

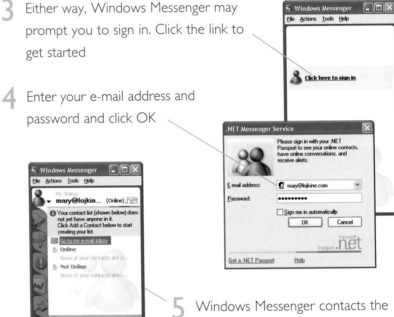

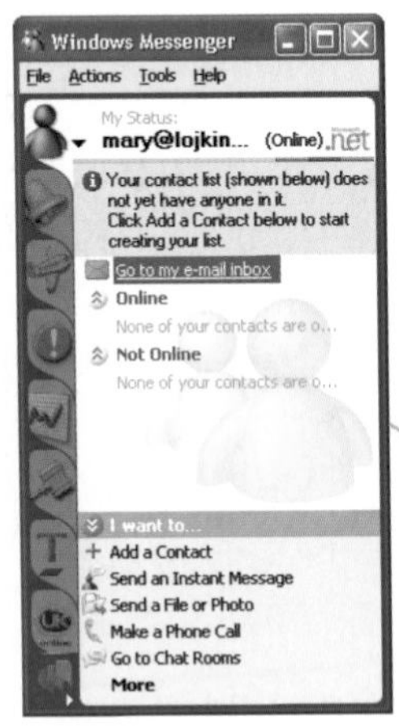

5. Windows Messenger contacts the central server and informs it that you're on-line and ready to receive messages

If you have a standard installation of Windows XP and have created a Passport, Windows Messenger will probably sign you in automatically. You'll go straight to the screen shown in Step 5.

Find your friends

The next thing to do is to add your friends to your Contacts list, so you can send messages to them easily. You'll need to know their e-mail addresses.

1 Click the 'Add a Contact' link in the 'I want to…' list at the bottom

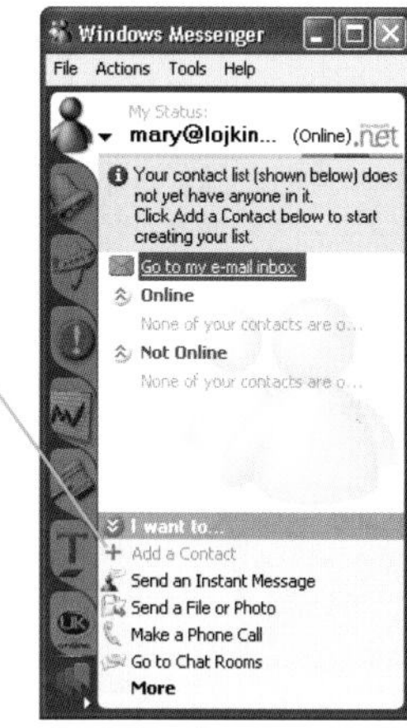

DON'T FORGET

If your friend has more than one e-mail address, you'll need to find out which one they use for their .NET Passport.

2 Select 'By e-mail address or sign-in name'. Click Next

3 Enter your friend's e-mail address

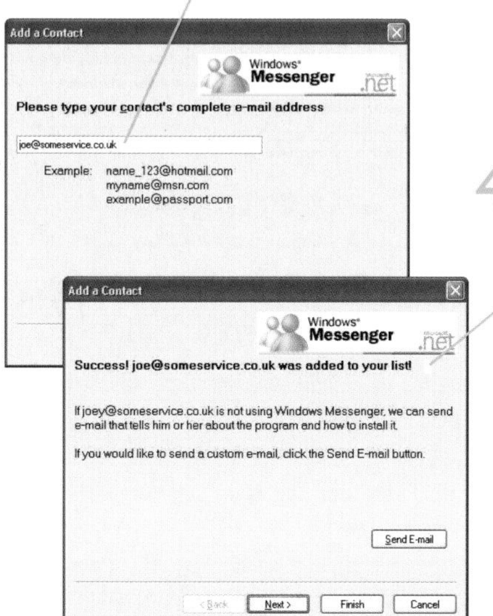

4 Windows Messenger checks with the central server and tries to locate your friend. If it succeeds, their name is added to your Contact list

5 If your friend isn't using Windows Messenger, you can't add them to your list. You're invited to send them an e-mail that explains how to download and install the software

When you add someone to your Contacts list (Step 4), Windows Messenger lets them know. They have two options: they can allow you to contact them or block all your messages. Likewise, when someone adds you to their list, you can let them in or shut them out. This prevents total strangers from bothering you with irrelevant messages.

1 If you know the person and want to communicate with them, select 'Allow this person...' You can add them to your own Contact list

To change the way your name is displayed or use a nickname instead, go to Tools>Options and click the Personal tab. Change the 'My display name' setting.

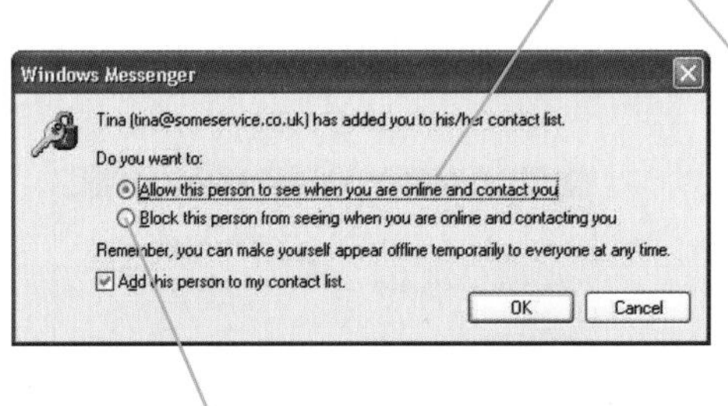

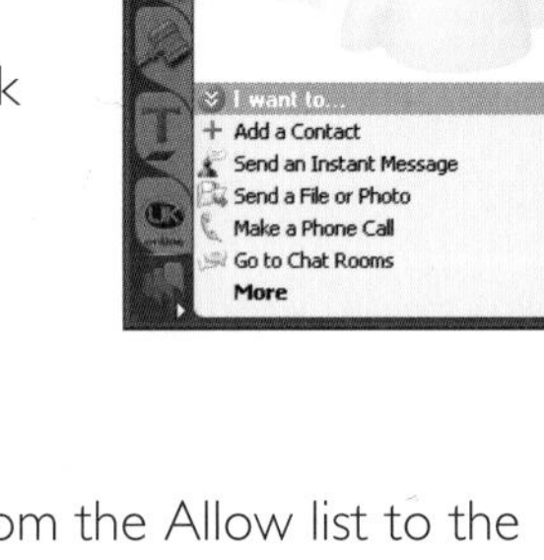

2 If you've been added by someone you don't know (or don't like), choose 'Block this person...'

3 If you change your mind about someone, go to Tools>Options. Click the Privacy tab and move the person from the Allow list to the Block list, or vice versa

Start a conversation

Windows Messenger divides your contacts into two groups: people who are on-line and people who aren't. Glance at the list to find out who's available.

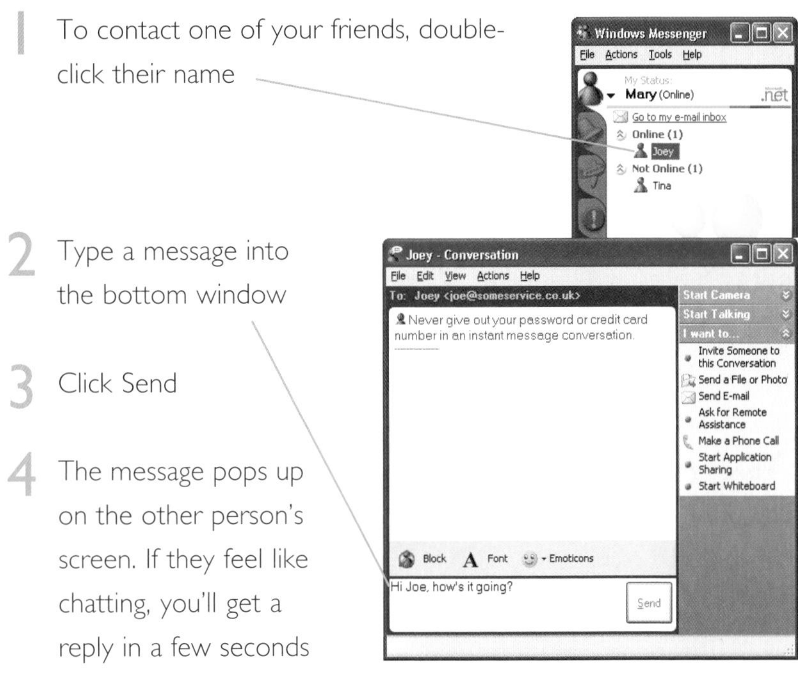

1 To contact one of your friends, double-click their name

2 Type a message into the bottom window

3 Click Send

4 The message pops up on the other person's screen. If they feel like chatting, you'll get a reply in a few seconds

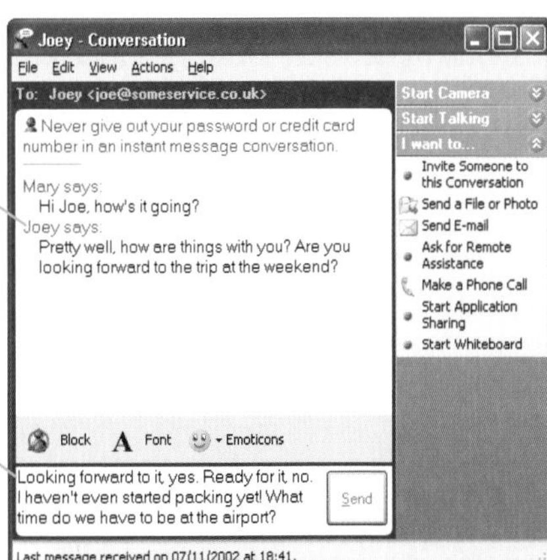

5 The reply appears in the top window

6 To carry on chatting, type another comment into the bottom window and click Send again

If you can't type very quickly, use abbreviations to speed things up. Try 'u' for 'you', 'cu' for 'see you' and 'l8r' for 'later'.

All the icons have keyboard shortcuts. To see the list, click the Emoticons button, then click the button with three dots [...]. See page 162 for more about emoticons.

7. To convey humour or emotion, click the Emoticons button and choose an icon

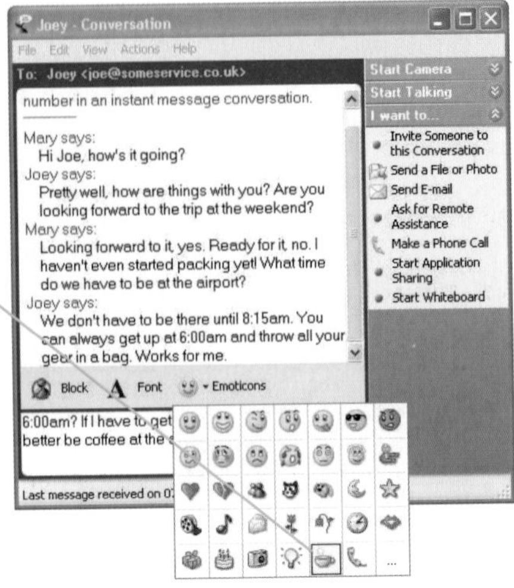

If you have a microphone or video camera attached to your computer, you can also conduct audio or video conversations. Go to Help>Help Topics for more information.

When one of your friends tries to contact you, the initial message pops up in the bottom right-hand corner of your screen.

1. Click the message to bring up the Conversation window

2. Carry on with the conversation by typing a reply into the bottom window

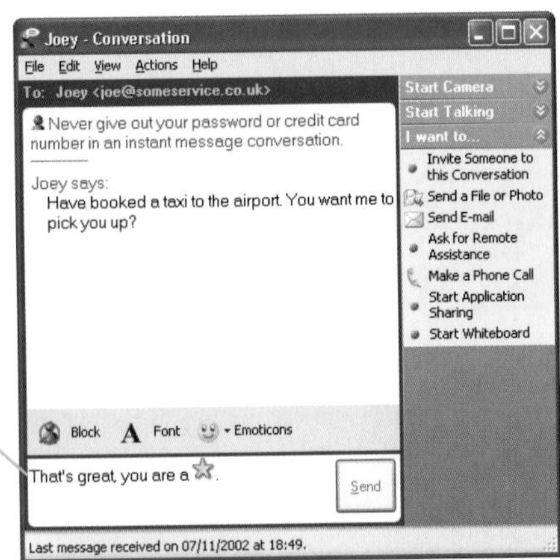

Build a Web site

Chapter Twelve

You came, you saw, you clicked… and now it's time to stop touring and start designing your own pages. A Web site can serve all sorts of useful purposes, from promoting your business to sharing the photographs from your wedding, or it can simply be something you create for fun. This chapter explains what's involved and helps you lay the foundations.

Covers

A site of your own

There'll come a day when you want to create Web pages. You'll be wandering around the Web, clicking from page to page, and suddenly you'll want a site of your own – a virtual home that promotes your business, showcases your interests and/or reflects your personality.

There are lots of reasons to create a Web site:

- **To advertise your services.** If you go on-line for business reasons, creating a Web site is probably near the top of your to-do list. It's a great (and inexpensive) way to explain what you offer and stay in touch with your customers.
- **To promote yourself.** If you're looking for a job, an on-line resume not only provides information about your education and experience, but also demonstrates that you're at home in the high-tech world of the Internet. On-line portfolios are also useful for people who work on a freelance basis, such as writers, photographers, programmers and consultants.
- **To share your interests.** If you have a passion for a particular subject, creating a Web site lets you make use of the material you've accumulated. You can pass on information to like-minded enthusiasts and extend your hobby. You might not want to go scuba diving in the middle of the winter, for example, but you can still work on your diving Web site.
- **Keep your friends and family up to date.** A personal Web site is the best way to share stories and photographs from family events and holidays. You only have to tell each story once and you can add as many pictures as you want.
- **It's fun.** Creating a Web site is like decorating your home, except you don't have to wash the brushes or wait for the paint to dry. You get to choose the subject, the colours, the fonts and the design. It's a chance to exercise your creativity and produce something that's uniquely yours.

This chapter won't teach you everything about creating a Web site. Web design is a big subject so please refer to other titles in this series if it's something you want to pursue.

Learn the lingo

Web pages are created using HyperText Mark-up Language, otherwise known as HTML. You can produce HTML files with a word processor, but most people prefer to use a dedicated HTML editor – a program designed specifically for creating Web pages.

Tag it and bag it

The simplest approach to HTML is to start with a file containing the text for your page. You then 'mark up' the text by inserting tags – commands that tell Web browsers how to format individual words, phrases and paragraphs.

Most tags come in pairs: an 'on' tag that goes before the text you want to format and an 'off' tag that goes afterwards. Both of the tags are surrounded by angled brackets. For example:

> This is my <b>very first</b> Web page.

The <b> tag turns on bold formatting and the </b> tag turns it off again, giving:

> This is my **very first** Web page.

There are tags that control different types of formatting, tags that tell browsers to insert an image file or create a link, and tags that take care of housekeeping tasks, such as giving the page a name. HTML is just a toolbox of instructions that enable you to turn a slab of text into a formatted Web page.

All your own <yawn> work

In the early days of the Web, people created their pages by hand. They started with a text file and added tags in all the right places, painstakingly inserting angled brackets until the page was complete.

The good thing about creating pages by hand is that you become intimately familiar with all the tags. The bad thing is that it's incredibly tedious. It's also easy to make mistakes. If you add a <b> tag and then forget to add the corresponding </b>, the bold formatting continues to the end of the page. Every page has to be checked in a Web browser, and edited, and checked again.

Visual HTML editors are also known as WYSIWYG (What You See Is What You Get) editors.

Today most people use visual HTML editors that display the actual formatting, rather than the tags. Instead of entering <b> and </b>, you highlight the text you want to format, then click the

Bold button or select Bold from the Format menu. The program inserts the corresponding tags.

You design a page like this...

...and your editor adds the tags

To learn more about HTML, look out for 'HTML in easy steps', another title in this series.

With a visual editor, designing a Web page is like formatting any other document. You can create an entire site without knowing anything about HTML. However, if you're serious about Web design, it helps to understand the basics. Some of the things you can do in a word processor don't work in HTML, and vice versa.

Choosing a HTML editor

You can use almost anything to design Web pages: a basic text editor such as Notepad, a word processor, a desktop-publishing program or even a graphics program. However, it's best to use a tool that was designed for the job. A dedicated HTML editor enables you to create attractive Web pages, quickly and efficiently.

Big-name HTML editors include Adobe's GoLive, Macromedia's Dreamweaver and Microsoft's FrontPage. However, these are professional programs with correspondingly impressive price tags. More affordable alternatives includes Namo's WebEditor, the program used for the step-by-step guides in this chapter.

You can get more information about all these programs from the following Web sites:

Adobe at: http://www.adobe.com/
Macromedia at: http://www.macromedia.com/
Microsoft at: http://www.microsoft.com/
Namo Interactive at: http://www.namo.com/

Plan your site

The key to successful Web design is to plan your site on paper before you start creating the pages. The structure of your site affects the construction of the links, so if you get it wrong, you'll have to go through your pages and change all the links – which is annoying, to put it mildly.

Start with a sketch

Find a piece of paper and draw a doodle that shows all the pages of your Web site and the most important links between them. For example, here's a plan for a personal Web site:

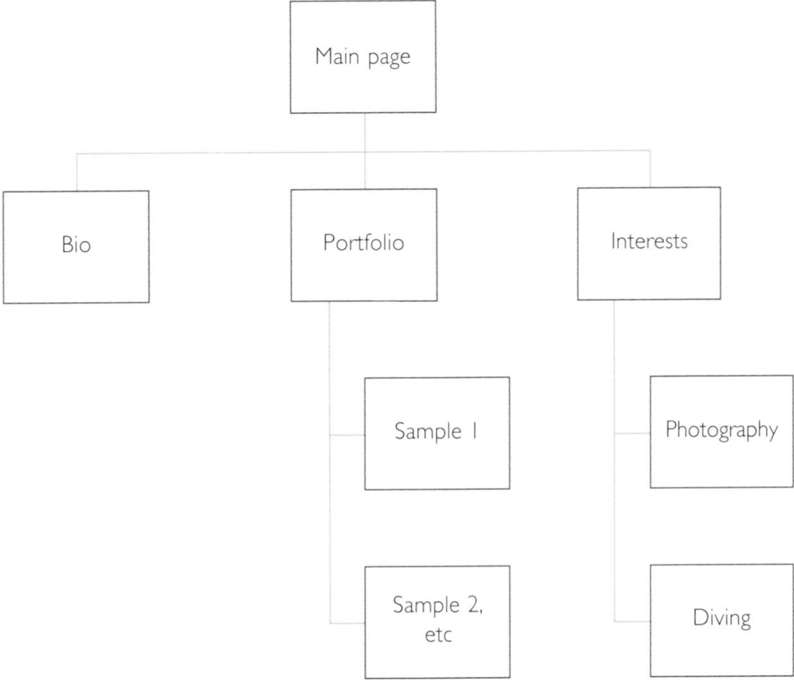

Think about pages you might want to add in the future. Where will they go? Make sure your plan is flexible enough to allow the site to evolve and grow.

Files and folders

For a small site, you can keep all your files in a single folder. For larger sites, it's a good idea to create a folder for the site, then add a subfolder for each section. Otherwise you'll end up with a big, unmanageable heap of files.

Be very careful when you name your files. Since people use all kinds of computers to access the Internet, it's a good idea to choose names that will work on any system. That means:

- Up to eight lower-case letters, followed by a dot (period), followed by a three-character extension.
- No punctuation, other than periods (.) and underlines (_), and no funny characters.
- The extension should be .htm for a Web page and .gif or .jpg for an image (see below).

Give your documents meaningful names such as bio.htm and portfol.htm. If you call them page01.htm, page02.htm and so on, you'll find it hard to tell them apart. Record the names on your sketch.

File formats

Web pages are saved as plain (unformatted) text documents, but with a .htm extension. Your HTML editor will take care of that (one of the advantages of using a proper HTML editor is that it automatically saves files in the correct format).

Pictures must be saved in either the GIF format (.gif extension) or the JPEG format (.jpg extension). In general, the GIF format is the right choice for artwork such as logos, diagrams, maps and cartoons. The JPEG format is used for photographs.

Find out more about Paint Shop Pro from Jasc's Web site: http://www.jasc.com/

Your images may already be in the correct format. For example, if you are using photographs from a digital camera, they are probably .jpg files already. If you are creating original graphics, or you have pictures in other formats, you'll need to use an image-editing program such as Paint Shop Pro to save them as GIFs or JPEGs.

An image editor also comes in handy if your images aren't the right size for your Web site. In general, images on Web sites are kept small to minimise the file size and reduce the download time. You may need to scale down existing images before you use them on your Web pages.

Work with words

The text forms the backbone of your Web page. You can type it directly into a new page or cut and paste the text from an existing document, such as an essay or report.

1 Run your HTML editor and create a new Web page. Save it

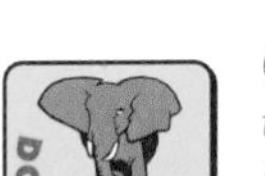

Only use fonts that other Internet users will have: Arial, Comic Sans, Georgia, Impact, Times New Roman, Trebuchet and Verdana.

2 Enter your text

3 Use the text-formatting tools to choose a font and change the size, colour and style

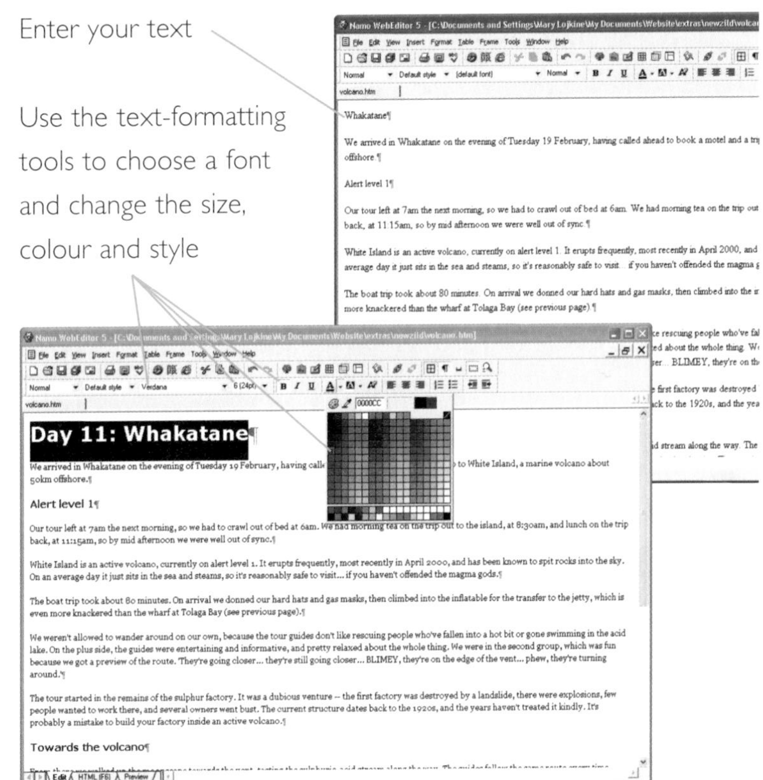

The title appears at the top of the Web browser window, in the blue title bar. Keep it short.

4 To give the page a title, go to File> Document Properties and click the General tab. Enter the title

5 Save the Web page

Add some pictures

Before you add an image to your Web page, ask yourself the following questions:

Computer images are made up of small square dots called picture elements or 'pixels'. A 17-inch computer screen is typically 1,024 pixels wide by 768 high; a smaller 14- or 15-inch screen displays 800x600 pixels. Images on Web pages are usually less than 200 pixels wide, although a large photograph might be 500-600 pixels wide.

- **Is the image the right size?** Open it in an image-editing program and check the dimensions, in pixels. You may need to reduce the size to fit it on to your page.
- **Has the image been saved in a Web-friendly format?** It must be a .gif or .jpg file.
- **Is the image in the correct folder?** You can put it in the same folder as the Web page document or create a special subfolder for image files. Be consistent, though.

1 Open a Web page in your HTML editor and position the cursor where you want the image to appear. It's a good idea to put it in a separate paragraph

2 Go to Insert>Image or click the Insert Image button

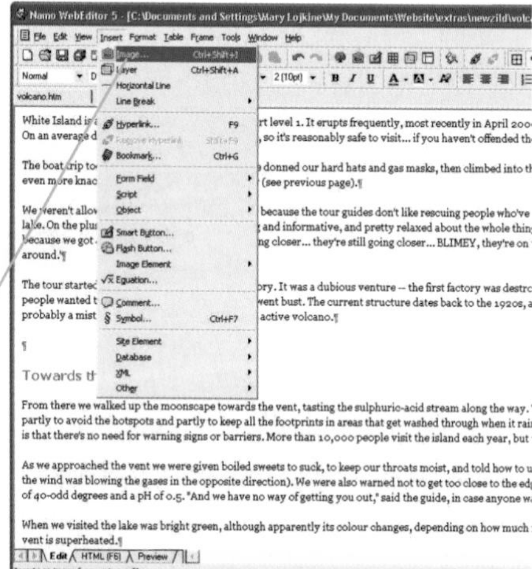

3 Click the Browse button and find the image file. Click Open and then OK to add it to the Web page

4 The image appears on your page

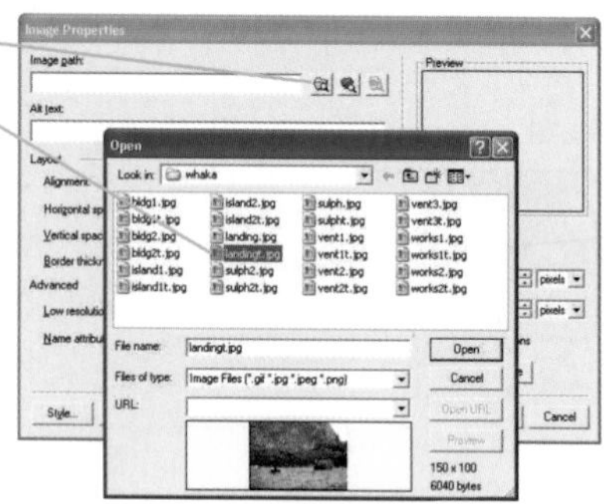

To centre an image, select the paragraph in which it appears. Use the text-formatting tools to centre the entire paragraph.

5 Insert more images in the same paragraph to produce a horizontal row of pictures

6 Add images in separate paragraphs to produce a vertical column

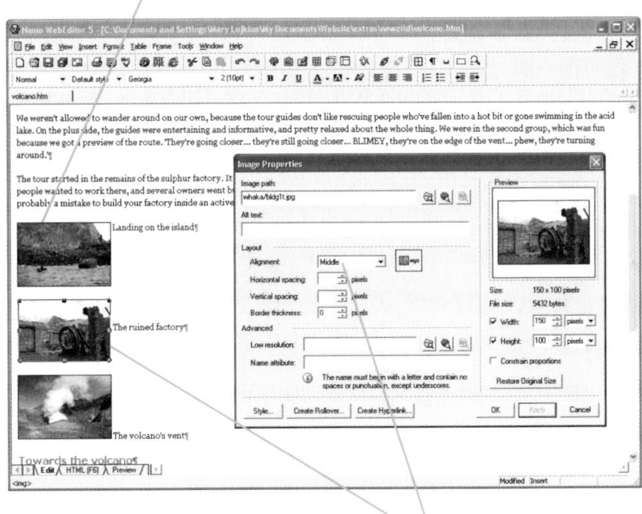

7 If you arrange the images vertically, you can type short captions alongside them. To adjust the placement of the caption, right-click on the image and select Image Properties. Set 'Alignment' to 'Top', 'Middle' or 'Bottom'. For a long caption, select 'Left'

Create hyperlinks

Creating a link is simple: you select the text (or image) you want to link from, then open a dialogue box and enter the address of the page you want to link to. There's just one catch: you must get your files and folders in order before you start creating links.

Suppose you have two Web pages stored in the same folder on your hard disk. When you create a link from the first page to the second, you add an instruction that tells your Web browser to go back to the folder where it found the first page and look for the second one. The link doesn't specify the name or location of the folder. It just says, 'Same again, Sam, but grab page2.htm'. In Web-design terms, it's a 'relative reference'.

The important thing about this system is that you can move both pages to a different folder – for example, a folder on your service provider's Web server – without breaking the link. As long as the pages are together, your Web browser can find the second one.

If you find this system confusing, keep all your Web pages in a single folder.

The pages don't have to be in the same folder to make this work. For example, you could put the second page in a subfolder. The link would then tell your Web browser to go back to the original folder, then down into subfolder Aaa, then find the second page. As long as you use the same folders on the Web server, and arrange them in the same way, the links will work.

1. To link two of your own pages together, select the text you want to link from

2. Select Insert>Hyperlink or click the Insert Hyperlink button

3. Click the Browse button and select the page you want to link to. Click Open and then OK

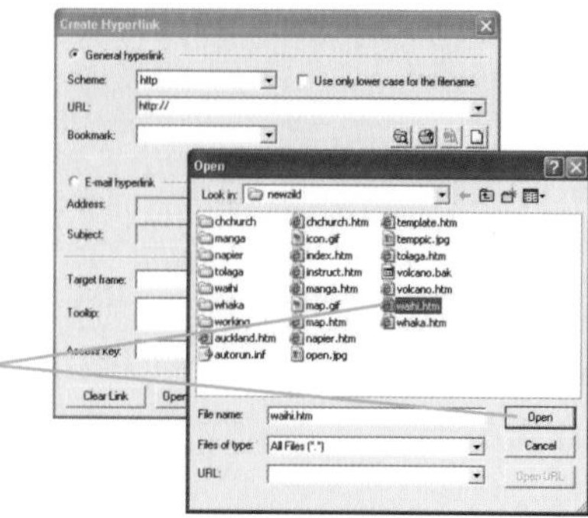

4 The text becomes a link

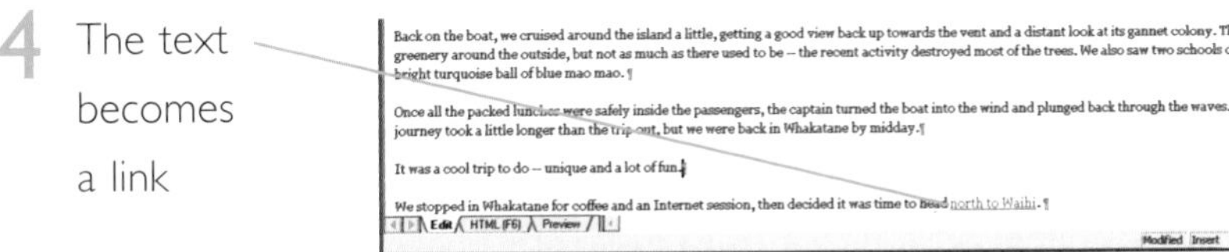

You may also want to link to other people's Web pages, or turn some of your images into links. The procedures are similar.

1 To link to a page on someone else's Web site, you must fill in the entire address, including the http://

2 To link from an image, for example to create a clickable button, start by inserting the image (see page 180). Click on the image to select it, then follow Steps 2 and 3 on the opposite page

Tidy up with tables

Tables are used to organise information into rows and columns. They're useful for price lists, schedules, competition results and so on. Less obviously, they can be used to control the layout of your Web page. For example, you might use a table to divide the page into two columns, one for pictures and one for text.

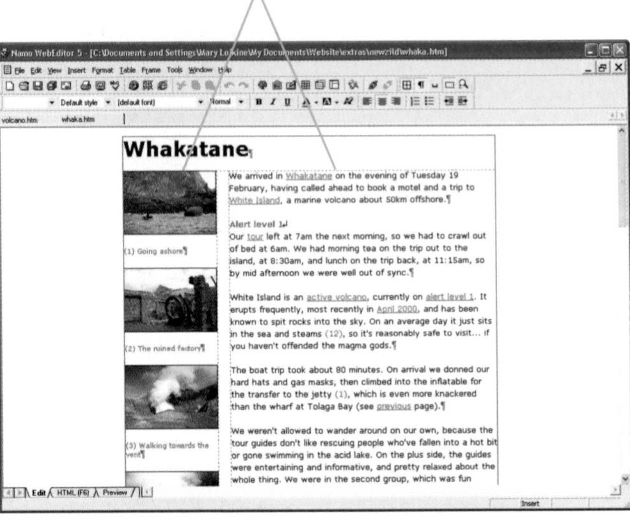

1. To create a table, place the cursor where you want it to appear. Go to Table>New Table

2. Specify the number of rows and columns you require

3. An empty table is inserted. The cells expand and contract as you fill in your information

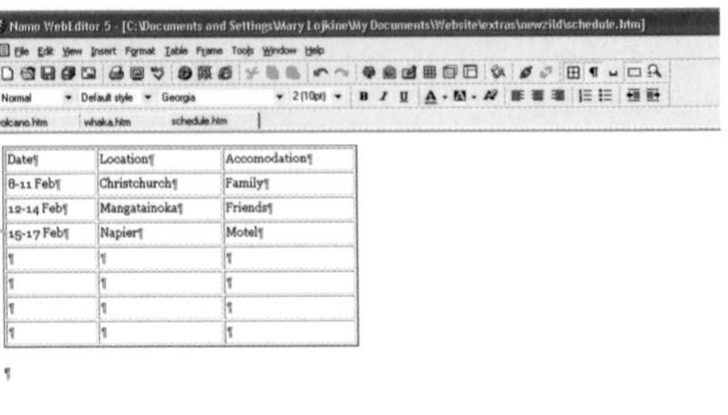

Date	Location	Accomodation
8-11 Feb	Christchurch	Family
12-14 Feb	Mangatainoka	Friends
15-17 Feb	Napier	Motel

HOT TIP: *You can also set the width of the table, in pixels or as a percentage of the browser window. 'Cell Spacing' sets the space between the cells; 'Cell Padding' sets the space between the cell border and the contents of the cell. If you set 'Border Thickness' to 0, the borders disappear.*

Find space for your site

Your Web pages need to be stored or 'hosted' on a computer that's permanently connected to the Internet, so everyone can access them. There are three options:

- Your Internet service provider may give you some space on its Web server as part of your Internet account. This is often the best option, because there's no additional cost involved. Check with your service provider to find out how much space you have and how you access it. Check the terms and conditions, too – sometimes you're only allowed to use the space for a personal, non-commercial Web site.

- If you didn't get any Web space with your account, you can sign up with one of the services that provide free hosting. Like Web-based mail services, companies that offer free hosting are supported by advertising. When people visit your site, they'll also see adverts that have been added by the hosting company. Popular services include Tripod (at http://www.tripod.lycos.com/) and Yahoo! GeoCities (at http://geocities.yahoo.com/).

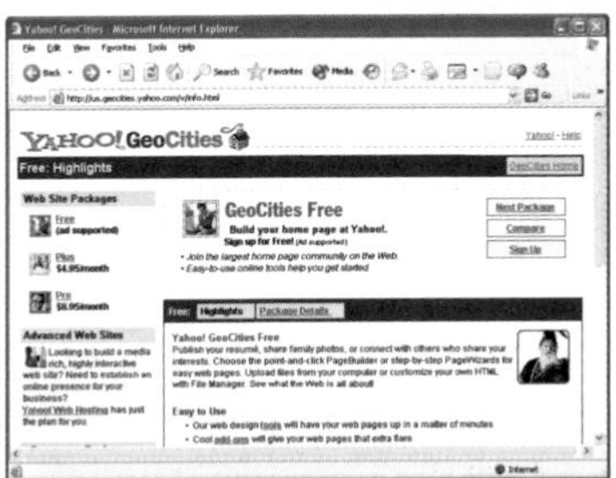

- If you're setting up a Web site for your business, you won't want to display someone else's ads. A more professional option is to rent space from a company that specialises in hosting Web sites. In return for a monthly or annual fee, you'll get plenty of space for your site. You may also get extra services such as technical support, information about your visitors and the option to add interactive features such as password protection or message boards. Flick through a couple of Internet magazines to find out what's available.

A name to be proud of

If your Web space is provided by your service provider, or by one of the free Web-hosting services, you'll end up with a complicated Web address such as:

http://www.someservice.co.uk/~joe/

See page 46 for more about domain names.

By the time you've spelled it out a dozen times for your family, your friends and your colleagues at work, you'll be wishing it was shorter and easier to remember. The solution is to register your own domain name, such as:

joeordinary.com

You can then change your Web address to:

http://www.joeordinary.com/

You can also have a new e-mail address, such as:

mail@joeordinary.com

Just as there are companies that concentrate on hosting Web sites, there are companies that specialise in registering domain names (and many that do both). Do a search for 'domain name registration' or look through adverts in Internet magazines to find a company that can help.

Domain names must be unique, so only one person can have joeordinary.com However, there can also be a joeordinary.org, a joeordinary.name, a joeordinary.co.uk and so on.

Some companies offer a budget package that includes the name of your choice (assuming it is still available) plus Web and e-mail forwarding. With Web forwarding, anyone who enters your new address is automatically taken to your existing Web site. You don't have to move the site or change it in any way. Likewise, if someone sends e-mail to your new address, it is sent on to your existing mail box. One advantage of this system is that it doesn't matter if you change Internet service providers. You simply update the forwarding details so people (and messages) get shunted to your new location.

If you rent Web space from a hosting company, you'll probably get a domain name thrown in. It'll be set up to point to your Web site, so you don't have to worry about forwarding.

Index

E

F

G

I

J

K

Q

R

S

T

U

Z

Worldwide Web Guide

Alphabetical list of sites

News

Whether you're looking for breaking news or archived stories, the Web is the best place to start. Most of the major broadcasters and publishers have Web sites that are updated throughout the day. Search functions and electronic cross-references make it easy to find stories of interest and follow them back to their roots.

Resources

Google News

http://news.google.com/

Google News pulls together stories from over 4,000 news sources and compiles them into a single page. Follow the links for more information or use the search function to hunt down particular items.

Northern Light Current News Search

http://www.northernlight.com/news.html

Northern Light's news search helps you find items from the last two weeks, current day or last two hours. You can also restrict your search to areas such as business, entertainment, politics, sports or weather conditions.

Guardian Unlimited World News Guide

http://www.guardian.co.uk/worldnewsguide/

Guardian Unlimited's attractively presented News Guide links you to news sources and government Web sites from around the world, by region or country. The directory is selective – you get the best sites, not a comprehensive list – making it a good place to start your research.

Abyz News Links

http://www.abyznewslinks.com/

Abyz News Links is functional rather than attractive. It provides a comprehensive database of on-line newspapers, broadcasters and other news sources, sorted by country. Details include the type of media, the focus (general, business, sport and so on) and the language used. The listings are searchable.

World-newspapers.com

http://www.world-newspapers.com/

This site is less specialised than it sounds. It deals in magazines as well as newspapers and has links to the main sources of news in various subject areas, including world, business, Internet and sport. It also lists sites that offer photographs, personalised news services, alternative news and criticism.

Onlinenewspapers.com

http://www.onlinenewspapers.com/

This site presents a well-organised database of on-line newspapers, sorted by country. There's no information about the papers, apart from an occasional note about the language, but you can find what you want very quickly.

HeadlineSpot.com

http://www.headlinespot.com/

HeadlineSpot is a US-oriented site that lists resources by type and subject. It's useful for specialised areas such as columnists, polls, industry news and obituaries.

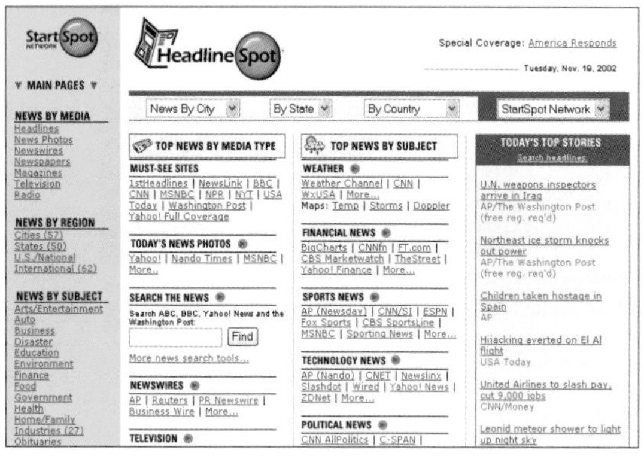

NewsNow

http://www.newsnow.co.uk/

NewsNow aggregates headlines from a range of (primarily British) on-line sources, presenting a single-page view of the day's top stories. You can also opt to focus on topical issues or areas, from Bin Laden and Iraq to soap operas and Harry Potter.

Crayon

http://www.crayon.net/

Crayon lets you CReAte Your Own Newspaper, not by scrawling on newsprint but by selecting your favourite on-line news sources. It's basically an easy way to organise a list of news sites.

BBC News by e-mail

http://www.bbc.co.uk/dailyemail/

If you don't have time for the Web, get the BBC to e-mail you a daily bulletin covering the subjects of your choice. Options include UK and world news, politics, business, health and sport.

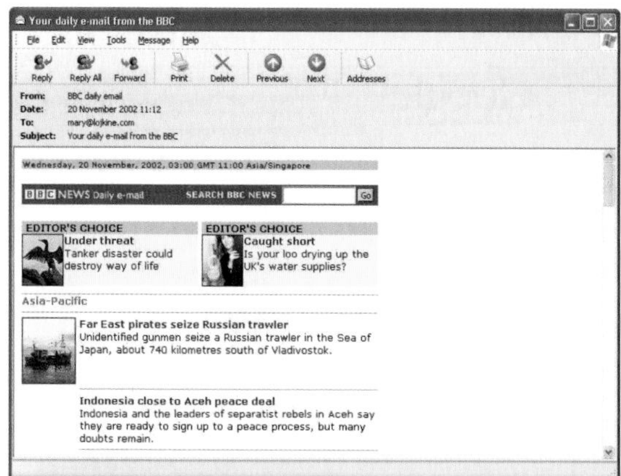

Broadcast news

BBC News

http://news.bbc.co.uk/

The BBC has an excellent news site with everything you could possibly want: UK, international and foreign-language editions, streaming audio and video, a text-only version for slow connections, in-depth features, Talking Point areas where you can have your say and, of course, a wealth of breaking news, all served up without adverts or other distractions. One of the best sites on the Web.

BBC World Service

http://www.bbc.co.uk/worldservice/

The World Service site comes in 43 (!) languages. It offers short audio bulletins on demand plus the opportunity to tune in to a 24-hour news channel or the regular World Service broadcasts.

CNN

http://www.cnn.com/

CNN offers three editions – US, Europe and Asia – and has sections for everything from US and world news to technology, politics, health and travel. CNN's long-standing interest in the US space programme makes it particularly strong in that area.

Voice of America

http://www.voanews.com/

The US government's broadcasting service transmits in 53 languages. Read the latest stories on-line or tune in to audio and video Webcasts. Special features include a pronounciation guide that helps you say the names of newsworthy people and places.

MSNBC

http://www.msnbc.com/news/

The US-oriented MSNBC site offers an upbeat take on the news with plenty of multimedia and interactive features.

ITN

http://www.itn.co.uk/

ITN provides news for the UK's commercial television channels – ITV, Channel 4 and Channel 5 – and virtually all the commercial radio stations. Its own site provides only a smattering of headlines, acting principally as a gateway to the sites where its stories appear. Follow the links for bulletins from your favourite broadcaster.

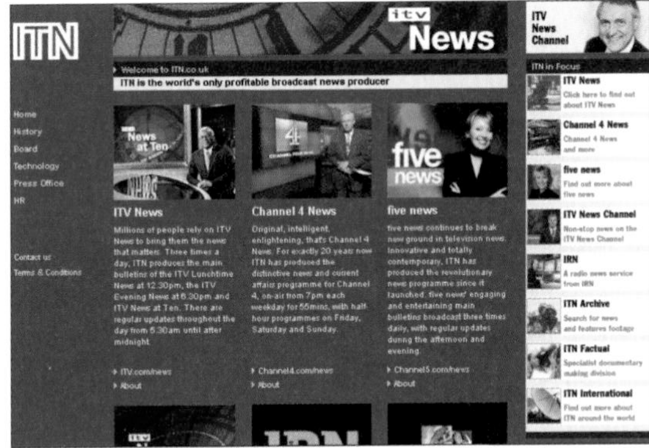

Sky News

http://www.sky.com/skynews/

The Web site of British broadcaster Sky News gives you more pictures than most. There are lots of photo galleries, often with an entertainment focus, and it has Webcams that enable you to spy on popular locations in London and Edinburgh and find out what's happening in the streets.

ABC News Online

http://www.abc.net.au/news/

The news section of ABC's site has both Australian and international news, with special sections for rural and indigenous news. Other features include audio, video, forums and news by e-mail.

Channelnewsasia.com

http://www.channelnewsasia.com/

Channel NewsAsia's Web site has Singapore, Asia-Pacific and world news. Special features include news formatted for handheld computers.

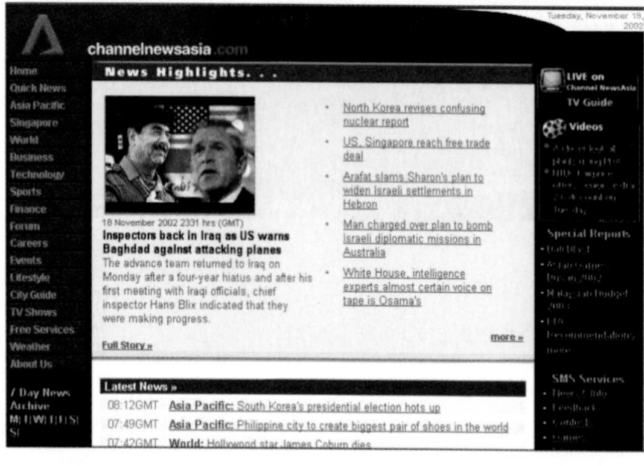

Radio New Zealand

http://www.radionz.co.nz/

Radio New Zealand broadcasts news bulletins and selected programs over the Internet, in Windows Media format. You can also click through to the Radio NZ International site for a selection of stories from the Pacific.

Newswires

Ananova

http://www.ananova.com/

Ananova's unique selling point is a green-haired, computer-generated virtual newsreader who delivers bulletins in a synthetic voice. You can opt for regular, light, sporty or quirky news, or simply read the stories yourself. Ananova also sends news to mobile phones on the UK's Orange network.

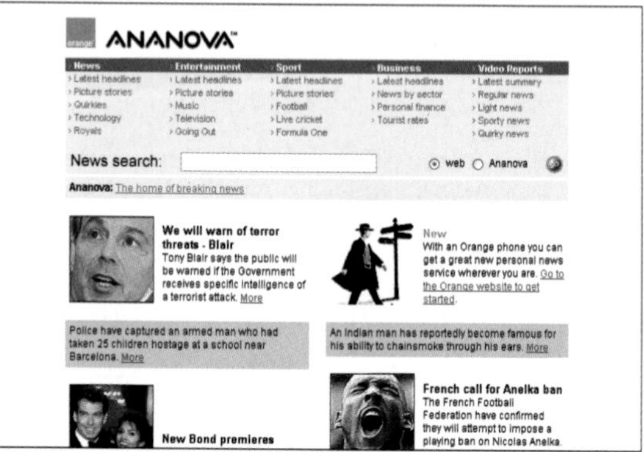

Reuters

http://www.reuters.com/

The famous news agency offers both regular and business news on a jam-packed Web site. Beyond the usual sections, there's an Oddly Enough area featuring stories such as 'Court punishes vandals with donkey rides'. The Reuters site also has extensive photo galleries dedicated to news, entertainment, sports and fashion.

Associated Press

http://wire.ap.org/

The Associated Press Web site doesn't provide news directly; instead, it links you to member sites in the US and elsewhere. For fast access to the main stories, click the link that takes you to a randomly chosen site. The Multimedia Archive has some interesting special features.

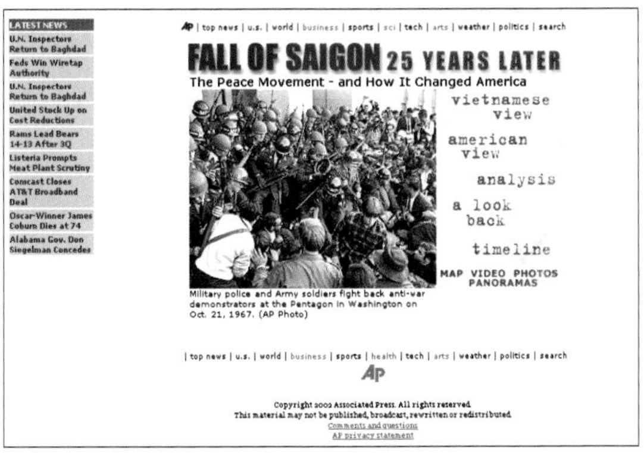

News24

http://www.news24.com/

News24 is a South African service providing local, African and international news. Convenient features include a Top Stories list detailing the most popular items over the last 24 hours and last seven days.

Newspapers and magazines

The New York Times

http://www.nytimes.com/

The on-line edition of *The New York Times* is so newspaper-like in both layout and content that you wonder why there's no ink on your hands when you finish reading. It's a literate, in-depth antidote to the infobite news that dominates the Internet.

Washington Post

http://www.washingtonpost.com/

The Washington Post's Web site has a special section for politics, where you'll find the latest news from the White House, the Senate and Congress. You may even find coverage of Watergate, a mere three decades after the paper first broke the story.

Chicago Tribune

http://www.chicagotribune.com/

Another US perspective, this time from Chicago. The *Tribune* has a strong sports section, even though the local teams aren't currently enjoying the glory the Chicago Bulls experienced in the 1990s.

USA Today

http://www.usatoday.com/

A more concise take on the news from America's national newspaper. The on-line edition includes fun features such as an interactive crossword.

Christian Science Monitor

http://www.csmonitor.com/

For a different perspective, try the on-line edition of *Christian Science Monitor*, an international, Pulitzer prize-winning daily newspaper published by the First Church of Christ, Scientist. Its mission is "to injure no man, but to bless all mankind."

Time

http://www.time.com/time/

News, in-depth features and photo essays from the weekly magazine. Check out the Time Favorites section for the person of the week, quotes, a parting shot and the best cartoons.

Guardian Unlimited

http://www.guardian.co.uk/

Guardian Unlimited is more sectionalised than most newspaper sites, enabling you to concentrate entirely on news, sport, politics or whatever else takes your fancy. Spin-off sections for film and football feel even more divorced from the main site. It's a more Internetty, less newspapery approach.

Telegraph.co.uk

http://www.telegraph.co.uk/

The UK's leading on-line newspaper has everything, including news, business news, sport, motoring, shopping, gardening, weather, opinions, horoscopes, crosswords (requires an annual subscription), letters, obituaries and cartoons. Best of all, it has an enormous, searchable archive going all the way back to April 1996 – and there's no charge for retrieving stories.

The Sun Newspaper Online

http://www.thesun.co.uk/

The UK's biggest-selling newspaper has a cheerful site that reflects its tabloid nature with punchy headlines, celebrity gossip and a huge gallery of Page 3 photographs.

Times Online

http://www.timesonline.co.uk/

The on-line edition of *The Times* presents itself in a more subdued, newspaper-like fashion. There's even an option to view virtual versions of the papers from the last seven days, so you can see which stories were published together. It also has a series of on-line specials, but it lacks the free archive that makes *The Telegraph's* site so useful.

News.com.au

http://news.com.au/

News.com.au brings together stories from the News Limited network, which comprises over 100 Australian newspapers. Members include *The Australian, The Daily Telegraph*, the *Herald Sun, The Courier-Mail, The Advertiser, The Mercury* and *The Sunday Times*. Special features include audio reports and news by e-mail.

Sydney Morning Herald

http://www.smh.com.au/

The Sydney Morning Herald's site covers the usual newspaper ground, with a couple of interesting additions. You can download a PDF file of the paper's front page, for the authentic newspaper experience, and there's a Web Diary that mixes commentary from one of the journalists with feedback from her readers.

The New Zealand Herald

http://www.nzherald.co.nz/

Across the Tasman, *The New Zealand Herald* has a simple site with New Zealand and world news, plus business, technology, sports, entertainment and travel sections. A separate marine section covers all things aquatic, from crippled oil tankers to the America's Cup.

Stuff

http://www.stuff.co.nz/

Stuff brings together stories from New Zealand newspapers such as *The Waikato Times, The Dominion Post, The Press* and *The Southland Times*. Rural, regional, national and world news stories all have their place.

Mail&Guardian Online

http://www.mg.co.za/

South Africa's Mail&Guardian Online has been publishing news on the Internet since 1994. In addition to South African and African news, it has specialist features such as a Notes and Queries section and an HIV/AIDS barometer.

Independent Online

http://www.iol.co.za/

Independent Online brings together stories from 14 South African newspapers. The site has a relaxed, informal feel that makes it pleasant to browse.

The Straits Times Interactive

http://straitstimes.asia1.com.sg/

Strait Times Interactive has a selection of stories from the current edition of *The Straits Times*, Singapore's most popular broadsheet. There's also a limited free archive with articles from the three previous days. For anything older, you have to pay.

Business news

Financial Times

http://news.ft.com/

Although the pages are white rather than pink, the on-line edition of Britain's best-known business paper is as authoritative as the printed one. Some features require a paid subscription.

Economist.com

http://www.economist.com/

If you're concerned about global economics, rather than your personal fortune (or lack of), try the on-line edition of *The Economist.* Useful features include country data files with facts, figures and articles about the economic and political outlook.

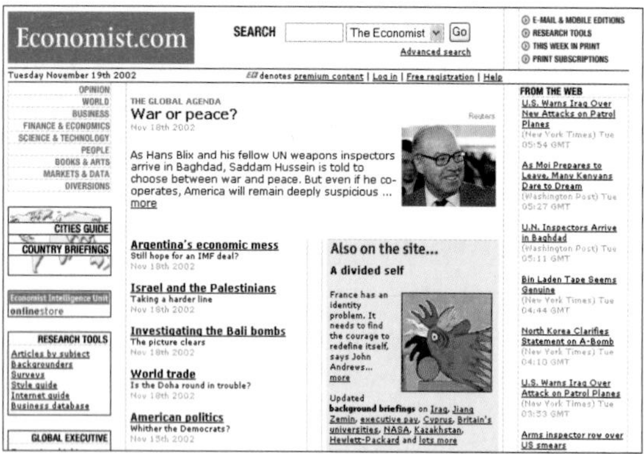

Wall Street Journal

http://online.wsj.com/

The on-line edition of *The Wall Street Journal* comes in three flavours, for the US, Europe and Asia. Brief stories on the front page lead you to more detailed articles in the interior, making it an easy site to browse – if you're prepared to pay for an annual subscription. Free content hides near the bottom of the front page and includes annual reports.

Bloomberg.com

http://www.bloomberg.com/

Bloomberg's Web site has financial news, market reports, stock prices and a range of financial tools.

Forbes.com

http://www.forbes.com/

Cast an envious eye over the names on the various lists – richest people, top celebrities and so on – then read the business, technology and market news to work out how to join them. Once you've acquired your millions, the Lifestyle section will help you spend them.

Business Week Online

http://www.businessweek.com/

Why wait a week when this US Web site brings you a daily dose of business news? Separate sections cover investing, global business, technology, small business and business education.

Business 2.0

http://www.business2.com/

Find out what's happening in the new economy with news, features and commentary from *Business 2.0* magazine. If you don't find what you're looking for here, there's also a Web Guide that catalogues the best business sites.

Sports news

CNNSI.com

http://sportsillustrated.cnn.com/

Featuring material from CNN and *Sports Illustrated,* CNNSI.com is dominated by US sports: baseball, basketball, football and ice hockey. It does a reasonable job of world sport as well, but don't expect obsessive coverage of sports such as cricket, football (soccer) and rugby.

EPSN

http://espn.go.com/

ESPN offers more variety, with extensive coverage of soccer (aka football), outdoor sports (fishing and hunting) and action sports (skateboarding, bike stunt and so on). Many other sports are covered in the Olympic Sports section.

BBC Sport

http://news.bbc.co.uk/sport/

BBC Sport covers football, cricket, rugby, tennis, golf, motorsport, boxing, athletics and other sports, with typical BBC thoroughness. You can watch, listen, vote or comment, or enjoy the lighter side of sport in the Funny Old Game section.

Sporting Life

http://www.sportinglife.com/

UK sports paper *Sporting Life* concentrates on all the sports that Britons might take part in (or, more probably, watch and place bets on): football, horse racing, cricket, rugby, Formula 1, golf and so on.

Eurosport

http://www.eurosport.com/

Cable/satellite channel Eurosport offers news and results in several languages. Like the channel itself, the Web site doesn't shy away from less popular sports such as cycling, sailing, ski-ing and swimming. You can tune in to its broadcasts over the Internet, although you may hear more than you see.

Sportal.com.au

http://sportal.com.au/

This Aussie sports portal covers a wide range of sports including cricket, soccer (aka football), Aussie Rules football and horse racing. It also has photo galleries, video, polls and games – including a memory game featuring pictures of Anna Kournikova.

Weather

The Weather Channel

http://www.weather.com/

Although some of the content is US-oriented, The Weather Channel's Web site provides forecasts for the entire globe. Just enter the name of your city for current conditions and predictions for the next ten days. You can choose between metric and imperial measurements and check the temperature and rainfall against the monthly averages.

BBC Weather

http://www.bbc.co.uk/weather/

The BBC's Weather site has five-day forecasts for the UK and the world, plus a wealth of weather-related information. Curious about climate change? Want to know the difference between ground frost and air frost? Wondering how the weather will affect upcoming sporting events? The BBC has all the answers.

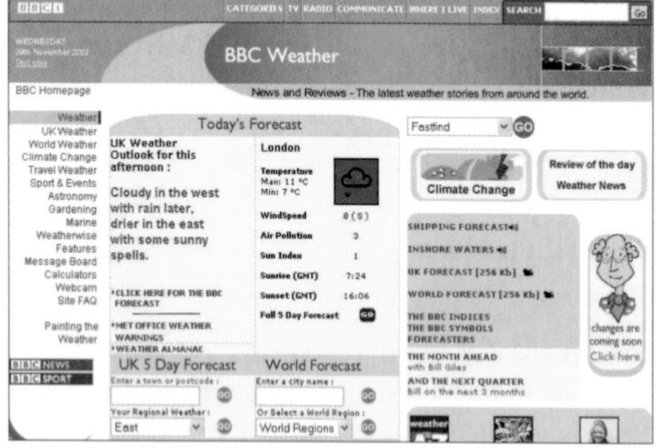

CNN Weather

http://www.cnn.com/WEATHER/

Still haven't found a forecast that pleases you? CNN gives you forecasts, temperatures and satellite maps, by continent or city. Try animating the maps to see cloud movements over the last six hours.

UK Met Office

http://www.metoffice.com/

The Met Office doesn't just forecast UK and world weather, it also provides a summary of the UK weather over the last month – just in case you weren't paying attention. It has an excellent range of satellite images and is setting up cameras that let you see exactly what's happening around the UK.

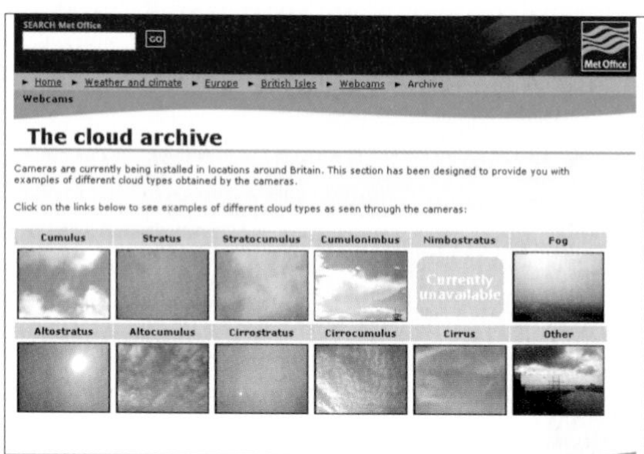

PA WeatherCentre

http://www.paweathercentre.com/

The Press Association's WeatherCentre is notable for its groovy animated maps showing conditions around the UK. British Internet users also get the option to download detailed, localised weather information, albeit over a premium-rate line.

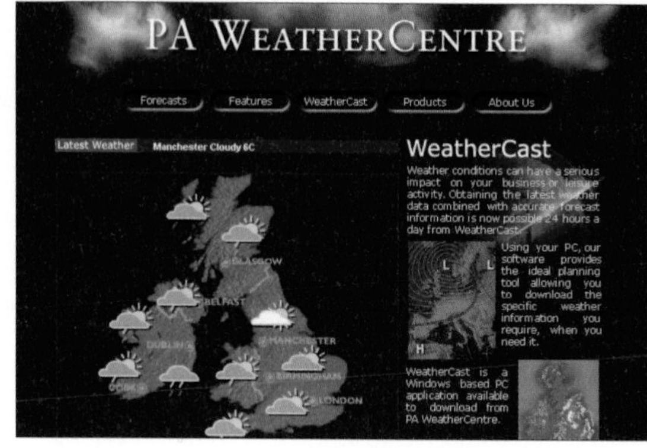

Australian Bureau of Meteorology

http://www.bom.gov.au/

The Bureau of Meteorology provides a bunch of forecasts, charts and radar and satellite images. There's also a special section for marine weather, with forecasts for coastal waters and high seas, current observations and links to tide tables. You'll need to be weather-savvy to interpret all the details.

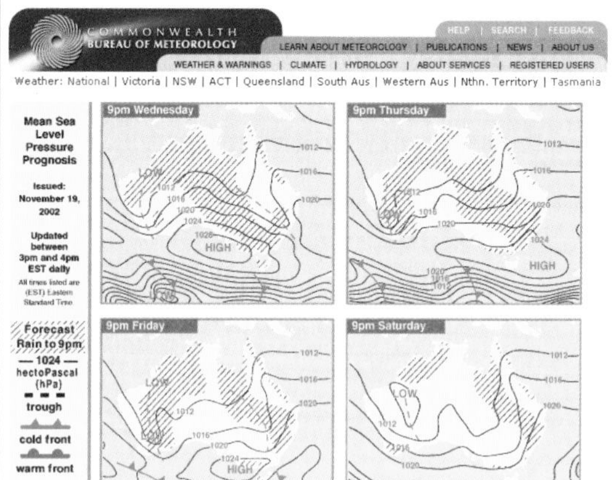

NZ MetService

http://www.metservice.co.nz/

The MetService has a chatty site that provides easy access to regular, mountain and marine forecasts. There's also a set of weather maps and an interesting article that explains how to read them.

National Environment Agency

http://app.nea.gov.sg/

Singapore's National Environment Agency (NEA) provides weather reports and haze readings. Forecasts are succinct, reflecting the predictability of Singapore's weather – try the station reports for more details. A frequently updated map of rain locations helps you work out whether you're experiencing an isolated shower or the opening salvo in a major storm.

South African Weather Service

http://www.weathersa.co.za/

The South African Weather Service provides general and specialised forecasts, radar and satellite images and real-time data. If you're making long-term plans, check out the seasonal forecast, which covers the next few months.

Information

The Internet isn't just entertaining, it's also incredibly useful. You can find everything from the capital of Kazakstan to the phone number of your next-door neighbour – if you know where to look. This section of the Worldwide Web Guide catalogues all the reference sites that come in handy when you're looking for facts and figures.

Resources

Bartleby.com

http://www.bartleby.com/

Bartleby.com has an extensive collection of reference books, including *The Columbia Encyclopedia, The American Heritage Dictionary, Roget's Thesaurus, The Oxford Shakespeare, The King James Bible* and *Gray's Anatomy*. While you don't always get the most recent edition, access is free and you can search individual titles, works of a particular type (such as Dictionaries) or the whole collection.

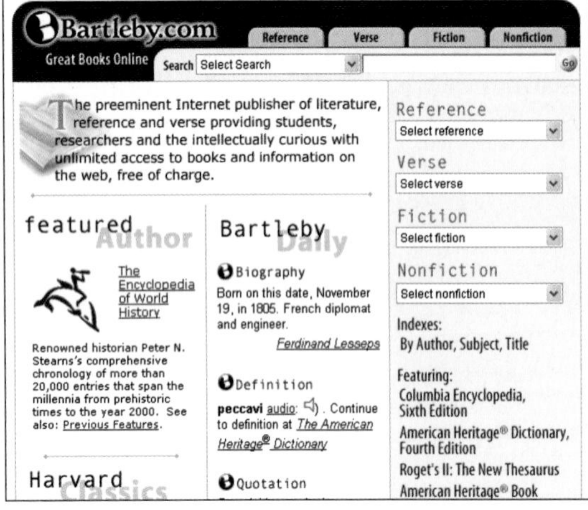

Refdesk

http://www.refdesk.com/

Refdesk is a gigantic catalogue of reference Web sites. It's well organised, pointing you to the most useful resources first and then allowing you to dig deeper if necessary.

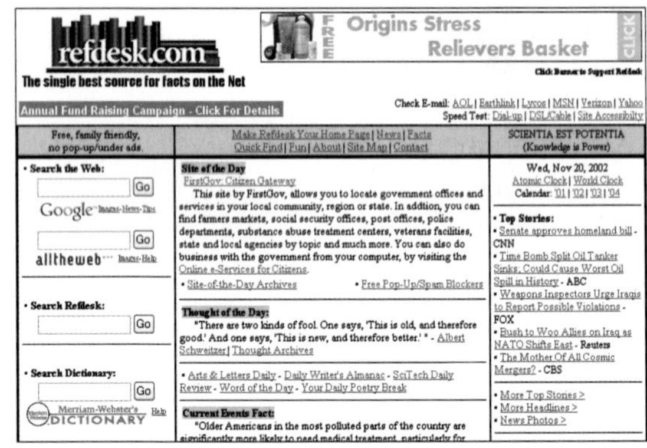

iTools

http://www.itools.com/

iTools provides easy access to a range of reference sites. Search the Web, look up words, find facts, convert currencies and look at maps.

Yahoo! Reference

http://education.yahoo.com/reference/

Yahoo!'s Reference page provides access to a selection of books and tools, including *The Brittanica Concise*.

MSN Learning & Research

http://encarta.msn.com/

MSN's Learning and Research section provides access to material from Microsoft's Encarta Encyclopedia, World English Dictionary and Dynamic Atlas. Some articles are only available to MSN subscribers.

Encyclopaedias

Encyclopaedia Britannica

http://www.britannica.com/

The 32-volume *Encyclopaedia Britannica*, on-line and searchable, no reinforced bookshelves required. The catch is that while some material can be browsed freely, you have to pay an annual subscription for full access. A free trial enables you to find out whether it's worth it.

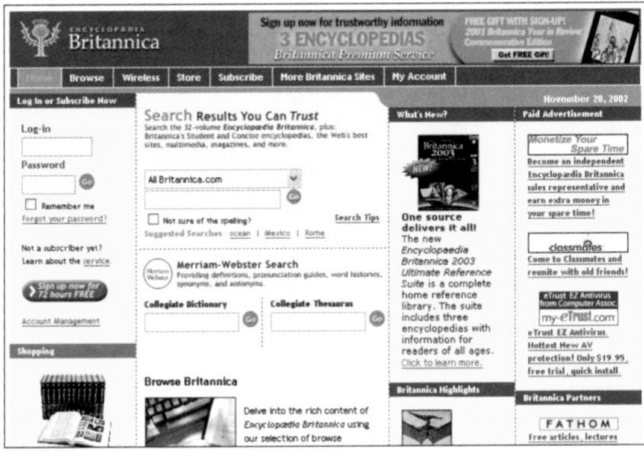

Encyclopedia.com

http://www.encyclopedia.com/

Free access to 57,000 articles from *The Columbia Encyclopedia, Seventh Edition.* If you subscribe to the eLibrary service, you can get further information by following the links at the end of each article.

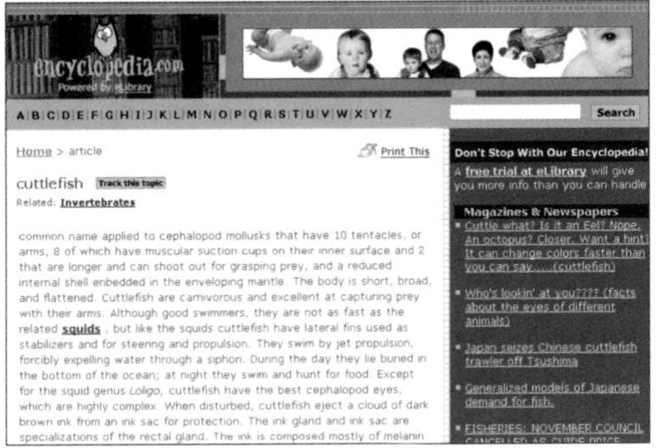

Dictionaries

OneLook Dictionaries

http://www.onelook.com/

Search for your word in over 800 on-line dictionaries using OneLook's simple interface. It's a useful tool that gives you quick access to multiple definitions. You can also find translations for foreign words.

Dictionary.com

http://dictionary.reference.com/

Dictionary.com also searches for your word in multiple dictionaries, although the selection is more limited. On the plus side, you can see the entries side by side and compare them. It also has a thesaurus, a translator and a Word of the Day feature.

Merriam-Webster OnLine

http://www.m-w.com/

Free access to the *Merriam-Webster Collegiate Dictionary* and *Collegiate Thesaurus*, plus subscription-based access to *Webster's Third New International Dictionary, Unabridged.* Probably the Web's most popular dictionary, mostly because it has been available on-line for several years.

WordCentral.com

http://www.wordcentral.com/

WordCentral.com is aimed at younger Internet users. It enables you to search Merriam-Webster's *Student Dictionary* and has fun features such as a buzzword of the day, a verse composer and a Build your own Dictionary section for made-up words.

AskOxford

http://www.askoxford.com/

Wordy offerings from Oxford Publishing, including a word of the day, word games, articles about words and an Ask the Experts section. You can also get very concise definitions from the *Oxford Paperback Dictionary and Thesaurus.*

Oxford English Dictionary

http://www.oed.com/

The famous and prestigious *Oxford English Dictionary*, available on-line – but only if you pay for an annual subscription. Otherwise you get a sample word each day. You never know, it might be the one you were looking for.

Cambridge Dictionaries Online

http://dictionary.cambridge.org/

Cambridge provides on-line access to seven dictionaries, including the *Cambridge International Dictionary of English, Cambridge Dictionary of American English, Cambridge Learner's Dictionary* and *Cambridge Dictionary of Idioms.* A well-designed interface enables you to switch dictionaries without changing words. There's also a Top 20 section that reveals the most searched-for words.

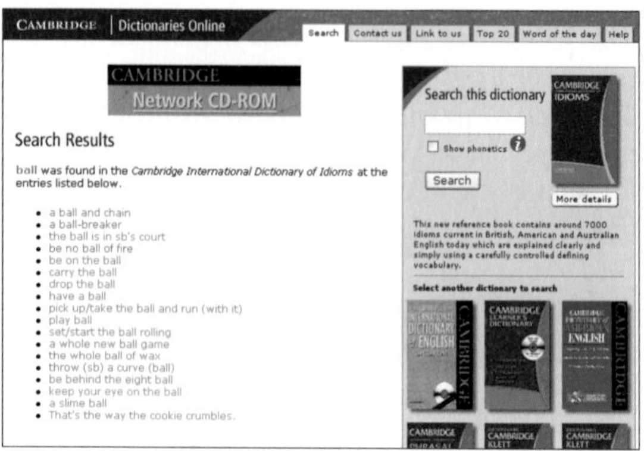

Roget's Thesauri

http://www.bartleby.com/thesauri/

A number of Web sites provide access to *Roget's Thesaurus*, but Bartleby's has the nicest interface. It provides synonyms from two versions, one from 1922 and the other from 1995.

Acronym Finder

http://www.acronymfinder.com/

Decipher annoying acronyms and abbreviations with the Acronym Finder, which has a database of over 250,000 confusing combinations of characters.

Jargon File

http://www.tuxedo.org/~esr/jargon/

Also known, in its printed form, as *The New Hacker's Dictionary*, the Jargon File is something of an Internet institution. It lists and defines the jargon used by computer enthusiasts – 'hackers' in the old sense, meaning people "who enjoy exploring the details of programmable systems and how to stretch their capabilities, as opposed to most users, who prefer to learn only the minimum necessary."

WordSpy

http://www.wordspy.com/

An entertaining site dedicated to new words and phrases. Each term gets a definition, an example of its use and a bit of background tracing its origin. Fascinating reading, even if you have little practical use for phrases such as 'parachute children' and 'corridor cruising'.

Symbols.com

http://www.symbols.com/

A dictionary without words. Looking up symbols is slightly tricky, there being no such thing as alphabetical order when you're dealing with nonalphabetic characters, but Symbol.com gets round this with a question-and-answer page that helps you describe your graphic. If you know the meaning of your symbol, you can also work backwards from the list of definitions.

Grammar and style

Garbl's Writing Center

http://garbl.home.attbi.com/

Useful round-up of writing resources with links to many Web sites covering punctuation, spelling, grammar, style and other troublesome subjects.

Times Style Guide

http://www.timesonline.co.uk/

Follow the links for the Style Guide from the front page of *The Times'* Web site and write like a topnotch journalist. It answers tricky questions such as whether to hyphenate 'deckchair' (no) and how to spell 'whiz-kid' (one 'z').

Internet Grammar of English

http://www.ucl.ac.uk/internet-grammar/

Comprehensive guide to English grammar from University College London. Currently available to everyone but may not remain free indefinitely.

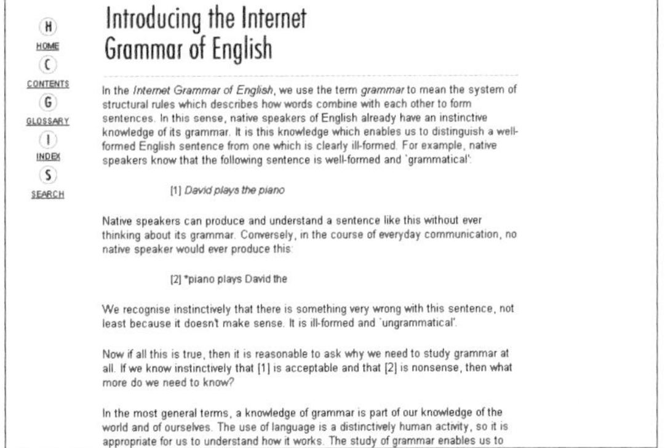

Guide to Grammar and Style

http://andromeda.rutgers.edu/~jlynch/Writing/

Miscellaneous collection of rules, comments on style and general advice on writing.

Quotes

Quotations at Bartleby.com

http://www.bartleby.com/quotations/

Over 80,000 quotations from three different sources. Bartleby.com scores again.

The Quotations Page

http://tqpage.com/

Long-established site with a searchable database containing over 15,000 quotes. You can also browse by subject or author.

Quoteland

http://www.quoteland.com/

Quotes by topic or author, plus special sections for sports and literary quotations.

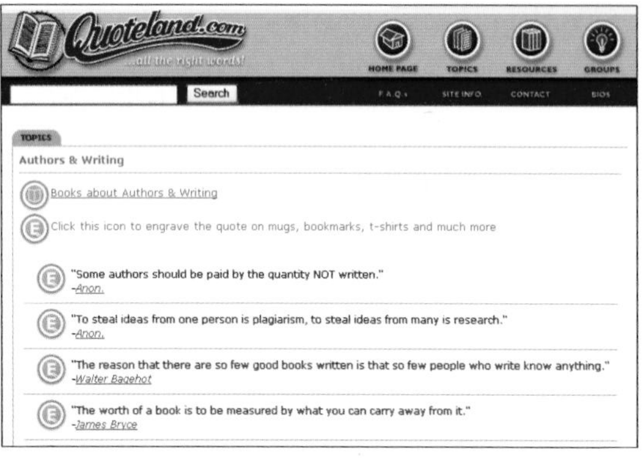

Mark Twain Quotations

http://www.twainquotes.com/

"The right word may be effective, but no word was ever as effective as a rightly timed pause." Huge collection of quotations from one of the masters of the pithy comment, organised by subject.

Shakespeare Quotes

http://www.allshakespeare.com/quotes/

Useful site that lists 100 of Shakespeare's most famous lines, then explains where they come from and what was happening at the time.

Translation

AltaVista Babel Fish

http://babelfish.altavista.com/

Translate short pieces of text by typing or pasting them into the box, or enter a Web address to translate an entire page. The translations are mechanical, so they aren't 100 per cent accurate, but you can get the gist of an article – and the errors are often amusing. Babel Fish translates French, German, Italian, Spanish, Portuguese, Russian, Chinese, Japanese and Korean text to English, and vice versa.

InterTran

http://www.tranexp.com:2000/InterTran

InterTran supports an even greater range of languages and lets you choose any supported pair, so you can translate Welsh into Greek, should you so desire.

FreeTranslation.com

http://www.freetranslation.com/

FreeTranslation has a limited range of languages, but it lets you enter 1,500 words of text, rather than the 150 supported by Babel Fish. It's useful for large chunks of French, German, Italian, Spanish and Portuguese.

Addresses and phone numbers

Telephone Directories on the Web

http://www.teldir.com/

This site catalogues on-line telephone directories and related resources for over 180 countries. It includes yellow pages and business directories as well as white pages (residential directories) and has a brief description of each site.

Postal Rates.info

http://www.postalrates.info/

Postal Rates.info does a similar job for postal information, directing you to sites that calculate postage, provide information about stamps and/or check postcodes.

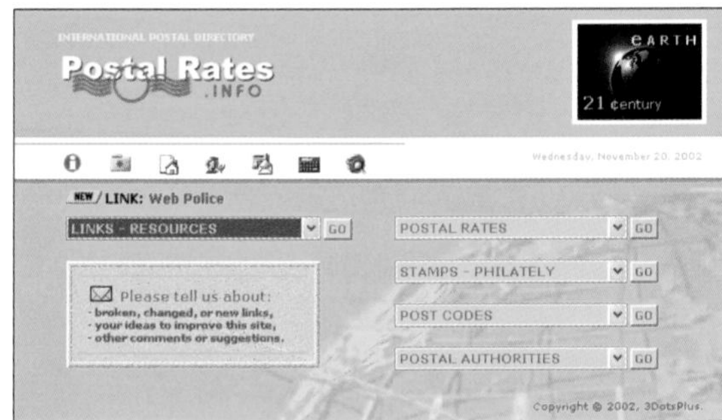

Infobel.com

http://www.infobel.com/world/

Infobel enables you to search for people and businesses in the UK, the US, Canada and a number of European countries. A simple interface makes searching straightforward.

Yahoo! People Search

http://people.yahoo.com/

Yahoo!'s People Search enables you to hunt for US street addresses or e-mail addresses from anywhere.

WhoWhere?

http://www.whowhere.lycos.com/

Tracking down e-mail addresses is mostly a matter of luck, so it's worth trying several databases. WhoWhere? gives you another chance of success.

AnyWho

http://www.anywho.com/

AT&T's AnyWho site helps you find people and businesses in the US. There's also a reverse search that turns a phone number into a name and address.

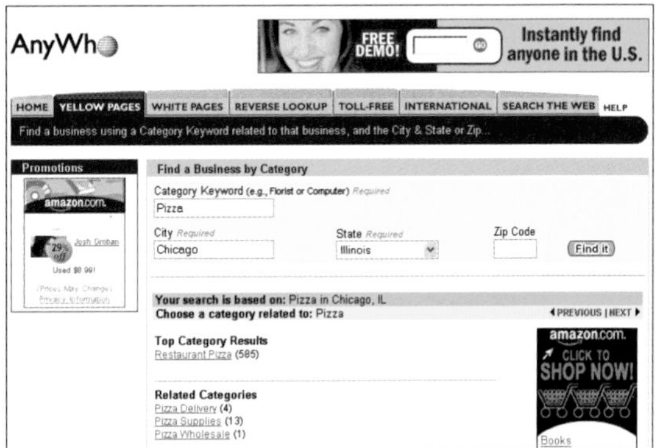

United States Postal Service

http://www.usps.com/

Everything you might want to know about sending mail within the US, including a ZIP code finder.

BT eDQ

http://www.bt.com/directory-enquiries/

The electronic version of BT's Directory Enquiries service gives you access to the complete UK phone book. Plug in a person's surname and town to find their number, assuming they're in the book. Casual visitors are restricted to ten searches per day.

192.com

http://www.192.com/

192.com draws its information from the UK electoral roll, so it can find addresses for people who don't have telephones (or don't have a phone in their name). However, you have to pay to access its database, so it's worth trying the other services first.

Friends Reunited

http://www.friendsreunited.com/

Friends Reunited lists its members according to their old school, university, workplace, team or club, enabling you to relocate people you've lost touch with over the years. Once you've registered, you can create your own entry and decide whether to contact any of your old mates.

Yell.com

http://www.yell.com/

Looking for a plumber in Manchester? Yell.com, the electronic version of the Yellow Pages, lets you search for businesses by location and name or function. It also has a nationwide Film Finder that tells you what's on at your local cinema.

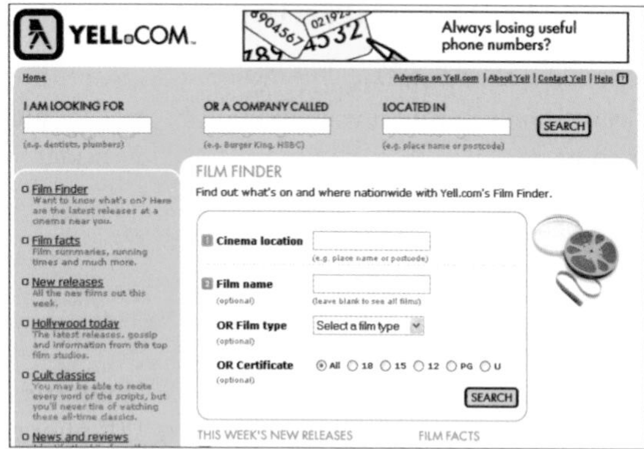

Scoot

http://www.scoot.co.uk/

Scoot is an alternative business directory, with very similar features to Yell.com.

Royal Mail

http://www.royalmail.com/

Useful features on the Royal Mail Web site include postcode and address checkers, a postal calculator and a Track & Trace option that checks the progress of Registered and Recorded Delivery items.

Australian White Pages Online

http://www.whitepages.com.au/wp/

Australia's White Pages are on-line, enabling you to track down people and businesses. There's also a postcode checker and you can follow the link to the Yellow Pages site for further business listings.

New Zealand White Pages

http://www.whitepages.co.nz/

The Internet White Pages Web site makes it easy to search for people, businesses, doctors and hospitals, and government departments.

Kiwis Reunited

http://www.kiwisreunited.co.nz/

Find your old friends with Kiwis Reunited, which lets you look up your old school or company and make contact with other people who studied or worked there. You can also post an account of your progress – spectacular or otherwise – since those long-forgotten days.

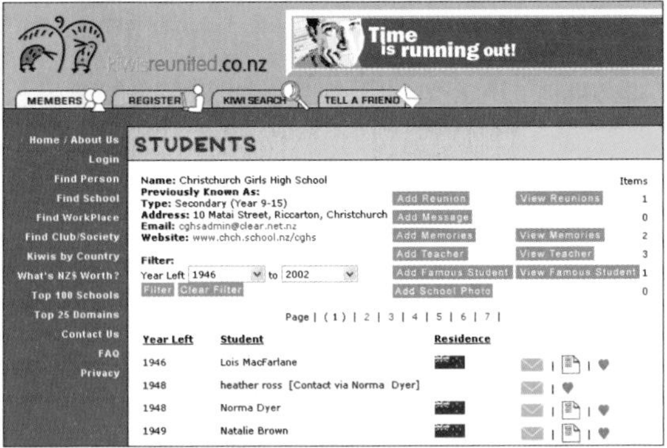

Singapore Phone Book

http://www.phonebook.com.sg/

Singapore's on-line phone book has residential, business and government listings, with a reverse search for business and government numbers. Use the map links to find out where you need to go.

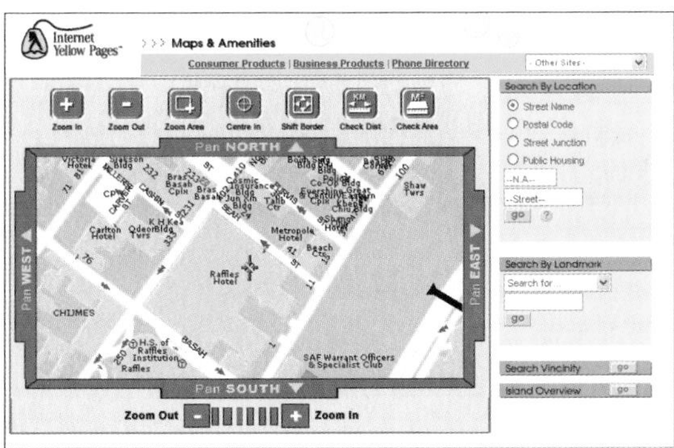

Singapore Post

http://www.singpost.com/

If you have to post a letter, SingPost's site makes it easy: there's a postcode finder, a post office and postbox locator and a table of rates.

Maps and country details

CIA World Factbook

http://www.cia.gov/cia/publications/factbook/

The World Factbook provides basic intelligence about every country in the world. Since it's a publicly available document, it concentrates on the not-so-secret stuff: location, geography, population, government, economy, communication and so on. It's an excellent source of facts and figures.

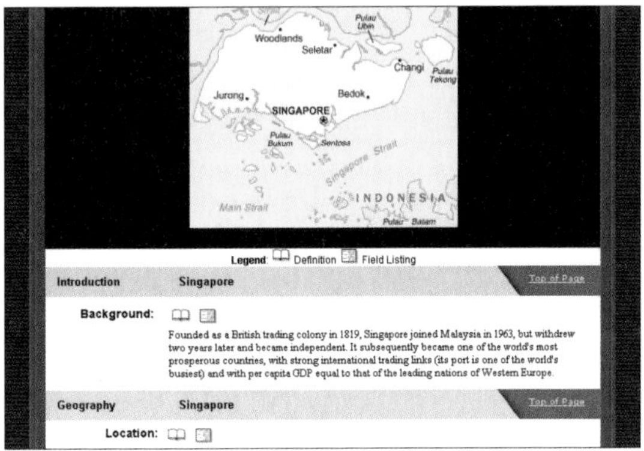

World Gazetteer

http://www.world-gazetteer.com/

If you're specifically interested in people, visit the World Gazetteer to check the population of any country, region or city you care to name. Useful features for impressing friends include a list of the worlds largest metropolitan areas (lead by Tokyo) and cities (topped by Mumbai).

Flags of the World

http://flagspot.net/flags/

Flags of the World is devoted to vexillology (the study of flags, unsurprisingly). Not contenting itself with a picture of the flag of each country, it provides a wealth of additional details: information about the design and origin, alternative flags, historical flags, marine ensigns, coats of arms and so on.

MapQuest World Atlas

http://www.mapquest.com/atlas/

The MapQuest site has attractive but not especially detailed maps of continents, countries, oceans and polar regions. It's worth a look if you just need a basic outline with major cities.

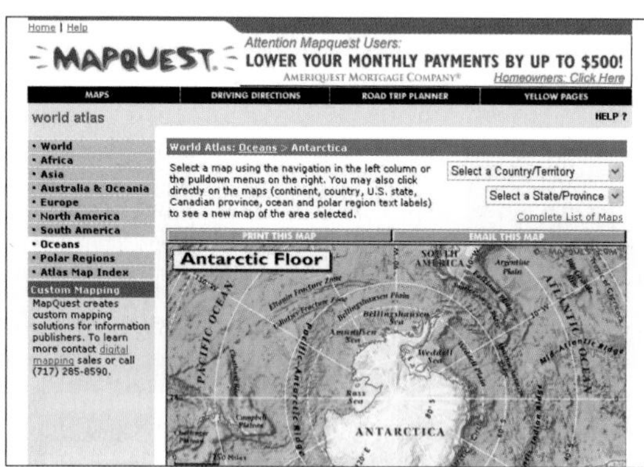

National Geographic Map Machine

http://plasma.nationalgeographic.com/mapmachine/

Give the Map Machine the name of a place and it'll find you a map. You can then change the theme to see anything from the physical relief or population density to the annual rainfall.

Expedia Maps

http://maps.expedia.com/

Expedia Maps has driving maps of the US and topographical maps of the entire world. The maps are available in three sizes – small, medium and large – and zooming in gives you a reasonable amount of detail.

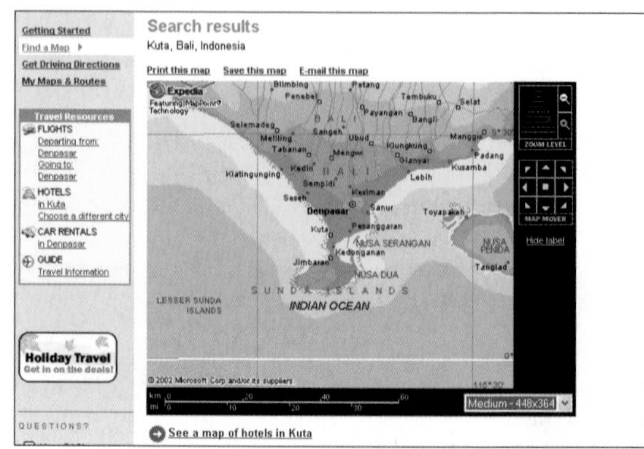

Terraserver

http://www.terraserver.com/

For a different perspective, try the Terraserver, which gives you access to aerial and satellite photography. Coverage is by no means complete, but it's still fun to look down on the world.

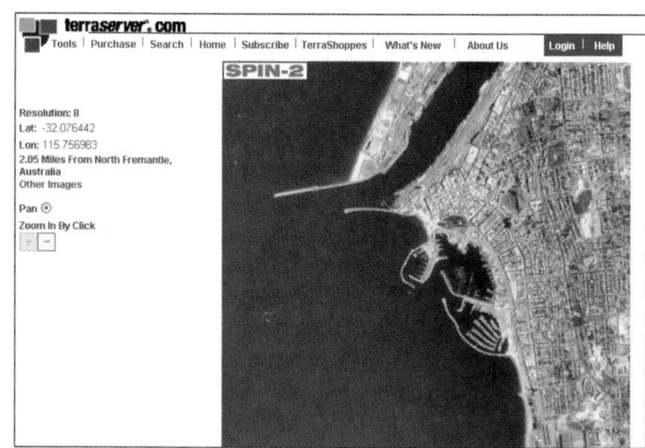

Multimap

http://www.multimap.com/

Multimap has street maps of the UK, Europe and the US and basic road maps of the rest of the world. Special features include aerial photographs of most of England and Wales.

Streetmap.co.uk

http://www.streetmap.co.uk/

Streetmap has street maps of all of mainland Britain, searchable by street, postcode, place name, grid reference, latitude/longitude and telephone code – so if you know anything at all about the place you're trying to find, it should be able to produce a map. Like Multimap, it has aerial photos of some areas.

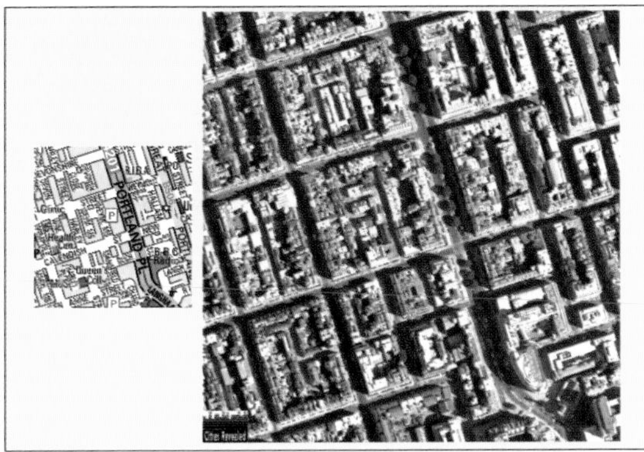

RAC

http://www.rac.co.uk/

Once you know where in the UK you're going, use the RAC's routefinder to get there. Simply plug in your current location and destination and it tells you how to drive between them. It even tells you how long the journey should take, assuming you don't run into roadworks or traffic jams.

Whereis Online

http://www.whereis.com.au/

Whereis doesn't just show you maps of Australian cities, it also tells you how to drive – or walk – from one place to another.

GeoScience Australia

http://www.ga.gov.au/map/

The GeoScience site lets you create your own maps by zooming in on its master map of Australia, then deciding whether you want to display roads, rivers, airports and so on. If that's too much effort, you can simply view assorted maps of the country.

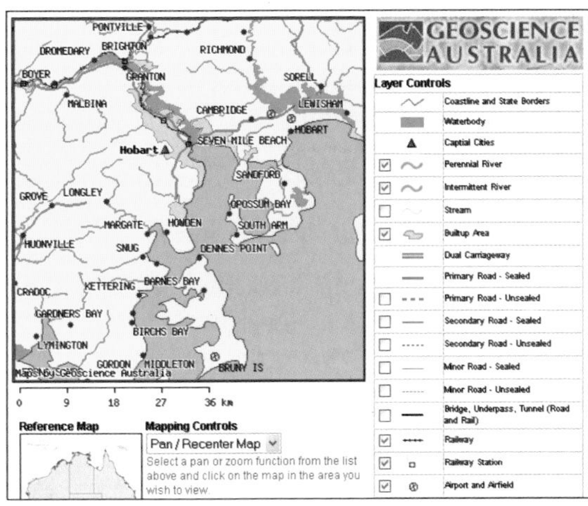

Can.com.sg

http://www.can.com.sg/

Select the canFind option for an interactive map of Singapore. You can search for almost anything, including streets, postcodes, companies, major buildings and attractions. When you zoom in, the map even shows individual houses.

Clocks and calendars

Timeanddate.com

http://www.timeanddate.com/

Convenient single-page display of the current time in over 250 cities around the world. Alternatively, you can create a customised view showing only the cities where you have friends or colleagues. You can also create a calendar for any month or year.

World Time Server

http://www.worldtimeserver.com/

Attractive world clock that provides the current time in the country or major city of your choice.

Today's Calendar and Clock Page

http://www.ecben.net/calendar.shtml

Although it isn't much to look at, this site catalogues lots of clock and calendar resources. If you're looking for any kind of calendar, be it Julian or Gregorian, Jewish, Islamic or Hindu, you'll find a link here.

Earth Calendar

http://www.earthcalendar.net/

Earth Calendar concentrates on the important dates: holidays, celebrations, anniversaries and gratuitous days off. You can browse the holidays by date, country or religion.

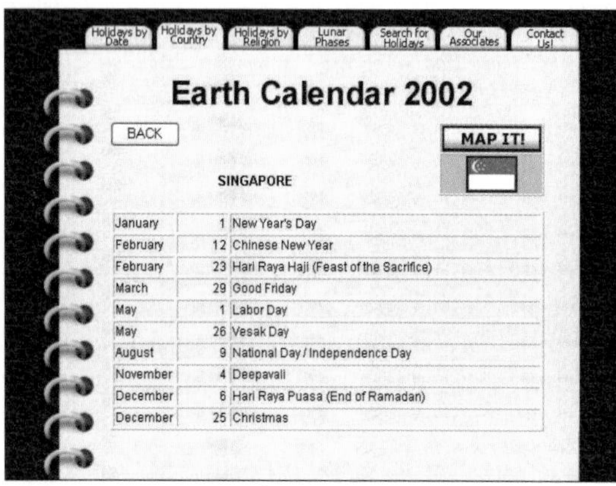

This Day in History

http://www.historychannel.com/tdih/

The History Channel's This Day in History page provides accounts of the major events that occurred on today's date in previous years. You can settle for general history or delve into specific areas such as crime, entertainment and technology. It also has separate sections for major conflicts, from the Civil War to the Cold War.

Moon Phases

http://www.googol.com/moon/

Attractive site that provides a visual calendar of the phases of the moon, for any month of any year.

Earth and Moon Viewer

http://www.fourmilab.ch/earthview/vplanet.html

Entertaining tool/toy that creates simulated views of the Earth and Moon at the current moment, showing you the areas of daylight and darkness.

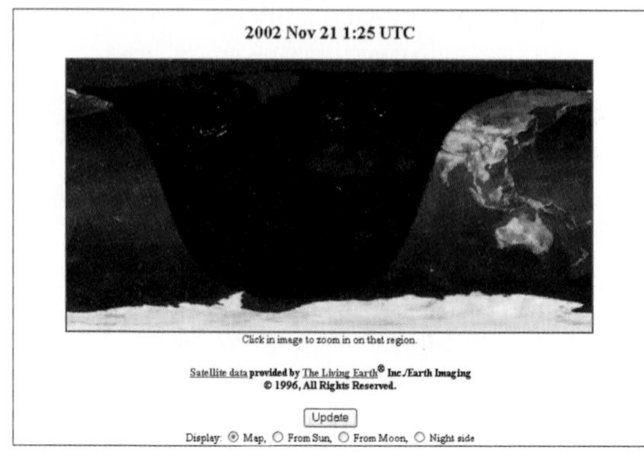

Numbers and measurements

A Dictionary of Units

http://www.ex.ac.uk/cimt/dictunit/dictunit.htm

A Dictionary of Units has lots of information about measurements, units, the Systeme International (SI) and metrification, plus a comprehensive set of convertors that take the strain off your brain.

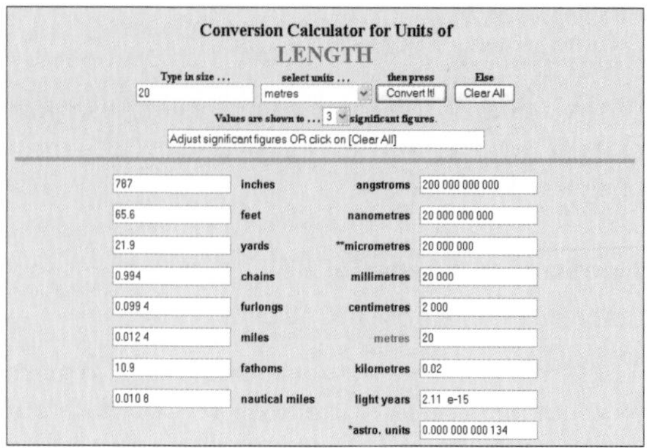

English Weights and Measures

http://home.clara.net/brianp/

Curious about drams, tods, sacks and London pounds? This site explains what they are (or were) and bemoans the rise of the metric system.

The NIST Reference on Constants, Units and Uncertainty

http://physics.nist.gov/cuu/

NIST is the (US) National Institute of Science and Technology. On this unfortunately named but nicely designed site it provides values for the fundamental physical constants, a thorough explanation of the Systeme International (SI) units and some notes about uncertainty.

WebElements Periodic Table

http://www.webelements.com/

Excellent resource for students and chemists, with information about all the elements – including photographs, cartoons and comments such as, "The most romantic way to extract gold is by panning it out from a stream in some pleasant valley but most such sources are now depleted." It comes in both professional and scholar editions – the pro version has more details.

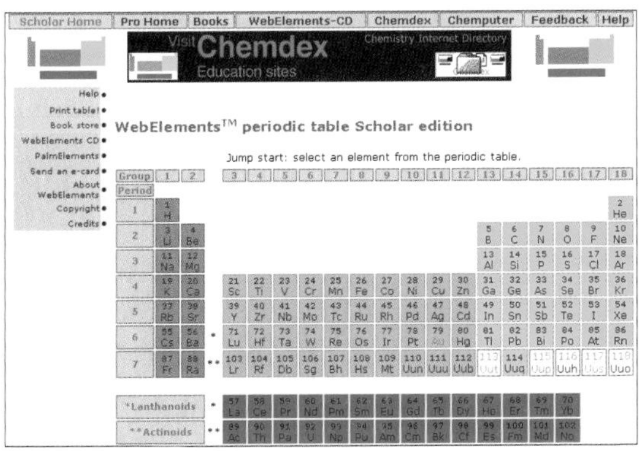

Government

FirstGov

http://www.firstgov.gov/

Your first port of call for information from the US Government, be it straightforward advice about birth certificates or voting or obscure details such as the current wait times at border crossing-points.

White House

http://www.whitehouse.gov/

Take a virtual tour of the US President's des res or find out about his activities and policies. The Vice President and First Lady get their own special sections and kids can read about the President's dogs, cat and cow (?!).

ukonline.gov.uk

http://www.ukonline.gov.uk/

Starting point for accessing UK government and public-service Web sites. Mostly you'll pass quickly through on your way to other places, but if you decide to hang around, you can have your say on topical issues or get government advice on everything from having a baby to death and bereavement.

10 Downing Street

http://www.number-10.gov.uk/

Not to be outdone by the Yanks, the UK Prime Minister also has a home in cyberspace, complete with panoramic images of his home. Once you've admired the decor, you can read the press briefings, watch videos of Prime Minister's Question Time and browse assorted fact files.

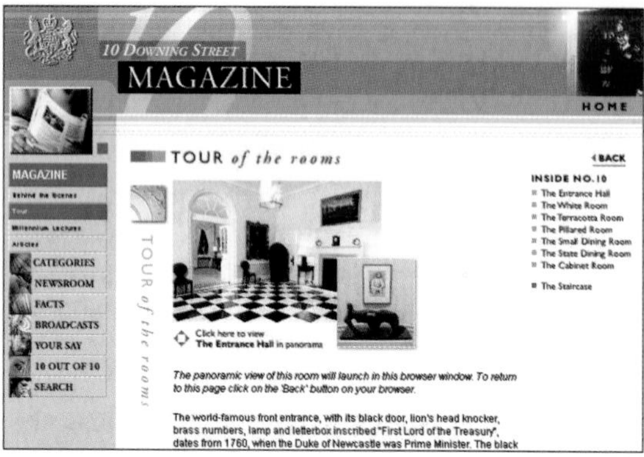

Fed.gov.au

http://www.fed.gov.au/

Another country, another portal that serves primarily to bounce you off to other sites. Australia's Fed.gov.au is divided into sections for individuals, students, businesses and non-residents, making it easy to access appropriate information.

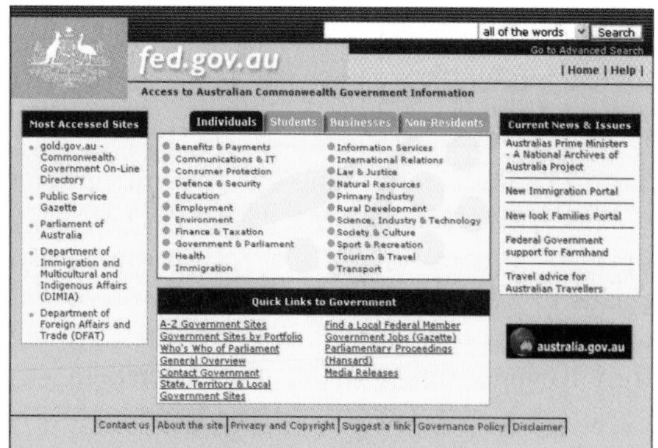

govt.nz

http://www.govt.nz/

govt.nz catalogues government and council information alphabetically, by type and by life event. You can also find out how to request information from an MP or government organisation or provide feedback on issues currently under debate. The About New Zealand section provides information for visitors.

SINGOV

http://www.gov.sg/

Singapore's SINGOV catalogues government services and keeps you informed about statements and speeches. Follow the link to the Singapore Statistics site for oodles of official numbers.

South Africa Government Online

http://www.gov.za/

Gov ZA is structured much like the South African Government, with sections for the President, Ministers, Deputy Ministers and government departments. It also covers provincial and local government and you can download documents, reports and forms.

Science and Technology

The great paradox of the Internet is that all the information you need to get connected is available on-line... but you can't access it until you've got your computer connected. By then you'll be interested in other things: finding Web sites, choosing new software and hardware, and/or laughing at geek humour. Fortunately there's loads of advice on these subjects as well.

Finding Web sites

Search Engine Watch

http://searchenginewatch.com/

Search Engine Watch lists and reviews search engines and provides advice on hunting for sites. The section on the major search engines, with descriptions of their features, is handy for beginners. Specialist and multimedia search engines are listed separately.

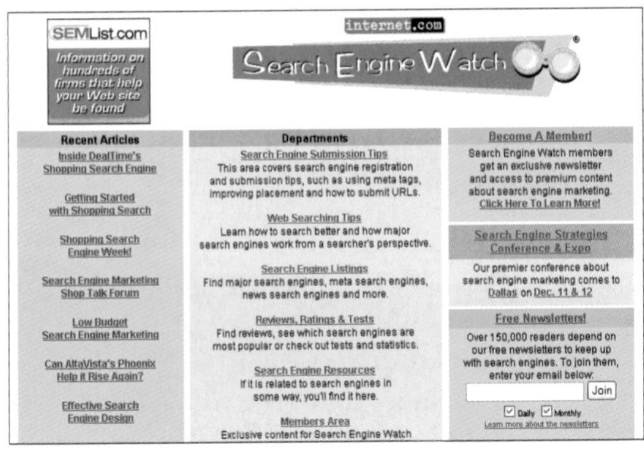

Google

http://www.google.com/

The critic's favourite, thanks to a clean interface and the ability to magic up relevant results. It also offers specialist image, newsgroup and news searches, plus a Web directory. With so much on offer here, there's little reason to look elsewhere.

Yahoo!

http://www.yahoo.com/

Yahoo! was one of the first really popular Web sites. It still gets the visitors today, although they come as much for its other offerings – Web-based e-mail, instant messaging and so on – as for the directory that started it all off. It's still worth a look when you're researching a broad area and just want the best sites. Localised versions cater to specific countries and regions, including the UK & Ireland, Australia & NZ, and Singapore.

AltaVista

http://www.altavista.com/

AltaVista was once the Web's leading search engine, but its popularity slipped when it diversified into other areas. Today the focus is back on searching, with general, image, MP3/audio, video and news searches. Numerous localised versions enable you to restrict your search to sites from a specific country.

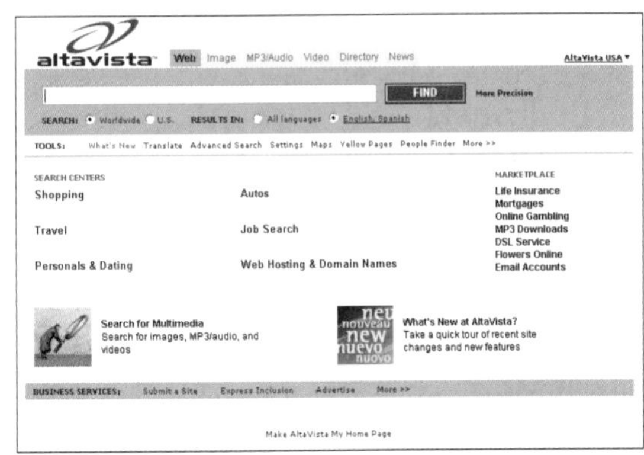

MSN Search

http://search.msn.com/

MSN offers a searchable directory of top sites, provided by LookSmart. You can also use the Advanced Search option to search the entire Web.

Excite

http://www.excite.com/

Like Yahoo!, Excite now offers so many extra features, from news and stock prices to personal horoscopes, that it's easy to miss the Search box in the middle of the page. You can search the entire Web or just Excite's directory, or look for photos.

Lycos

http://www.lycos.com/

Lycos offers Web, news and shopping searches, plus a range of other services.

Ask Jeeves

http://www.ask.com/

Ask Jeeves responds to plain-English questions, saving you the bother of posing your query in computer-speak.

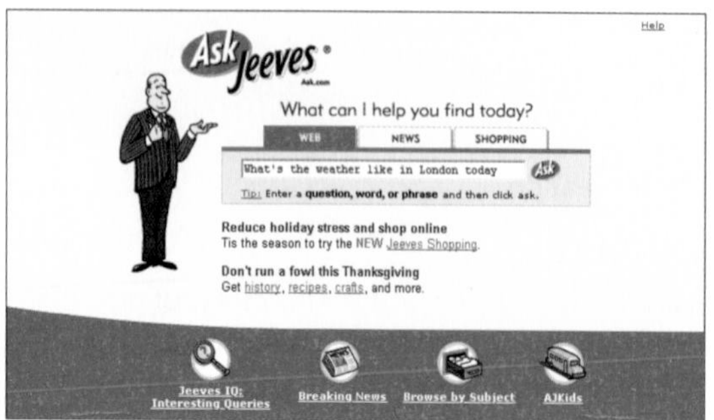

Web Wombat

http://www.webwombat.com.au/

Web Wombat is an Aussie search engine cum directory cum portal site with news, weather, horoscopes and so on. It's useful if you're specifically interested in Australian Web sites.

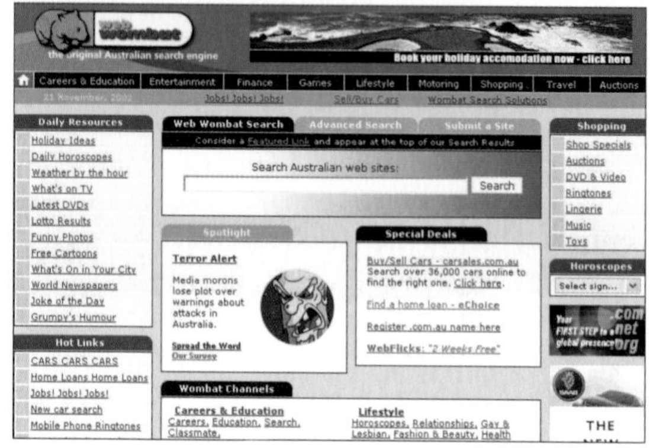

LookSmart

http://www.looksmart.com/

LookSmart offers a categorised directory of Web sites with brief comments from the LookSmart reviewers. There are separate versions for the UK, Australia, New Zealand and Canada.

Yahoo! Daily Picks

http://dir.yahoo.com/new/

If you're just looking for something new and/or topical, Yahoo!'s Daily Picks section highlights recent additions to the directory and sites worth seeing. A good choice for a rainy afternoon.

Netsurfer Digest

http://www.netsurf.com/nsd/

Netsurfer Digest is an e-zine (electronic magazine) that highlights topical Web sites and Internet trends. Sadly, you now have to pay an annual subscription to receive the weekly bulletins. Offshoots deal with science, education, books and robotics.

Encyclopaedias

PC Webopaedia

http://www.pcwebopaedia.com/

Look up those mysterious technical terms in the PC Webopaedia, an on-line dictionary that not only provides explanations but also gives you links to sites where you can explore the subject in more detail. A list of the top 15 search terms lets you see what's puzzling other Internet users.

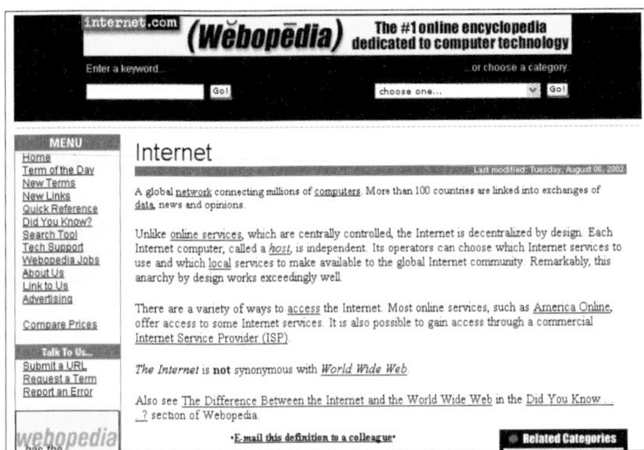

Whatis?com

http://whatis.techtarget.com/

If you're still mystified, try Whatis?com, a slightly geekier dictionary that covers some of the more obscure computing terms.

NetLingo

http://www.netlingo.com/

NetLingo is an Internet dictionary that explains all the strange terms that are used on-line. Find out what is meant by 'cornea gumbo', 'kevorking' and 'meatspace'. It also has a collection of smileys – little faces made out of keyboard characters.

PC Technology Guide

http://www.pctechguide.com/

The PC Technology Guide concentrates on the stuff inside (and attached to) your system box. If you're been baffled by a sales assistant or just want to know how your computer works, this is the place to start. It begins gently but gets quite technical.

General computing

CNET.com

http://www.cnet.com/

Vast site with technology news, features, product reviews, software to download and advice for Web designers. It was easier to find your way around when the site was smaller and less successful, but there's plenty here that's worth reading. Reviewers are clear about their likes and dislikes and there's some useful material for beginners... somewhere.

ZDnet

http://www.zdnet.com/

Technically part of the CNET Network, ZDNet still feels separate and different. Like CNET.com, it has news, features, reviews and a download library, but offers more depth and weight. Watch out for the buyers' guides, which explain what to look for in your new toys.

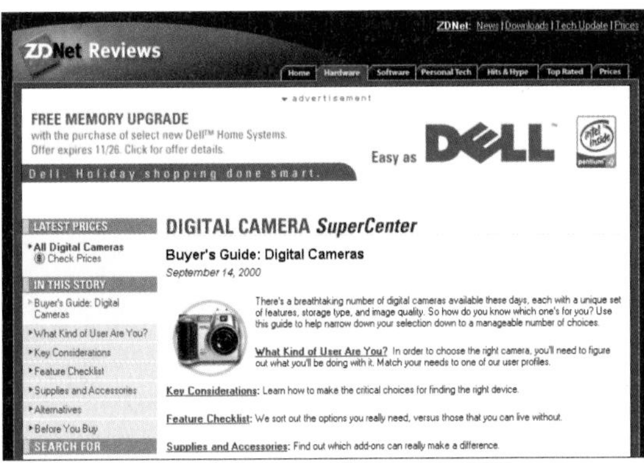

MaxPC

http://www.maxpc.co.uk/

MaxPC collates reviews, features and tutorials from the computer magazines produced by Future Publishing, a UK-based company. You can also click through to the sites of the individual titles for a more focused approach.

Computer Buyer

http://www.computerbuyer.co.uk/

Produced by the UK magazine of the same name, the Computer Buyer site succeeds where so many others fail: it's easy to navigate. Start with the latest news, reviews and features, then plunge into the archives, which integrate material from sister titles *Computer Shopper, PC Pro and MacUser.*

The Register

http://www.theregister.co.uk/

The Register is a UK-based news site that offers opinionated reports on the latest developments in computing. Its willingness to snipe at anyone and everyone (the site's tagline is, "Biting the hand that feeds IT") makes it more readable than the average technology site.

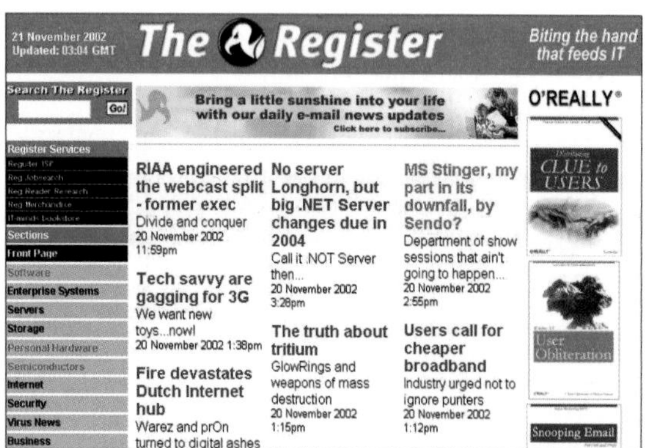

Australian PC World

http://pcworld.idg.com.au/

The PC World site has the usual mixture of news, reviews and features, but with an Australian twist. Highlights include the Buying Guides, which cover everything from motherboards to antivirus software, and the HelpScreen section, where you can post a problem and get help from other readers and the *PC World* staff.

Internet

Wired News

http://www.wired.com/news/

The latest on the Internet, in fluorescent colours, from the iconoclastic *Wired* magazine. It's easier on the eye than the printed version, because the wild colours are pushed off into the margins, and it has the most interesting stories. Always worth a look, especially if you have a penchant for the offbeat.

.net

http://www.netmag.co.uk/

UK Internet magazine *.net* covers the Internet from an ordinary user's point of view. Highlights of its site include the In-depth Articles section, which is packed with features from previous issues of the printed magazine, and the Web Builder section, which helps you create your own Web site.

Internet Magazine

http://www.internet-magazine.com/

The star attraction of *Internet Magazine's* site is the ISP section, which offers advice on choosing a service provider plus an extensive database of UK ISPs. If you don't know where to begin, try the list of recommended services – ten top ISPs that seem to please most people. Broadband has its own section.

All About the Internet

http://www.isoc.org/internet/

Dry, minimalist guide from the Internet Society. It's mostly of interest for its links to other sites, which include several histories of the Net.

Expedition Internet

http://www.worldlinklearning.net/ei/home.htmlConcise

Produced by AARP, the American Associated for Retired People, this set of tutorials takes you on five voyages around the Internet. Each tutorial is broken down into manageable chunks, with activities to try and quizzes to test your understanding.

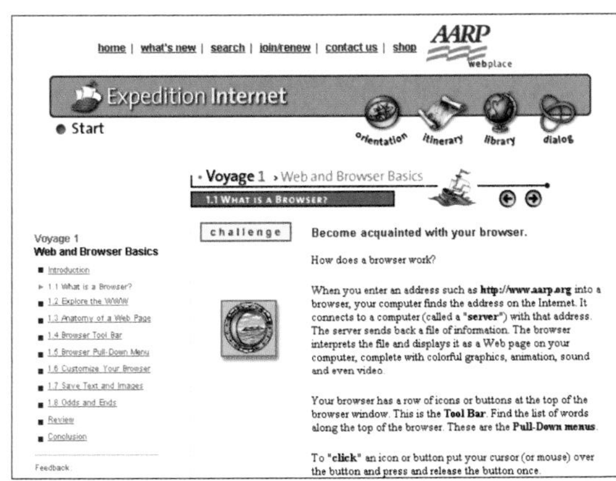

Internet Tutorials

http://library.albany.edu/internet/

These on-line tutorials from the University at Albany Library start with the basics and then provide in-depth advice on using the Web for research. Worth a look if you're a student, teacher or academic.

Webmonkey

http://hotwired.lycos.com/webmonkey/

Learn how to build your own Web site with material from *Wired* magazine. Separate introductions for beginners, builders and masters help you find appropriate tutorials and advice.

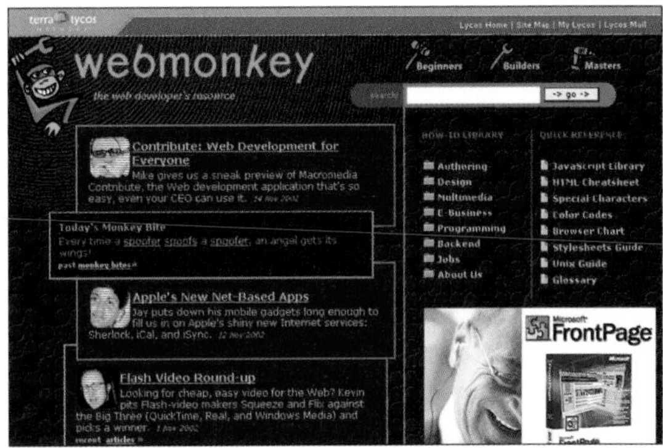

Intel

http://www.intel.com/

Find out what makes your computer tick, compare your processor with Intel's latest and greatest offering and see what else the company is up to. You can even take a virtual tour of the Intel museum. Intel also has localised Web pages for many countries.

IBM

http://www.ibm.com/

Like most manufacturers, the inventor of the PC doesn't just tout its new computers on-line, it also helps you keep your current one in shape. Visit the Support and Downloads section for solutions to your technical problems and updated drivers.

Dell

http://www.dell.com/

Dell sells over the Internet in many countries – select yours from the drop-down list. Find out what's available and specify the system of your dreams, without grappling with pushy salespeople.

Hewlett-Packard

http://www.hp.com/

HP makes everything from desktop computers to printers, scanners and digital cameras, so its site doesn't just sell you individual products, it also shows you how they all fit together. It has local sites for many countries, but is inclined to flip you back to the US site when you request more information.

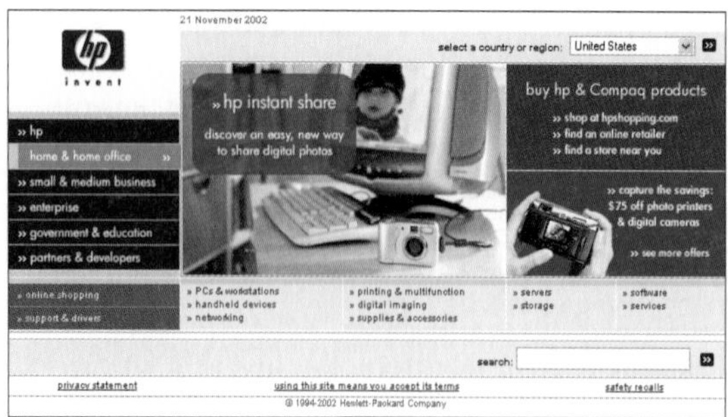

Apple

http://www.apple.com/

Think different(ly) at Apple's site, which attempts to lure you away from the Windows world with information about its friendly and colourful computers. This is also the place to get information about software products such as QuickTime.

Epson

http://www.epson.com/

Epson's well-organised sites provide lots of information about its printers and scanners. They also help you make them most of them with downloadable software and on-line problem solvers. In the UK, check out the Photo Expert site (`http://www.photoexpert.epson.co.uk`) for advice on digital imaging.

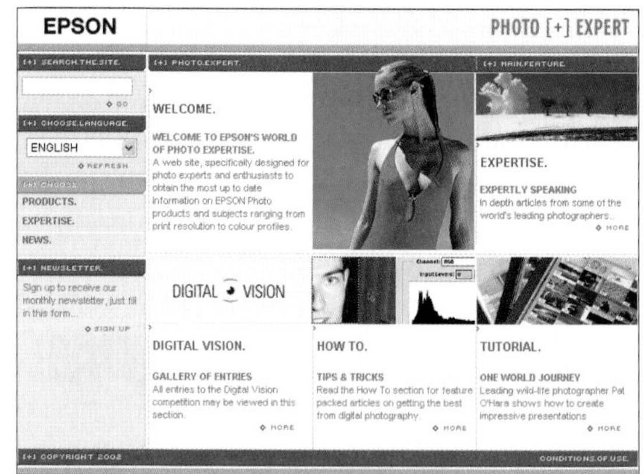

Scantips

http://www.scantips.com/

Having problems getting pictures on to your computer? This site provides reams of information on scanners, scanner software and scanning. Detailed explanations of concepts such as resolution are followed by advice on the settings to choose and tips for improving the results.

Iomega

http://www.iomega.com/

Iomega's sites provide information about its myriad different drives – Zip, CD-RW, hard and Mini USB – and help you choose one. Depending on your location, you may be able to purchase it on-line. You can also download the latest version of the drive software and sometimes you'll find fun activities such as games and competitions.

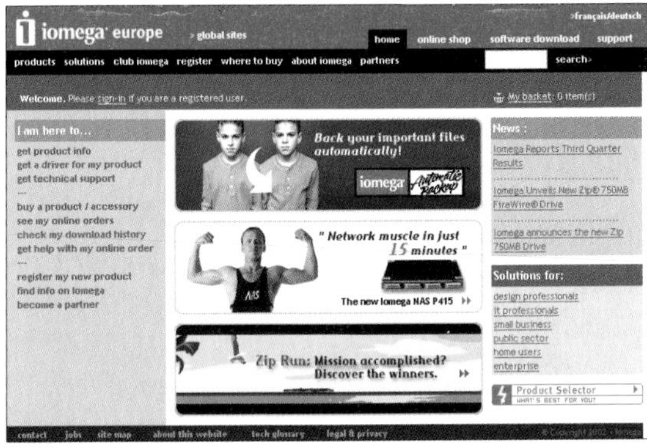

USRobotics

http://www.usr.com/

Check out the latest modems from USRobotics, learn more about the technologies they use and download drivers, upgrades, data sheets, manuals and troubleshooting guides.

Zoom Telephonics

http://www.zoomtel.com/

Click your country's flag to find out which of Zoom's modems are available in your area. You can also click through to the Hayes site for the Hayes range of modems (now owned by Zoom).

Curt's High-speed Modem FAQ

http://curt.vee90.net/modems.html

If you want to know how your modem works (or why it isn't working), Curt's page is a good place to start. It explains everything from connection speeds to the ins and outs of 56kbps technology and software modems. It's particularly helpful when you're trying to achieve a happy relationship between an older computer and an older modem.

Logitech

http://www.logitech.com/

Input specialist Logitech sells mice, keyboards and Webcams. Its stylish site has all the details and makes it easy to compare products.

Typing Injury FAQ

http://www.tifaq.com/

Sore hands? Aching wrists? The Typing Injury FAQ advises you on the proper arrangement of your desk, chair, keyboard and screen. It also covers alternative keyboards and pointing devices.

SONICblue

http://www.sonicblue.com/

The companies formerly known as S3 and Diamond Multimedia have morphed into SONICblue, purveyor of modems, MP3 players and video recorders. Peruse the products here and purchase music or download free tracks.

Palm

http://www.palm.com/

Is that a handheld in your pocket, or are you just pleased to see me? Admire the latest Palms, inspect the accessories and stock up on software.

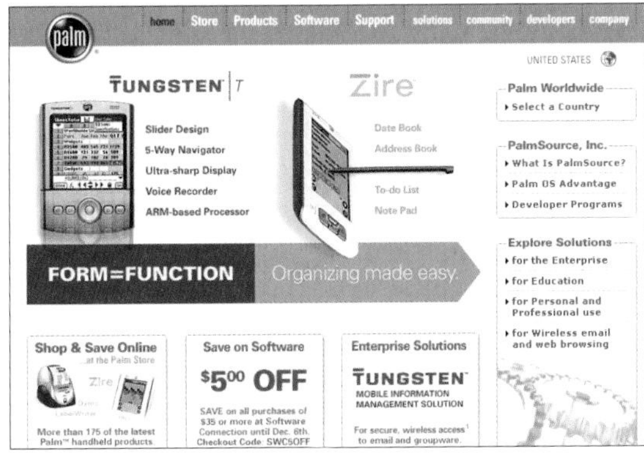

Software

Microsoft

http://www.microsoft.com/

A gigantic site for a titan among companies. Here you will (eventually) find information about all Microsoft's products and programs. If one of your applications is misbehaving, go to the Support section and search the Knowledge Base, a huge database of reported problems and their solutions. You can also visit Bill Gates' personal home page and try to divine the secrets of his success.

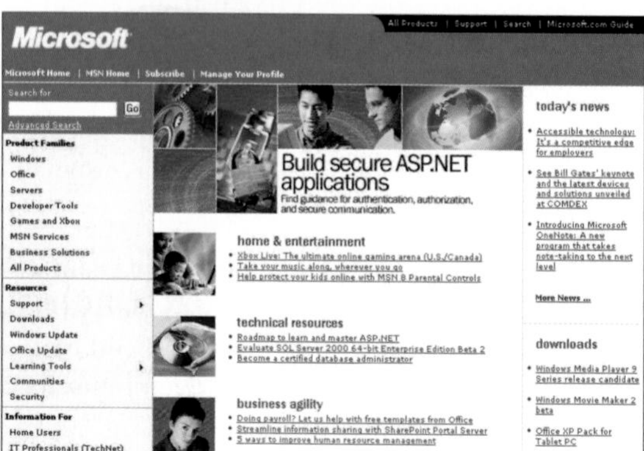

Linux

http://www.linux.com/

Linux is an alternative operating system that can be used in place of Windows. Linux.com provides news and information, an introduction for beginners and links to relevant Web sites. The associated Freshmeat site (http://freshmeat.net/) catalogues Linux software.

LinuxQuestions.org

http://www.linuxquestions.org/

You've got Linux... so now what? Post your questions in the forums on this site and get advice from other Linux users. Topic areas include software, hardware, networking and security.

Adobe

http://www.adobe.com/

Adobe's professional graphics and design programs include Photoshop, Illustrator, PageMaker, GoLive and Premier. Find out more about them, download tryout versions and upgrades, and get tips and advice. This is also the place to come if you need a copy of Acrobat Reader to display PDF files.

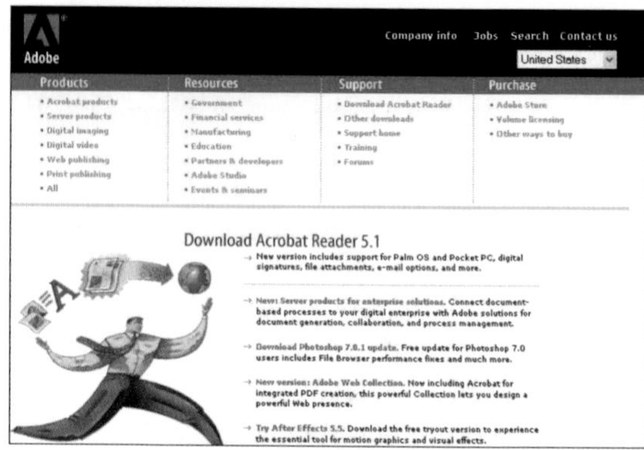

Corel

http://www.corel.com/

Corel produces two big-name applications – CorelDraw Graphics Suite and WordPerfect Office – plus a number of less familiar ones. Its Web site has product information, trial versions, updates and a database of questions and answers. For tips and freebies, click through to its other Web sites, Designer.com (http://www.designer.com) and OfficeCommunity.com (http://www.officecommunity.com/).

Macromedia

http://www.macromedia.com/

On the Internet, Macromedia is best known as the producer of Flash Player and Shockwave Player. In the real world, it produces a range of graphics and Web-design programs, including Dreamweaver, Macromedia Flash (the program used to create Flash animations), Authorware and FreeHand.

Jasc

http://www.jasc.com/

Jasc is best known for Paint Shop Pro, which is available from this site as a trial version or to purchase and download. You can also find out about its other products, download freebies and work through the tutorials in its Learning Center, which covers digital photography, Web design and computer art.

Symantec

http://www.symantec.com/

Symantec produces software that protects and optimises your computer, including antivirus programs and the perennially popular Norton Utilities. If you have a fast connection, you can purchase the programs on-line and download them to your hard disk. If you're concerned about viruses (and who isn't?), visit the Security Response section for details of the latest threats.

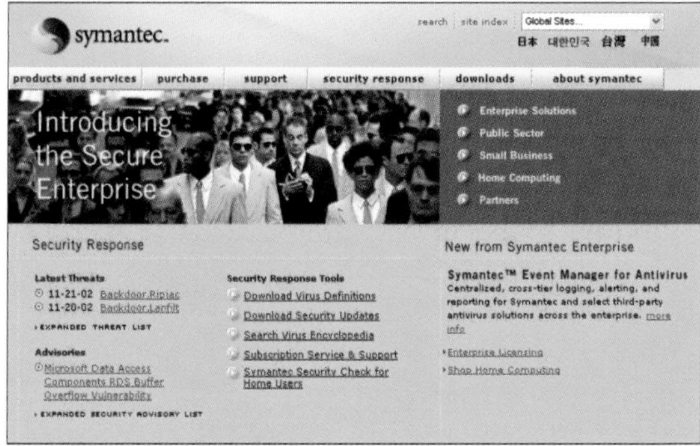

Netscape

http://www.netscape.com/

Netscape's site doesn't focus on software the way it used to, but if you look closely you can still find and download its Web browser and e-mail program.

Nullsoft

http://www.winamp.com/

Join the MP3 generation by downloading Nullsoft's popular (and free) Winamp player. The Web site also has free music, a huge library of skins (add-ons that change Winamp's appearance) and a load of laid-back humour.

Tucows

http://www.tucows.com/

Blown your software budget already? Visit Tucows for over 30,000 freeware and shareware programs, themes, skins and screensavers. The search engine lets you specify your operating system and the programs have brief descriptions and ratings.

Simtel

http://www.simtel.net/

Another shareware and freeware library. The Spotlights area highlights the best programs and there's an intriguing Top 100 list that shows you what other people are downloading.

Download.com

http://download.com.com/

Brought to you by CNET Networks, this site has all manner of downloadable software, from demos of commercial programs to shareware and freeware. There's plenty of information and you can browse by program type or search for specific applications.

Screensaver.com

http://www.screensaver.com/

Download Windows eye candy from this site, which not only features screen savers but also desktop themes – coordinated wallpapers, icons, cursors and sounds. Some are free, others are shareware.

1001 Free Fonts

http://www.1001fonts.com/

Free fonts for Windows and Mac, sorted by style: calligraphic, decorative, dingbat, graffiti, hard to read, retro and so on. Each font has a preview page showing all the letters and numbers.

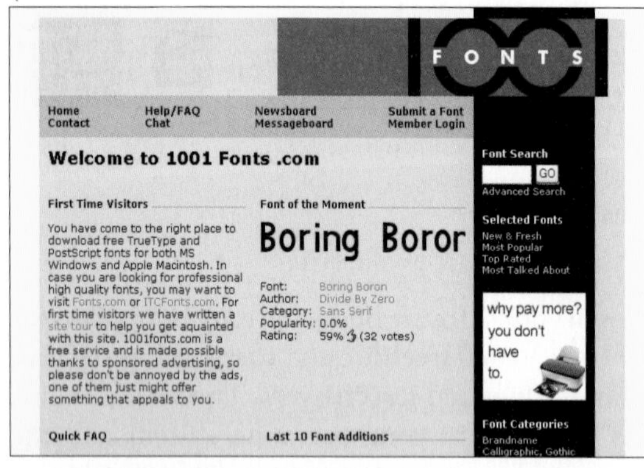

Computer games

Happy Puppy

http://www.happypuppy.com/

Long-standing games site that covers all the major platforms, from humble handhelds to the shiny new Xbox. It also has a section for Web games with links to oodles of Java, Shockwave and browser games that you can play on-line, right now.

Gamespot

http://gamespot.com/

Very busy and professional site with news, reviews, previews, demos, patches, tips, articles, interviews… everything a gamer could desire, for all the major platforms. You'll need to pay an annual subscription to access all the material, but there's no shortage of free content if you're skint.

PC Gamer

http://www.pcgamer.com/

The Web site of "the world's best-selling PC games magazine" has game reviews and a chart of the top 50 demos. They're available for download, although you'll want a fast connection.

id Software

http://www.idsoftware.com/

Visit the home of Wolfenstein, Doom and Quake, the first-person shoot-'em-ups that have rampaged round the globe, bringing terms such as 'frag' and 'bfg' to previously sedate offices. id's site has the lowdown on all its games, from its very first efforts (anyone remember Commander Keen?) to its latest blockbusters, with demos and updates for the more recent titles.

Electronic Arts

http://www.ea.com/

EA publishes gazillions of games for PC, PlayStation, Nintendo and Xbox. Titles you've probably heard of include Sim City and The Sims, Need for Speed and Command & Conquer. It also produces film tie-ins for the likes of the James Bond and Harry Potter movies and sports games featuring everything from football and basketball to snowmobile racing. In short, whatever type of game you like, you'll find information, demos and tips here.

Sierra

http://www.sierra.com/

Sierra's titles range from the explosive Half-Life to the family-friendly Incredible Machine. Most games have their own Web sites, which you can reach from the Sierra home page.

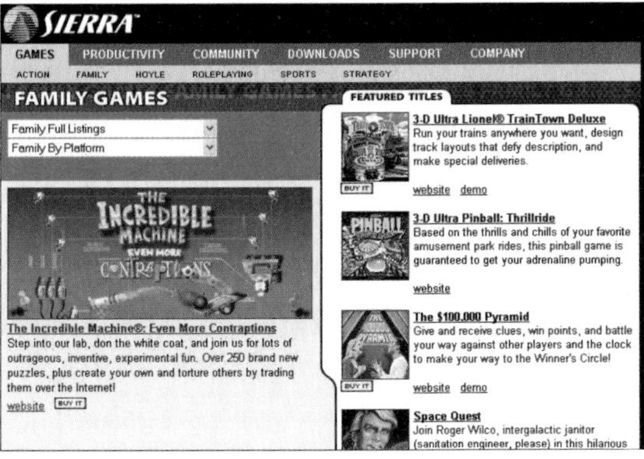

LucasArts

http://www.lucasarts.com/

Get your *Star Wars* games here, basically. LucasArts makes the odd diversion into other areas with the likes of Indiana Jones games and sword-and-toga epic Gladius, but *Star Wars* spin-offs dominate its range. If you're struggling, visit the Support section and put your questions to Yoda.

PlayStation

http://www.playstation.com/

The PlayStation Web site has news, game details, hardware specifications and forums, all wrapped up in an animated interface.

Xbox

http://www.xbox.com/

Find out what's happening with Xbox hardware and games, then visit the Xbox Live section to learn how to play games over the Internet. There's also a community area where you can chat about specific games or general Xbox issues.

ClassicGaming

http://www.classicgaming.com/

Hankering after the games of your youth? This site explains how to install an emulator and relive the days of the Amstrad CPC, Atari 2600, Apple II and Commodore 64. It also has many arcade games.

Geek things

Useless pages

http://www.go2net.com/useless/

The pages listed here have few aesthetic merits and serve no practical purpose, but they're entertaining in their own useless way.

Complete Guide to Cows

http://userpages.umbc.edu/~dschmi1/text/cow-list.txt

Why settle for a smiley face made out of keyboard characters when you could have an entire cow? Here's the definitive herd.

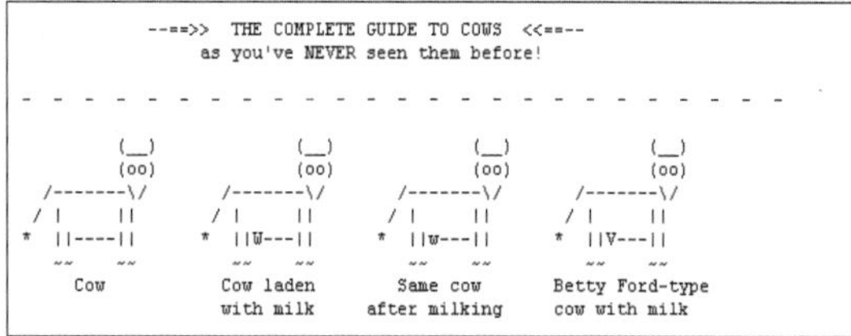

Hamster Dance

http://www.hampsterdance.com/

Very annoying animated hamsters that bop round to a very annoying tune. One of the more inexplicable Internet fads.

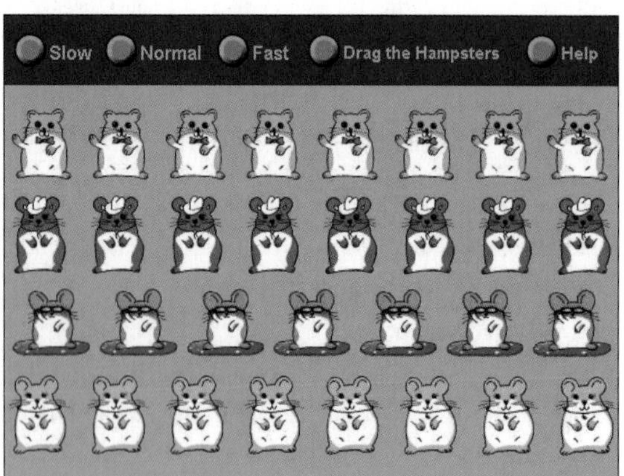

I Kiss You

http://www.ikissyou.org/

The Mahir Cagri phenomenon can't be explained, it simply has to be experienced. This site collects together Mahir-related material, from parodies and games to press articles and links to fan sites. It also provides some background on the amiable Turk who became an Internet celebrity, but don't expect to be much the wiser after reading it.

Dancing baby

http://www.dancing-baby.net/

Take a computer model of a baby, superimpose a cha-cha motion and this is what you get – a surreal animation that toured the Internet and then took on a life of its own. There are all sorts of dancing babies out there now, but this site has the original file.

All Your Base

http://www.planettribes.com/allyourbase/

In the beginning, there was a video game. And the introduction was translated into English, very badly, producing the phrase, 'All your base are belong to us,' which then reappeared on signs, in magazines and adverts, on computers and in other strange places. What does it mean? Nobody knows.

Stick Figure Death Theatre

http://www.sfdt.com/

Tasteless but blackly humorous, Stick Figure Death Theatre is a collection of crudely drawn animations in which people come to sticky ends. There are no surprises – the stick figure always ends up in a pool of red pixels – but it's compulsive viewing.

Science

New Scientist.com

http://www.newscientist.com/

The Web site of *New Scientist* magazine has news and articles, as you might expect. Less predictable material includes The Last Word, a collection of questions about everyday phenomena such as dripping taps and nodding pigeons. There's also a huge directory of recommended science Web sites with detailed write-ups.

Scientific American

http://www.sciam.com/

More science news and features, plus weekly polls and an opportunity to put your questions to the experts. Nanotechnology gets a section of its own, so this a good place to come if you're interested in "a vast grab bag of stuff that has to do with creating tiny things that sometimes just happen to be useful." Bring your magnifying glass.

Discovery

http://www.discovery.com/

The Web site of the Discovery Channel (and its many spin-offs) supplements its programs with multimedia and interactive features. You rarely just read anything – there's almost always something to do, whether it's diving in a virtual submarine, building your own dinosaur, exploring the space station or monitoring the polar bear cam.

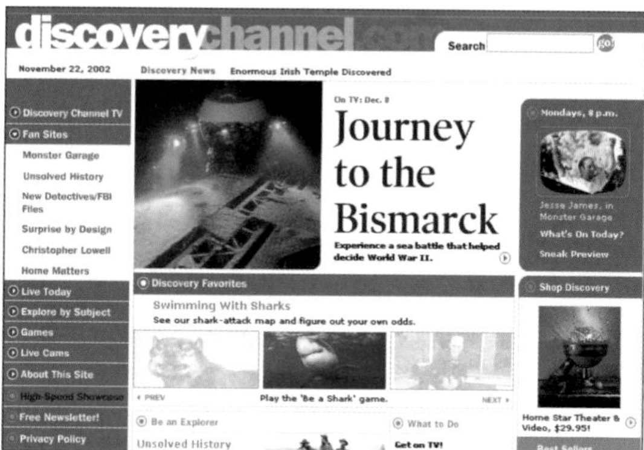

Scientific American Frontiers

http://www.pbs.org/saf/

The *Scientific American Frontiers* doesn't just tell you about the series of science specials hosted by Alan Alda, it enables you to watch them over the Internet. There's hours (literally) of intriguing entertainment here.

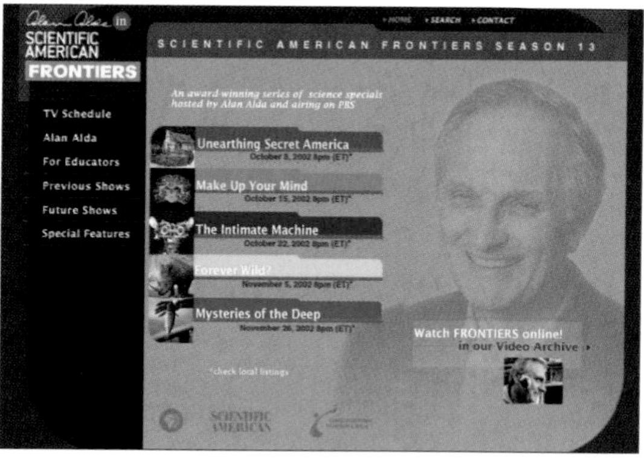

HowStuffWorks

http://www.howstuffworks.com/

Excellent and very popular site that does exactly what it says in the title bar: it explains how stuff works. By 'stuff' it means everything from car engines and computers to tattoos, caffeine and Christmas. The articles are clear and entertaining, with lots of cross references and links to other relevant Web sites.

Bill Nye.com

http://www.billnye.com/

Bill Nye the Science Guy has a sophisticated site with experiments to try at home, miscellaneous interesting facts and a question of the week. The experiments ('demos' in Nye-speak) use everyday household items and don't seem likely to cause cataclysmic explosions in your kitchen.

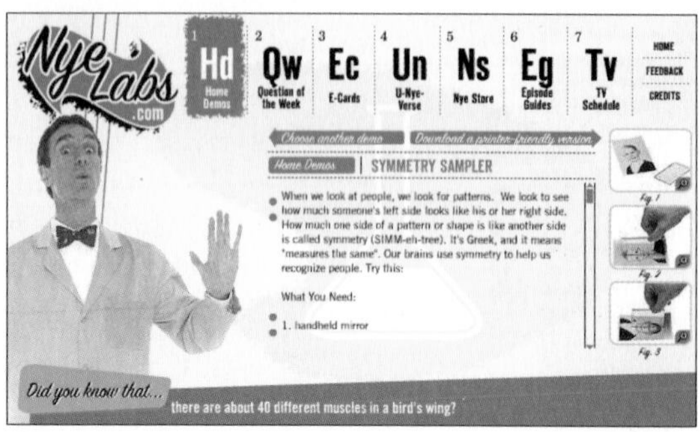

Animal Diversity Web

http://animaldiversity.ummz.umich.edu/

Not much to look out but immensely useful for school projects, the Animal Diversity Web has thousands of articles about animal species, written by university students. They are sorted into a proper taxonomic hierarchy, but you can use the search engine to skip all the Latin and go straight to a page on your favourite beast. As the all-inclusive title suggests, it covers everything from creepy-crawlies to lions, tigers and elephants.

BBC Nature

http://www.bbc.co.uk/nature/

Lots more natural history from the BBC, including a Wildfacts database covering hundreds of animals, a special section on British wildlife, features about pets, live Webcams, electronic postcards and information about all its nature programmes.

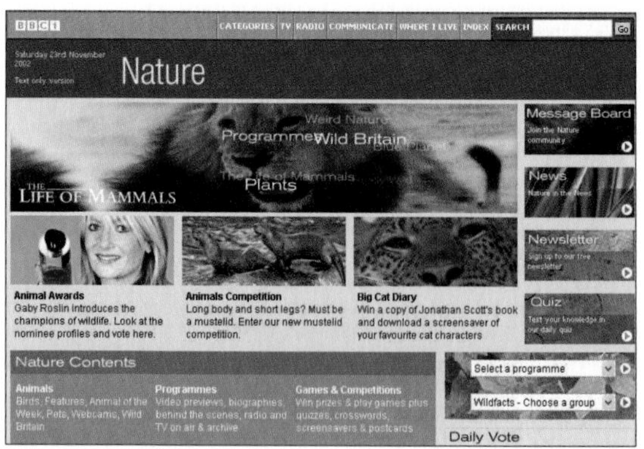

The Why Files

http://whyfiles.org/

The Why Files explains the science behind the news, in detail but without using too many big words. Accessible and even humorous, it adds a new feature every week. The front page also points you back to stories that are relevant to this week's events and you can browse the archive by topic or search for particular subjects.

Physics Central

http://www.physicscentral.com/

$E=mc^2$ and all that. This whiz-bang Web site is brought to you by the American Physics Society and has sections for physics in action, people in physics, physics pictures and physics news. The authors attempt to keep everything on a layperson's plane, although the odd technical term creeps in.

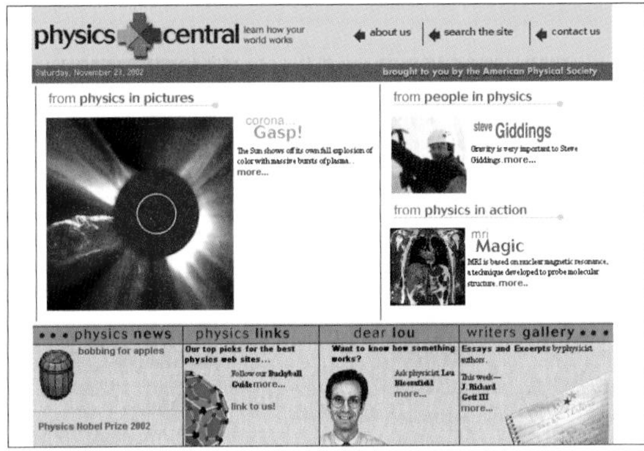

NASA

http://www.nasa.gov/

Don't be put off by the dull appearance of the NASA home page. From here you can click through to the space agency's more dynamic subsites. The Human Space Flight site (http://spaceflight.nasa.gov/) is the highlight, with information about every manned flight from the first Mercury mission to the latest Shuttle and Space Station adventures. The Gallery has photographs and videos and you can tune into NASA's own TV channel for 24-hour coverage of missions and other activities.

Space.com

http://www.space.com/

When you get done at NASA's site, Space.com promises "something amazing every day". It has space news, science and astronomy features and a Space Views section with image galleries, desktop wallpaper, screensavers and electronic postcards.

A.L.I.C.E. AI Foundation

http://www.alicebot.org/

Chat with A.L.I.C.E., twice the winner of the Loebner Prize for artificial intelligence. To win, the chatterbot had to sustain a typed conversation with the judges. Only one person confused 'her' with a human, and once you've indulged in a surreal conversation with the artificial entity, you'll realise 'she' still needs to work on her social skills.

Robots.net

http://robots.net/

Useful resource for robotics enthusiasts, with links to articles from around the Web and a Robomenu where you can show off your creations.

Cool Robot of the Week

http://ranier.hq.nasa.gov/telerobotics_page/coolrobots.html

This NASA Web site links you to a new robotics Web site every week. Since the NASA people actually know something about robots, the choices are generally interesting. They aren't sniffy about amateur projects, either, including everything from Lego bots to university and commercial projects.

Entertainment

As well as being entertaining in its own right, the Internet also has lots of information about real-world amusements. Find out about the latest movies, check up on the music world, see what's on the box, read about books, view art and find something to laugh about.

What's on

Whatsonwhen.com

http://www.whatsonwhen.com/

What's on. And when. And where, which is just as important, especially given that this site covers the globe. If you're feeling practical, choose your country or city (or the place you're about to visit). Those with money to burn can pick a theme and a date, then call their travel agents with instructions.

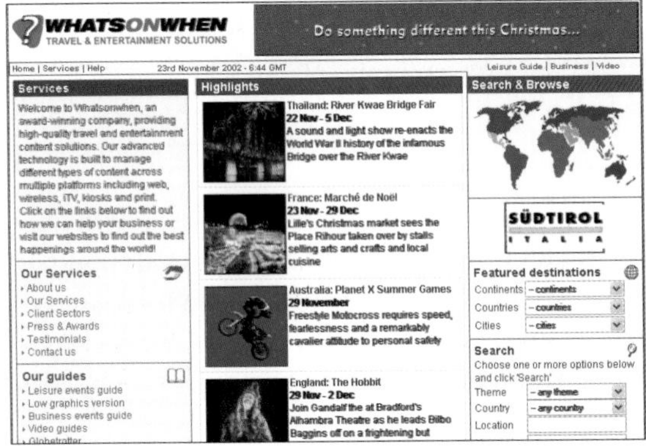

Festivals.com

http://www.festivals.com/

Festivals.com catalogues festivals and celebrations around the globe. It has subsections for arts, kids, motor, music, sports and cultural events, with features to get you enthused before you peruse the listings. You can also search for events by country.

Time Out

http://www.timeout.com/

The Time Out Web site has guides to over 30 cities, with reviews of restaurants, bars, cafés, hotels and shops, plus a roundup of the month's events. If you're still stuck for something to do, follow the links to local Web sites for each city.

Ticketmaster

http://www.ticketmaster.com/

Ticketmaster sells tickets for concerts, shows and sporting events in North America, the UK, Ireland, the Netherlands, Norway and Australia. Events are sorted into categories and the most popular ones are highlighted. Listings have information about both the event and the venue, including seating plans, and you can purchase tickets on-line.

Aloud.com

http://www.aloud.com/

Aloud.com sells tickets for gigs, concerts and festivals. You can search by artist, location or genre, but you have to know what you want to see because there's no information about the events. An on-line ticket tracker helps you find out what has happened to your precious scraps of paper.

Ticketek.com

http://www.ticketek.com/

Ticketek covers Australia, New Zealand, Hong Kong and Argentina. It sells tickets for concerts, performances, sporting events and festivals and provides information about both the events and the venues. Tickets can be purchased on-line and in Australia you can even purchase electronic tickets for some events – instead of queuing up at the box office, you print your own ticket.

Sistic

http://www.sistic.com.sg/

Sistic sells tickets for events taking place in Singapore. You can search by event name, venue or month, or browse the categorised listings.

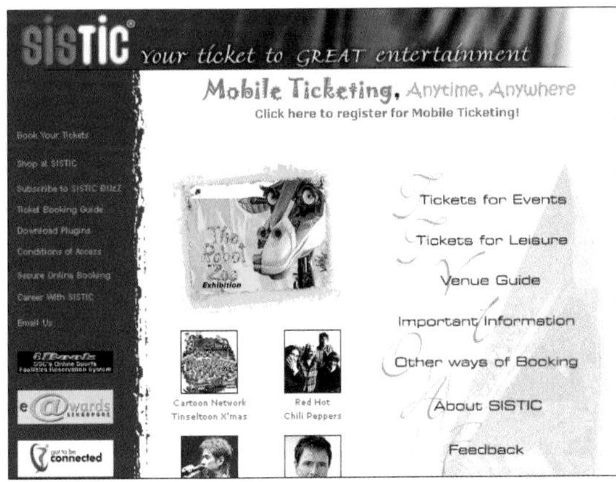

Artslink.co.za

http://www.artslink.co.za/

Artslink.co.za has arts news, a show database and a visual arts diary for South Africa. Navigate carefully, because it has links to two different ticketing sites.

Computicket

http://www.computicket.com/

South Africa's Computicket site lets you book tickets for the cinema and for live events. You can also buy bus tickets – handy if you need to travel.

General sites

Entertainment Weekly

http://www.ew.com/ew/

Like the magazine, the Entertainment Weekly Web site has something for everyone. It covers movies, videos, DVDs, television, music, books and popular culture. Check out the box office and television charts to find out what Americans are watching and text your hipness with the pop quizzes.

People.com

http://people.aol.com/people/

People.com deals with the famous and the beautiful. It has lots of profiles and photographs, a fashion section and the answers to questions such as who had the best and worst hair in 2002.

E! Online

http://www.eonline.com/

E! Online is entertaining about the entertainment scene, with smartly presented news, features, reviews and gossip. Don't miss the Fun & Games section, where you'll find gems such as the 'N Sync-erator, a tricky jigsaw puzzle that requires you to distinguish one member of the boy band from another.

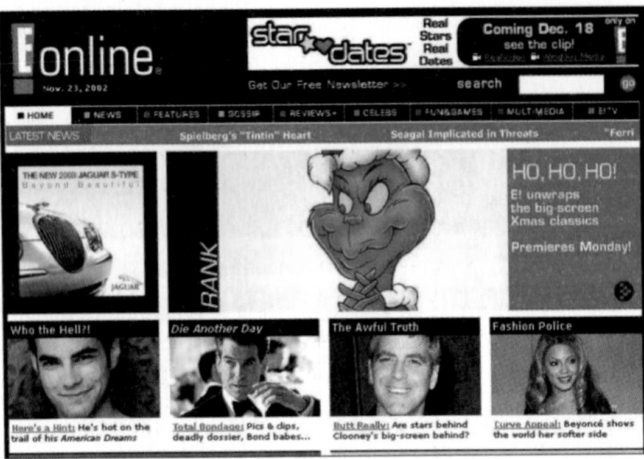

ScoopMe!

http://www.scoopme.com/

ScoopMe! is another fun site that uses snappy design and opinionated writing to encourage you to read its movie and television reviews. If you disagree with the comments, you can "rant, rave, mock, talk, gossip, and more" in the site's forums.

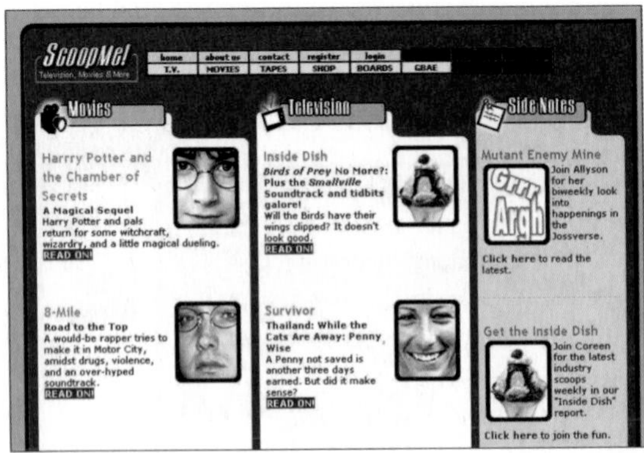

Movies

Internet Movie Database

http://www.imdb.com/

The Internet Movie Database (IMDb) is the definitive movie Web site. Here you'll find everything your film-loving heart desires, from cast lists and synopses to trivia and goofs to links to reviews from all around the Web. It also covers television, although not with quite the same attention to every minor detail.

Ain't It Cool News

http://www.aintitcool.com/

Obsession takes another form at Ain't It Cool News, where the red-headed Harry Knowles dishes the dirt on Hollywood. This is where you'll find rumours about scripts, comments from test screenings and stills from yet-to-be-released movies, bundled up with Harry's take-no-prisoners commentary and LOTS OF CAPITAL LETTERS.

Leonard Maltin's Movie Crazy

http://www.leonardmaltin.com/

At the opposite end of the spectrum, well-known movie critic Leonard Maltin offers measured opinions on new films and DVDs. His journal offers further commentary on the movie business and he includes some personal photographs.

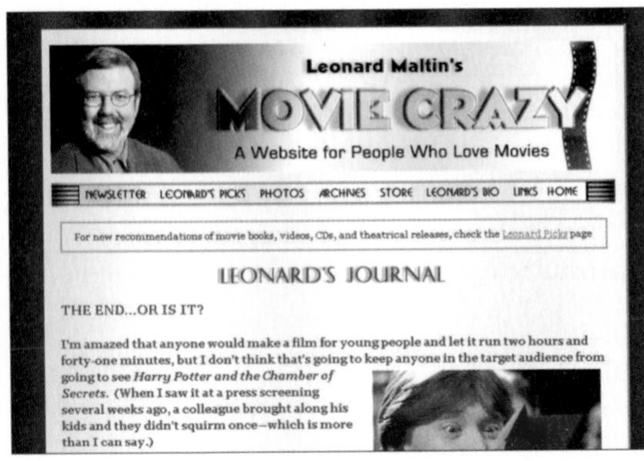

Hollywood.com

http://www.hollywood.com/

US movie site with news, features, reviews and trailers. There's a calendar showing the films that are due out over the next few months, a Top 5 list of recommended movies and a box-office chart. If you purchase a subscription, you can also watch independent films over the Internet.

Movies.com

http://movies.go.com/

More movie news, more reviews. If you don't feel like reading, you can listen to audio reviews by Robert Ebert and Richard Roeper. Other interesting features include the Buzz Bin, which lists the 20 hottest upcoming movies.

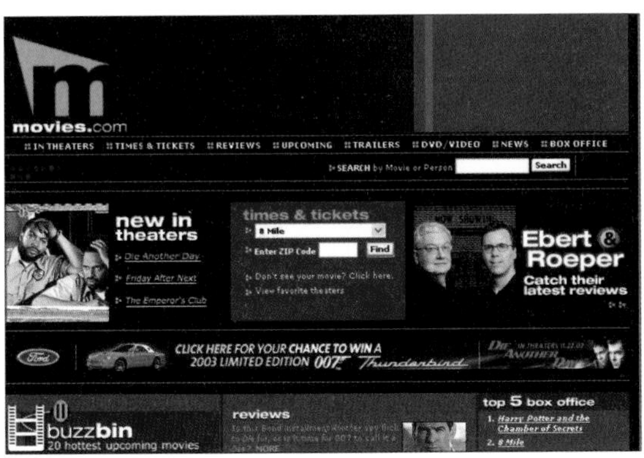

Premiere

http://www.premiere.com/

US film magazine *Premiere* concentrates on reviews. There's also a little bit of gossip about films currently in production, a collection of features and a daily poll. Who was the best Bond? Sean Connery, said 70 per cent of visitors.

Film Unlimited

http://film.guardian.co.uk/

The Guardian's film site has the usual news and reviews, plus interviews (and interview transcripts) and a Brits in Film section with brief biographies. Fun features include a Mood Matcher that selects films for such occasions as, "When you're learning to drive," and, "When the planet's being invaded." The Games section has light-hearted quizzes.

Empire Online

http://www.empireonline.co.uk/

Popular British film mag *Empire* has a vast Web site with lots of reviews, a Future Films section that tracks the progress of the most eagerly awaited movies and a set of buying guides that help you fill out your DVD collection. Premieres get in-depth coverage and you can relieve the highs and lows of recent years with its annual reviews.

Movie Mafia

http://www.moviemafia.com.au/

Find out what's happening in Australian cinemas (and on television) with Movie Mafia, a local publication that gives extra screen inches to the likes of Nicole Kidman and Russell Crowe. It has lots of gossip (both in the Gossip section and elsewhere) and plenty of opinions.

Miramax Cafe

http://www.miramax.com/

These days if it doesn't have a Web site, it isn't really a movie. The Miramax site provides easy access to information about the films it is distributing. Each film gets brief cast and crew details and a synopsis. You can usually view the trailer as well.

Dreamworks SKG

http://www.dreamworks.com/

Catch the trailers for Dreamworks movies and find out what's coming out on DVD and video. The studio seems to put almost as much effort into its Web sites as it does into its films, so expect lots of animated presentations and special effects.

Walt Disney Pictures

http://disney.go.com/disneypictures/

Find out what's coming next from Disney and watch the trailers, then extend the movie experience with on-line games and downloadable screensavers.

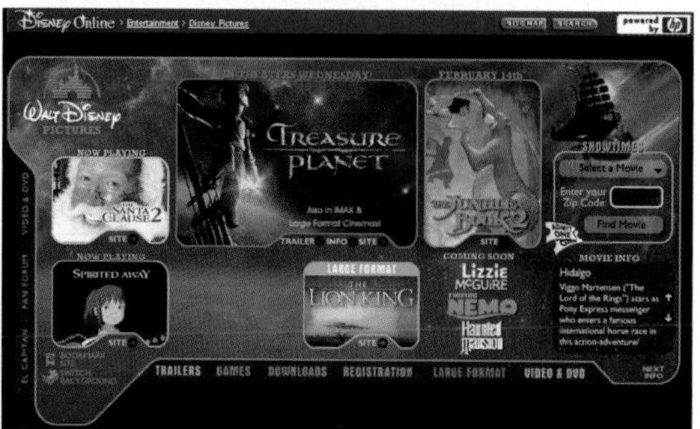

QuickTime Movie Trailers

http://www.apple.com/trailers/

There are lots of sites that have movie trailers, but Apple's is the best option when want to cut to the chase. It's a no-muss, no-fuss site that just lists the trailers by studio, then lets you play them. Most come in several sizes, so you can choose something appropriate to your connection speed.

Drew's Script-O-Rama

http://www.script-o-rama.com/

Find out what your favourite character actually said with Drew's Script-O-Rama, which links you to scripts and transcripts from around the Web. If you can't face all those words, try the Haiku page for the short versions of popular films.

Oscar.com

http://www.oscar.com/

The official site of the Academy Awards has everything you love about the Oscars – the films, the frocks, the small gold men – and everything you hate – including the speeches. Come here first when you're looking for nominations or results.

Sundance

http://www.sundance.org/

Start here for the official sites of both the film-making institute and the festival.

Music

Music Newswire

http://www.vh1.com/news/newswire/

VH1's newswire brings you the top stories, features and reviews from the top music news sites around the Web. It's a convenient one-stop shop for the latest in pop.

Rolling Stone

http://www.rollingstone.com/

Rolling Stone's Web site feels very much like a magazine, with all the current features and reviews listed on the front page and everything else stored neatly in categorised archives. The distinctive and magazine-ish page layout also sets the site apart and makes the articles easy to read. Don't miss the Photos section, which has lots of stylish images.

Ultimate Band List

http://www.ubl.com/

Everything you ever wanted to know about every band in the world... probably. Read a brief account of your favourite solo artist or group, peruse their greatest (and not so greatest) albums, listen to songs and follow the links to official and unofficial Web sites. It also lists related artists, although you have to work out the relationships yourself.

MTV.com

http://www.mtv.com/

Like the television channel, MTV.com brings you popular music, 24 hours a day. There's music to download, videos to watch and a fantasy music game to play, plus music news and a database of bands. You can also get the lowdown on shows such as *Celebrity Deathmatch* and *The Osbournes*.

dotmusic

http://www.dotmusic.com/

dotmusic is a UK-based electronic magazine with news, reviews, features and interviews, plus official charts with commentary and sound clips. You can access the material by genre, making it easy to get your fill of pop, dance, indie, rock, hip hop, soul and R&B and classical music.

Q4music.com

http://www.q4music.com/

Although it sounds like a place where you can join a long line of people waiting for free CDs or concert tickets, Q4music.com is actually the on-line edition of the UK's *Q* magazine. Novelty features include polls, a Listomania section with essential dozens and celebrity record collections and a Ringtones area that lets you arm your mobile phone with annoying electronic versions of the latest hits.

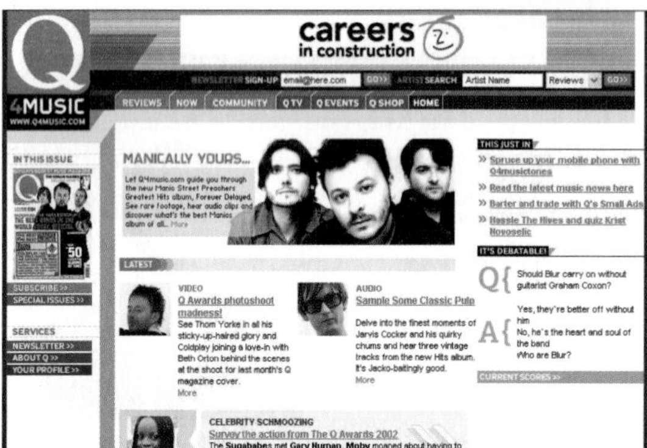

BBC Radio 1

http://www.bbc.co.uk/radio1/

Check out the Official UK Top 40 Singles Chart, then listen to the entire countdown over the Internet. You can listen to other Radio 1 shows, too – at your convenience rather than in their normal time slots – and a selection of documentaries. The One Music section has advice for aspiring musos.

Juice

http://www.juice.net/

Australian mag *Juice* squeezes the music industry and separates the pith (news and gossip) from the fresh juice (reviews and features) to create a healthy cocktail of world and Australian stories.

NoiZyland

http://www.noizyland.com/

NoiZyland covers the New Zealand indie music scene. It also has lots of links to other New Zealand music sites, so it's a good place to start even if your tastes run more to jazz or classical. The Reviews and Interviews sections catalogue all the material published about New Zealand artists, with links to the source Web sites.

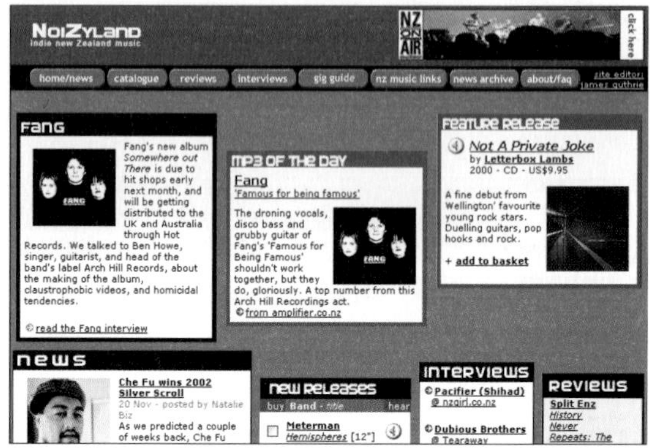

Vivamusic.com

http://www.vivamusic.com/

Vivamusic.com covers the Asian music market, with separate sections for pop, j-pop, dance, k-pop, South East Asian music and others (classical, jazz, new age and so on). It also covers events taking place in its real-world store/venue in Singapore.

Essentials of Music

http://www.essentialsofmusic.com/

Start getting your head around classical music with the Essentials of Music site, which is built around Sony's Essential Classics series of discs. The site provides overviews of the six main eras of music, with information about the composers and examples of their music that you can listen to on-line.

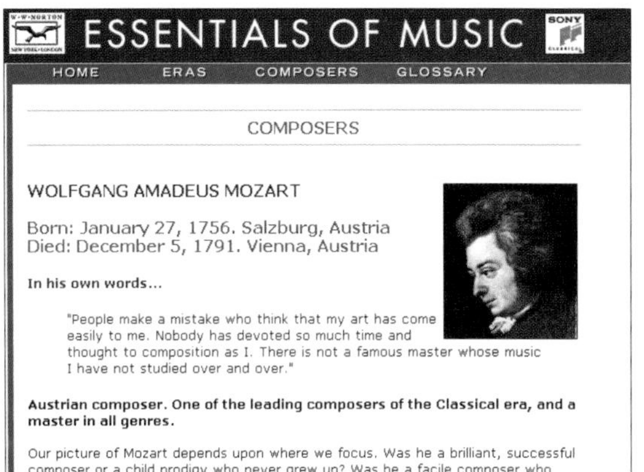

Classical Net

http://www.classical.net/

Unattractive but informative site with reviews of over 2,400 discs, advice on building a collection of classical music, lists of recommended discs and links to over 4,000 other classical music sites.

Jazz Online

http://www.jazzonline.com/

This long-standing jazz site has reviews, artist Q&As and a Jazz 101 section that introduces the main styles and recommends discs. If you still have questions, put them to the Jazz Messenger. A quick trawl through the archives reveals the answers to everything from, "Do you think 'smooth jazz' or 'contemporary jazz' is really jazz?" to, "Why did they call Charlie Parker 'Bird'?"

SOHH.com

http://www.sohh.com/

SOHH.com specialises in hip hop. Check out The Wire for the latest news, or The Core for in-depth articles. It also has forums where you can rant, rap and generally express your opinions.

MP3.com

http://www.mp3.com/

MP3.com introduces you to the world of MP3 music with software and hardware guides and reviews and lots of music to listen to or download. Top 40 charts reveal the most popular tracks of the day, overall or by genre.

Television

TV Guide Online

http://www.tvguide.com/

TV Guide's listings are only useful if you live in North America (or assorted Central and South American countries), but since many American shows make their way to other countries, the news, gossip and features are still worth reading. The ShowGuide section covers hundreds of programmes (including programmes produced outside the US), with overviews, episode guides and links to features and old cover images.

TV Land

http://www.tvland.com/

TVLand is a funky site covering classic American shows such as *All In The Family, The Brady Bunch* and *Taxi*. You'll find episode guides, details of the actors and characters, and sounds and pictures. The site also has theme tunes, 'retromercials' (old commercials) and interviews with TV legends.

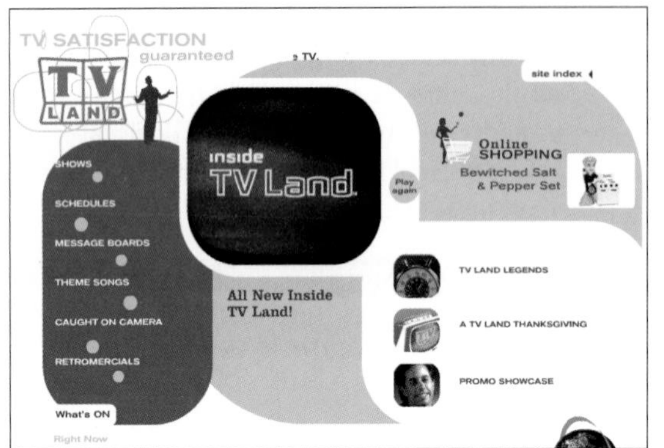

Television Without Pity

http://www.televisionwithoutpity.com/

Television Without Pity (TWoP to its friends) provides biting recaps of popular US shows such as *Angel, CSI, Six Feet Under* and *The West Wing*. Part episode guide and part review, the recaps are often funnier than the programmes themselves.

epguides.com

http://epguides.com/

Find out what you missed with episode guides for over 500 shows and episode lists (titles and air dates) for 1,500 more. Plot summaries are brief but you get the general gist of each episode.

BBCi

http://www.bbc.co.uk/

The BBC's Web site is organised by topic: Business & Money, Children's, Education, Entertainment and so on. There's also an A-Z of programme sites that enables you to go straight to the page for your favourite show. There's an enormous amount of everything here, from character guides and video clips to on-line games, recipes and instructions for decorating your home. If the BBC makes a programme about it, there'll be information here.

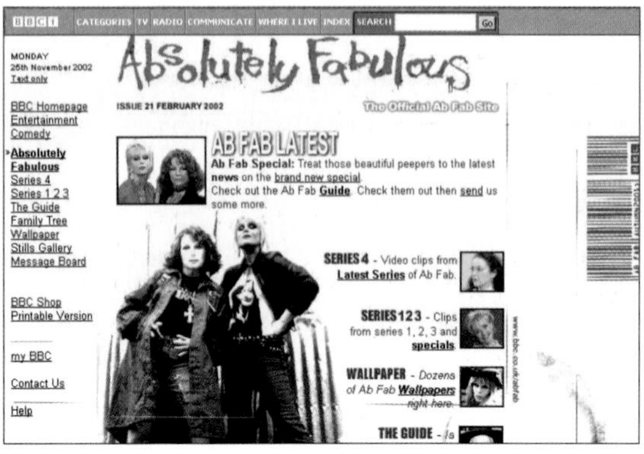

Channel 4

http://www.channel4.co.uk/

The UK's Channel 4 can't compete with the BBC, but it makes a valiant effort, providing on-line support for its own shows and also for the programmes it imports. Get the word on everything from the lowbrow *Big Brother* to the archeological *Time Team* to Mesh, its digital animation scheme. It also has listings for the current week.

thecustard.tv

http://www.thecustard.tv/

Thecustard.tv is an independent site aimed at "young, intelligent, selective television viewers". It lists the programmes that are worth watching, day by day, with Top Ten lists for people who really can't be bothered to make their own choices. Rhubarb Rhubarb reviews the previous week and The Crumble serves up crunchy quotes and other memorable moments. The name comes from rhyming slang: custard and jelly, telly.

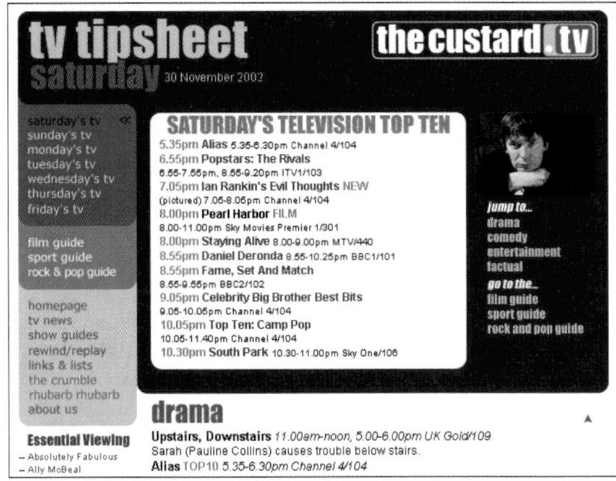

DigiGuide

http://www.digiguide.com/

DigiGuide is a Windows program that enables you to download programme information and create customised listings for the UK and Ireland or the United States. You can also purchase a version for handheld PCs or simply view the listings on-line.

Sofcom TV Guide

http://www.sofcom.com.au/tv/

Australian couch potatoes can find out what's on at the Sofcom site, which lets you create complete listings or focus on particular genres. It also has programme information and television gossip.

NZOOM OnTV

http://ontv.nzoom.com/

NZoom's OnTV section has schedules for New Zealand's five channels. It also has a handful of features, the latest TV ratings and links to other sites that cover New Zealand television.

MediaCorp TV

http://www.mediacorptv.com/

Singapore's MediaCorp TV is responsible for four television channels: Channel 5, Channel 8, Suria and Central. Its Web site provides daily highlights, biographies of MediaCorp artists and an electronic programme guide.

SABC Television

http://www.sabctv.co.za/

SABC's site has listings for SABC 1, 2 and 3, viewable up to seven weeks in advance. Select the individual channels for information about new and popular shows and behind the scenes details.

ER

http://www.ertv.co.uk/

Most popular TV shows have their own Web sites and some have more than one. The official UK site for medical drama *ER* has cast and episode guides, panoramic images of the sets, a screensaver and a glossary of those incomprehensible medical terms, wrapped up in an all-singing animated interface.

The West Wing

http://www.warnerbros.com/web/westwingtv/

Warner Bros promotes popular drama *The West Wing* with the usual mixture of cast details, episode guides and background material. You can watch a few interviews in the Theater section and there's a weekly poll on issues from the show.

Coronation Street

http://www.coronationstreet.co.uk/

The popular UK soap has an entertaining site with UK and international episode guides and gossip about upcoming developments. There's a Who's Who section for those who don't know their Curly Watts from their Mike Baldwin and fans can chat about the show in the forums.

Neighbours

http://www.neighbours.com/

The Web site for Australia's most famous soap covers the history of the show and its stars – most notably the box-and-girl-next-door combo of Kylie Minogue and Jason Donovan – and provides episode and character guides. You can also peek behind the scenes or download screensavers and wallpaper.

Star Trek

http://www.startrek.com/

Rumours that the Internet was created solely for the benefit of *Star Trek* fans have yet to be confirmed, but there's certainly no shortage of *Trek* sites. This is the official one, with information about all the different series and films, character bios, photos, videos, games, a technology library, a database of foods eaten around the *Star Trek* universe and an opportunity to question some of the characters. It's truly Trekkie in scope.

Theatre

Broadway.com

http://www.broadway.com/

Broadway.com has the buzz, the star bios, the interviews, the reviews and the tickets for shows on Broadway and in London. You can also put your own questions to various actors and read the replies, which are published on the site.

Playbill On-line

http://www.playbill.com/

The on-line edition of *Playbill* isn't pretty, but it gives you plenty to read. It has theatre news from around the world, listings for the US and London and lots of features, interviews and columns. If you think you know a lot about theatre, try the quizzes.

Whatsonstage.com

http://www.whatsonstage.com/

Whatsonstage.com covers the UK theatre scene, including drama, music and dance. It has listings and seating plans, details of opening and closings, and reviews of West End, fringe and regional performances. Other highlights include a 20 Questions section that profiles leading performers. Once you've looked at the list of recommended performances, you can purchase tickets on-line.

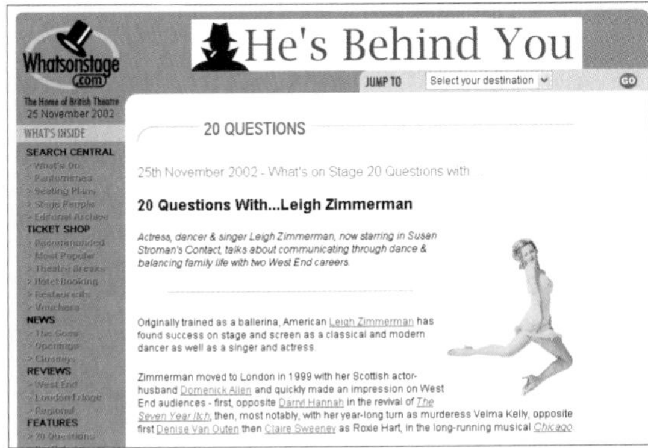

TheatreNet.com

http://www.theatrenet.com/

Also focused on the UK, TheatreNet has a weekly news and gossip column, advice on how to book tickets and where to sit, and a useful collection of theatre links.

ArtLex

http://www.artlex.com/

Make sense of arty jargon with ArtLex, an illustrated art dictionary that defines over 3,000 terms used by artists, art historians, critics and other people who not only know what they like, but also know how to describe it. Some of the entries have expanded into articles with links to relevant works.

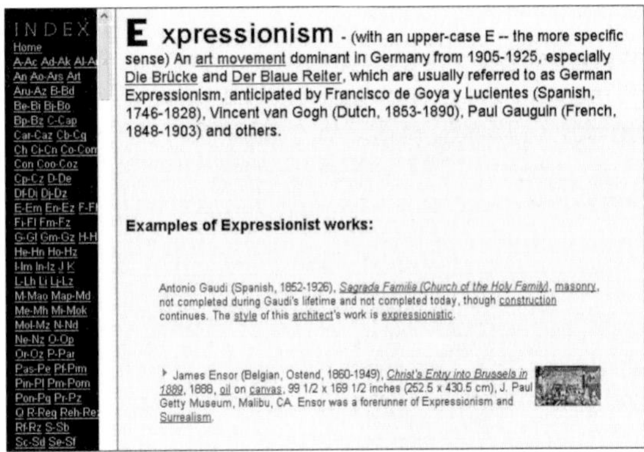

Artonline

http://www.artonline.it/eng/

Italian art site with a History section covering the major artists of the past and a XX Century section for modern works. You can also try your hand at jigsaw puzzles made from works of art or track down the Web sites of the world's major museums and galleries.

Metropolitan Museum of Art

http://www.metmuseum.org/

The highlight of the Met's site is the on-line collection, which features about 3,500 items from the museum. You get 50 highlights from each department plus the entire European paintings collection and you can browse or search by artist, type of work, country of origin, creation date or keyword. The site also has a timeline of art history and information about the museum.

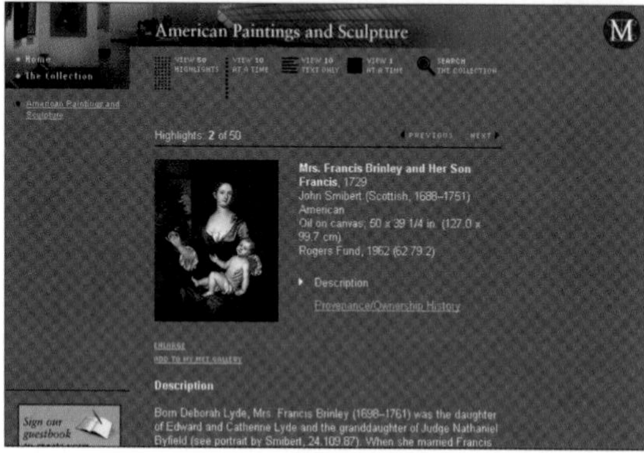

Museum of Modern Art

http://www.moma.org/

New York's Museum of Modern Art (MoMA) also shares its collection on-line. Selected items from the six departments – architecture and design, drawing, film and media, painting and sculpture, photography and prints and illustrated books – are available for browsing. Most have commentary so you can appreciate their place in the art world.

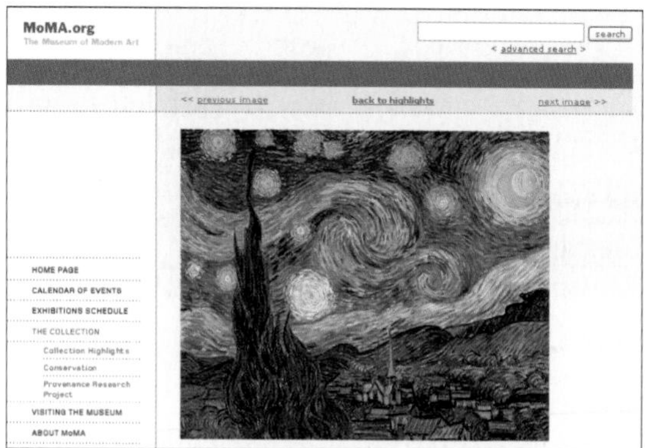

National Gallery

http://www.nationalgallery.org.uk/

The UK's National Gallery presents 12 of its most famous works on-line. You can view them all together, or by artist or time period, but after a while you'll get bored. That's when you should click across to the Full Collection Index, where you'll find all the other artworks, sorted by artist, with commentary and good-sized reproductions. The site also has beginner's guides that explains some of the stories and subjects depicted in the paintings.

Tate

http://www.tate.org.uk/

The Tate collects British art from 1500 to the present day and modern art from around the world. Details of all the works in the collection are available on-line, although not all the entries have pictures. Still, you can find out where your favourite items are displayed and go and see them in the flesh. You can also find out what's on at the various galleries.

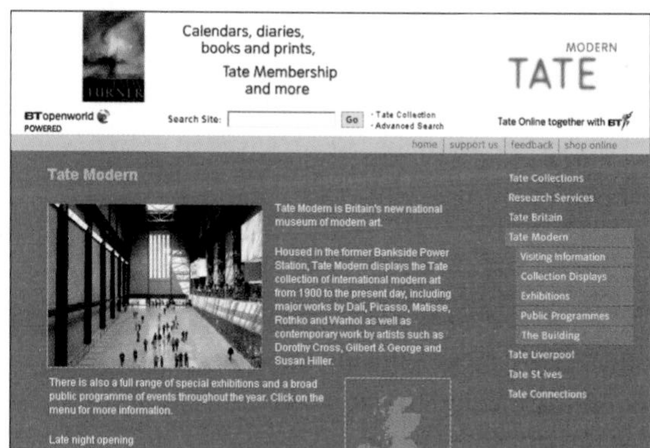

Le Louvre

http://www.louvre.fr/

Le Louvre goes one better than its rivals with a virtual tour featuring 360-degree panoramas that let you spin round inside its galleries. The site also features selected works from the museum's collections of antiquities, sculptures, paintings and drawings – including its most famous work, Leonardo da Vinci's Mona Lisa.

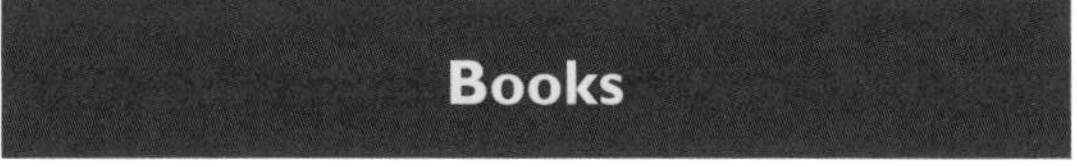

BookBrowser

http://www.bookbrowser.com/

Subtitled "the guide for avid readers", BookBrowser is aimed at those who not only finish the book, but also buy the sequel – or even the entire series. It has Reading Lists sorted by genre and author, enabling you to find all the books about a particular character. If you're looking for something new, you'll also find Best Of... and If You Like This... Try... lists.

Booknotes

http://www.booknotes.org/

The Booknotes site accompanies an author interview programme of the same name that appears on a cable channel in the US. You can read transcripts of the interviews or watch them over the Internet.

ChapterOne

http://www.washingtonpost.com/wp-srv/style/books/chapterone.htm

Why bother with a review when you can simply read the first chapter of a book and see what you think? That's the idea behind *The Washington Post's* Chapter One site, which provides excerpts and initial chapters from recently published works. Most are linked to *The Post's* review, just in case you want a second opinion.

London Review of Books

http://www.lrb.co.uk/

The bimonthly *London Review of Books* carries lengthy and literate book reviews, plus essays and columns. Some articles are only available to subscribers, but there's plenty here for casual visitors as well. If you're looking for literary love, check out the personal ads from the latest edition.

Independent Enjoyment

http://enjoyment.independent.co.uk/books/

The Independent newspaper's Enjoyment section has a user-friendly Books subdivision with literary news, features, interviews and plenty of reviews. Simply run your eye over the list of titles until something takes your fancy.

Project Gutenberg

http://www.gutenberg.net/

Project Gutenberg produces electronic versions of out-of-copyright works and makes them available on-line. If you're looking for classics, you'll find several thousand of them here.

Humour

Comedy Central

http://www.comedycentral.com/

Comedy Central is the home of the badly animated but immensely popular *South Park*. It also broadcasts other comedy shows and stand-up. Find out more here, then waste time in the Time Wasters section, which has jokes, games and interactive toys.

The Onion

http://www.theonion.com/

"America's Finest News Source™" satirises current events. It looks like a newspaper, right down to the datelines and informative graphics, but the stories are… different. Read and enjoy.

Private Eye

http://www.private-eye.co.uk/

The on-line edition of the UK's *Private Eye* replaces the cheap newsprint of the original with tidy Web pages that don't crease or smudge. It offers a selection of jokes, columns and cartoons from the current issue, plus a very small selection of older material.

Comics.com

http://www.comics.com/

Comics.com features over 90 comic strips and editorial cartoons. It has current and recent strips, desktop diversions such as icons and cursors, and assorted other entertainments. The Dilbert and Peanuts sections are the highlights.

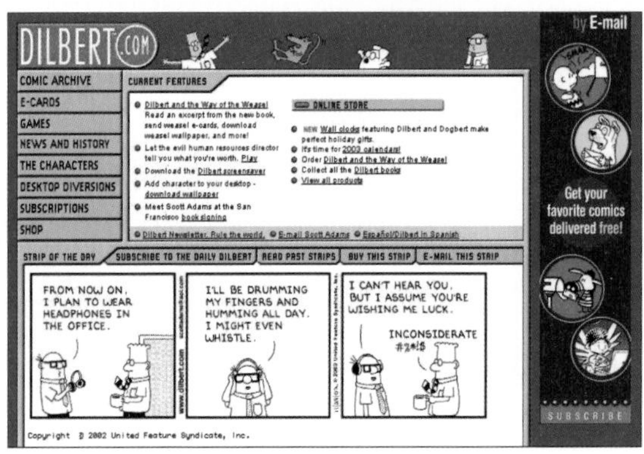

Jokes.com

http://www.jokes.com/

Thousands of jokes, of variable tastefulness and rated for explicitness. Browse them by category – blonde jokes, lawyer jokes and so on – or simply click the Random Joke button for unspecified laughs.

Random Joke Server

http://www.randomjoke.com/

Select your favourite type of joke for a random offering. The Joke Server offers classic one-liners and light bulb jokes as well as jokes for nerds (don't go there) and a Bill Clinton Zippergate section.

Recreation

You know you ought to spend more time doing things and less time in front of the computer... but let's be honest, sometimes it rains and you don't want to go out. And even your indoor projects require some research. The Internet has plenty of sites about sports and pastimes. You can immerse yourself in facts, theories, statistics and plans... and then get more out of your off-line activities.

Food

Epicurious

http://eat.epicurious.com/

Eat, drink and learn at Epicurious. There's a champagne primer and a wine guide, a food dictionary and a set of videos demonstrating everything from the frying of eggs to the zesting of lemons. The star attraction, though, is the recipe collection: over 14,000 of them, browsable by category or searchable by all manner of criteria.

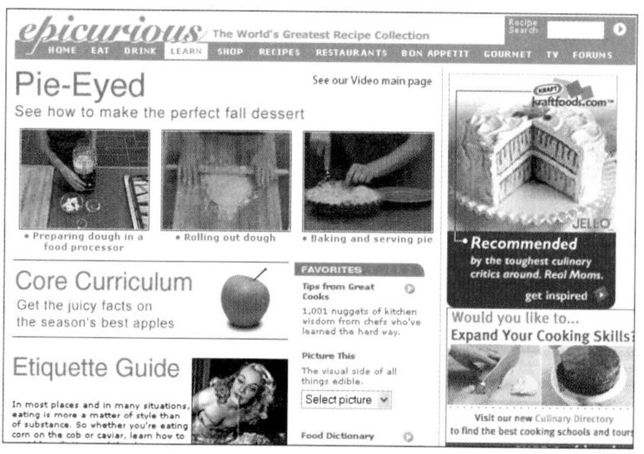

StarChefs

http://starchefs.com/

At StarChefs the cooks are as much of an attraction as the food. Pick a chef, check their bio, read their tips, find out where they work and then – if you like what you've seen so far – try their recipes. It features both restaurant chefs and cookbook authors.

Delia Online

http://www.deliaonline.com/

The egg queen has a cool and collected site with three main sections: Recipes, Ingredients and Cookery school. The last has illustrated guides to cookery techniques, including – of course – instructions for boiling eggs. Once you've got the dinner out of the way, you can read Delia's diary or visit her shop.

BBC Food

http://www.bbc.co.uk/food/

The BBC does food as well and as thoroughly as it does everything else. Here you'll find biographies of its chefs and presenters, Web pages for all its food programmes and a searchable database of recipes. It's left to you to decide whether Rick Stein's Thai Fish Cakes with Green Beans will go with Jamie Oliver's Easiest Sexiest Salad in the World.

All Recipes

http://www.allrecipes.com/

Recipes, recipes and more recipes, by course, ingredient or occasion. If you're overwhelmed by the choice, try the Top Ten section of the Recipe

Index – it lists the best recipes from each of the collections. There's also a Cooking Basics section that tells you what to make and how to make it.

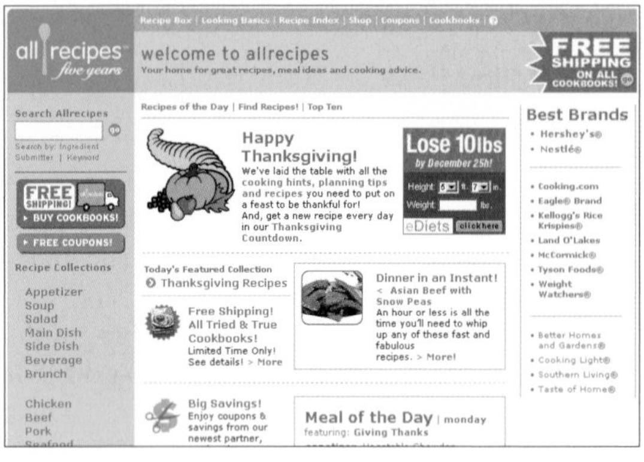

Webicurean

http://www.webicurean.com/

Webicurean makes the most of the Net by linking its articles to material on other sites. It also has forums where you can add comments and recipes.

Messy Gourmet

http://www.messygourmet.com/

Cack-handed and experimental cooks will like Messy Gourmet, a site that proclaims that "cooking is an experience to be savored by all senses… the steam, the aromas, the colors… the mess." Only the articles from the current issue are immediately obvious – check the archives for more.

KidChef

http://www.kidchef.com/

KidChef serves up advice and recipes for younger chefs. The Before You Start section emphasises safety and clearing up afterwards, and the Cooktionary explains all the terms. From there you can proceed to the recipes, which are categorised by type and skill level.

Accidental Scientist

http://www.exploratorium.edu/cooking/

You aren't just making a meal, you're engaged in practical chemistry. The Cooking section of The Accidental Scientist explains the science behind your culinary endeavours. Find out what happens when you bake bread, make a naked egg (!) and learn how smell affects flavour.

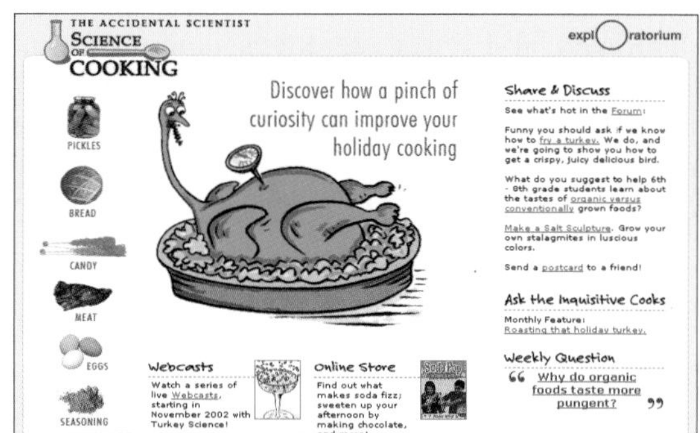

Cook's Thesaurus

http://www.foodsubs.com/

You've got all the ingredients except one – and it's something you've never heard of. Can you use something else instead? The Cook's Thesaurus tells you (and shows you) what things are, then recommends alternatives.

House and garden

iVillage Home & Garden Channel

http://www.ivillage.com/home/

The Home & Garden section of this US megasite covers architecture, home improvement, decorating, crafts and even cleaning and organising. Find out how to place your furniture, choose the right colours for your walls or learn about 20 surprising uses for salt. Sources include *House Beautiful, Country Living* and *Good Housekeeping.*

Channel4.com 4homes

http://www.channel4.com/4homes/

Channel 4's 4homes site explains how to buy, sell and renovate houses in the UK. Learn how to make your home attractive to potential buyers, then read about the area you plan to relocate to. You can also find out how to volunteer for programmes on all these subjects.

This Old House Online

http://www.thisoldhouse.com/toh/

This Old House Online accompanies the US magazine and television series of the same name. It has articles and project guides for doer-uppers, plus useful extras such as materials calculators and discussion forums. For inspiration, look at the section on the houses featured in the television series. You'll find virtual tours, floor plans, timelapse movies and Webcams.

Changing Rooms

http://www.bbc.co.uk/homes/changingrooms/

The Web site of the BBC's budget decorating programme has details of many of the makeovers, with brief instructions to help you recreate the looks. You can also find out about the presenters and even peek into some of their homes.

HomePro.com

http://www.homepro.com/

Find a plumber, painter, paver, pool installer or other tradesperson in the UK, then use the jargon buster to find out what they're talking about. There's also a style magazine with products and projects for everything from the loft to the patio.

Better Homes and Gardens Australia

http://www.bhg.com.au/

The Web site of Australia's *Better Homes and Gardens* magazine has sections for gardening, food, home improvement, craft and better living. Special features include encyclopedias on everything from food and drink to plants, pests and diseases, and DIY. It also has measurement and loan calculators.

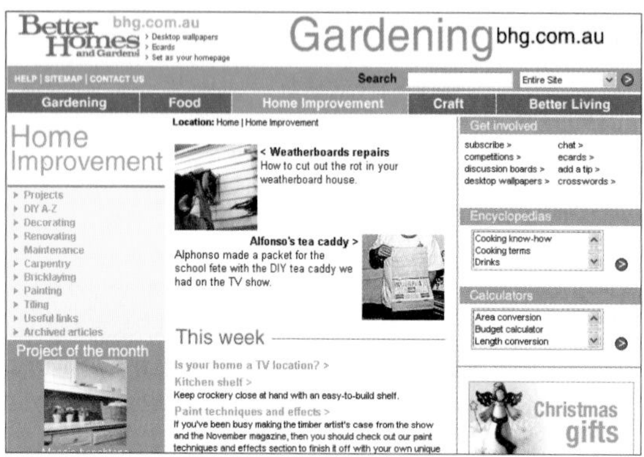

Habitat

http://www.habitat.co.za/

South Africa's *Habitat* magazine covers interior design, art, motoring and wine. Selected articles from recent issues appear on its stylish Web site.

GardenWeb

http://www.gardenweb.com/

The GardenWeb site has lots of resources for gardeners, including a plant database and a botanical glossary, plus over 90 forums covering everything from antique roses and butterfly gardens to tractors and woodlands. Localised versions of the site cater for European and Australasian gardeners.

Garden Advice

http://www.gardenadvice.co.uk/

Find out how to create or renovate a lawn, build and maintain a water garden, or get the best out of your house plants. There's also a special section for kids with projects such as seed collecting and hairy monster pots.

Carry on Gardening

http://www.carryongardening.org.uk/

Carry on Gardening encourages you to keep exercising your green fingers despite accidents, illnesses, disabilities and plain old ageing. It has advice on making your garden accessible plus lots of projects to consider. There's also a Tools section that explains how to use and adapt regular garden implements and reviews specialised tools.

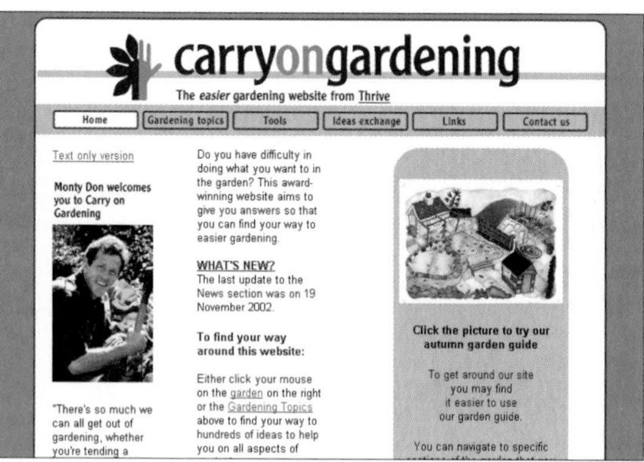

The National Gardens Scheme

http://www.ngs.org.uk/

Find a garden to visit with the NGS's on-line database of UK properties that are open to the public. You can select your county or search by name, opening dates or specific features.

NZ Gardens Online

http://gardens.co.nz/

Find a garden to visit in New Zealand or peruse the articles and advice. There are special sections for roses and native plants and it has links to other Web sites about gardening in New Zealand.

Care for Animals

http://www.avma.org/careforanimals/

The American Veterinary Medical Association has put together an animated site that provides basic advice on selecting and caring for pets. The Kids section has worksheets to print out and complete.

InfoPet

http://www.infopet.co.uk/

The UK-based InfoPet site provides general information and advice about common and uncommon pets, including cats, dogs, chinchillas, hedgehogs and snakes. It also compiles news and research from various sources and has book reviews and a list of useful contacts.

RSPCA

http://www.rspca.org.uk/

The RSPCA's Web site has information about its campaigns, pet-care advice and a Tricky Problems FAQ that explains what to do if you encounter cruelty or find your cat stuck up a tree.

Battersea Dogs' Home

http://www.dogshome.org/

The Battersea Dogs' Home site covers the four Rs: rescue, reunite, rehabilitate and rehome. It mixes information about the home with advice for anyone who has lost their pet or is looking to rehome.

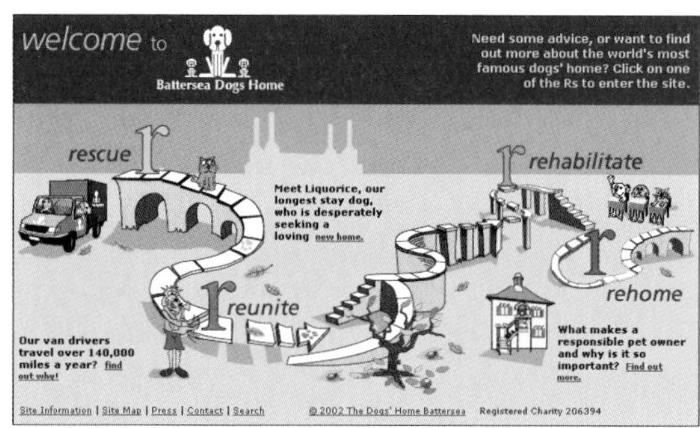

The Dog Hause

http://www.doghause.com/

The Dog Hause is a fun site for pet owners. You won't find much advice here, but it has lots of animal quotes and proverbs, fun facts, clip-art, fonts and sounds. It also has a Spay and Neuter section that encourages pet owners to avoid unwanted litters.

Hobbies

The Genealogy Home Page

http://www.genhomepage.com/

Well-organised collection of links to on-line genealogy resources. The What's Really New section is updated daily.

RootsWeb.com

http://www.rootsweb.com/

Genealogy site that enables you to get in touch with other genealogists and share your findings. It's sponsored by Ancestry.com, a subscription-based reference site. It also has a guide to tracing your family tree, with links to on-line resources.

FamilySearch

http://www.familysearch.org/

The FamilySearch site provides on-line access to genealogical information compiled by The Church of Jesus Christ of Latter-day Saints. Resources include records from the 1880 United States, 1881 British Isles and 1881 Canadian censuses.

Linns.com

http://www.linns.com/

Linns.com is the Web site of the weekly stamp-collecting magazine. It has stamp news, how-to information for beginners and a collection of reference material, including a glossary of philatelic terms. The related Stampsites.com (http://www.stampsites.com/) enables you to search over 15,000 Web pages dealing with stamps.

CoinSite

http://www.coinsite.com/

If you don't fancy stamps, how about coins? CoinSite has a numismatic FAQ covering coins and paper money, reference material, a list of recommended books and an Ask the Coin Doc section that lets you put any remaining questions to the resident expert.

Smithsonian Kids: Collecting

http://kids.si.edu/collecting/

The Collecting section of the Smithsonian's Kids site introduces youngsters to the art of accumulating miscellaneous objects. It explains why people collect things and how to start a collection, then provides information about some of the Smithsonian's collections. It also has video clips in which young collectors show off their booty.

Museum of Dirt

http://www.planet.com/dirtweb/dirt.html

Proof that anything is collectable, the Museum of Dirt dishes up earth and other ground coverings collected from around the world. Some of it comes from famous places, some of it was provided by famous people, and some of it is just dirt.

Classic Stitches

http://www.classicstitches.com/

Classic Stitches magazine has lots of free charts on its Web site, in PDF format. Some are only available to members of the Classic Stitches Club, but it's free to join. There's also a Know How section with guides to needlecraft techniques and a message board where you can discuss your projects with other stitchers.

World Wide Quilting Page

http://ttsw.com/MainQuiltingPage.html

Useful rather than attractive, the World Wide Quilting page has how-to articles, directions and diagrams for lots of traditional quilt blocks, a message board and links to other quilting sites.

Center for the Quilt

http://www.centerforthequilt.org/

More of a looking site than a doing one, the Center for the Quilt Online details various projects to preserve America's quilting heritage. You can read interviews with quiltmakers, view quilts and quilting ephemera and put your questions to the experts.

Pottery Making Illustrated

http://www.potterymaking.org/

The highlight of *Pottery Making Illustrated's* Web site is the Techniques section, which has step-by-step slideshows covering various tasks. There's also a collection of glaze recipes and a small selection of articles from the current issue.

Woodworker's Central

http://www.woodworking.org/

Get chopping, sawing, carving and turning with Woodworker's Central, a vast resource with links to articles and plans from around the Web. It also has tool reviews, book reviews, a sampler with photographs of different woods and a message board.

art-e-zine

http://www.art-e-zine.co.uk/

UK site "for everyone that's interested in playing and having fun with paper, paints, inks and stamps, and any other exciting mediums." Here you'll find tag art (creative luggage labels), collages, art journals, a paper doll gallery and other papery concoctions.

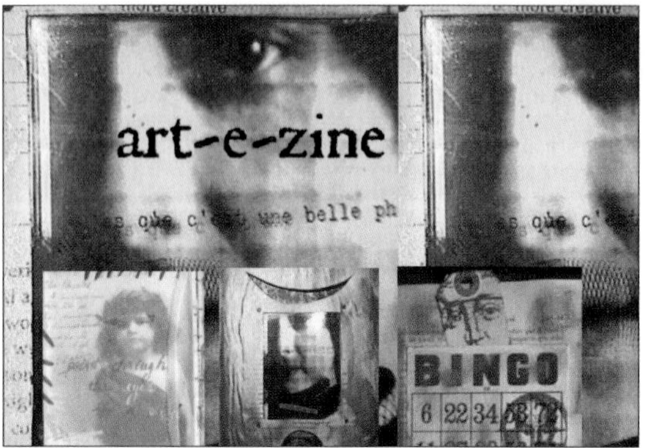

Oriland

http://www.oriland.com/

Novel origami site that displays folded characters and structures in virtual worlds. Instructions for some of the models are available in the Origami Studio. The Learning Center has a guide to origami, an explanation of the symbols and a set of lessons.

Alex's Paper Planes

http://www.paperairplanes.co.uk/

Build yourself a fleet of aeroplanes with the diagrams and instructions on this site. Projects are classified as easy, medium or hard to make and come with flying instructions. You'll also find a helicopter, a blimp, a rocket and a paper frisbee.

photo.net

http://www.photo.net/

Vast photography Web site with lots of great images to inspire you. It has equipment reviews, advice, busy forums and a gallery where you can upload your photos and have them criticised. There's also a Travel section with illustrated travelogues.

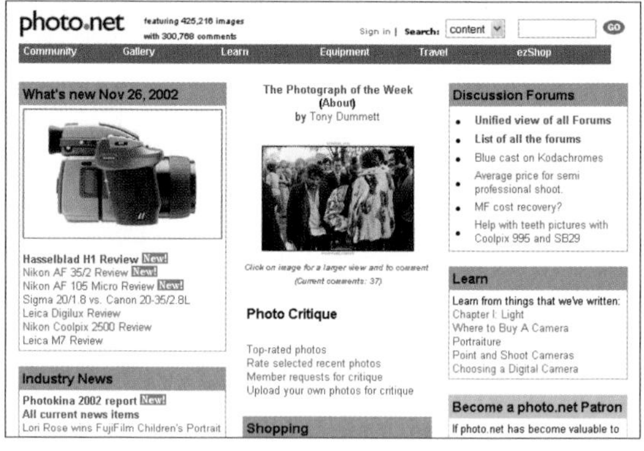

Digital Photography Review

http://www.dpreview.com/

If you're looking for a digital camera, Digital Photography Review has all the latest news plus in-depth reviews of most of the cameras on the market. Other features include an imaging glossary and forums where you can find out what other Internet users think about particular cameras.

ShortCourses

http://www.shortcourses.com/

Find out how to choose and use a digital camera with this collection of electronic books. Despite the 'ShortCourses' monicker, the guides are comprehensive and clearly written. It also has printable pocket guides for popular cameras.

Motor Trend Online

http://www.motortrend.com/

US site with industry news, road tests and features from *Motor Trend* magazine. Check out the Future Vehicles section for predictions for the next few years, concept cars and sneak previews of forthcoming models. You can also read about the car, truck and sport/utility vehicle of the year.

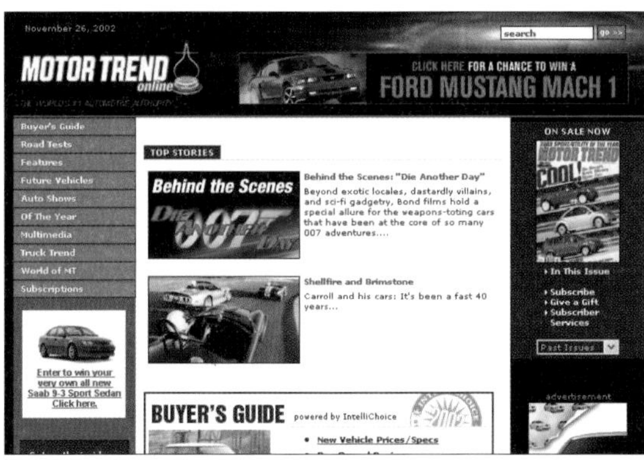

Car and Driver

http://www.caranddriver.com/

Car and Driver's Web site has buyer's guides for new and used cars, reviews, comparison tests and user's road tests. There's also a report on the supercar challenge to find "the baddest in all the land" and a 10 Best Cars section with cars from the last 20 years.

Top Gear

http://www.topgear.beeb.com/

The site of the UK television programme and magazine has lots of everything: news, features, opinion columns, reviews, advice on buying and owning a car, valuations and readers' letters. The inimitable Jeremy Clarkson appears at the top but doesn't (at the time of writing) have much to say.

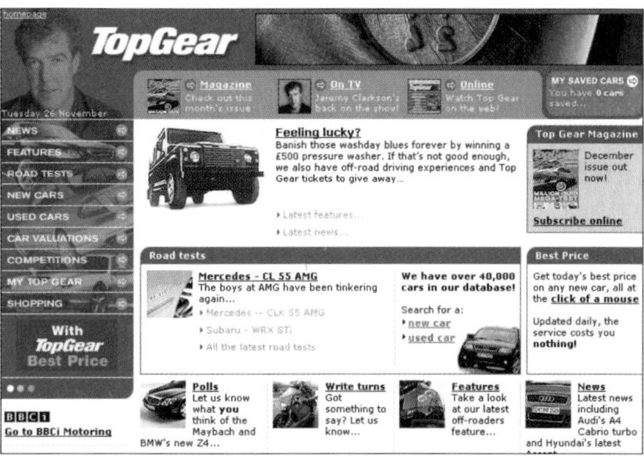

CarTalk

http://cartalk.cars.com/

CarTalk is a US radio show featuring mechanics Tom and Ray Magliozzi. Listen to the latest broadcast on-line or read all sorts of entertaining articles and columns. There's a lot here that's just for fun, such as the electronic traffic tickets you can send to your friends, but there's also plenty of useful advice.

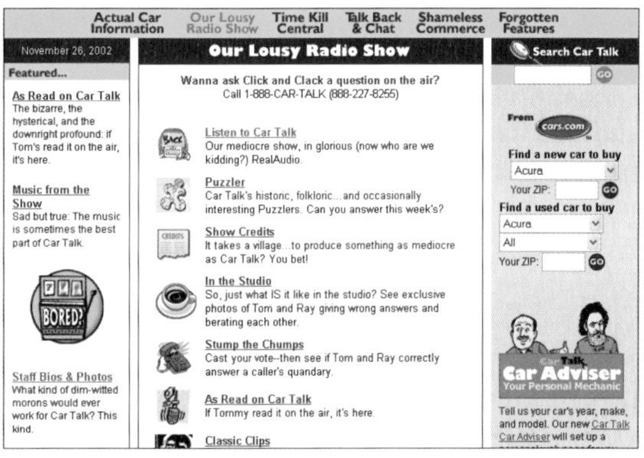

American Woman Road and Travel

http://www.roadandtravel.com/

American Woman Road and Travel provides a female perspective on going places, by car or otherwise. It has buying guides, reviews, safety and security advice and road humour – minus the endless cracks about women drivers, obviously.

MINI.com

http://www.mini.com/

Find out about the funky new Mini from this stylish site. It has games, video clips and interactive features as well as the lowdown on the car. Localised versions are available for many countries.

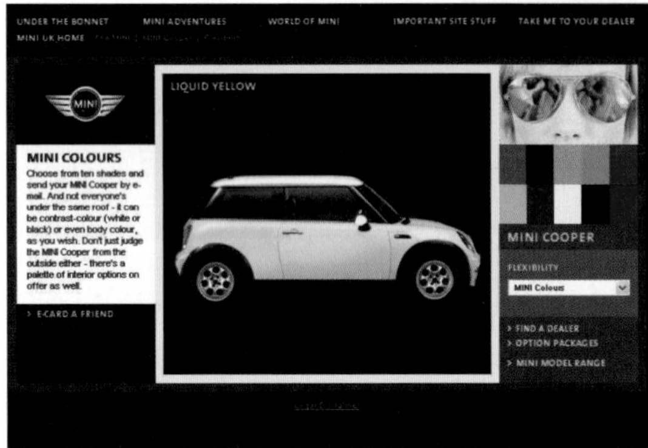

MCN

http://www.motorcyclenews.com/

UK motorcycling magazine *MCN* has a busy Web site with news, bike and product reviews, advice and tips, and classified ads. Racing and off-road riding get their own sections.

Bikersweb

http://www.bikersweb.co.uk/

Bikersweb is an independent on-line magazine covering the UK bike scene. It has news, coverage of the major shows, an events calendar, forums and reader's photographs.

Harley-Davidson.com

http://www.harley-davidson.com/

Feel the wind in your hair at the Harley-Davidson site, which has riding and maintenance advice as well as details of the bikes. You can also find out about renting a Harley or going on an official tour.

The Antique Motorbike Club of America

http://www.antiquemotorcycle.org/

The main attraction on the Antique Motorbike Club's site is the virtual tour of its museum. Panoramic images give you a 360-degree view of the interior. Click through to the Extended Museum for more details and rotating images of 36 bikes.

Sport

football365.com

http://www.football365.com/

Football365 is updated 365 days a year – hence the title. It offers a daily newspaper delivered by e-mail plus lots of news, views, humour and games. Where else are you going to find a football dictionary with definitions for 'lager lout' and a Gary Lineker entry that begins, "Greying crisp salesman and former international goal-hanger with sideline of hosting the **BBC's** entire portfolio of live football..."

Soccernet

http://www.soccernet.com/

Long-standing football site that's now part of ESPN. It covers the English and Scottish Premier Leagues, Europe, the Champions League and global football.

Extras include a fantasy league and reports from fans of the English Premiership teams.

FIFA

http://www.fifa.com/

The official site of the official body (the Fédération Internationale de Football Association, to give it its full name) has round-ups of recent events, lots of fact sheets, regulations and the rules of the game.

UEFA

http://www.uefa.com/

UEFA's site has the lowdown on the Champions League, with audio and video to liven things up. It's also developing a Training Ground section with information on playing, coaching and refereeing and there's a Fanzone with games and forums.

Planet Rugby

http://www.planet-rugby.com/

Planet Rugby has lots of news that can be viewed on the main page or sorted by country. It also has opinion columns, a regular discussion of rules and refs, a rugby lookalikes feature that matches up players and celebrities, and some fun and games.

Scrum.com

http://www.scrum.com/

Scrum.com gives you more news, by country or tournament, plus features, columns, a fitness section, a primer for beginners and a rugby dictionary. There's even a section for women's rugby.

World of Rugby

http://www.worldofrugby.com/

World of Rugby has yet more news, plus subsites for Web Rugby, Tri Nations, Six Nations and Super 12. The Web Rugby site provides links to rugby sites from around the world, sorted by country or type. There's also a What's Cool category that lets you charge straight to the good stuff.

NFL.com

http://www.nfl.com/

Find out what's happening in the American football world with the official site for the NFL. It has scores, stats, schedules and standings, plus many other things not beginning with 's'. There's news, of course, plus radio broadcasts that you can listen to over the Internet, depth charts and links to the official sites of all the teams. If you have a broadband connection, don't miss the NFL Films TV section.

Play Football

http://www.playfootball.com/

Play Football is the NFL's site for kids and thus has brighter colours, shorter words and fewer numbers. It explains the positions, the equipment and the field, tells kids what it's like to be a player and posts the latest scores. Kids can also play football-related games or get off the couch and get involved.

AFL

http://afl.com.au/

Follow football with an Aussie accent at the official site of the Australian Football League. It has audio and video coverage as well as news, results and details of all the clubs and players. There's also a Laws section and a collection of info sheets. Fun features include games, screensavers and wallpaper.

NBA.com

http://www.nba.com/

The National Basketball Association gets covered with typical American thoroughness on NBA.com. Here you'll find news, previews, reviews, player files and more statistics than Michael Jordan could dunk. And when you get tired of reading, you can look at the photographs and watch the videos. A companion site covers the WNBA.

Inside Hoops

http://www.insidehoops.com/

Inside Hoops covers the entire (American) basketball spectrum, from the pro leagues to college and high school basketball to streetball. Highlights include a rumours page, a daily editorial and fan commentary.

SLAM Online

http://www.slamonline.com/

On-line edition of the basketball magazine with attitude. Read the features, grab some cool desktop wallpaper and crash the (message) boards to chat with other bball fans.

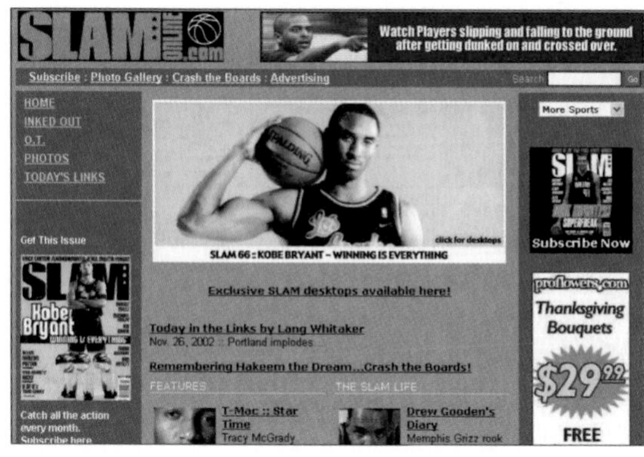

NHL.com

http://www.nhl.com/

Another game, another fine collection of news, scores, schedules and stats. This time it's ice hockey, with live audio from the games and video highlights for those who're prepared to pay. It also has a rulebook, features on the history of the game and a special section on the Stanley Cup.

SLAM! Sports: Hockey

http://www.canoe.ca/Hockey/

The Hockey section of SLAM! Sports provides a Canadian perspective on ice hockey. Select your favourite team for news and results or read the commentary in the Puckmaster column.

CricInfo

http://www.cricinfo.com/

It's just cricket at CricInfo, the stat-happy home of the game that takes breaks for afternoon tea. Features include live ball-by-ball scorecards for selected matches, stats, player files, more stats, a database of grounds, a StatGuru, ratings, photographs and forums where you can talk about… stats, of course.

Cricket365

http://www.cricket365.com/

Cricket news and views, 365 days a year… except when rain stops play. Even then it has plenty of fun features to keep you entertained, including a lookalikes feature and a Mouthing Off column with quotes such as, "There's Neil Harvey standing at leg slip with his legs wide apart waiting for a tickle."

Major League Baseball

http://www.majorleaguebaseball.com/

The MLB site is eerily similar to the NFL and NHL sites – and not just because of its penchant for initials. Once again, there's audio and video (and as with the NHL site, you have to take out a subscription for full access). Exclusive features include a Hot Stove report with news about free agents and trading.

Baseball

http://www.usatoday.com/sports/baseball/front.htm

A joint effort brought to you by *USA Today* and *Baseball Weekly* (now *Sports Weekly*), this site has scores and stats, ratings by Jeff Sagarin, team notebooks and a week-by-week archive that lets you click back in time.

The Tennis Server

http://www.tennisserver.com/

Long-standing tennis site with links to news stories from around the Web and an interesting set of columns covering everything from the state of the game to the science of tennis to advice for amateurs.

Wimbledon

http://www.wimbledon.com/

The most famous of the Grand Slam tournaments gets the cyber treatment and comes up green and purple. Highlights include a virtual tour with panoramic images, stills and Webcams. There's also a Video Vault with clips from classic matches. The shop ships official merchandise around the world, so you can fill your bathroom with green and purple Wimbledon towels.

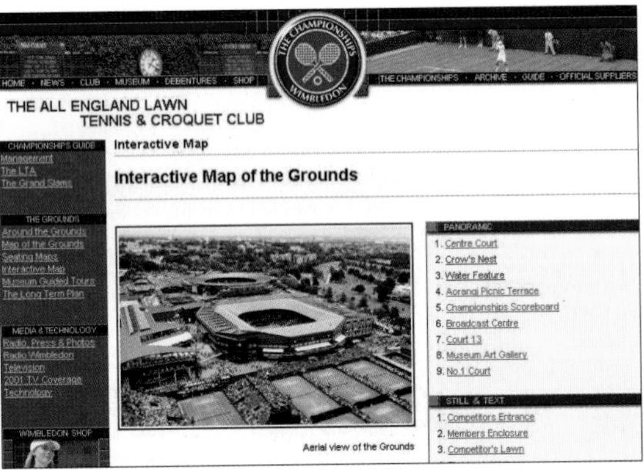

Davis Cup

http://www.daviscup.com/

Find out which countries are still in the Davis Cup with the official site, which has details of the history and structure of the competition, a list of champions going back to 1900, drawsheets, updates and results.

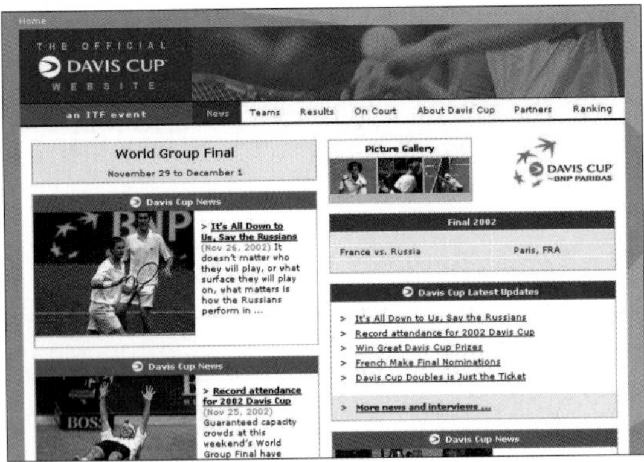

PGA.com

http://www.pga.com/

Spoil a good walk at the official site of the Professional Golfers' Association of America. It has event and tour schedules with links to the relevant Web sites, a Lesson Book covering everything from swing fundamentals to the mental side of the game, instructional videos and a section for juniors.

Golf Today

http://www.golftoday.co.uk/

Golf Today has news and tour coverage, course directories for the UK and Ireland (plus limited coverage of the rest of the world) and a set of on-line tutorials. There's also a virtual golf club offering various discounts and other benefits for members.

Olympics

http://www.olympic.org/

The official site of the Olympic movement profiles over 250 Olympic heroes from the summer and winter games. Each athlete gets a write-up and photo gallery and there are videos of some performances. It also has a Sports section with details of all the disciplines that are (or were) included and an Olympic Games section with accounts of all the games since 1896.

IAAF.org

http://www.iaaf.org/

The Web site of the International Association of Athletics Federations brings you track and field news, results, records and rankings. The most interesting feature is the athletes' journals.

Track and Field News.com

http://www.trackandfieldnews.com/

Don't come here for news, although it does link you to results from recent events, but for stats. The Lists section details the top performances from the current year; the Rankings section gives you the top ten performers for each event for every year from 1947 onwards. The Records section has the world records.

Cyclingnews.com

http://www.cyclingnews.com/

The "world centre of cycling" has an immensely busy front page linking you to dozens of features and reports. A random sampling of items includes a review of a seat post, an interview with Laura Van Gilder, Lawrence Armstrong's comments on his quest for a fifth Tour de France victory, news of another doping scandal and results from races in Australia, Belgium, France, Spain and the USA.

Tour de France

http://www.letour.fr/indexus.html

The official site for cycling's most famous event has details of the next race and results from the most recent one. Highlights include an animated map.

SquashTalk.com

http://www.squashtalk.com/

Independent squash site covering events from around the world. It has several regular columns, a Player of the Month and a Hall of Fame section.

MegaSpin

http://www.megaspin.net/

MegaSpin covers table tennis, otherwise known as ping-pong, "the game that is usually played in the basement with an opponent, with plastic paddles in hand that [make] the distinctive noises when a ball [is] struck." This site covers everything from the equipment required for the basic basement game to the results from international events.

International Gymnast

http://www.intlgymnast.com/

Somersault to the Web site of *International Gymnast* magazine for a frequently updated news page and live reports from major events. It covers both artistic and rhythmic gymnastics.

Gymn

http://www.gymn-forum.com/

Gymn has brief biographies of gymnasts, a gymnastics FAQ, a calendar of upcoming events and lots of links to other gymnastics resources.

SkateWeb: The Figure Skating Page

http://www.frogsonice.com/skateweb/

SkateWeb catalogues figure skating Web pages. The front page highlights recent and upcoming events, making it easy to find coverage of competitions. New sites also enjoy a brief spell on a front page before being moved into the appropriate category: Reference, News & Features, Elite Skaters and so on. Brief descriptions are provided where necessary.

Transworld Skateboarding

http://www.skateboarding.com/skate/

Enter the world of ollies and salad grinds with Transworld Skateboarding. It has photos and a few videos, trick tips, message boards and a buyer's guide that tells you what the pros are riding.

formula1.com

http://www.formula1.com/

This site was being redeveloped into the official Formula 1 site at the time of writing. It has always been good, with lots of news, pages for all the teams with car specs and driver bios, reports on all the races, attractive circuit maps, games, quizzes and a caption competition. The new version will definitely be worth a look.

itv.com/f1

http://www.itv-f1.com/

ITV's Formula 1 coverage merits a special section of the ITV site, with real and spoof news, photo features, pictures of pit babes, humorous digging by The Mole and a diary by ITV's man at the track, Murray Walker.

GORP

http://www.gorp.com/

The Great Outdoor Recreation Pages should be the first place you visit when you get the urge for fresh air. It's huge, energetic and most of all enthusiastic, with lots of get-out-and-do-it guides to places, activities – from biking and camping to snorkelling and skiing – and the necessary equipment.

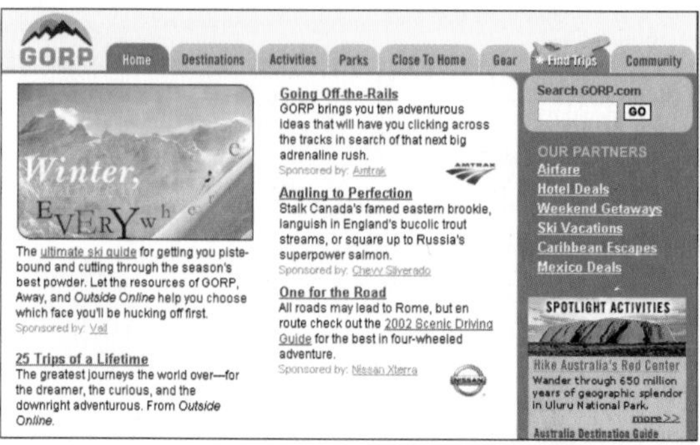

Outside Online

http://outsidemag.com/

Another great site, this is the on-line edition of *Outside* magazine. It has four main sections: Gear, Travel, Bodywork (getting fit) and Features. The last has articles from the magazine – such as 'Knives in the Water', a preview of the America's Cup, and 'Arcs over the Arctic', an account of kite-skiing on Baffin Island in northern Canada.

Backpacker.com

http://www.backpacker.com/

Read the reviews to choose the best boots, rucksacks and other equipment, then go hiking in the US and Canada. It also has a Technique section covering health, nutrition and nature. Want to know how to prevent blisters or make gourmet meals in the wilderness? The answers are here.

Outdoor Britain

http://www.visitbritain.com/uk/outdoorbritain/

Outdoor Britain encourages you to "experience the beauty of Britain's countryside by snorkelling through a bog or chasing cheese down a hill". Or if those very British activities don't take your fancy, you can take inspiration from authors, composers and artists who have described or depicted the countryside. Once you're ready to leave your desk, the site recommends locations for walking, cycling, horse riding, water activities and extreme sports.

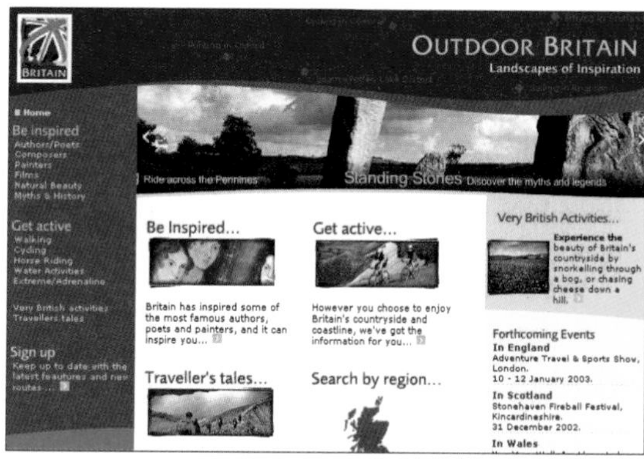

Geocaching

http://www.geocaching.com/

Discover geocaching, a new sport where you use your GPS unit to track down a cache – a hiding place where items can be concealed. You can then make an entry in the logbook, take something from the cache, leave something for the next person to find and go on your way. It's a high-tech treasure hunt.

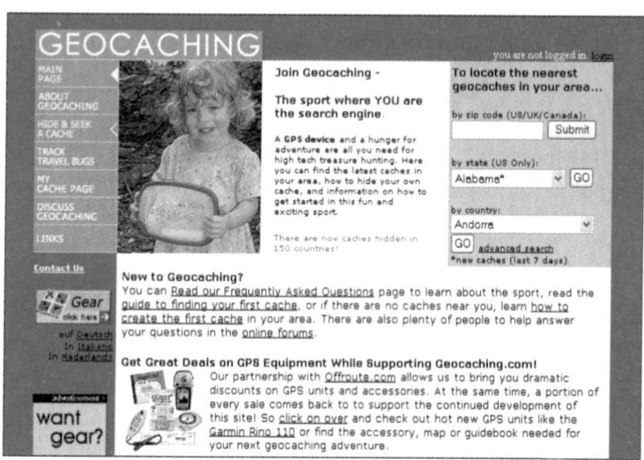

mtbREVIEW.com

http://www.mtbr.com/

Forsake the highways at mtbREVIEW.com. It has a product database with reviews by riders, details of over 6,000 trails around the US and Tech Talk message boards covering everything from wheels and brakes to riding and training techniques.

Mountain Biking UK

http://www.mbuk.com/

Web site for the popular UK mountain biking magazine, under redevelopment at the time of writing but hopefully back in business by the time you read this. If not, you can still access the forums.

Birding on the Web

http://www.birder.com/

Extensive resource for birdwatchers, with lists of birding hotspots, advice for backyard birders and links to lots of other birding sites.

BirdSource

http://www.birdsource.org/

Interesting site that enables US birders to get involved in research projects by recording and sharing their observations. The instructions and results – especially for the FeederWatch project – are worth reading even if you're based elsewhere.

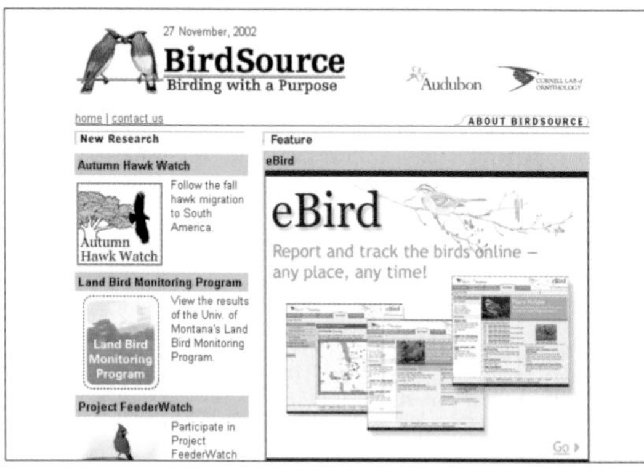

Outdoor Life

http://www.outdoorlife.com/outdoor/

The on-line edition of US hunting and fishing magazine *Outdoor Life* has lots of advice on catching your own dinner. The Fish Finder covers over 90 game fish, with techniques and gear tips, and the Game Finder explains how to shoot everything from mourning doves to black bears. The site also has reviews of everything from socks to trucks.

Tales of the Ultimate Sportsmen

http://www.ultimatesportsmen.com/

Lots of stories about the ones that got away – and more to the point, the ones that didn't.

The Daily Sail

http://www.madforsailing.com/

The Daily Sail is a UK-based site with sailing news and features. The emphasis is on racing, with separate sections for offshore, inshore and dinghy events. If you're feeling mean, go straight to the Disaster pages and read about other people's misfortunes.

The Boating Info Centre

http://www.boating.co.nz/

New Zealand boating site, with the emphasis on sailing. There's advice on preparing for and sailing in races and improving your speed.

DiverNET

http://www.divernet.com/

The UK's *DIVER* magazine republishes most of its features on the Web. Its informative site has articles on training, travel, marine life and photography, gear reviews and a regularly updated News section. It also has forums where you can make contact with other British divers.

Scuba Board

http://www.scubaboard.com/

Popular and busy diving message board covering everything from learning to dive to deeply technical wreck and cave diving. It's a good place to ask questions, get opinions on gear and read about dive destinations around the world.

SkiNet.com

http://www.skinet.com/

Find the snow at SkiNet.com, an extensive site with North American and international snow reports, gear reviews and photo essays. If you're struggling to stay on your feet, check out the Instruction section, where you'll find features on fitness, technique and avoiding accidents.

thealps.com

http://www.thealps.com/

Check out the snow at both ends of the world with thealps.com. It covers resorts in Europe, Utah and New Zealand, providing details of the ski areas, facilities, activities and accommodation. It also has weather reports for some resorts.

MountainZone.com

http://www.mountainzone.com/

MountainZone.com takes you to the top of the world, by bike, crampon and karabiner, and then down again on skis or a snowboard. It also covers the newly popular sport of adventure racing. For inspiration, look at the spectacular images in the Photography section.

Lifestyle

In the real world, you might feel isolated, but on the Internet, there's always someone who shares your concerns. Whether you're looking for help with health problems or want to get in touch with people who are confronting the same issues, there are lots of great resources on the Web.

HealthFinder

http://www.healthfinder.gov/

HealthFinder directs you to on-line health information. The links were compiled by the US Department of Health and Human Services, so the sites should be reputable – but you should still read critically and exercise your judgement. Resources can be accessed by topic or interest group.

WebMD Health

http://my.webmd.com/

WebMD's Health section has two basic types of material: medical information about diseases and conditions, and health and wellness advice to help you avoid needing the medical stuff. It's aimed at laypeople and the articles are attractively presented and clearly written.

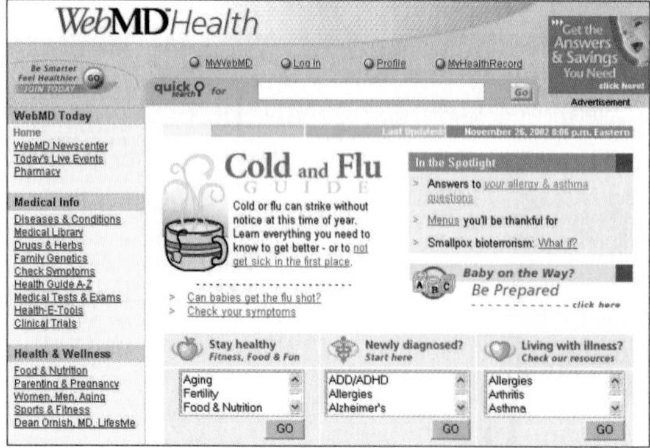

MEDLINEplus

http://medlineplus.gov/

MEDLINEplus features health information from the US National Library of Medicine. Find out about diseases and conditions, look up medicines, explore the medical encyclopedia and check medical terms in the dictionary. If you still aren't satisfied, go to the Other Resources section and follow the links to MEDLINE itself, a searchable database with information about articles published in over 4,000 medical journals.

NHS Direct Online

http://www.nhsdirect.nhs.uk/

The UK's NHS Direct Online is another gateway to health information. It has a health encyclopedia, a self-help guide to help you interpret your own symptoms and a section on healthy living.

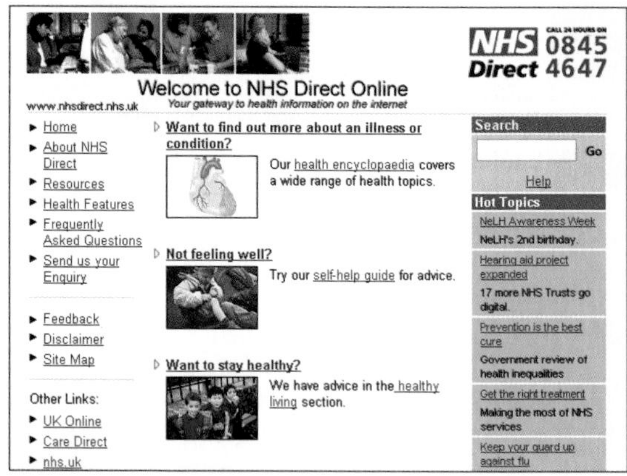

Australian Department of Health and Ageing

http://www.health.gov.au/

The Australian Department of Health and Ageing provides an A to Z guide linking you to Web sites on its programs, subjects and initiatives. For general advice, click through to Health Insite (http://www.healthinsite.gov.au/). It has lots of health information accessible by lifestyle, disease or condition, life event and population group.

OncoLink

http://www.oncolink.com/

OncoLink specialises in cancer. Created by experts at the University of Pennsylvania, it has articles about different types of cancers, treatment options and coping strategies. If you need cheering up, try the art gallery, which features work by cancer patients – many of them children.

KidsHealth.org

http://www.kidshealth.org/

KidsHealth has separate areas for parents, children and teenagers. The Kids section is fun and has an interactive tour of the body as well as articles and advice. A glossary defines the big words and explains how to say them. Parents miss out on some of the entertainment, but they do get information about everything from first aid to behavioural problems.

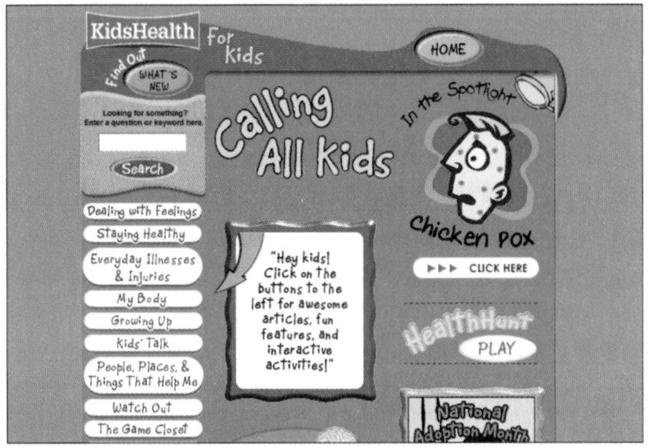

Go Ask Alice!

http://www.goaskalice.columbia.edu/

Go Ask Alice! is a medical question-and-answer site run by Columbia University. School and university students (and anyone else) can ask questions anonymously and read the replies on the site. Since Alice has been answering questions for a long time, there's a good chance your question has already been asked – in which case you can find the answering by browsing or searching.

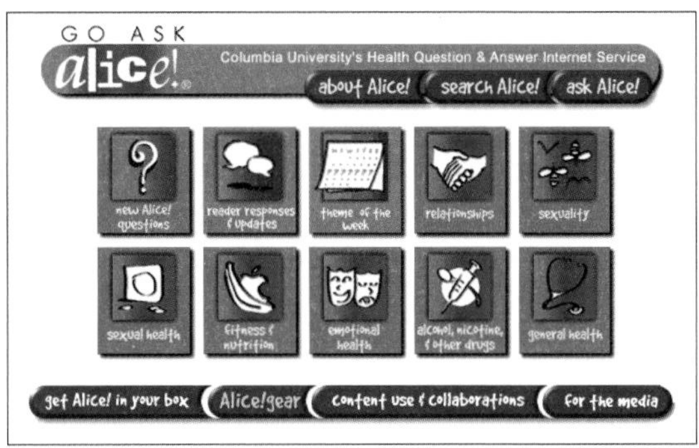

Men's Health

http://www.menshealth.com/

The Web site of *Men's Health* magazine has "tons of useful stuff" about fitness, weight loss, health and sex. Find out how to shed that stomach and get a cover-model body while avoiding a heart attack and giving your girlfriend a night to remember.

Health on Oxygen

http://www.oxygen.com/health/

The Health section of women's lifestyle site Oxygen covers diet and nutrition, fitness and staying healthy. Use the calculator to find out your Body Mass Index and see how you shape up, type in a food item to find out how many calories it contains and sort out a fitness plan that suits your lifestyle.

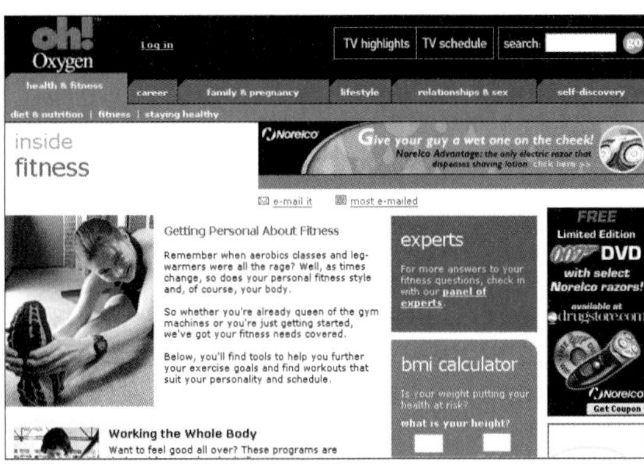

Disabilities

Disability Now

http://www.disabilitynow.org.uk/

The Web site of UK campaigning newspaper *Disability Now* has news and features from the latest issue plus an archive of older material. The Links section features categorised links to other disability sites.

Youreable.com

http://www.youreable.com/

Youreable was created as the result of a television competition to win business support for a new Internet venture. The nicely designed site provides information for disabled people, including headline news, plus details of products and services. It also has forums where you can discuss subjects such as benefits, equipment, motoring and work.

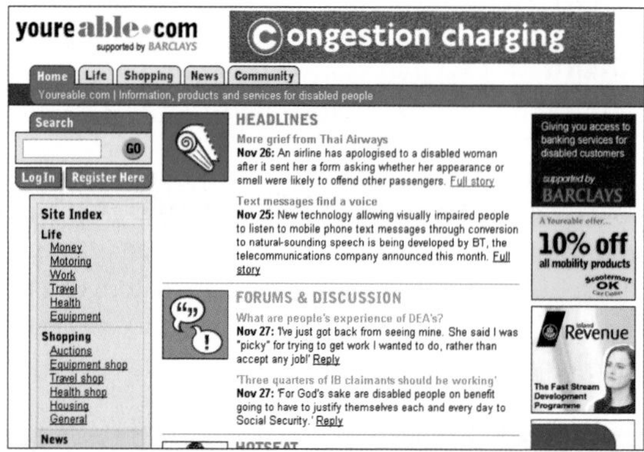

RNIB

http://www.rnib.org.uk/

The UK's Royal National Institute for the Blind uses its Web site to provide the answers to questions such as "What can blind and partially sighted people see?" and, "Who can register as blind?" It also has lots of information about living with a sight problem and a directory of useful Web sites.

British Deaf Association

http://www.britishdeafassociation.org.uk/

The British Deaf Association is run "by deaf people, for deaf people". Its Web site has news and fact sheets for both deaf and hearing people, plus a mini dictionary of British Sign Language (BSL). Each sign is illustrated with a short video clip.

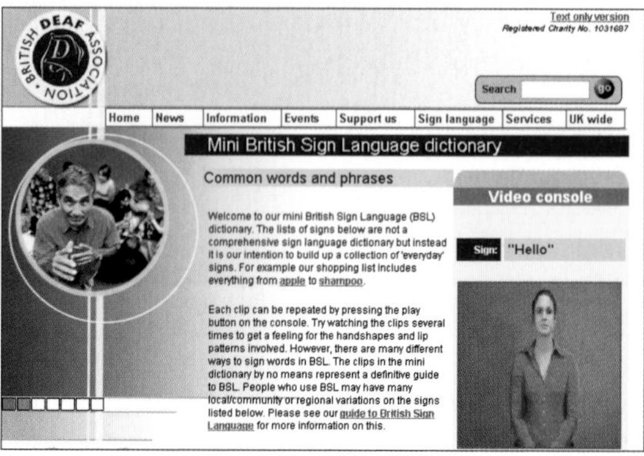

EnableNet

http://www.enable.net.au/

Australia's EnableNet aims to be a resource on disabilities and a meeting place for people who are affected by them. Currently it has news headlines, a chat area, message boards, a directory of Web sites and books that provide further information and pointers to on-line services that make life easier for people with disabilities.

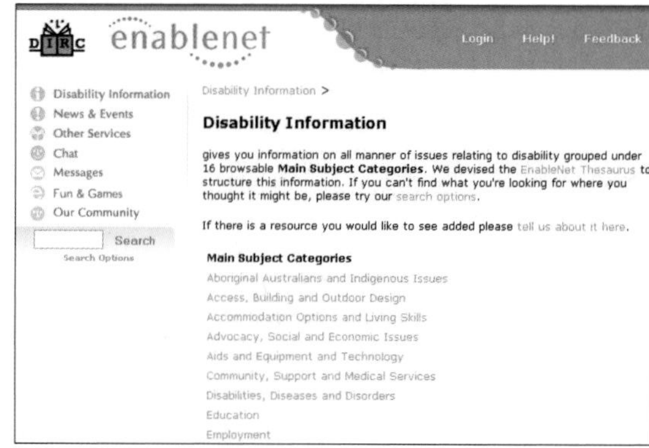

EnableNZ

http://www.enable.co.nz/

Enable NZ assists people who are affected by disabilities. Its Web site has a range of resources, including information about funding, a searchable equipment database, an catalogue detailing items in its library (which can be requested on-line) and a directory of relevant Web sites.

Family

Yahooligans!

http://www.yahooligans.com/

Yahooligans! is a version of the Web directory designed for young browsers. It works just like the grown-up version, but concentrates on sites for kids. Special features include Ask Earl, a weekday column in which cartoon characters Earl and Stray Kat use the Web to answer questions submitted by children. There's also a section for parents with information about safe surfing.

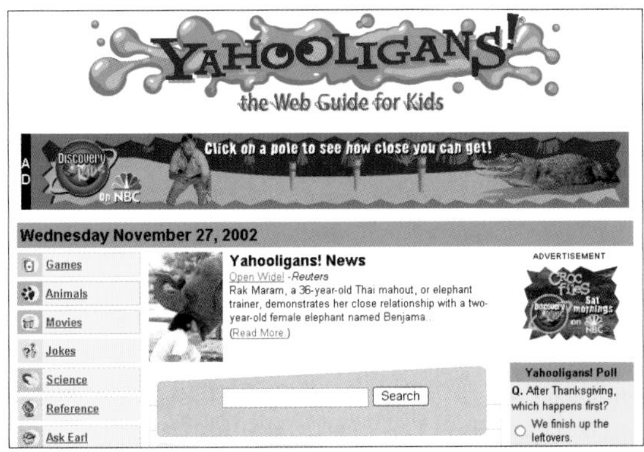

Nickelodean Online

http://www.nick.com/

The Web site of the popular children's television channel is all about fun, games, cartoons and interactivity. Kids can select their favourite show for character files, clips, message boards and lots of games, or simply click around the sections and see what they find. It'll keep them happily occupied for hours on end.

National Geographic Homework Help

http://www.nationalgeographic.com/education/homework/

National Geographic's homework site brings together all the fact-filled features that'll be useful for projects and reports. If there's an assignment on animals, science, history or, of course, geography, you'll find material here. Once the homework is done, there are games and activities in the Kids site.

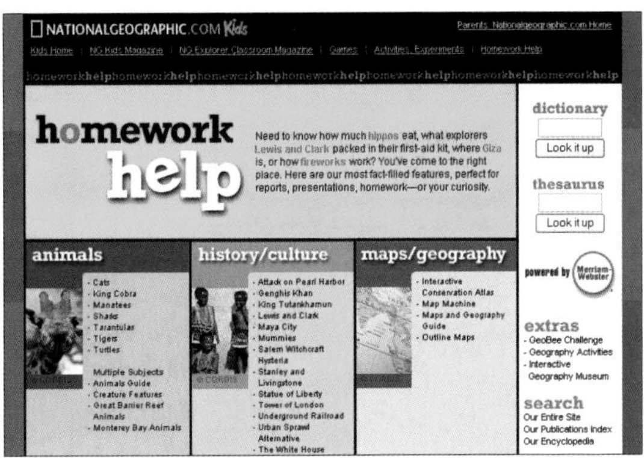

SOFWeb

http://www.sofweb.vic.edu.au/

SOFWeb is an reference site with resources of its own and links to the best education sites around the

Web. It's run by the Department of Education and Training in Victoria, Australia, but students and teachers from other countries will also find it useful.

Oxfam's CoolPlanet

http://www.oxfam.org.uk/coolplanet/

Oxfam's CoolPlanet covers global issues such as poverty and fair trade in a kid-friendly manner. Check out the Amazing World section for information about some of the countries where the charity works, then visit the Active 8 section for things to do, both in the real world and on-line.

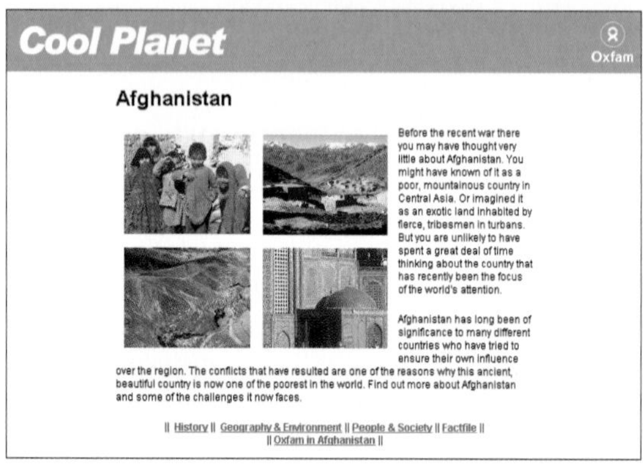

Raising Kids

http://www.raisingkids.co.uk/

Find out what to do with your kids (no, you can't just leave them on the bus) with Raising Kids, a UK site that covers youngsters of all ages and stages. Learn what to expect from your baby, how to toilet train your toddler or encourage your child to eat properly at school, and get advice on the troublesome teenage years. There are lots of articles here, and if you don't find what you're looking for, you can put your questions to an expert.

Mumsnet

http://www.mumsnet.com/

The UK-based Mumsnet enables mothers – and fathers – to share their experiences. Find the best childcare products (and submit your own opinions), get advice from childcare experts, find out how to teach your child to count, read or swim, and talk to other parents via the message boards.

Mumsweb

http://www.mumsweb.com.au/

Australia's Mumsweb is a community site that enables parents to discuss everything from pregnancy to helping kids through a divorce. Add your comments to the articles, contribute a feature of your own or join other parents in the chat rooms.

Older people

Senior.com

http://www.senior.com/

The best-known site for older Internet users was being redeveloped at the time of writing, but it'll be back. Become a member for health and travel advice, personalised news and entertainment headlines and the opportunity to chat with other 'silver surfers'.

ThirdAge

http://www.thirdage.com/

ThirdAge caters to people who aren't quite seniors: "first-wave baby boomers, adults in their mid-40s through 50s". If your kids have moved out – or are about to – and you have more free time, visit this site for beauty and style advice, a tech section for people who weren't born with joysticks in their hands, a genealogy section and articles on health, love, money and travel.

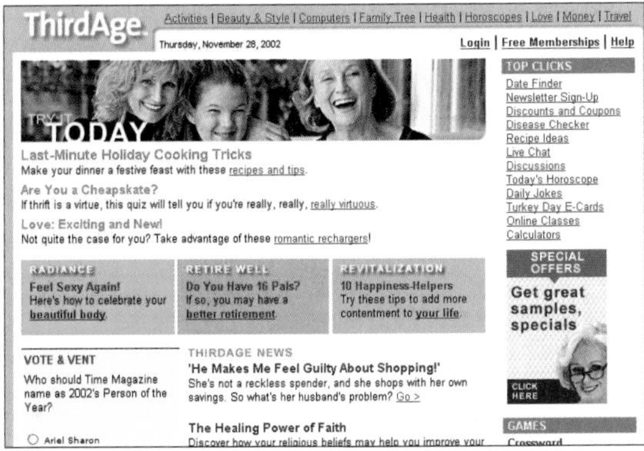

Over50s.com

http://www.over50s.com/

Over50s.com is a UK-based site with news, features on finance and health and a legal section dealing issues such as divorce and will-making. It also covers subjects such as travel, careers, motoring and relationships.

Adventures in Ageing

http://www.adventuresinageing.org/

Adventures in Ageing is a new site that looks at developments in science and economics that will affect our futures. At the moment it has links to stories on pensions, government policy and biomedical science.

GoldenYears

http://www.goldenyears.co.nz/

GoldenYears is a New Zealand site that covers products and services to help you enjoy your retirement. It has links to Web sites with financial advice, information about accommodation, products for the elderly, medical services and support. There's also a chat room.

Sexuality

PlanetOut

http://www.planetout.com/

PlanetOut is a US portal for lesbians, bisexuals and gay men. It has articles on money and careers, family issues, health and fitness and romance, plus coverage of Pride events around the world and a busy personals section.

Gay.com

http://www.gay.com/

In addition to the global site, Gay.com has offshoots for various countries, including the UK. It has political, financial and entertainment news, features on lifestyle, health and HIV, and a travel section. Members also get access to chat rooms, personals, e-mail and message boards.

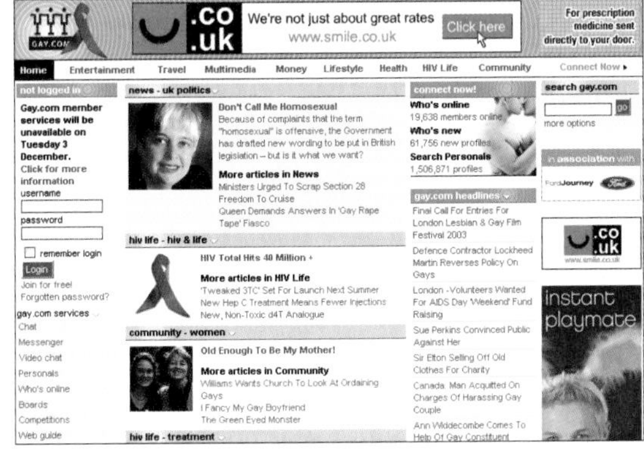

RainbowNetwork.com

http://www.rainbownetwork.com/

RainbowNetwork is a UK site for lesbians and gay men, with news, shopping and travel sections, members-only areas for men and women, forums and personal ads. There are lots of fun features as well, including a not-all-serious agony column and "half-assed" tips on everything from surviving the Christmas party to becoming a porn star.

Gay History

http://www.gayhistory.com/

Serious and rather academic site with a timeline covering gay (male) history from 1700 to 1900. The next section is currently being developed.

New Mardi Gras

http://www.mardigras.com.au/

On-line home of Sydney's world-famous gay and lesbian Mardi Gras, currently resurrecting itself after some financial problems. Find out what's happening this year, volunteer your services or make a donation to support the festival.

ReligiousResources.org

http://www.religiousresources.org/

Extensive and well-organised database of religious (mostly Christian) resources on the Internet. Find religious texts, theology sites, religious organisations, electronic communities, clip-art and Web graphics, music and much more.

BuddhaNet

http://www.buddhanet.net/

BuddhaNet provides information and educational resources for people from all Buddhist traditions. Features include a basic Buddhism guide, a library of electronic books and a Web directory.

The Hindu Universe

http://www.hindunet.org/

The Hindu Universe is a resource centre with news, horoscopes, an event calendar, lots of educational materials and a Web directory. Find out about Hindu philosophy and customs, read about Ayurveda and yoga or chat in the forums.

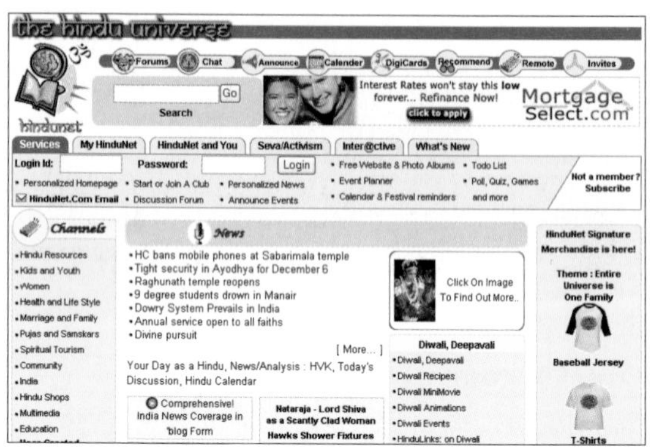

Al-Islam

http://www.al-islam.com/

The multilingual Al-Islam has information from the Qur'an and Hadith, an Islamic dictionary, prayer-time and Zakah calculators, and a guide to Hajj and 'Umrah. There's also a Discover Islam section that introduces the concepts and principles.

Godulike

http://www.godulike.co.uk/

Irreverent site that provides an unbeliever's overview of more than 100 faiths. Find out what people believe and which gods they worship, then review the Godulike scorecard. Religions are rated on such qualities as "belief in any sort of existence after death", "clear and understandable explanations" and "chance of world domination". Whether it amuses, intrigues or offends depends on your point of view.

Shopping and services

Internet shopping has exploded over the last few years, thanks to the development of encryption technologies that protect your credit-card details as they travel across the Internet. You can buy all sorts of things, from books and CDs to computers and cars – but do check that the store can deliver to your area. You can also use the Internet for banking, job hunting and travel.

Guides

ShoppingSpot

http://www.shoppingspot.com/

ShoppingSpot is a US-based site that links you to price-comparison tools, advice and product reviews as well as on-line stores. It only lists major retailers, but sometimes that's all you need. You'll need to check whether the shops can deliver to your country.

DealTime

http://www.dealtime.com/

DealTime is a price-comparison tool that searches for products in lots of different stores, then shows you the prices. You can then click through to the store with the best deal and place your order. There are separate versions for the US and the UK.

ShopSmart

http://uk.shopsmart.com/

ShopSmart is a UK shopping portal with a directory of on-line shops, price comparisons and shopping guides. Each store gets a brief review and a rating.

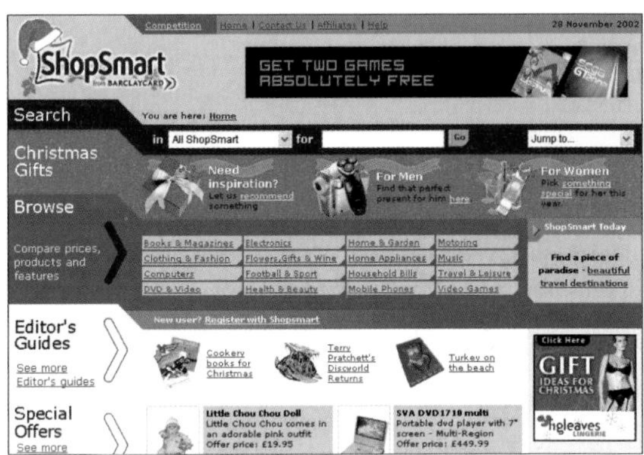

2020Shops

http://www.2020shops.com/

2020Shops is another UK guide to on-line shopping, with a directory of reviewed and rated stores, price comparisons from DealTime and details of bargains and special offers.

GoodShoppingGuide.com.au

http://goodshoppingguide.com.au/

GoodShoppingGuide showcases bargains and offers from selected Australian on-line shops. The range of stores is quite limited, so you may not find everything you're looking for.

Books

Amazon.com

http://www.amazon.com/

Probably the best-known store on the Internet, Amazon started out as a bookseller, but now offers all sorts of things, including CDs, videos and DVDs, toys and games, electronics and clothing (customers outside the US can only purchase books, music and video products and some software titles). Despite its megastore aspirations, it's still best known for books and has lots of features that make it easy to pick something off the virtual shelves. You can read customer reviews, see what other titles were bought by people who bought the book you're considering and even look at sample pages from some titles. Amazon also has local stores in several countries, including the UK.

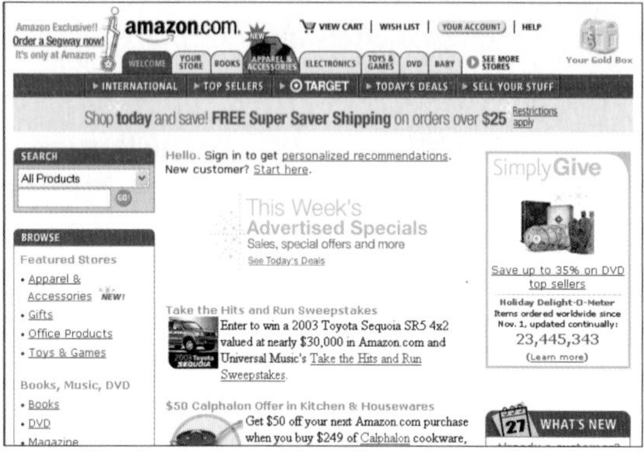

Barnes & Noble

http://www.barnesandnoble.com/

If you don't find the book you're looking for at Amazon, try the on-line home of real-world US bookstore Barnes & Noble. In addition to regular fiction and nonfiction, it has sections for business and technical books, college textbooks and children's books. You can also look for bargains in the half-price section or track down out-of-print books.

Bookbrain.co.uk

http://www.bookbrain.co.uk/

BookBrain is a useful tool for UK bookbuyers. Enter the title, author or ISBN of the book you're looking for and it'll search for it in 14 on-line stores, then show you who has it and what they're charging. Surprisingly worthwhile, because even paperbacks can vary in price significantly.

bol.com

http://www.uk.bol.com/

BOL sells books in the UK, several European countries, Japan and China. The UK branch concentrates on value rather than range and offers significant discounts: at least 60 per cent off best-sellers and at least 20 per cent off everything else. To take advantage of these prices, you have to become a member, which involves making a second purchase within six months of your initial one.

Collins Booksellers

http://www.collinsbooks.com.au/

Collins Booksellers is an Australian chain with real-world and on-line stores. The Internet branch enables you to browse by department or search by title, description, author or ISBN. There's also a bargain bin with discounted titles.

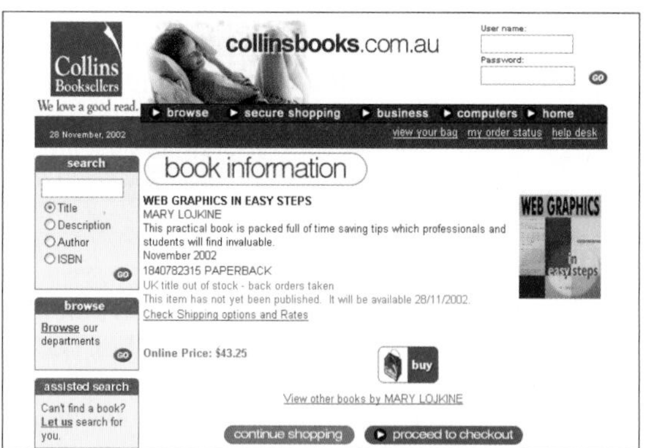

Kalahari.net

http://www.kalahari.net/

South Africa's Kalahari.net sells books, music, videos and DVDs, software and more, in English and Afrikaans. Useful features include a wishlist that keeps track of products that you'd like to buy but aren't quite ready to purchase. It delivers internationally as well as within South Africa.

Music and film

CDNOW

http://www.cdnow.com/

US store CDNOW sells CDs, tapes, vinyl, videos and DVDs, plus related products such as t-shirts and accessories. The album info usually includes track listings and sound samples so you can make sure you're buying the right thing.

CD Universe

http://www.cduniverse.com/

Find further music at CD Universe, which lets you browse by genre; search for artists, titles, songs, soundtracks or labels; or look at hot sellers, recent releases, future releases and music charts. It has track listings and sound samples, cross references to other albums and customer reviews.

101cd.com

http://www.101cd.com/

101cd.com is a UK-based music and video store that ships internationally. It carries over 1.6 million titles, including over one million imports, plus related merchandise such as t-shirts and calendars. Themed mini stores enable you to concentrate on specific artists, films or shopping problems – such as Christmas presents for gran and grandad.

SecondSpin.com

http://www.secondspin.com/

SecondSpin.com sells (and buys) used CDs, videos and DVDs, enabling you to stretch your budget or pick up hard-to-find titles. It ships internationally and will replace any item that's scratched or faulty.

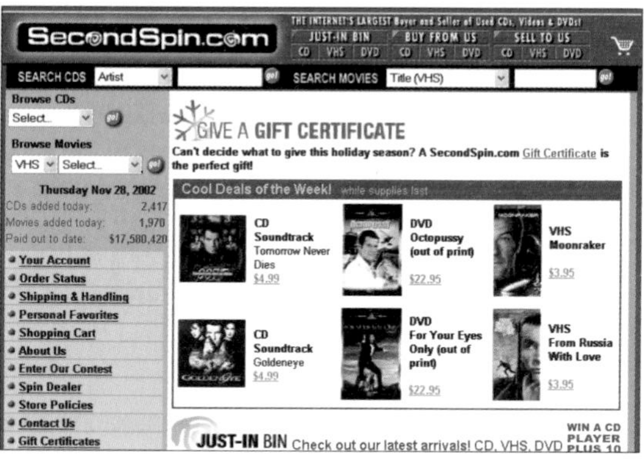

DVD Empire

http://www.dvdempire.com/

DVD Empire is a US store that ships internationally. The upside is that films are usually released in the US long before they come out anywhere else. The downside is that the discs are Region 1 and NTSC, so make sure you'll be able to play them before you place your order.

BlackStar

http://www.blackstar.co.uk/

BlackStar is a UK-based video and DVD store. Special features includes zones for cult favourites such as *Doctor Who* and *Buffy the Vampire Slayer*, an e-mail service that notifies you when current cinema releases make it to video or DVD and a video hunt service for hard-to-find titles. As long as you're happy with PAL VHS videos and Region 2 DVDs, it'll ship internationally.

Take 2

http://www.take2.co.za/

Take 2 sells music, videos, DVDs, games and electronics to customers within South Africa and in neighbouring countries. A Best-sellers page provides easy access to the most popular titles in all formats and you can pre-book the top future releases.

Food and drink

Tesco

http://www.tesco.com/

Save yourself a trip to the supermarket with Tesco's home delivery service. Simply select your groceries from the virtual shelves, then sit back while someone else does your shopping and brings it round. Enter your postcode to find out whether your part of the UK is covered.

Woolworths HomeShop

http://www.homeshop.com.au/

Woolworths offers Internet grocery shopping in Sydney, Canberra and Melbourne. You can browse the shelves by category or search for particular products. Items you order regularly can be recorded on a reusable shopping list. Woolworths plans to expand the service into a national operation, so if your area isn't covered, it might be added.

Cold Storage

http://www.coldstorage.com.sg/

Cold Storage's Dial and Deliver service offers over 3,500 grocery items that you can order on-line for delivery throughout Singapore. You need to be reasonably familiar with its range to interpret the terse descriptions, although some items have pictures. It also lets you save a personal shopping list to speed things up.

TheDrinkShop.com

http://www.thedrinkshop.com/

TheDrinkShop.com stocks beer, wine, spirits and soft drinks. It sells single bottles as well as cases and also has bar accessories, so you can even order a bottle opener. It delivers within the UK and to some European countries.

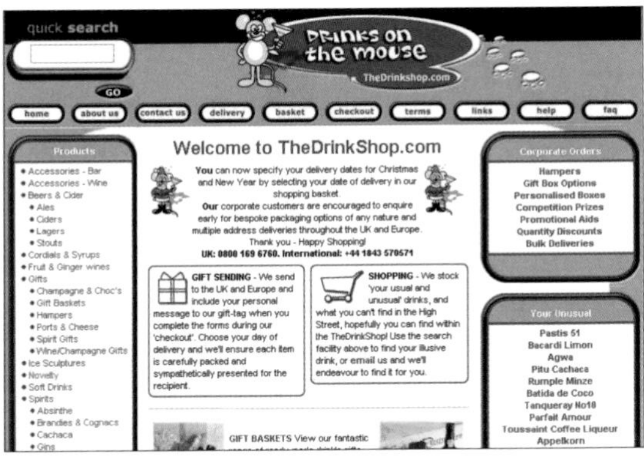

Cellarmasters

http://www.cellarmasters.com.au/

Cellarmasters delivers wine throughout Australia. You can order regular or mixed cases, or subscribe to a wine plan for regular deliveries. There's plenty of information to help you make your decision.

Flowers

1-800-Flowers.com

http://www.1800flowers.com/

1-800-Flowers.com delivers flowers, plants, gourmet treats, sweets and gifts to the US. It can also arrange international delivery of flowers – select the recipient's country to see what's on offer.

Fleurop Interflora

http://www.interflora.com/

Fleurop Interflora's Web site lets you select flowers for delivery to any country. The range depends on the destination – for the UK it includes bouquets, baskets and the traditional dozen roses. You can also specify a colour and let the florist make up a bouquet of seasonal blooms.

Flowers2Send.com

http://www.flowers2send.com/

Flowers2Send is a virtual florist that delivers to the UK. The striking, modern arrangements are cut and packed in Holland, then whisked across the Channel for next-day delivery.

Australian Flowers

http://australianflowers.net/

Australian Flowers is a Melbourne-based florist that delivers flowers – including Australian natives – locally, nationally and around the world.

Virtual cards

Blue Mountain

http://www.bluemountain.com/

If it's too late for flowers, send a card by e-mail. Blue Mountain has animated, musical cards for all occasions and circumstances, from birthdays and weddings to announcing a new e-mail address. You need to be a paid-up member to access all the designs, but there are plenty that anyone can send.

Shockwave.com

http://www.shockwave.com/sw/create/

Shockwave.com's Create section has sophisticated animated cards and tools for creating cards and puzzles from your own photographs. You can then send your masterpiece to your friends.

Corbis

http://www.corbis.com/

If you want to send a picture of something specific, visit the Corbis image library, enter a keyword and search for E-cards. Unless you select something extremely obscure, you'll get a collection of photos and artworks that you can turn into cards.

Cards.co.za

http://www.cards.co.za/

Cards.co.za is a South African site with a wide selection of attractive cards. It has designs for all the usual occasions, humorous cards, party invitations and plain cards for uncategorisable communications.

Miscellaneous

eBay

http://www.ebay.com/

eBay is an auction site that lets you unload your unwanted junk on to other Internet users and purchase the treasures they've carelessly spurned, for whatever you think they're worth. It works like any other auction, although you don't have to worry about scratching your nose – simply make your offer, and if it's the top bid when the auction closes, you win. eBay has local sites for many countries, including the UK, Australia, New Zealand and Singapore.

dabs.com

http://www.dabs.com/

dabs.com is a UK mail-order company turned Internet retailer that offers a huge range of computer hardware and software. You can browse by product type or manufacturer, or opt for speed and search for a specific product.

Crucial

http://www.crucial.com/

Crucial is a memory specialist that makes it easy to order memory upgrades for your computer, even if you're a technological ignoramus. Select your computer's manufacturer, and then your model, and it'll tell you what you can install. It has local sites for several countries, including the UK, plus an international site that ships around the world.

Carphone Warehouse

http://www.carphonewarehouse.com/

UK blabbermouths can purchase mobile phones and accessories from the Carphone Warehouse site. If you're one of the three people who doesn't yet have a mobile, the Encyclopaedia Mobilia will fill you in on the state of the market, the technology, the tariffs and the phones.

Jessops

http://www.jessops.com/

Capture the moment with a camera from Jessops. The UK's largest chain of photographic stores has an on-line branch that sells regular and digital cameras and camcorders, plus the whole range of accessories. You can also search the database of used equipment or upload your digital photos and get them printed.

iQ TOYS

http://www.iqtoys.co.nz/

iQ Toys is a New Zealand-based store that specialises in educational toys. You can browse by age, type or brand, making it easy to select something appropriate. It ships all over the world, although Australian customers get their own site.

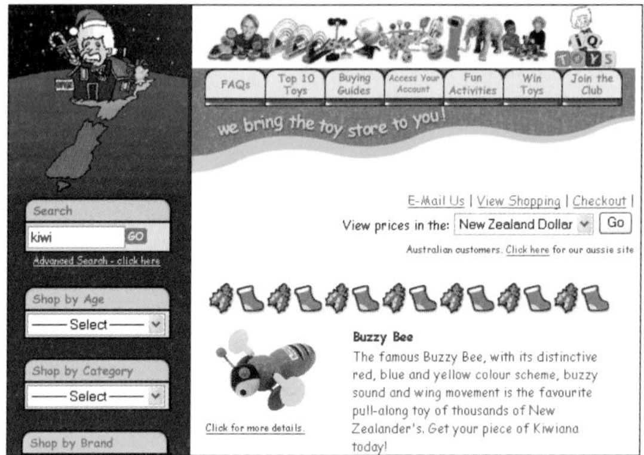

Finance and banking

The Motley Fool

http://www.fool.co.uk/

The Motley Fool provides accessible advice on financial matters, from credit cards and loans to investments and pensions. You can also set up an on-line portfolio and track your stocks. There are separate versions for the UK and the US so you don't get your dollars mixed up with your pounds.

HSBC

http://www.hsbc.co.uk/

The UK branch of the multinational bank offers an on-line banking service that enables you to check your accounts and pay your bills. Unfortunately it can't send crisp new fivers down the line, so you'll still have to make the occasional trip to the cashpoint.

Smile

http://www.smile.co.uk/

Smile is an Internet-only bank set up by the UK's Co-operative Bank. It offers current accounts and credit cards, loans and on-line share dealing. And since the Co-operative Bank is committed to ethical investing, you should end up with something to smile about. It does help if you like pink, though.

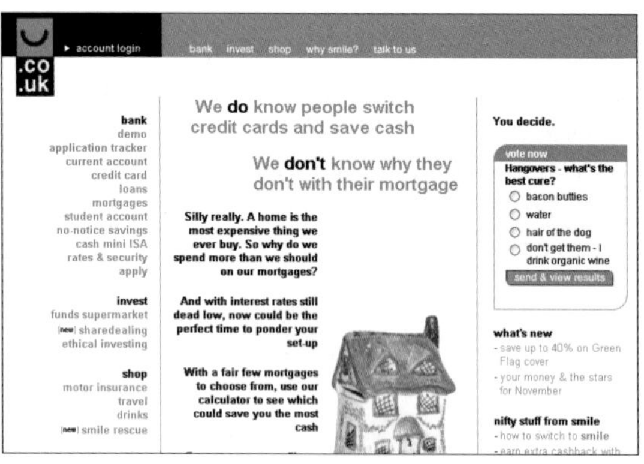

E*TRADE

http://www.etrade.com/

E*TRADE offers on-line trading in the US, the UK, Australia and several other countries. As well as placing buy and sell orders, you can track stocks, get personal market updates, set up customised charts and access company profiles.

eChoice

https://www.echoice.com.au/

eChoice is an Australian mortgage-matching service that lets you enter your requirements over the Internet. A consultant then calls you up to discuss any issues and tell you about matching products. It also has fact sheets and calculators that help you make sense of the whole business.

Employment

Job-Hunt.Org

http://www.job-hunt.org/

Job-Hunt.Org catalogues career and job-hunting Web sites. It has advice on creating an on-line resume and using the Internet to find a job, plus links to over 7,000 job-search sites.

Monster

http://www.monster.com/

Gigantic job-search network with sites for many countries. You can search for jobs on a one-off basis or set up an agent that will run searches periodically and e-mail you the results. You can also create an on-line CV and use it to apply for jobs, although you should read the privacy policy carefully first.

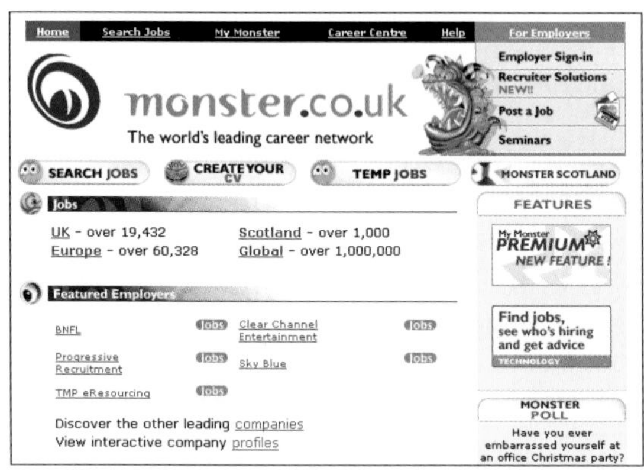

Guardian Unlimited Jobs

http://jobs.guardian.co.uk/

The Guardian newspaper's Jobs site has details of all the jobs advertised in the paper, plus additional Internet-only adverts. Like the paper, it has special sections for education, media and society jobs, or you can browse by employer or sector or conduct detailed searches. Registered users can be alerted to new jobs by e-mail, save job ads and searches and create on-line profiles and CVs.

Australian JobSearch

http://www.jobsearch.gov.au/

Australian JobSearch is a government-run site with a searchable database that includes jobs advertised in Job Network Services around the country, published in some national newspapers and/or entered by employers. It also has a resume builder and information about Work for the Dole activities.

Travel

World Travel Guide

http://www.worldtravelguide.net/

World Travel Guide is a huge on-line factbook with travel information about every country in the world, from Afghanistan to Zimbabwe. Find out what documents you'll need and what kind of weather to expect, get contact details for tourism boards and consulates and read a wealth of background material. It also has city and airport guides.

Foreign & Commonwealth Office

http://www.fco.gov.uk/

Read the UK Foreign & Commonwealth Office's country-specific travel advisories to find out where you shouldn't go and what you shouldn't do. It also has a Before You Go section that encourages travellers to prepare for potential problems and a discouragingly named If It All Goes Wrong section that tells you what to do when the worst happens.

Lonely Planet

http://www.lonelyplanet.com/

The attractively presented Web site of the Lonely Planet guidebook series has a world guide for independent travellers, discussion boards where you can share your experiences, links to other travel sites and a travel ticker that summarises current travel warnings.

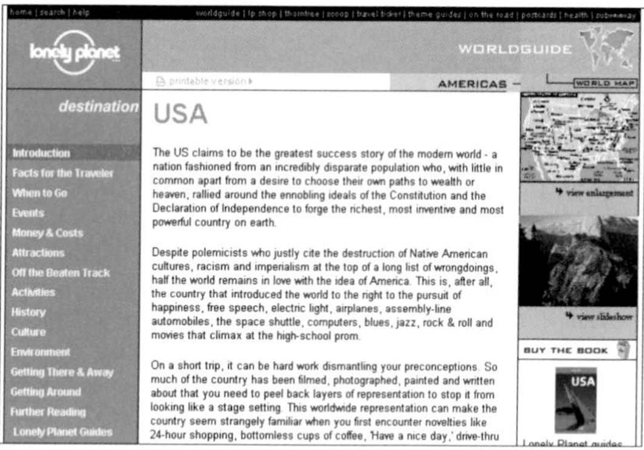

Rough Guides

http://www.roughguides.co.uk/

Rough Guides has a similar site with material from its guidebooks, discussion forums and space for registered members to create on-line journals.

Expedia

http://www.expedia.com/

Expedia is a travel-booking site with branches in several countries, including the US and UK. People from any country can use any Expedia site to make hotel and car reservations, but you can only purchase plane tickets from your own site. Enter your departure city, destination and dates, then click the Search button to find out what's available.

Travelocity

http://www.travelocity.com/

Travelocity is an alternative to Expedia with sites in the US, Canada, the UK and Germany. It pulls its flights from a different database, so it's worth checking both sites.

Travel.com.au

http://www.travel.com.au/

Travel.com.au enables Australians to book flights, hotels, cars and day tours over the Internet. As well as general tools it has dedicated pages for various countries and regions, with features and offers.

Visit Britain

http://www.visitbritain.com/

The British Tourist Authority has created a glossy sight that highlights the best that Britain has to offer. It customises the site depending on where you're coming from, picking out appropriate attractions. You can also take a virtual tour through the landscapes, seasons, cities and regions.

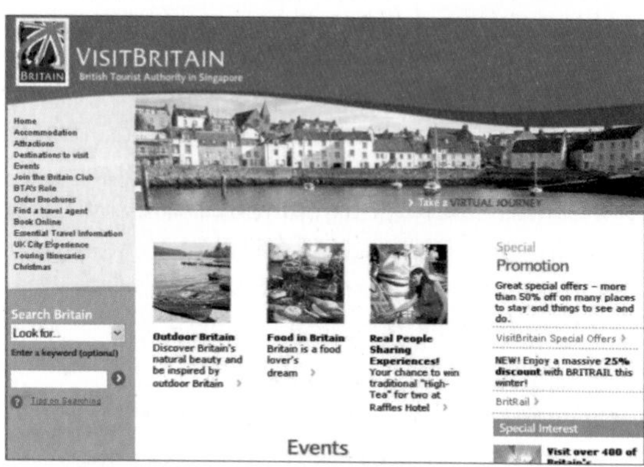

Australia.com

http://www.australia.com/

Australia.com helps you plan your trip to the sixth largest country in the world. It has facts and figures, panoramic images and videos, advice on where to go, what to do and what to buy, and a calendar of major events. You can even compile the pages you like best into a personal travel brochure.

PureNZ

http://www.purenz.com/

PureNZ has features and facts to help you plan a trip to Kiwiland, plus travel journals in which New Zealanders recount expeditions to various parts of the country.

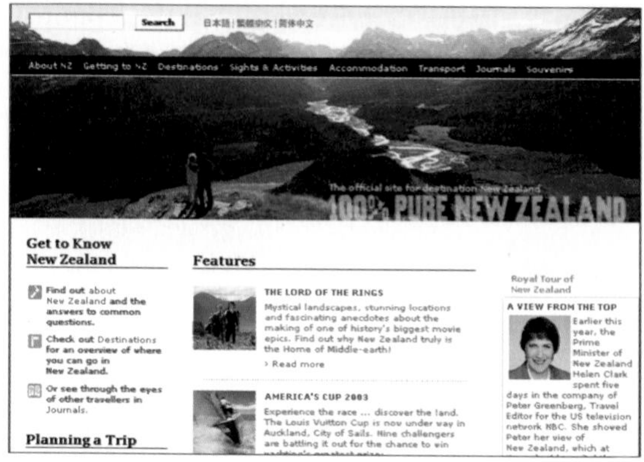

Visit Singapore

http://www.visitsingapore.com/

The Singapore Tourism Board's Visit Singapore site has lots of information about things to do in the Lion City. There's a list of 101 ways to live it up, with details of foods to try and places to hang out, and a directory of tours. Any pages that seem useful can be transferred to the Print Cart, which compiles them into a single document for easy printing.

Encounter South Africa

http://www.encounter.co.za/

South African Tourism's Web site explains why the country is unique: among other things, it's where you'll find "the world's oldest rocks, the world's oldest fossils, and the world's newest democracy." It also has sections on where to go and what to do, plus a trip planner with reference material and a calendar of upcoming events.